Grabbing the Tiger by the Tail

NGOs Learning for Organizational Change

MW00912663

Published by the
Canadian Council
for International Co-operation

Canadian cataloguing in publication data

Kelleher, David

Grabbing the tiger by the tail : NGOs learning for organizational change

Issued also in French under title: Prendre le taureau par les cornes.

ISBN 1-896622-00-3

1. Organizational change—Management. 2. Non-governmental organizations. I. McLaren, Katherine I. II. Bisson, Ronald III. Canadian Council for International Co-operation IV. Title

HD58.8.K45 1995   658.4'06   C95-900737-7

Authors

David Kelleher is a consultant based in St. Anne de Prescott, Ontario. Over the past twenty-five years he has worked with voluntary, government, and non-governmental organizations, involved in all stages of the organizational-learning process. He is a part-time faculty member in the Applied Social Science Department at Concordia University in Montreal. His publications include books and articles on managerial and organizational learning.

Kate McLaren has worked for twenty years for international-development NGOs as an educator and a program manager in Canada and overseas. She is a partner in South House Exchange, an Ottawa-based consulting practice specializing in organizational development, research and evaluation, and human rights.

Ronald Bisson is a consultant specializing in strategic management, service improvement, and capacity building in government, non-government organizations, and the private sector. He has twenty-five years' experience as a volunteer, board member, staff, and executive director in local, provincial, and national community-based organizations. He is a lecturer on Organizational Behaviour at the University of Ottawa.

Credits

Cover design: Holly Kelleher
          Tom Dart, First Folio

Text design and illustrations: Tom Dart, First Folio

Printed in Canada.

Contents

Acknowledgments

The inspiration for this book came from a series of workshops for member agencies of the Canadian Council for International Co-operation (CCIC). The insight, creativity, and commitment of the organizational leaders attending the four "Tiger by the Tail" programs ("Prendre le taureau par les cornes") helped to shape many of the key ideas in this book. We thank the participating organizations: Association québécoise des organismes de coopération internationale (AQOCI), Atlantic Council for International Cooperation, Broadcasting for International Understanding, Camrose International Institute, Canada World Youth, CAUSE Canada, Canadian Crossroads International, Canadian Environmental Network, Carrefour Tiers-Monde, Centre de solidarité internationale, Comité de Solidarité Tiers-Monde/T.R., CREDIL, CUSO, (national, Québec, Atlantic regions), Disabled Persons International, Friends of the Earth, International Development & Refugee Foundation, Jesuit Centre for Social Faith and Justice, Jeunesse du monde, Manitoba Council for International Cooperation, Marquis Project, MATCH International, Mennonite Central Committee Manitoba, Newfoundland Youth for Social Justice Network, Nous tous un soleil, Nova Scotia–Gambia Association, OXFAM-Canada, Pollution Probe, Primates World Relief and Development Fund (Anglican Church of Canada), Réseau acadien pour la solidarité internationale, Save the Children Fund of British Columbia, SOS Children's Villages Canada, United Nations Association in Canada, World Accord.

Throughout the writing, we initiated several discussion groups with a number of our NGO colleagues whose feedback and constructive criticism has been immensely useful in clarifying what we are attempting to convey. All this feedback, as well as numerous discussions with NGO friends and co-workers over the years, has enriched our own thinking and the final text. We would like to thank those who participated in discussions for the book: Marc Allain, Matthieu Brennan, Roger Clark, Lawrence Cumming, Jacquie Dale, Monique Dion, Tim Draimin, Carol Faulkner, Bill Gilsdorf, Bob Goodfellow, Franklyn Harvey, Jacques Lacarrière, Richard Marquardt, Christine Ouellette, Rose Potvin, Kendall Rust, John Saxby, Eva Schacherl, Carol Séguin-Kardish, Magda Seydegart, Carol Sissons, Rieky Stuart, Brian Tomlinson, Beth Woroniuk.

We owe a special thanks to the co-facilitators of the Tiger workshops: Reiky Stuart and Hilary Van Welter who worked with David Kelleher on the two English workshops, Ron Bisson with Monique Dion for the French workshops in Quebec, and Ron Bisson who facilitated the bilingual workshops in the Atlantic region.

We are very grateful to the organizations that allowed their experience to be used as case studies in the book. The cases were essential in grounding our analysis and in subjecting our concepts and frameworks to the questions and challenges that organizational leaders and staff are facing as they reinvent their organizations. While each case is based on interviews with persons at all levels of the organization, the interpretation and presentation are the sole responsibility of the authors.

Our liaison on the organizational development team at the Canadian Council for International Co-operation, Monique Dion, has been a source of creative energy, guidance, and inspiration from the beginning of the "Tiger" project. Without her, this book and its accompanying video would not have been conceived and produced. Linda Brassard, who provided administrative back-up at CCIC, and Micheline Laflamme, who has translated the text into French, each deserve our thanks for their fine work and attention to deadlines. Gilles Rivet reviewed the translation, deftly preserving every nuance in the English text.

We are indebted to Charis Wahl, whose editorial skill, good humour, common sense, and penetrating questions have kept both our thoughts and our prose on track.

The video companion for this book is the creative work of Broadcasting for International Cooperation, a Canadian NGO that both participated in the "Tiger" program, and recorded parts of it for the video. We wish to thank Peter Lockyer, who headed up the crew that prepared the script, design, and film for this project.

Funding for the preparation and production of both the video and the book has been provided in large measure by the Canadian International Development Agency. We are grateful for their support and belief in the value of this work.

Finally, the authors wish to extend sincerest thanks to the Canadian Council for International Co-operation for the opportunity to work with member agencies in the "Tiger" program, and for the support and encouragement we received to write this book.

David Kelleher and Kate McLaren
Ottawa, October 1995.

Foreword

Canadian NGOs are being pushed from many directions: shrinking government funds, the greater presence of southern NGOs, new forces in the global economy, new opportunities for policy dialogue, and the need for a better-informed public. Such buffeting is putting a lot of pressure on boards of directors, staff, donors and volunteers; however, it is also releasing a new creative energy focussed on maximizing the opportunities that a period of intense change generates.

The Canadian Council for International Cooperation (CCIC), an umbrella organization of more than 110 NGOs, works creatively with its members to ensure that Canadian NGOs remain relevant and in the forefront of the work for social justice. NGOs need to be clear about their vision for international cooperation and to manage change proactively rather than being rocked by political and economic upheaval.

This book has grown out of a CCIC program developed to address these needs. Called "Grabbing the Tiger by the Tail," the process involved a series of workshops to help NGO staff and board members to learn about organizational change from other NGOs. One of the most exciting discoveries for participants was learning that they were not alone. Many organizations are experiencing organizational questioning, conflict and confusion as they try to adjust to new environments.

Sharing these experiences and examining organizations in the private and public sector engendered support and new ideas for the program participants. The insights from the workshops were so valuable that they have grown into a video and now this book. The book presents theoretical discussions of the dynamics of organizational change, case studies drawn from the experience of Canadian NGOs that participated in the CCIC process, and a selection of practical "tools for change."

We hope this book will enhance the discussion as you reinvent your organizations for new times and new challenges. The insights and experiences offered here will also contribute to dialogue in the larger NGO community about how to create new forms of organization to support our work in the struggle for social justice.

Betty Plewes
President - CEO
Canadian Council for International Co-operation
September 1995

Introduction

Paul Tremblay is the executive director of a medium-sized
non-governmental organization with a good reputation for
international-development work. Yesterday he heard from a
major funder that the annual sustaining grant was to be cut
by 40 per cent; it is one month to the start of the next fiscal
year. His first reaction was that he just didn't have the energy
to go through another round of consultations and planning
decisions – and neither did his staff. That seemed to be all
they were doing these days, what with funding cuts and the
changes in the organization. What would happen, Tremblay
wondered, if he just brought together the chair of the board
of directors, his two program directors, and the finance director and made a decision.

Tremblay is experiencing what a lot of organizational leaders
and staff are feeling in these times of cutbacks and change.
He has been through strategic-planning exercises, has
restructured the organization, built teams that are working
reasonably well, involved the board, and tried to be open-
minded about the problems that come with cutbacks and
downsizing. But people are tired. Huge amounts of energy go
into the process rather than into the actual work. This new
cut means more of the same, but the organization has little
energy and few financial resources to manage the change.

This book is an effort to address these organizational dilemmas, which many public-sector organizations are facing in
Canada and elsewhere. It is not our intention here to examine the nature of the external challenges that non-government organizations (NGOs) are facing around the world;
many other writers are considering these questions. The

Things are not going to get easier. People working in organizations need new skills and orientations for dealing with change. ...managing change is now a big part of our work.

purpose is to help organizational leaders and programming staff, particularly in the not-for-profit sector, to understand the dynamics of change in their organizations and to act in ways that strengthen the organization in a tough external environment.

Things are not going to get easier. People working in organizations need new skills and orientations for dealing with change. In addition to professional and programming skills, they need "change skills," for managing change is now a big part of our work.

This book evolved from a series of workshops between 1993 and 1995. The workshops, called "Grabbing the Tiger by the Tail," ("Prendre le taureau par les cornes" in the French workshop) were organized for member agencies of the Canadian Council for International Co-operation (CCIC), and were held in four Canadian cities. The "Tiger Program" was in direct response to the growing need for managing change in the international-development NGO sector in Canada. Each agency was invited to send two participants: the executive director and the volunteer chair of the board of directors. The assumption was that these two positions are pivotal in making things happen in an NGO, but the individuals are often in different cities and rarely spend substantial time together working on agency matters. This workshop was going to provide both a framework for action and the time for two key persons to begin to map out a change plan that they could take back to their organizations.

Each workshop was preceded by a full day with the two agency participants working through an organizational assessment. The results of these meetings provided the facilitators with important information about the changing dynamics and issues affecting participating agencies. In each city the workshop proper brought together the two participants from each of approximately ten agencies. It was carried out in two phases: the first part, lasting three days, set out some of the key ideas and gave each agency time to develop a plan based on the issues it had identified during the assessment day. Six months later, a second two-day workshop brought the same people back together to report on how their plan was working, and to get feedback from one another on the next steps.

The follow-up evaluation, done by CCIC several months later as a phone survey of the majority of participants, indicated that many of the participants had succeeded in implementing some or all of their organizational change plan or strategy. Almost everyone felt that the workshops had given them both the practical guidance and the confidence to move ahead.

This book is an elaboration of the "Grabbing the Tiger" experience. It is not a recipe – there are no simple, foolproof recipes. What works at one time for one agency may not work later or for another. What is important is to develop processes for each situation, based on a firm grasp of the fundamentals: a good understanding of the immediate context in which you are working, a realistic assessment of the human and financial resources of your organization, and a good hunch about what might work or not. An organization open to learning, to asking tough questions, and living with the answers has an increased likelihood of survival.

Of course even if you do everything "right," there are no guarantees. Not all the organizations that have done as we are suggesting are living happily ever after. Nonetheless, these ideas are our best current understanding of what helps, for it's only through experimentation that we get better at managing change. Each change effort is different; it should build on the last one, asking new questions and trying out new approaches.

This book is based on the authors' experience and that of many NGO colleagues in Canada and overseas. Our experience is in the public sector: with non-government organizations at the community, national, and international level; with school boards, hospitals, unions, and government departments. We have worked as managers in NGOs and as external consultants and facilitators.

We know that the public sector is in the process of massive restructuring, as the private sector has been. This is part of a global process that is having a profound impact on all public- and private-sector organizations and those who work in and with them. Government cutbacks and policy changes have altered forever the "social contract" between the government and the public, between public-sector employees and employers. The line between the public and private sectors is blurring as the private sector takes over many functions traditionally carried out or funded by government. These changes mean that NGOs in Canada are being confronted with major financial and ethical dilemmas about their future.

"The emerging trends in the governing process have the potential to significantly enhance the importance and impact of the voluntary sector, but will necessitate that the leaders of national voluntary organizations begin to adopt new modes of thinking and new ways of doing things."

— S. Phillips, "On Visions and Revisions: The Voluntary Sector Beyond 2000."

Because of this sea change, many of our assumptions about growth, service, job tenure, and even the nature of our work are being swept away. Individuals and organizations are now rethinking their missions, commitments, relevance, and relationships with their clients, supporters, program partners, and donors, including government. Many NGOs are turning to the private sector for ideas, setting up for-profit businesses, fee-for-service activities, and joint ventures with the private sector and other NGOs. Some are taking on the role of public-sector contractors – providing services to government. At base, however, not-for-profit organizations are different from the private sector: their rationale is not profit, but effective programming or service. Although their funding environment is increasingly competitive, they are not market driven, as private sector, for-profit firms must be. They are driven as much by values as by survival; and by multiple – sometimes conflicting – accountabilities to supporters, donors, volunteers, partners, and major funders. NGO boards of directors, therefore, are managing a different set of dilemmas.

The challenge for NGOs is to survive without sacrificing the social purpose of the organization. This, after all, is what sets social-justice or change organizations apart from the for-profit sector.

There are a number of theories of organizational change, based on different ideas about what organizations are. Some focus on structure and formal relationships, others on culture and how individuals interpret and relate to change. We have attempted to incorporate the most helpful elements of each model in our approach to change and learning. Underlying our approach are a number of assumptions about organizational change. These are key themes that will be examined throughout the book:

Assumptions about change

1. Change is not new. Managing ongoing and often tumultuous change, however, requires a new set of competencies and attitudes. Many of the old ideas about management need to be questioned.

   Change requires a new set of competencies and attitudes.

2. Managing change is not solely a "management" issue. Change involves everyone in the organization, not just leaders. The collective experience, knowledge, and needs of participants are the raw material for change. Collective ownership of the outcome is the best guarantee of success.

   Change involves everyone in the organization, not just leaders.

3. Involvement and participation is not enough, however; direction, guidance, planning, clear decision making - a measure of "control" - are also essential. Finding the balance between being flexible and open while staying focussed and in control is essential.

   Finding the balance between flexibility and control is vital.

4. Managers are not always in control. Sometimes they must trust the process to take the organization where it needs to go, even if the destination is not entirely clear when

   Managers are not always in control.

you start out. Letting go in a gale may feel self-destructive, but as all sailors know, in a storm you must run before the wind, not fight it. Outcomes are not always as planned; lots of unplanned things will happen. Some of the most innovative approaches can emerge when you relax your grip.

Organizations are open systems.

5. As open systems, organizations are permeable to external influence. Managing change involves paying attention to the organizational environment - both immediate and large scale – first to understand it, then to figure out how to deal with it. For NGOs this means paying attention to their network of accountabilities – to donors, members, partner groups, staff, board, government.

Organizational change and restructuring shifts the balance of power in organizations.

6. Change is about power, so change and restructuring shift the balance of power within organizations. It causes, and is sometimes caused by, conflict inside or outside the organization. How individual participants interpret the impact of change in terms of their status, program, and loyalties is critical to their supporting, facilitating, or resisting the change. Organizations are not mechanistic, rational, problem-solving entities. They are also messy, contradictory, and ornery. Therefore, paying attention to people and to their needs and feelings is essential.

Change is a good thing ultimately.

7. Change is a good thing, ultimately. It may be thrust on us, but it represents an opportunity to renew our organizations and shake loose old assumptions that may be blocking our effectiveness. Major change can transform organizations for the better.

The goal of change is not organizational survival for its own sake.

8. The goal of change is not organizational survival for its own sake. Some organizations will go under, but new ones will emerge to carry on the work. The purpose of change is to deal with changing circumstances, to ensure relevance, and to renew commitment to the mission of the organization.

This book is divided into three parts. Part I, Chapters 1 and 2, lays the groundwork by examining blocks to change and ways to overcome these blocks through a process of organizational learning. Chapter 1 identifies the internal dynamics of organizations that can prevent an effective response to crisis and change – things such as bureaucratic and overly rational thinking, failure to adequately consider one's internal and external relationships, and the traditional patriarchal way of organizing work and relationships. Chapter 2 considers an effective response to these dilemmas or blocks: a learning response that makes the best possible use of the experience, information, and knowledge of people who work in and with the organization.

Part II comprises three chapters and deals with three different levers for change: the culture of the organization; the strategy, i.e., position and perspective of the organization; and the structure, i.e., formal relationships, systems, and decision-making mechanisms of the organization. All three must be involved in a change effort. Several case studies describe experiences of NGOs in Canada and overseas.

Part III provides practical suggestions on how to go about the change process in a non-government or voluntary organization. In Chapter 6, we discuss different types of organizational change, from small scale to large scale, and present a "map" for large-scale change that pinpoints what change leaders must pay attention to at each step or phase of the process: start-up, transition, and resolution. Chapter 7 describes a number of tools that we and others have used in the change process. These are accompanied by worksheets and step-by-step descriptions of what was done or what is to be done. These can be copied and used or modified to suit the needs of your organization.

What about Paul Tremblay[*], the frustrated executive director

---

[*] Paul Tremblay and his organization are a composite drawn from many real organizational experiences.

introduced above? What might this book suggest to him? First, that he should think very carefully about the readiness of his organization for the different approach to decision making he is considering. Second, he should weigh the negative implications on trust, ownership, and morale, and balance these against the need to deal quickly with the problem. It may be that he's right: perhaps a fast, decisive, and simple process would be best, building on the change work already done. Whatever the decision, our message to Paul is that managing change is not something he must get through in order to get on with the "real" work; it is now part of his job, of all our jobs, and will be into the future.

The Problematic: Turbulence, Vulnerability, and Control

"After the meeting I was really dejected. I felt I wasn't doing my job — there were all these problems...all these conflicts.... Sometimes I think maybe I've stayed here long enough."

– NGO Manager

THE WOMAN WHO SAID THIS IS A DEEPLY COMMITTED, SKILLED manager of a development agency doing ground-breaking work all over the world. She is experienced, energetic, and well respected by her colleagues. She is also overwhelmed by the pressures: multiple demands, change, conflict, and a growing feeling that maybe it is time to find another job. She is not alone. Staff and board members in voluntary and non-governmental organizations around the world are involved in a struggle to revitalize, renew and, rebuild organizations that are facing uncertain futures from a deeply troubling present.

What is all this effort for? What is driving us to turn our organizations upside down, to spend nights and weekends agonizing over new strategies, structures, and approaches?

Many have written about the turbulence faced by NGOs.[1] Whether we're thinking of the post-welfare age, millennial change, globalization, or the triumph of transnational capital, these times are not kind to NGOs. It may not be possible – or in some cases desirable – to preserve many of our organizations or our current way of doing things. The focus of our efforts must be to preserve the development *impetus* – the desire, knowledge, experience, and relationships that allow us to be involved in one another's efforts to create a world free from hunger, violence, and poverty – a world that is more tolerant and equitable.

Preserving this capacity requires organizational learning, enhancing the NGOs' ability to generate and act on knowledge about their environment, programs and their ways of functioning because the current environment threatens the very life of NGOs, perhaps communities of NGOs. This is not a prediction; it is a description of the present.

In a recent workshop on alternative fund raising offered by the Canadian Council for International Co-operation (CCIC), the average budget cut suffered by international-development NGOs attending was found to be over 20 per cent. One large Canadian-based international development NGO had more than 400 staff worldwide as recently as 3 years ago. It now has about 260. As we write, the leaders are considering a further staff cut of 40 per cent, following increased government cuts and the adoption of a new strategic vision. As a result of the recent Canadian federal budget, some 90 development education NGOs and 7 provincial councils of international development NGOs lost all their federal-government funding.

Most organizations, public and private, have been caught up in similar turbulence in recent years. Many have survived through creativity, risk taking, and sometimes radical surgery. But others remain vulnerable, and are ill prepared to cope. In NGOs this vulnerability derives from:

- poor accountability – outmoded relationships to donors, members, partners, and other NGOs, and

- inappropriate organizational "metaphors" shaping organizational thinking and acting.

Both of these conditions derive from strongly held beliefs about control and autonomy. Most, if not all, organizations are constructed to entrench control, through constitutions, by-laws, funding criteria, administrative policies, and programming guidelines. We set up safeguards to prevent undue external or political interference with our purpose.

Yet we need outside influence and feedback to bring fresh thinking, to challenge the status quo, and to hold us accountable to our larger constituencies and stakeholders. In other words, we need to relinquish some control in order to learn, and thereby to withstand the gales of a turbulent organizational environment.[2] Outside influence can affirm us in our work, in our mission, and in our ongoing strategic choices.

Our tendency to maintain authority and control is rooted in the metaphors of our organizational consciousness. The deep structure of our thinking about organization – ideas such as bureaucracy, patriarchy, and rationality – is formed around control and a particular kind of authority.

Control and authority are not necessarily bad: if you are in a stable environment and have a winning formula, control is exactly what you want. But if you are in a turbulent environment and looking for new ideas, then new ways of thinking about control and authority are required. New thinking is needed most to consider the question of organizational

> We need outside influence and feedback to bring fresh thinking, to challenge the status quo, and to hold us accountable to our larger constituencies and stakeholders.

accountability – a major issue for NGOs and community-based organizations.

Accountability: Autonomy and Control

Accountability is a relationship between individuals and groups inside and outside the organization. NGOs are "accountable" when stakeholders can hold us responsible for accomplishing our mission in a principled and ethical manner. NGOs have "accountable" relationships with major funders, partners overseas and in Canada, with clients, members, staff, and donors, although each has a different perspective and needs. We provide a service, product, or expertise that the stakeholders wish to purchase or receive. In return for funding, we provide information on how the funds are used.

Accountability can also be thought of as a path for information about the environment, desires, expectations, and needs of our partners, donors, members, and staff. Accountability is a two-way relationship.

Accountability relationships nurture and sustain an organization. High levels of accountability also make an organization more open to external pressure, challenge, and learning from its various publics. This openness or two-way accountability is a check on "go-it-alone" leadership styles. Accountability constitutes an ongoing pressure to perform to particular standards and expectations, and is a key element of a learning organization.

Of course it also sets up a tension. Underresponsiveness prevents learning; overresponsiveness to external demands results in opportunistic decision making. For example, in a competitive funder's environment, it is tempting to bend one's programs to fit funder's criteria – to become the "flavour of the month," even if doing so undermines genuine accountability to

Accountability can also be thought of as a path for information about the environment, desires, expectations, and needs of our partners, donors, members, and staff. Accountability is a two-way relationship.

partners, members, and donors. All in all, however, accountability is a positive pressure on an organization.

External Accountability Relationships

If accountability is generally a good thing, why then has it not
been welcomed and pursued by NGOs? Indeed NGOs often
oppose greater accountability mechanisms for fear of losing
autonomy over programming decisions – or out of fear of
criticism or misunderstanding. Yet surrender of some autonomy and control is necessary in order to engage with the
outer world, to learn, change, and thrive.

Consider the question of accountability to individual donors.
How many NGOs do not fully describe to their donors what
they do or how they do it? There are many reasons for not
bothering people with too much detailed information.
Donors are kept at arm's length, contented, the organization
assumes, with encouraging stories of the good work their
contributions support. Donors are not engaged in policy or
implementation discussions – about the importance of political action, for example, or of work in Canada, or the cost
breakdown of working overseas. How might this relationship
change, and what would be the consequences, if it were
more open?

Some of the same questions arise in the relationship with the
Canadian International Development Agency (CIDA), which
has been a major funder of many Canadian international-
development NGOs. This relationship is complex and can
change with the political winds. Financial dependence on
the state can be hazardous. NGOs have therefore often avoided wider or more open contact out of fear of co-optation,
criticism, and loss of funding. A certain wariness and mistrust
exists on both sides, yet many NGOs remain highly dependent
on their relationship with CIDA for survival; it is a key
accountability relationship, which comes with certain

responsibilities. What would be the consequences of a more forthright dialogue? Would NGOs be more or less vulnerable and effective as a result?

Within the NGO community, there is considerable collegiality and a number of joint initiatives, but few intrude on agency autonomy. Recent discussions within CCIC of a code of ethics are instructive. The members have adopted a Code of Ethics, but it is self-administered. By June 1997, compliance will be a requirement of membership, with an accompanying complaints mechanism.

The relationship of northern NGOs with their southern partners may be the most crucial and enriching. Yet in all the strategic planning, board retreats, management seminars, and annual general meetings held in the past five years, where are the voices, perspectives, and observations of these partners? Most NGOs visit partners regularly and some build deep, long-term relationships of mutual influence and trust; yet when it is time to think about where we are going, those partners' voices are represented if at all by sympathetic northerners. The partners are, a colleague has pointed out, far removed in time, space, and resources from membership, board, and donors.

Difficulties with accountability have slowed the development of tools for learning. Growing competitive pressures have made for-profit business very clear about the ongoing need for information.[3] This understanding has led to innovative mechanisms for being accountable to customers, suppliers, and other business partners. For example, the concept of the "value chain" enables a business to look at each stage of the process of creating value and ask if they are proceeding with the highest possible quality, at the lowest cost, and at the fastest speed.[4] This level of conceptualization is missing from most NGO work. If NGOs had a better understanding of the nature of the processes and methodologies involved in their work (and that of their partners), they could systematize what is being learned. As it is, a lot of information and experience is not translated into organizational learning. (The problem is accentuated by the need to communicate across cultural and national barriers.)

NGOs are, however, taking steps toward reducing the distance between themselves, their donors, partners, and the general public. The question of accountability is very much on the minds of NGOs and must be seen as a serious commitment.

Some Examples of Accountability Measures

- Some NGOs regularly take board members on project tours to meet southern partners and discuss the projects

- CCIC's recently developed Code of Ethics has stimulated several other members to develop their own codes of ethics, or to adopt the CCIC code as their own

- Some NGOs in Europe are undergoing "social audits" – outside appraisals of the NGO's functioning that become public documents

- Some NGOs have deliberately created a culture that respects and involves their partners at all levels of the organization

- A number of NGOs have put particular emphasis on donor feedback in an effort to find effective ways of communicating their message, and raising more funds; individual donors have little opportunity, however, to influence programming decisions

- One NGO plans a series of member opinion polls (some of which would be binding) on key policy issues

- A few NGOs do regular market-research studies of their donors

To sum up, accountability relationships function as a constructive pressure on an organization to remain relevant to its constituency and mission. Accountability mechanisms serve as sources of information about what is needed and what the organization is providing. Little accountability means little information and little pressure – two key factors in organizational learning.

Internal Accountability: Boards and Strategic Leadership

The leadership of an organization, both staff and board, should be at the intersection of the relationships described above – immersed in a flow of information, engaged in creating knowledge through dialogue, and sustained by the solidarity of these relationships. Knowledge and solidarity need to be the *prima materia* of discussion within the organization: who we are, what we care about, what we are called to do, what we love doing, what our unique contribution is ...

These questions are the primary agenda of the board. Although voluntary organizations and NGOs typically involve staff and others in these discussions, it is the board that holds the legislative mandate, the responsibility to commit the organization to a strategic direction.

Strategic discussion must be ongoing to ensure that the organization remains relevant in a changing environment. This work involves being clear about the organization's identity, acquiring needed information, and making *choices*. For example, a recreation board recently decided to support community recreation and to stop delivering direct service. An NGO board decided to decrease its focus on sending volunteers to southern countries and increase its capacity to build strategic alliances among southern and northern NGOs. Such decisions to stop or decrease one activity in order to work on another reflect the ultimate purpose of the organizations.

Boards have difficulty with such strategic choices, which require a board to reconceive its fundamental role. Many a board still sees itself as the overseer of the executive director, its job to receive reports from the staff, scrutinize staff decisions, and approve the budget. Boards exercising strategic leadership, however, must see themselves as *owners in trust*, responsible for the long-term survival and development of the organization.[5] This means focusing on the big questions. It necessitates building a board with diverse points of view, rooted in the constituencies of the organization; it requires that the board be well informed about the realities facing the organization, clear about its role, willing to think in new ways and to make hard decisions, sometimes contrary to staff advice.

Is this a prescription for a board without much coherence? Coherence is important, but it comes out of dialogue, consensus building, skilled planning and communication mechanisms, not through homogeneous membership and inadequate accountability.

Outmoded ideas of autonomy and control have prevented many NGOs from building the kind of relationships necessary to ensure learning and genuine accountability. They have inhibited the development of the strategic leadership so badly needed at present. The next section looks at another set of control pathologies – three metaphors that have defined our organizations and how we experience them.

> Outmoded ideas of autonomy and control have prevented many NGOs from building the kind of relationships necessary to ensure learning and genuine accountability.

Toxic Metaphors: Bureaucracy, Patriarchy, and Rationality

Our socialization in a bureaucratic and patriarchal culture has left us with inappropriate metaphors to think about organizations. Although many of us no longer believe in highly rational, authoritarian, and patriarchal leadership, we still harbour beliefs in a bureaucratic paradigm that colour our understanding about organizations and how they change.

Bureaucracy

To understand how metaphors of bureaucracy dominate our thinking about organizations, picture an effective NGO: it probably has clear goals, objectives, management systems, reporting structures, and policies. It also has people in a hierarchy, meetings, and offices. Now, imagine other metaphors for picturing organizations: a rain forest, the human brain, or an orchestra. That's much more difficult. These images just don't seem as, well, "natural" as the bureaucratic one.

The deep structure of modern bureaucracy was laid down in the eighteenth century by Frederick the Great of Prussia. He had inherited an army of conscripts, criminals, and foreign mercenaries, and decided to transform the unruly mob into a logical war machine. He introduced ranks and uniforms, extended regulations, and standardized equipment, training, and army drill. Almost two hundred years later, Max Weber described bureaucracy in terms that Frederick would have recognized immediately: " ... an organization routinizes administration exactly as the machine routinizes production. [Bureaucracy] emphasizes precision, speed, clarity, regularity, reliability and efficiency achieved through the creation of a fixed division of tasks, hierarchical supervision and detailed rules and regulation."[6]

Weber's study was the groundwork for "scientific management," designing jobs for the highest possible efficiency, often breaking them down to a series of simple, routinized tasks that could be performed with minimal skill.

Such thinking produced the notion that orders issued from the top of the organization would have the intended effect at the bottom, because the working conditions were all controlled. It also assumed that organizational effectiveness requires the exercise of authority.

In fairness, bureaucracy was a major advance. It introduced a rule of law into organizations. Nepotism, favouritism, and arbitrary managerial action were condemned; promotion on merit, objective decision making, and fair, even-handed treatment of staff was encouraged. Hiring practices were codified, pay scales standardized, and organizational behaviour subjected to rules and procedures beyond the arbitrary power of managers and owners.

Bureaucracies also introduced impersonal mechanisms for managing conflict. Rules, procedures, and policy anticipate events and specify action. Organization members don't have to be continually burdened with making decisions that reward some and penalize others.

NGOs and voluntary organizations have been known for being less bureaucratic than for-profit or government organizations. They have been proud of their accessibility, their closeness to the people they work with, and their ability to respond to changing situations.

However, even as we fought it, we retained an unquestioned, deep belief in the core of the bureaucratic paradigm – that organizations are rational, goal-seeking mechanisms, hierarchically structured, and focused on the efficient use of resources to accomplish clearly defined goals.

A rational, efficient, goal-seeking organization doesn't sound all that bad, but our experience tells us that organizations are not, in practice, all that rational. People act on flashes of genius and brown-outs of dysfunction, buffeted by the demands of multiple stakeholders, and sustained by the encouragement and energy of their supporters. Nor, if we were committed to efficiency, would we tolerate the time it takes to reach consensus from diverse points of view. "Efficiency" wouldn't allow the investment of the hours and days in the dialogue required to make a partnership flourish.

As for being "goal seeking," traditional goal statements force us to think about achievable, observable, and measurable ends – things that are in some way predictable. Yet, focusing on the predictable eliminates the serendipitous tangents that might go somewhere worthwhile. The very act of planning and implementing according to these goals undermines our ability to *see* beyond them. Only parts of our work – sometimes the least interesting parts – are amenable to traditional goal setting and measurable results: for example, the number of people attending the workshop, the amount of money disbursed, the number of training programs held ...

The problem with the bureaucratic paradigm is not that goals and efficiency are wrong, but that when we place them in the centre of our organizational consciousness we block out the fullest possible understanding our work: what it is and what it might be.

Our heritage of bureaucratic assumptions has prevented, until recently perhaps, the serious consideration of:

- complex, organic, biological structures rather than a simple mechanistic one;

- a multi-perspective view of organizations rather than an objective one;

- concern with involvement, communication, participation not weighed against the narrow criteria of measurable impact and efficiency.

The anthropologist Gregory Bateson reminds us that there is nothing more toxic than a bad metaphor.[7] Bureaucracy, with its authoritarian, sexist, mechanistic baggage certainly qualifies.

It is not surprising that bureaucracy is so entrenched. Rationality, hierarchy, and objectivity are core values of Western society.

Two powerful grounds of critique of these assumptions that have particular cogency for voluntary and non-government organizations have come from discussions of gender and rationality.

Patriarchy

Until recently, organizational theory and practice has been gender blind, the different experience of men and women in organizations invisible and, therefore, unexamined. Although many organizations have made significant efforts to hire more women, include more women on the board of directors, and think about program in terms of the different impact on men and women, the substructure of organizations remains essentially patriarchal: designed by men, led by men in ways compatible with men's interests.[8]

Patriarchy continues to colour our understandings of relationships, authority, and control. Not surprisingly, patriarchal assumptions about authority and control are at the heart of the bureaucratic paradigm. When we organize, we unthinkingly import the patriarchal assumptions connected to bureaucracy.

It is only lately that feminist theorists have pointed out that organizations are "gendered." Although there is no consensus on what a "feminist organization" might be and whether it would be broadly desirable, much can be learned from the feminist perspective on organizations.

For example, leadership in voluntary organizations requires long hours, work on weekends, and an ability to travel. In a society that still leaves child care largely in the hands of women, these requirements significantly advantage men over women. Moreover, as Dorothy Dinnerstein points out, as long as child care is the responsibility of women, women will be seen as "problem workers": it is for them that we need to

> ...as long as child care is the responsibility of women, women will be seen as "problem workers."
>
> – D. Dinnerstein

consider day care, make special travel arrangements, adjust work hours to child-related boundaries, and so on.[9] If it wasn't for women, we could run the organization in the "normal" way: long hours unconstrained by family responsibilities, and a primary focus on work, to the exclusion of other "problems" of life.

Organizations are often gendered in their decision-making processes. Many NGOs have departed from male, authoritarian decision making, but it has been replaced by an adversarial democracy that retains much of an individualist (one man, one vote) approach to decision making. Feminist organizational theory brings with it a critique of elitism, hierarchy, and oppressive inequality. Robin Lidener contrasts an ethic of "care" with the ethic of "fairness" that underlies liberal organizational democracy.[10] An ethic of care implies a consideration of minority points of view and, even more important, points of view not in good currency within the majority culture. The deep, often unquestioned, structure of male democratic process is that there will be a debate and then a vote leading to one side losing and one winning. The losers must be consoled by the "fair process". This fair process, agreed on in advance by the majority, is more important than the outcome, which may be deeply hurtful. Whether the difference between a caring ethic and a fairness ethic is a matter of gender has not been determined, but it seems that more women function better within a caring ethic and more men function more comfortably within a fairness ethic.

The linguist Deborah Tannen[11] has demonstrated that there are significant differences in the style of language used by men and women, and much of that difference relates to control, power, and hierarchy. Much of men's interaction is concerned with attaining a one-up position – or at least avoiding being one down. Much of women's conversation is about finding equality or expressing solidarity. As most organizations are gendered in their definitions of competence – definitions that can include high levels of self-confidence – many women are seen as "not ready for promotion" because they don't seem aggressive enough or sufficiently sure of themselves.

Male-gendered bias extends to the quality of programming. Anne Marie Goetz, a development scholar, points out that much international development activity ostensibly focused on issues and sectors that involve women (such as agricultural work) excludes women in planning and often in outcomes. She recently estimated that in Africa, where women are responsible for 80 per cent of food production, women farmers receive approximately 2 per cent of extension contracts. In Bangladesh, apart from some micro-credit agencies that focus on women, the credit women receive is lower than that extended to men, and the training women receive is for low-profit, sex-stereotyped activities. Some training and credit is also conditional on the acceptance of family-planning measures.[12]

If NGOs and voluntary organizations are going to transform the lives of both men and women, their programs must include the perspectives of both women and men. This means that organizations must be places where men and women can work at their best. This will require changes in the basic working methods of many organizations both in their internal ways of working and their program.

Rationality

As our environment gets more complex, we have tended to think harder and longer about what is happening. Unfortunately, that thinking often falls into the traditional linear, rational rut, reducing intricate problems to simple categories of right and wrong, and to quantitative measurement. The inability to factor values into logical thinking, and the impossibility of using logic to resolve paradox, make this mode of thinking inadequate to our situation.[13] It is becoming increasingly clear that effective management involves being able to resolve dilemmas so that apparently conflicting values are maximized.[14]

For example, one critical issue in voluntary organizations concerns flexibility, creativity, and empowerment on one hand and focus, control, and integration on the other. Both combinations are necessary for effective organizational functioning, but finding the balance at any given time can be a challenge.

Another issue is how much to invest in providing services (productivity) and how much in the health of the organization – participation, involvement, training, governance. It is not helpful to state flatly that we exist to alleviate hunger and everything else must take second place. Agencies with this mindset are usually understaffed, underqualified, and rife with the martyrdom that inhibits effective work. Conversely, we all know organizations that have indulged in sterile ideological discussions, unrelieved by considerations of impact and accomplishment.

This critique of linear rationality is not a call to abandon thought – it is a call for more complete thought, which admits to conflicting values and swiftly changing realities – thinking for change.

> Traditional analysis is the product of one smart person or group. In a learning organization, thinking for change must be everyone's work.

Traditional analysis is the product of one smart person or group. In a learning organization, thinking for change must be everyone's work, drawing on all our creativity and sensing skills. It includes story, allegory, experience, values, and feelings. Stories matter to us; we are moved when our work makes a difference in people's lives.

In this chapter we have begun with the belief that NGOs and voluntary organizations are facing challenges that demand fundamental change. We have argued that voluntary and nongovernmental organizations are handicapped in this effort by their lack of accountability, and by the capacity of their leadership for strategic thinking. At a deeper level, they are handicapped by traditional metaphors of organization. Bureaucracy is designed for stability and the exercise of authority; it cannot deal easily with change and distributed authority. Two particularly compelling sources of learning have been the feminist critique of organizations and the current discussion of the limits of rationality.

This chapter immediately raises the question, Does a different paradigm exist that can deal with these complex issues? It is this question that the rest of this book endeavours to answer. We begin, in the next chapter, by describing the learning organization, the foundation of this paradigm.

References

1. J. Clark, *Democratising Development:The Role of Voluntary Organizations* (London: Earthscan, 1991); Coalition of National Voluntary Organizations, *Taking Voluntarism to the Year 2015* (Ottawa, 1994); L. Cumming, with B. Singleton, "Organizational Sustainability – An End of the Century Challenge for Voluntary International Development Organizations," paper presented to the Annual Conference of the Canadian Association for the Study of International Development (Montreal, 1995); R. Marquardt, "The Voluntary Sector and the Federal Government: A Perspective in the Aftermath of the 1995 Federal Budget," discussion paper prepared for the CCIC Annual Meeting, May, 1995; S. Phillips, "Of Visions and Revisions: The Voluntary Sector Beyond 2000," in *Bulletin of the Coalition of National Voluntary Organizations* 12, no. 3 (Winter 1993); J. Saxby, "Who Owns the Private Aid Agencies? Mythology ... and Some Awkward Questions," draft chapter for Transnational Institute publication, Amsterdam, 1995; I. Smillie, and H. Helmich, eds., *Non-Governmental Organizations: Stakeholders for Development* (Paris: Development Centre of the OECD, 1993).

2. R. Stacey, *Managing the Unknowable: Strategic Boundaries Between Order and Chaos in Organizations* (San Francisco: Jossey-Bass, 1992).

3. R. Howard, *The Learning Imperative: Managing People for Continuous Innovation* (Boston: Harvard Business Review Books, 1993).

4. M. Porter, *Competitive Strategy: Techniques for Analysing Industries and Competitors* (New York: Free Press, 1980).

5. J. Carver, *Boards That Make a Difference* (San Francisco: Jossey-Bass, 1988).

6. G. Morgan, *Images of Organization* (Beverly Hills: Sage, 1986), 24.

7. G. Bateson, *Mind and Nature: A Necessary Unity* (New York: Dutton, 1979).

8. A. Mills, and P. Tancred, *Gendering Organizational Analysis* (Newbury Park: Sage, 1992).

9. D. Dinnerstein, *The Mermaid and the Minotaur: Sexual Arrangements and Human Malaise* (New York: Harper, 1976).

10. R. Lidener, "Stretching the Boundaries of Liberal Feminism: Democratic Innovation in a Feminist Organization," in *Signs* 16, no. 2 (1991), 263–289.

11. D. Tannen, *Talking From 9 to 5* (New York: Morrow, 1994).

12. A. Goetz, "Gender and Administration", *IDS Bulletin* 23, no. 4, (1992).

13. C. Hampden-Turner, *Charting the Corporate Mind* (New York: Free Press, 1990).

14. R. Quinn, *Beyond Rational Management* (San Francisco: Jossey-Bass, 1988).

Learning Organizations

2

"One of the things that has frustrated me for as long as I've worked here is that we have accumulated so much incredible experience and knowledge in our work, but we can't seem to learn from it at the organizational level. It stays in the heads of individual staff and partners – out there somewhere. There's no learning that is institutional."

– NGO Manager

HOW MANY TIMES HAS A SIMILAR LAMENT BEEN HEARD IN OUR organizations, especially in larger and older organizations with ingrained routines and responses? What does it take to create a learning organization? Strategic planning and evaluation help but do not guarantee change. All of us feel the urgency of working out new ways of thinking about our work, our global relationships, and our organizations. What worked in the past is not going to work in the future. We can't manage for the status quo, for stability, growth, and predictability.

What is needed, as we have suggested, is a different orientation, a willingness to turn things on their heads by asking new and sometimes difficult questions and to live with the ambiguity while new processes are developed. This is frightening as well as energizing, for managing the learning organization demands much more of leaders and staff, of members and partner organizations. It demands thinking and learning together, with compassion, humility, and genuine empathic understanding.

The approach to organizational learning we describe in this chapter has been developed with a large number of voluntary organizations during the past several years. It formed a central framework in the "Grabbing the Tiger" workshops that preceded this book. It requires work in different areas and levels in the organization – what we call organizational "fields." Four such fields cover all the "territory," or relationships, of an organization, both inside its boundaries and outside.

Organizational Learning Fields

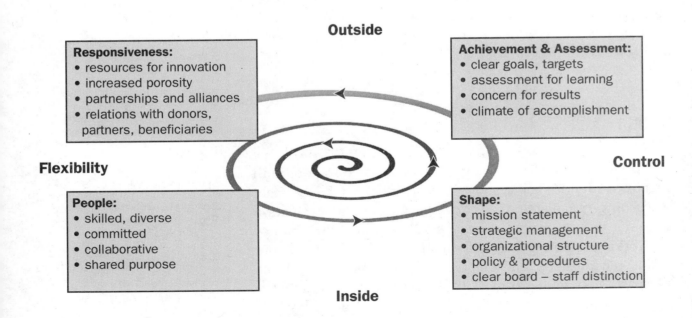

Outside

Responsiveness:
- resources for innovation
- increased porosity
- partnerships and alliances
- relations with donors, partners, beneficiaries

Achievement & Assessment:
- clear goals, targets
- assessment for learning
- concern for results
- climate of accomplishment

Flexibility

Control

People:
- skilled, diverse
- committed
- collaborative
- shared purpose

Shape:
- mission statement
- strategic management
- organizational structure
- policy & procedures
- clear board – staff distinction

Inside

This diagram depicts a set of dynamic relationships that characterizes all organizations. Organizational learning requires continuous work in all these fields and a dynamic balance among them. Two of these fields (achievement and responsiveness) are focussed on the *outside* of the organization; two (people and shape) are focussed on the *inside*. Similarly, the "people" and "responsiveness" fields require flexibility, while the "achievement" and "shape" fields require greater control.[1] Where an organization fits in this diagram depends on its purpose, values, history, and culture, as well as on the current context. Social-justice organizations often emphasize the "people" orientation over systems control. Well-funded organizations in a growth period may relax some of the control functions related to assessment or efficiency. When revenues are tight, however, or in a downsizing phase, more effort is put into the control and structure fields. A healthy organization finds an ongoing balance among all four fields rather than fluctuating back and forth from one field to another.

People

Whatever the orientation, learning begins with – and keeps coming back to – people, to their understanding, experience, and contribution. Supportive workplace relationships, working conditions, and management style are both a cause and effect of a learning organization. The way people behave in an organization – the culture and the policies – should be congruent with the social purpose and espoused values; this is especially the case with social-development organizations.

A focus on people involves:

• Attracting and keeping a skilled, diverse, gender-balanced group of staff, board, and volunteers who are committed to the organization, open to learning, and capable of working together

- Organizing teams that can withstand the pressures of collaborative learning

- Building a climate conducive to unleashing the energies of creative people

- Building a shared understanding about the purpose of the organization and its core values

Responsiveness

This field includes creativity, openness to information, responsiveness to members, donors, and partners as well as an attitude that encompasses daring to think and act in new, exciting ways. Considerable private-sector research has focused on the need for organizations to relate to their external environment through enhanced information gathering, stronger relationships with networks comprising suppliers, other producers, and customers. In a turbulent and unpredictable business environment, a responsive and flexible attitude to external relationships can be the difference between surviving or not.

In the NGO and voluntary sector, the same external conditions apply, although the end purposes are different. In a paper called *Operationality in Turbulence*, a British NGO, ACORD, makes a number of insightful recommendations for living in a changing world:[2]

- Listen to beneficiaries and to donors; and increase the "porosity" of the agency to feedback from people most directly affected by the programs.

 Dialogue between beneficiary groups and NGOs entails sensitivity to issues of privilege (including class, race, and gender), and valuing indigenous experience and knowledge, not just expert knowledge.[3] This recommendation is at the core of the organizational learning process, especially for international-development NGOs working to redress injustices and inequalities of vulnerable groups. Outsiders to the development process – northern donors and NGOs – must listen to and learn from the experience and indigenous knowledge of local people.[4]

- Ensure resources for continuous innovation and creativity. People need the space, both physical and emotional, to engage in creative problem solving. It's not enough to exhort people to make greater efforts.

- Build partnerships and alliances. No organization can go it alone. Networks, mergers, coalitions, consortia are emerging as new organizational forms. They increase the impact of the work – and learning – across organizational boundaries.

The ACORD document suggests some interesting bases on which to judge success in terms of responsiveness. What percentage of program staff time is spent with front-line staff and key decision makers in other organizations? What percentage of action-research projects, pilot projects, and budget are devoted to this? How often do we speak to funders? Is there quality control by funders and partners? How many funder visits to programs, and program visits to funders, are there? And our favourite – how many unnecessary procedures, regulations, meetings, and committees are *renounced* per month?

Shape

Structures and systems are about control and definition – not about quashing energy or initiative but channelling them through organizational goals, appropriate structures, and accountability mechanisms. Some of these are:

- Clear delineation of staff and board responsibilities, based on a shared and conscious purpose. There are many workable arrangements, but every organization needs to period-ically revisit this agreement.

- A mission statement or statement of purpose and values – a formal declaration of the core purpose of the organiza-tion. (See Chapter 4.)

- An organizational structure that facilitates important rela-tionships (vertical and lateral), focuses attention on critical tasks, and facilitates key accountabilities. (See Chapter 5.)

- A set of policies and procedures that stimulates both indi-vidual and organizational learning, from the traditional, (such as performance appraisal for both board and staff) to a research policy, program and institutional evaluations, and project visits. (See Chapter Seven.)

All these structuring activities need to be implemented with the exigencies of the other fields in mind. The control aspects of policy and procedure are often thought to be at odds with enhancing staff creativity and motivation. In fact, however, the two need to work together.

Achievement and Assessment

Work in this field builds a climate of accomplishment. Goals, targets, a commitment to achievement, a concern for mea-surement and greater impact are the central preoccupations of this field. This field has been highly problematic for volun-tary organizations and NGOs, and the subject of considerable debate and research. Evaluations tend to be undertaken because they are required by the funder rather than as an essential aspect of planning and learning. A recent analysis of the sustainability of Canadian international-development NGOs found nearly unanimous agreement among intervie-wees that the lack of meaningful assessment and evaluation is a serious shortcoming of NGO work in Canada.[5] The current discussion of the meaning and implications of "results-based" management is contributing fresh perspectives and approaches to the assessment of the non-quantitative, and often invisible, impacts of our work.

In summary, organizations learn by paying attention to all the organizational tasks and relationships in each of these four fields: to the people, to the systems, structures, and procedures; to the external world, and to the task at hand.

Managing for Learning

"Our organization has always worried about these things," you say. "How is this any different?"

A learning organization demands a fundamental shift in the way we think and relate to one another. Managing for the status quo means striving for predictability, stability, individual accountability, decisiveness, and consistency. Status-quo organizations value people who know what they are doing, who have the "right answer." Managing for learning requires that we admit that we don't really know the answer – indeed, that there is no certainty. The writer Boris Pasternak has Zhivago speak about the hubris of a rational, purposive method of reshaping how people work together:

> Reshaping life! People who say that have never understood a thing about life – they have never felt its breath, its heart – however much they have seen or done. They look on it as a lump of raw material to be processed by them, to be ennobled by their touch. But life is never a material, a substance to be moulded. If you want to know, life is the principle of self-renewal, it is constantly renewing and remaking and changing and re-configuring itself, it is infinitely beyond your and my theories about it.[6]

Thinking for change requires us to live with uncertainty,

ambiguity, and complexity, to realize that answers can emerge only from the collaboration of people with different interests, knowledge, and points of view who are willing to "craft" an answer together.[7]

The Problem with Problem Solving

Managing an organization for learning means leaving behind one of our most cherished (often male) management practices. For years we have valued "problem solving" and the manager who clearly defines the problem, sets out solutions, and takes swift decisive action.

So what's the problem with problem solving? Let's look at problem-solving logic and how it sometimes blocks real learning.

Traditional problem solving starts with the awareness that something needs fixing – and then sets about seeking to understand it through research and analysis. It is a methodology firmly focused on finding the best possible solution.

Steps in Traditional Problem Solving

1. Define the problem

2. Collect information

3. Analyse the information

4. Generate possible solutions

5. Select the best solution

6. Implement, or pilot, the best solution

7. Evaluate the outcome

It is comfortable, low-risk, predictable, directed at completing the task with as few mistakes as possible, and socially acceptable. As such, it is not disorderly, unpredictable, high risk, or inefficient, qualities associated with what George Prince has termed "speculative and creative" thinking.[8]

The difficulty with this method is that by focusing on the problem and the best solution, we tend to stay within the very logic that may have caused the problem in the first place. For example, a problem of staff workload could suggest the solution to add more staff or cut the amount of work. It may not necessarily lead to questions about the nature of the work and whether staff should be involved at all. More speculative or creative processes will be discouraged by a lack of time and resources, and by a mentality that prides itself on "making tough decisions" efficiently.

Possibility Creating

An alternative to traditional problem solving is "possibility creating." The process begins the same way – with an awareness that something is wrong. But instead of narrowing the discussion to concentrate on solutions to the problem, the process opens up to questions that do not limit but rather extend, questions that may seem illogical or out of line – even "unacceptable."

In the staff-overload issue, the discussion might pose questions such as, What do we want our organizational lives to be like? We might use metaphors, stories, or word associations; go off on tangents; look for possibilities that energize and inspire, ones that move the discussion, and the eventual solution, to unexpected places. This involves letting go of the need to stay focused on the outcome – on the conscious purpose of the effort.

Gregory Bateson reminds us that conscious purpose blinds us to complexity in ecological and social systems. Conscious purpose narrows our attention to the goal and the best means for achieving it. This logic ignores more holistic ways of understanding relationships – indeed, international-development projects have been criticized for not valuing, or not understanding, the many social and psychological impacts of their carefully planned projects.[9]

Bateson's condemnation of conscious purpose is a radical critique of management practice and culture. If we admit that the world is complex, unpredictable, and somehow interdependent, then we have to admit that we need to look at the problem in its broader context, that any given action will have an impact on other parts of the system, and that the best solutions can be generated only by a group of people with knowledge of the various aspects of the whole. Recognizing this complexity means avoiding the temptations of simplistic "bottom-line" thinking. Some examples illustrate the importance of avoiding simple solutions for complex organizational-learning tasks:

- Research by Richard Pascale describes how successful companies lose ground if they don't challenge their current theory of success. His research found that organizations need both "fit," (i.e., control, coherence, and adaptation to their environment) and "split" (i.e., de-centralization, variety, and individual freedom). It is the tension between fit and split that makes learning possible.[10]

- Charles Handy sums up the nature of "dilemma" as the following: "Most of the dilemmas we face in this time of confusion are not the straightforward ones of choosing between right and wrong, where compromise would be weakness, but the much more complicated dilemmas of right and right. I want to spend more time on my work *and* with my family; we want to trust our subordinates *but* we need to know what they are doing."[11]

- Danny Miller's recent work describes how companies that have a particular strength may fail because they neglected the opposite of that strength. For example, companies whose strength is the design of quality products may fail because they emphasize quality design to such an extent that they are incapable of the compromises demanded by the marketplace.[12]

- A study of managerial learning found that managers were most likely to learn when they experienced both pressure and support. A study of school innovation came to the same conclusion.[13]

- In a famous *Harvard Business Review* article, a Canadian steel company found that they had to think about both "bubbles and boxes." Bubbles were the softer issues of morale and teamwork; boxes were the harder issues of costs and technology.[14]

It is the tension between fit and split that makes learning possible.

- Robert Quinn's book on leadership, *Beyond Rational Management*, emphasizes the importance of the leader's ability to manage competing values – sufficient flexibility for innovation and responsiveness to changing situations, sufficient control to insist on accomplishment and the assessment of results. [15]

Taken together, the requirements for a learning organization add up to a different way of managing.[16] It may not be entirely accurate to call this a "feminist" approach, but it is certainly "post-patriarchal," de-emphasizing heroic individual struggle, competitiveness, hierarchy, and rational problem solving. This style would admit to complexity, and work toward inclusiveness and dialogue while injecting an urgency that calls for effective, timely decision making, innovation, accomplishment, and ongoing responsiveness to the changing world. It calls for a balance between flexibility and control, between process and content. Erring too much on one side or the other can have serious consequences down the road. This post-patriarchal style is, at its core, a way of managing that reconciles apparent opposites.

Organizational Learning in Practice: Two Cases

The two short cases that follow illustrate the contrast between a "common-sense" problem-solving approach and an approach more oriented to organizational learning:

Case #1: Canada

Recently, a medium-sized Canadian social-justice NGO ended the year with a sizable deficit after their annual fundraising campaign. It was immediately clear that the organization had to scale back its operations. The board executive and senior management debated ways to deal with this issue. The "prac-

Case Example

tical" thinkers saw it as a simple problem with a straightforward solution: cut the budget and redouble efforts to raise more money. In other words, be the same organization, only $1 million smaller.

Cutting the budget necessitated cutting staff. The pragmatists argued that the best approach was to establish priorities among current activities and lay off staff accordingly. (The staff, of course, would be offered fair compensation.) This group viewed the crisis as a chance to streamline the organization and make it more fiscally conscious.

The difficulty with this apparently straightforward approach is shown in the diagram below. Recent private-sector research finds that this practical approach does not necessarily lead to financial stability. Reducing staff and programs leads to dispirited staff, less accomplishment, and less commitment. This leads to conflict and a general lessening of organizational effectiveness. The result is yet greater financial difficulty.[17]

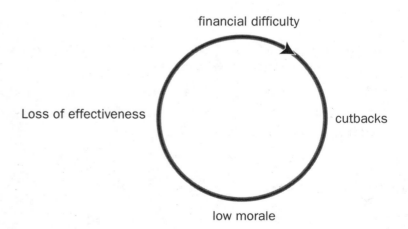

The opposing group opted for a learning approach that recognized the complexity of the situation. They proposed to rethink the organization in terms of the environmental changes that had resulted in the shortfall, and to link this to major changes in the development field. This option eventually won out.

An early event in this process was a workshop and consultation that produced a vision of what the organization might be. A number of parallel processes were also developed with the staff to ensure their participation and to deal with stress and personal needs for support – including financial and personal counselling and voluntary-termination packages. This humane approach allowed the staff to bring considerable energy to very difficult discussions. What followed was a consultative process that asked the question, How can we make the vision operational within our current budget?

Although the outcome of the two approaches meant budget and staff cuts, important learning took place as a result of choosing the second approach. The organization has a new vision, a new approach to working with members, and a new programming approach. This has left the organization well positioned to deal with the ongoing challenges.

This is not to say the latter option was easier, and indeed it has been less than a resounding success. The pragmatists on the board and in the membership fought hard for their views. The conflict split the organization and ate up enormous professional and emotional energy at a most critical time. This conflict, however, was an important developmental step and allowed the organization to work out a basic value dilemma. The outcome is reflected in a newly elected board that seems to be committed to the learning approach. A period of healing and relative peace has returned to the organization.

It is worth examining the assumptions underlying the second approach:

1. The spirit, commitment, and engagement of the staff, board, and members are essential to effective organization-

al change. This level of engagement must be preserved in cost-cutting programs.

2. Clarifying or rebuilding an organizational vision can be critical to resolving tensions and conflict. The resolution process can energize staff, board, and membership.

3. A precipitous change in the external environment, such as a dramatic drop in donor support, may be about more than just revenues and deficits. There may be other reasons behind the shortfall that the organization does not understand. This situation should be viewed as an opportunity to rethink the organization's position and perspective in all areas of work.

4. Accountability to members, board, and donors matters. It is the foundation of democratic change.

5. A significantly smaller organization is not just smaller – it is different. It may require a new structure, new ways of working with members and partners, and a new way of working with one another.

6. A turbulent environment demands a commitment to learning.

Case Example

Case #2: Asia

The second case example is drawn from the experience of a large Asian development NGO engaged in a number of development projects with women. In the past few years, it has attempted to improve the quality of its support to these projects. The leaders realized that improved service to women would require changing the attitudes of its largely male staff, but there was little understanding of the role of gender in development thinking and the changes required to implement a more gender-equitable program.

There were those in the leadership group who saw this as a problem to be solved rather than an exploration to be charted. The problem-solving solution was to design the best possible training program, run as many of the staff through the program as possible, and assume that staff, equipped with their new understanding of and sensitivity to gender issues, would make the organization more amenable to female staff and the programs more gender sensitive.

After considerable discussion, an alternative approach emerged. It started with the recognition that improving gender relations is not something anyone knows much about; therefore, what is needed is not training but exploration and learning. Moreover, this learning cannot be individual: change is needed in the culture and functioning of the organization itself.

The process developed was the following:

- Commit to a process of organizational and individual learning

- Put together a team: insiders with knowledge of the organization and its programs and outsiders with knowledge of gender and organizational change

- Develop an understanding of changing gender relations in the context of this organization (this was done by the team in discussion with managers and staff)

- Carry out a large-scale needs assessment that developed knowledge about gender relations in the organization

- Design and carry out an action-learning program that ties exploration of gender issues to specific action plans for change

- Hold trainers and managers accountable for accomplishing the goals agreed on

Let's look at the assumptions underlying this approach:

1. Left on their own, most staff will continue to act in a way that does not change gender relations; therefore, direction is required from the top.

2. Our beliefs about gender are culturally and socially determined. They are often unconscious and unquestioned, and not responsive to exhortations to change. A learning process is required that works on basic beliefs.

3. Commitment is more important than constraint: staff need to develop their own understanding of what is necessary and commit to a set of changes that makes sense to them in their situation.

4. Although this is a process of exploration, it needs to be tied to programming goals. People need to be accountable for change.

Key Aspects of Organizational Learning

These two cases reveal several important aspects of the organizational learning process.

1. Knowledge Building

Both organizations immersed themselves in a flow of information about the issue at hand, the broader environment, the feelings and beliefs of staff and leadership, and ideas from the outside. Significantly, important information came through "accountability structures": donors, board, and members. This information was used to create new organizational knowledge.

2. Thinking Together

The solutions that emerged were the product of many people thinking together. But just getting people together is not enough; both organizations effectively used staff consultations, a search conference, management planning conferences, questionnaires, and workshops.

3. Relationships

When they were at their best, both processes were characterized by a respectful, collaborative search for truth. At their worst, they were characterized by competition, lack of respect for other points of view, and the rigid defence of entrenched beliefs that may no longer be appropriate.

4. Complexity

Both organizations went beyond simple problem-solving approaches. Dealing with contradiction was particularly evident in the second case. In order to change gender relations, the NGO used a mixture of pressure from the top and involvement of the staff in determining their own goals for change.

5. Individual Learning

In both cases there was a requirement for staff and leadership to learn as individuals. This learning included ideas about the context, about fund raising, about change, about gender relations.

6. Accountability

Both organizations felt accountable in particular ways to their executive director, board, members, donors – i.e., to the constituencies that support and nourish their work. This aspect, however, is probably the least developed part of both change processes.

7. Gender and Patriarchy

Both organizations are evolving toward a post-patriarchal method of leadership that can integrate all these ideas and avoid the simplistic "common-sense" solutions usually rooted in the convictions of a small group of people at the top of the organization.

In summary, many NGOs and voluntary organizations are faced with internal and external forces that threaten their survival. Traditional approaches are not up to the job of organizational change on the scale now required. In this chapter we have argued that new approaches to problem solving are essential to transformation. These approaches must come from an orientation to organizational learning that draws on the experience, knowledge, and commitment of the people, that aligns organizational structures and strategies behind a vision, that is capable of assessing results, and that balances the need for adequate control/accountability mechanisms with the need for flexible, creative responses to the external environment.

References

1. R. Quinn, *Beyond Rational Management* (San Francisco: Jossey-Bass, 1988).

2. ACORD, "Operationality in Turbulence: The Need for Change," draft discussion paper, London, November 1992.

3. U. Narayan, "Working Together Across Difference: Some Considerations on Emotions and Political Practice," *Hypatia* 3, no. 2 (Summer 1988).

4. R. Chambers, *Rural Development: Putting the Last First* (London: Longman, 1983).

5. L. Cumming with B. Singleton, "Organizational Sustainability – an End of the Century Challenge for Canadian Voluntary International Development Organizations," paper for the eleventh annual Conference of the Canadian Association for the Study of International Development, Montréal, 1995.

6. We are indebted to Marie Gillen for this quote from Pasternak's *Dr. Zhivago*, in M. Gillen, "Religious Women in Transition: A Qualitative Study of Personal Growth and Organizational Change," Ph.D. thesis, University of Toronto, (OISE), 1980.

7. M. Schrage, *Shared Minds: The New Technologies of Collaboration* (New York: Random House, 1990).

8. G. Prince, "Creativity and Learning as Skills, not Talents," *The Phillips Exeter Bulletin*, June–July, and September–October 1980.

9. G. Bateson, *Steps to an Ecology of Mind* (New York: Ballantine, 1972).

10. R. Pascale, *Managing on the Edge* (New York: Simon and Schuster, 1990).

11. C. Handy, *The Empty Raincoat* (London: Hutchison, 1994).

12. D. Miller, *The Icarus Paradox* (New York: Harper, 1990).

13. D. Kelleher, P. Finestone, and A. Lowy, "Managerial Learning, First Notes from an Unstudied Frontier", *Group and Organizational Studies*, September 1986; M. Huberman and M. Miles, *Innovation Up Close* (New York: Plenum, 1984).

14. D. Hurst, "Of Bubbles, Boxes and Effective Management," *Harvard Business Review*, May–June 1984.

15. R. Quinn, op. cit.

16. F. Kofman, and P. Senge "Communities of Commitment: The Heart of Learning Organizations," *Organizational Dynamics*, Fall 1993.

17. D. Noer, *Healing the Wounds* (San Francisco: Jossey-Bass, 1993); *Globe and Mail, Report on Business*, "Survivors Also Suffer in Downsizing: Expert," Tuesday, May 23, 1995.

PART II

Levers for Change: Culture, Strategy, and Structure

Part I of this book has presented some of the key ideas about organizations and change. Chapter 1 reviewed fundamental ways of thinking about how our organizations work: ideas about bureaucracy; patriarchy and how it affects relationships in the workplace; and rationality as a particular way of relating to problems and solutions. Chapter 2 set out the framework for a different way of understanding organizations if we see them as places for learning as well as for doing.

The second part of this book will examine three key levers for organizational change: culture, strategy, and structure. Successful organizational change efforts need to work on each of these and to consider the interplay among them.

Culture and Organizational Change

3

THE CONCEPT OF ORGANIZATIONAL CULTURE FIRST CAUGHT THE attention of managers almost thirty years ago. Management training programs were focusing on issues of leadership and motivation of workers. Through experiential learning approaches and sensitivity training, the programs had a powerful impact on the managers attending. They returned to their organizations excited about working in new ways. Then came the letdown: they had changed, but their organizations had not. Their new skills received a hostile reception.

Later research confirmed that new management attitudes and skills alone were not enough to translate into organizational change.[1] Nevertheless managers and consultants had learned an important lesson: there is an organizational set of values, beliefs, and rules of behaviour beyond the power of individual managers to change. Therefore, training individuals does not result in change in the larger system of organizational ways of being, or "culture."

This was the beginning of the understanding that individual learning is only one part of organizational change. The "culture" has to change as well.

Organizational researchers, practitioners, and educators discovered that culture may facilitate change as well as block it, that some cultures are more amenable than others to change, but that all cultures are changeable, deliberately or not. This chapter will explore this relationship between culture and change.

What Is Organizational Culture?

Organizational culture is the pattern of shared beliefs and values that has worked to solve important organizational problems in the past.

Organizational culture is the pattern of shared beliefs and values that has worked to solve important organizational problems in the past. These beliefs and values reflect the assumptions that people make about their work. Fundamental values and principles are set out in mission statements and reflected in the way work is organized. They govern how people relate to one another in the workplace, how decisions are made, how clients are treated, how authority is exercised, and a myriad of other issues fundamental to collaborative work.[2]

Some organizations care about serving customers, and it shows in everything they do; some expect that senior members will be accorded respect and deference; and others are more informal and egalitarian. Culture can be thought of as the values and behaviours that make one organization "feel" different from another, although culture is often not noticed by those within an organization.

Many of the values and deeper assumptions underlying workplace behaviour are not fully obvious or conscious; indeed, sometimes these hidden assumptions and values run counter to the organization's formal value statements.

For example, a public-housing authority recently spent much time and some money on a process to engage tenants in the management of their community. However, whenever the tenants developed ideas about how the community could manage aspects of their life in a different way, staff always seemed to have good reasons why it wouldn't work. While claiming to value tenant participation, the organizational culture of the housing authority actually valued engineering above all else. What counted were efficiency and material considerations. If an idea could not be justified by a cost-benefit analysis, or if it upset existing engineering routines, it was unacceptable. Participation never had a chance.

Another NGO built a reputation for very high quality programming, developed and carefully controlled from the head office. However, as conditions changed in various regions of the world, the head office found it increasingly difficult to adapt. Many organizational members felt that the best way to deal with this issue was to decentralize program planning and authority. People in the centre worried that this might compromise quality. What emerged from the ensuing debate was the deeply held assumption that quality could be guaranteed only by central control. Decentralization was thus impossible until the culture changed.

A number of writers have tried to analyse the key dimensions of culture. For example, cultures can be classified as formal or informal, as centralized or decentralized. "Universalistic" organizations believe that rules and standard procedures are crucial to effective functioning; "particularistic" organizations believe that situations vary over time and in different locations, and what is required is a capacity to innovate and be responsive to a particular situation. Such classification schemes are helpful, but can blind us to the subtleties of a specific organizational culture. (These categories are a little like calling someone "outgoing" – the word differentiates her from others who may be quieter, but it does little more.) Organizational culture, like personality, emerges on longer acquaintance.[3]

Power is one characteristic of culture that is not always explicitly named, yet it has tremendous influence on the structure and character of an organization. Power is distributed formally, through job titles and areas of control, as well as informally. Rarely, if ever, is it evenly distributed among persons and groups. Even in egalitarian organizations, certain persons and groups have disproportionate influence over how things are done. Everyone in an organization knows about power centres, cliques, insiders and outsiders, and the coercive power of "group think." It is a fact of organizational life. Understanding the cultural values surrounding issues of power is imperative to leading organizational change.[4]

Organizational Culture and Change

We have mentioned that organizational culture inhibits or facilitates change and that organizational culture itself can change or be changed. Let's look first at how culture blocks change. Consider what happens when an organization first starts out. The organization is set up to address a problem or need in the marketplace or in a particular community. The problem is solved in the first instance by the leader(s) whose answers, behaviour, and vision eventually become embedded in the culture. What and whom the leader pays attention to, what behaviour is rewarded, and how resources are allocated eventually become a set of integrated cultural norms. Leadership is central to organizational culture and change.

For example, a trade union was born in fierce conflict with management. The early leaders were warriors, whose legitimacy was based on a history of confrontation. The culture that evolved was one focused on conflict, and as the union grew it solved problems within this framework. Succeeding generations of leaders came out of the same tradition and espoused the same principles. The union was thus not likely to take a conciliatory approach to resolving problems or to heed would-be leaders who suggested collaborative methods.

As the example shows, organizational culture affects the range of choices or strategies that an organization will consider. Some potential strategies are dismissed, and others are simply not visible to insiders. Thus, we might say that culture is a conservative force: it defines the way of working that solved problems in the past. Cultures do not change easily because organizations are not likely to let go of ways that have made them successful. It often takes considerable pressure, or a serious crisis, to unblock a culture stuck in the past.

How does organizational culture change? Most cultural change is evolutionary and unconscious. Organizations continuously change as they confront problems demanding new responses. Change might be a by-product of other factors, such as major technological change or the sale and reorganization of the company. Sometimes the change is rapid and discontinuous – a sudden shock to the system. Many changes are not managed, merely survived. As we come to understand how important culture is to the goal of organizational change, we become more interested in how to modify or work with the culture in a deliberate way. In order to do this, leaders and managers must understand their organizational culture. A lack of understanding of its own culture can lead an organization into change efforts that are unexpectedly difficult or impossible, as we will see below.

Because changing culture is so difficult, it is not to be undertaken lightly. Often it needs an external trigger, usually financial or political pressures that call into question the ability of the organization to continue as it is. Conscious and deliberate evolution begins when people in the organization realize they are confronted with a problem that challenges their core assumptions. This can set off a process of reflection, cultural analysis, and "puzzle solving" that establishes new directions, identifies new values, new ways of behaving and organizing work. This process can cause conflict because it brings to the surface hidden assumptions and values, and because it can shake up customary power centres and relationships.

A school board undertook an exploration of the culture and how it functioned. The hierarchical and traditional ways of working were at odds with a stated belief in creativity and innovation. The consulting team worked with the staff to make the culture of the school board more open, communicative, and supportive of innovation. Important forces in the change process were the director of studies, and other leaders among the principals and at the board office. The team used an organizational-development method that relied on lots of information collection and residential workshops to discuss the culture and its effects on learning and managing. The team confronted issues of power, team membership, and the goals of schooling. Like all efforts at cultural change, this one sometimes involved conflict, but the conflict was important. Without it, there is no change.

Culture change often requires the involvement of outsiders – as observers or consultants, or as advisers who can challenge things that insiders take for granted. Often the observations of outsiders bring cultural assumptions and artifacts into the open. Another way to probe organizational culture, especially if it is only partly visible or conscious, is to examine areas of disagreement or tension, to look for points of friction that can reveal not fully conscious attitudes and assumptions that nevertheless have an impact on behaviour and expectations. All the material revealed by the process must be discussed and worked through by members of the organization. This incremental, puzzle-solving method builds greater organizational understanding of the culture, and clarifies how aspects of the culture can deeply affect how the organization functions.

Finally, culture change is sometimes the result of new leadership in an organization. (By leaders, we mean people with influence, not only executive authority.) Leaders legitimize a certain way of understanding and behaving – those things that are rewarded or sanctioned. Leaders can affect culture if they actively intervene to change the way things are done, but this takes time.

A new leader was central to a cultural change in a municipal buildings-permit department. The department went from a culture of enforcement and concern with the "book" to a concern for service to the citizen, from authoritarian leadership by the supervisor to professional responsibility, and from individual action to teamwork. This change emerged from deep public dissatisfaction with the department, and the appointment of a new leader who enunciated a change of direction for the department. He undertook a three-year consultative process, which used every possible tool to change the culture: promoting well-educated people who embodied the new values; putting people into teams; insisting on service; using statistics to track work; and introducing management consultants, trainers, surveys, meetings, workshops, and other management approaches.

A number of our observations on culture are illustrated in the story of "INGO" – a non-governmental international-development organization based in Canada. We chose this organization because the dilemmas it faced are not unusual among North American international-development NGOs, and should also resonate for people in other voluntary sectors as well. The INGO case describes two very different change efforts several years apart. The first effort failed to achieve its particular objectives, and the second one succeeded. What was different the second time around? What role did organizational culture play in both attempts? And what was learned?

Case Study

INGO: International NGO

This is not the full story of the organization we are calling INGO. In some ways INGO is a composite, although none of the events is fictional. It is the story of change from the perspective of the staff in the head office of the organization.

Organizational Change at INGO: Phase 1

For several decades, INGO has worked overseas to provide development assistance in education, health, agriculture, and community development. In the early years, INGO worked primarily through overseas governments, as there were few southern NGOs. By the 1980s, INGO was a multi-million-dollar organization, with offices overseas and in Canada, working exclusively with southern NGOs. It received the majority of its funding from the Canadian government, through the Canadian International Development Agency (CIDA). It had an international board with overseas and Canadian representatives, and a union representing all but the management staff and nationals of other countries. Through the 1970s and early 1980s, funding was not a problem, and INGO grew steadily.

From the beginning, INGO attracted strong "believers," people committed to the ideal of a more equitable world. Like all social-development organizations, it was, and is, values driven.

Major programming decisions were made in staff meetings at the regional level, and then taken to an international staff meeting, known as the Forum, which comprised staff representatives and managers from every region where INGO worked. INGO plans and budgets were approved at the Forum and then recommended to the board for formal approval. Managers in the head office and overseas formed a management group, but did not make programming decisions, although managers had considerable influence as members of the Forum. There was often considerable jostling and conflict in Forum meetings; the conflicts were often political or ideological in nature, and were rooted in loyalties to regional programs. In the early years, there was no overarching organization-wide program, just a loose compilation of regional programs tied together by a mission statement. Nevertheless, there was an effort to reach decisions by consensus and through consultation, not by vote.

Toward the end of the 1980s, annual CIDA grants to INGO began to be reduced in a cost-saving measure by the Canadian government. The changing financial picture underscored the need for organizational decisions in a number of areas: INGO needed overall goals and objectives, criteria for allocating – and cutting back – program funds, more efficient information and administrative systems, and greater co-ordination. The management group began to co-ordinate work in each of these areas, moving slowly into territory normally occupied by representational bodies such as the semi-annual forum.

The Forum, November 1989

In the summer of 1989, management forecast a serious deficit in the current budget and further government cuts. Under a board guideline to balance the annual budget, INGO management began to think about consolidating office structures overseas and in Canada. In early September, managers started a series of secret meetings to consider budget cuts that might include staff layoffs in the head office and elsewhere. The meetings were tense and difficult, with no agreement reached for a number of weeks.

Throughout the autumn, the executive director was preparing the staff for cuts, possibly up to 10 per cent of the current operating budget, which had already been trimmed substantially. Memos and financial statements were sent around the world and copied to the union. Despite these efforts, at each staff meeting people would challenge the figures: were they complete and accurate?

The union was convinced that the purpose of such communication was to soften up the staff for layoffs. One program officer describes the dynamic: "Mistrust of the budget was at the centre of the struggle. Many staff felt it would be used by management to defend cuts of staff. So the union kept demanding more information. We discovered in the end that the budget figures were real."

The tension reached a crescendo at the Forum meeting in November 1989. Preliminary budgets for the next fiscal year were to be approved before going to the board. As part of the budget preparation, the executive director asked the participants to prepare a cutback scenario for each region and the head office. The acrimonious debate that followed challenged the assumptions of the exercise, and pitted one region against another. It became obvious that only a vote would settle the dispute, but a vote would be won by management as they were in the majority. Rather than call a vote with such clearly destructive ramifications, the chair called for adjournment and turned the problem back to management.

The management took the scenario, more or less as defined in the Forum, and prepared to implement it. (It involved cuts of staff and offices in several Canadian centres as well as overseas.) In Canada, an intense lobbying effort fought to have the board put a stop to the management plan. Board members were contacted by Canadian regional staff, union representatives, and other members. The lobbying achieved its objective, for at its next board meeting in February 1990, the board rejected the management plan. Instead, management was asked to conduct a review of INGO's work in Canada, to be presented to the board in six months' time.

The Report of the Canadian Review adopted the position of Canadian regional staff and board: it pointed out that INGO's mission and strategic goals gave high priority to building a stronger base in Canada. It recommended that a greater portion of agency resources be allocated to work in Canada. The report was tabled at the next Forum meeting, in June 1990, to a tense and polarized gathering. But a plan and budget had to be recommended to the board. After considering various options, participants proposed to cut resources to the head office, to slightly increase resources for Canada, and to leave overseas programming levels more or less the same. The Canadian Review provided the rationale for this shift in budget percentages.

This plan was then recommended to the board of directors, which accepted it with few changes. When the results were announced, head-office staff were shocked and very angry. As one staffer put it:

> *The objectives of the change weren't clear, or weren't agreed upon. So people got hung up on the budget, especially the lower percentage for head office. What right did the board have to make this kind of decision? The board was not seen as a legitimate body. It was composed of the same Canadian-based interest groups. It was not perceived as speaking for us. Who speaks for staff in the head office?*

The board decision now made organizational change and restructuring inevitable. It sent a clear message to the organization, setting out which approaches were acceptable, and which were not. And it underscored the importance of paying attention to the membership of INGO, a constituency to whom Canadian regional board members were accountable. A new political coalition of the union, some members of the board, and Canadian regional staff had emerged to outmanoeuvre the management. Management was now isolated from the board and effectively disempowered. During the summer, the executive director resigned from INGO, leaving his successor to tackle the problem of how to downsize head office.

Case Study Analysis

This organizational change attempt failed in its objectives: to restructure and downsize. In so doing it unleashed powerful forces and conflicts, which had to be resolved for the change process to succeed. What prevented otherwise skilled and committed people from resolving these conflicts? What do these events demonstrate about organizational culture?

Roger Harrison, an American management consultant, has delineated the primary features of different organizational cultures, which might help us look at INGO.[5] One of these is defined as a "political" culture: a culture that is not driven by authority or task accomplishment but by attachment to particular values.

INGO's culture had many elements of a political culture. It valued participation in the decision-making process over management's right to manage. INGO had evolved a culture of inclusiveness in decision making; it was not expected that managers would make decisions behind closed doors. INGO valued decentralized structures more compatible with the organization's philosophy of development. It also valued personal commitment to the values espoused in the mission statement. Conflict around political and ideological issues were common; lobbying of the board by staff, union, and members was well within normal organizational behaviour.

INGO's political culture was one of high commitment and high involvement; it was egalitarian and informal. The management change plan and process was top down, low participation, and profoundly counter-cultural. It was driven by a desire to circumvent an unwieldy, time-consuming, and conflictual decision-making structure.

In such an organizational culture, management did not have the legitimacy to carry out their plan without the support of staff. Nor did they have the authority to make such decisions without the support of the regional membership represented by the board.

INGO: Phase 2

A New Era: Healing Open Wounds

The new executive director arrived in an organization that had been bruised by several years of conflict. She was an outsider with no recent history with INGO, and a very different leadership style from that of her predecessor. She asked the board for an extension on the downsizing deadline, and set about rebuilding broken relationships. As she described it:

> *I was excited by the challenge. I came into the organization not knowing it or the people. I did not know where people were coming from, or the internal dynamics. The main issues I saw were the tension between labour and management, and the board and management. There were tensions within the management team as well – a lot of historical baggage. It wasn't easy. I had a hard time discovering the culture. I always try to work with the culture, to work with what is there. I joined an organization which had just spent the past five years developing its vision – a vision I believed in. It's not my style to come up with and promote my own vision. In any case, this would not have worked in INGO. It took time for people to understand my style. Part of the problem was that people were not confident. I always tell people that we got ourselves into this mess, and we can get ourselves out. If we cannot solve our own problems, then who will do it for us?*

The staff were highly receptive to this open and transparent style. The new executive director moved through the office making contact with management and staff, secretaries and officers. Rumours that the executive director picked up in her travels were brought into staff meetings and discussed. She spoke at union meetings and legitimized union issues by

Case Study

ensuring they were placed on the organizational agenda. Union representatives were included in organizational meetings. These efforts helped to bring to the surface and then diffuse the tensions, and to deal openly with the destructive assumptions and behaviours that had warped the organization. They also helped to clarify the separate roles of management, union, and board, and to build a greater sense of unity. The executive director insisted over and over that INGO was one organization, not seven, and that working together for a common purpose was the only way to survive.

This repair work was an essential precursor to the tough decisions ahead. But it was not enough to propel INGO into making the decisions. What was needed was a push from outside.

It came two days into the next fiscal year, hours after the last session of a tough planning and budgeting meeting with the managers. A phone call from CIDA informed the executive director of a major cut to INGO's overseas-program budget. It was clear that change was now an organization-wide problem, not just a local one for the head office. Decisions of this magnitude needed to be co-ordinated around agreed principles, programming criteria, and fair procedures.

Managing Organizational Change

It took some experimentation and some failed attempts before a workable change process and structure was in place. What did *not* work was a formal, representative, "Organizational Change Committee" and subcommittees headed up by managers. The committee got bogged down just as previous structures had, in reliance on representing a particular perspective, in difficulties reaching consensus, and with little motivation or resources to move toward action; as well, the managers were too preoccupied with operational work to devote adequate time to the committee's work. After two months of going around in circles, the committee was disbanded by the executive director.

A "change team" of three staff was seconded from their permanent positions to work part-time with an external consultant to build some energy and momentum around a process that would ensure decisions within the set deadline. The change team reported directly to the executive director, not to management, and had no management members. Instead, it was staffed by three former union leaders who applied to share the job after a debate within the union resulted in a union agreement to collaborate in the change process. One manager describes this sea change:

> *The hiring of a full-time change team was a turning point. It signalled that the union was open, since three union leaders applied for the one position. The executive director was wise enough to go with this. This was the spark on the tinder box. This removed two of the biggest blocks: the labour-management divide, and the board-management divide, since one of the applicants was both a union leader and on the board. She was close to a number of people on the board who were influential, and were also most critical of management.*

The change process, developed by the change team, focused on building consensus throughout the organization, especially in the head office. It ensured greater participation, cross-unit communication, and the generation of a broader pool of ideas about the content of change. The process served as a model for the kind of organizational behaviour that was more compatible with INGO's stated values. A program officer described the process:

> *The meetings were breaking down traditional barriers - there were some battles but they were face to face rather than in their separate groups. There is a political correctness in INGO, and people shy away from confronting each other openly, or worse, they dismiss those who do not agree. In order to have real participation, you need to look at the barriers to equal participation - they are intellectual, gender, hierarchical -*

support staff versus program management. People need the confidence to speak. The cross-unit meetings were a good approach.

The interesting thing about this approach is that it completely ignored the traditional decision-making structures – management meetings, the Forum, and other representative staff structures. The executive director opted instead for a change structure based on different principles, and parallel to, not part of, the ongoing operational structures. Participants in special planning and transition meetings were selected not according to their position or geographic location in the organization or according to whom they represented but according to their ability to contribute to the change process – to create, to problem solve, and to work for the good of the organization as a whole.

One of these meetings, in October 1991, designed a new structure for the head office. This "meeting" was accountable to the executive director, and through her to the board. Once the plan had been approved by the board, management developed the details of the downsizing process and worked with the union to implement the changes. Close to 20 per cent of the head office staff, as well as staff from other regions of the organization, volunteered to leave INGO. There were no involuntary layoffs. A number of other working units were restructured, new units were added, and a matrix structure was introduced for the major programming functions. When the restructuring was over in the head office, there was a clear sense of achievement and a pride in having overcome a major organizational crisis.

Lessons INGO Learned from Organizational Change

- People who are without influence in the change process can feel "victimized" – anxious, confused, angry.
- Open, transparent, regular, and clear communication with staff and members is central. Present the facts, dis-

cuss the rumours, answer questions. Use staff meetings, written communication, and one-on-one meetings. Offer lots of support.

- Define clearly what information is public and what needs to be confidential.

- Follow and/or develop clear policies, criteria, and processes for change to encompass program and staffing. Avoid ad hoc or one-on-one negotiations.

- Find a fair balance between full consultation and participation, and efficient decision making. Processes that drag on add costs and stress, but participation is very important. Be clear about deadlines and where final decisions rest, and about who is accountable for what.

- Ongoing monitoring and evaluation are essential, to catch problems before they become serious. Be open to hearing about and dealing with problems.

- Monitor staff workload. In the transition, adapting to new work without fully dropping the old can add stress and time.

- Support the transition with additional resources – research, planning, training, and support for grieving, as people let go of old ways and say goodbye to staff who are leaving.

- Pursue every alternative to staff layoffs, especially involuntary layoffs.

- Consider the process to be a "program," and allocate necessary time and resources to it. Organizational rebuilding is not an "add-on."

What differentiated this process from the earlier one?

- The leadership change helped unblock polarized and conflicted relationships. The executive director worked from an explicit feminist value stance and clearly articulated her management principles: openness, fair treatment, inclu-

Case Study Analysis

sion, clear lines of accountability, unity and shared responsibility, and a commitment to people first. She ensured that decisions were made within the alloted time frame. Where processes broke down, she stepped in.

- The political coalition that defeated the earlier management plan was now part of the change process; the board was clearly taking the lead. The management and board relationship was rebuilt with the active intervention of the executive director and outside facilitation. The executive director took responsibility for the process and was held accountable to the board. This time around, everyone knew where decisions were being made, and the criteria for making them.

- The first management-led process aimed to cut part of the Canadian regional structure – a structure whose membership base had considerable influence on the board. This base essentially defeated the first change effort. On the other hand, the second change process was not contentious among the members or regional staff. If anything, the opposite was the case: there was support at the board to trim what some saw as the over-resourced bureaucracy at the centre.

- The union was brought into the change process as a colleague rather than an adversary, with the support of the executive director.

- The change process was managed outside the established decision-making structures, short-circuiting customary behaviour and structural blocks. The change team, acting as "agents of change," had considerable organizational legitimacy, given their links to the staff, the union, and the board.

The second time around, the change process built on organizational principles of participation and transparency. The work of the change team was completely accessible to the union and to management through the executive director, and through regular communication. Throughout, emphasis was placed on building organizational coherence, although the process was dominated by staff in the head office. While downsizing was under way in the head office, considerable effort was going into strengthening program principles and changing programming guidelines to ensure that all programs fitted clearly within the mission and organizational priorities. This work continued after the head-office changes and developed its own change dynamics and dilemmas. In hindsight, the lack of more substantive regional input into the head-office restructuring weakened some of the new structures, which required collaboration with regional colleagues.

The change process and restructuring gave a number of staff the opportunity to leave the organization voluntarily. As an organization undertakes new directions, there are always some staff who decide not to be part of the new organization. Staff renewal can result from people leaving, receiving additional training, or moving into new positions. These personal decisions were aided by the availability of a voluntary severance package that provided ample financial incentives.

Finally, the management issue at INGO was resolved through a series of planned interventions – board/staff retreats, management team building – that clarified the role and legitimacy of the management function. Some of these were part of the strategic-planning processes mentioned above, but others were exercises designed to mend fences between former combatants. As clarity and trust grew, it was possible to let go of the defensiveness and blame that had characterized earlier behaviour.

The international staff Forum never met again. Many of its programming and operational functions were taken up without controversy by the revitalized management team. The organization had reached a healthier balance between flexibility and control.

INGO's two experiences highlight several important things about organizational change and culture. First, fundamental change requires understanding of the organizational culture and how to work with it – not against it. This means learning how to bring to the surface underlying assumptions and values that shape both individual and group behaviour and feed into conflict around the change. (Sometimes this culture change is an unanticipated outcome of planned change.) This process can be difficult for insiders to accomplish alone.

In summary, culture is the pattern of conscious – but often unconscious – beliefs, values, and ways of working that can either block or facilitate change. Cultures also delineate how power is spread and managed throughout an organization. Working with the organizational culture means managing power, especially in politicized organizations in which unity requires building coalitions of interests to confront a common problem rather than one another. In this process, some "old behaviour" will give way to new behaviour, and the culture itself will change. A strengthened and renewed organization will be well placed to manage the changes that lie ahead.

References

1. C. L. Cooper and I. Mangham, *T-Groups, A Survey of Research* (Toronto: Wiley, 1971); W. Schutz, "The Effects of a T-Group Laboratory on Interpersonal Behaviour," *Journal of Applied Behavioural Science* 2, 1966.

2. C. Hampden-Turner, *Creating Corporate Culture from Discord to Harmony* (Reading: Addison-Wesley, 1990); C. Handy, *The Gods of Management* (London: Souvenir Press, 1978); S. Sackmann, *Cultural Knowledge in Organizations: Exploring the Collective Mind* (Beverly Hills: Sage, 1991); E. Schein, *Organizational Culture and Leadership*, 2d ed. (San Francisco: Jossey-Bass, 1992).

3. E. Schein, op. cit.

4. L. Greiner, and V. Schein, *Power and Organizational Development: Mobilizing Power to Implement Change* (Reading: Addison-Wesley, 1988).

5. R. Harrison, "Understanding Your Organization's Character," *Harvard Business Review*, May–June 1972.

Strategy Making

COMMUNITIES INTERNATIONAL IS A MEDIUM-SIZED NGO WITH A head office in Canada and field offices in a number of overseas countries. They have just ended their February strategic-planning meetings. The planning and policy team at headquarters, led by a visionary executive director, revises their strategic plan in February of each year, evaluates annual reports from the field, and forecasts trends that will affect the work of the agency. The planning team then puts together the strategic plan to be implemented by program staff. Regular progress reports will measure outcomes against plan criteria.[*]

What's wrong with this picture?

This is not a strategic-planning process, it is a patriarchal control fantasy. Although few NGOs plan this way, this system embodies many of the assumptions underlying what people think strategic planning *should* be. This is the model of effective management of the 1960s and 1970s and continues to be the benchmark of managerial virtue, although there is little evidence that this approach to planning improves organizational effectiveness. As

---

[*] Communities International is a fictional NGO.

the planning writer Aaron Wildavsky explains, "... planning is not defended for what it accomplishes but for what it symbolizes – rationality. Planning is conceived as the way intelligence is applied to social problems.... Planning is good because it is systematic rather than random, efficient rather than wasteful, coordinated rather than helter-skelter, consistent rather than contradictory and above all rational rather than unreasonable.[1]

Strategic planning purports to be a mechanism to ensure accountability and control. Yet this control may be largely illusory.

During the past ten years, it has become accepted that good organizations have strategic plans, although some managers in voluntary organizations remain ambivalent about importing corporate processes into NGOs. Staff have often felt that strategic planning is a centralizing and controlling process; some boards have welcomed it, while some have rebelled at the formality and the time commitment required. Its major attraction for boards and donors is that it purports to be a mechanism to ensure accountability and control. Yet this control may be largely illusory.

Strategic planning reduces a complex set of tasks and organizational relationships to carefully described (and ideally quantified) strategic issues, strengths, weaknesses, strategic directions, goals, objectives, activities, schedules, and measurable indicators of success. This process is then shrink-wrapped into text by analysts and planners often far from the "front lines," and imposed on managers and field staff.

Strategic thinking, planning, and management can be very useful to NGOs; but what *kind* of strategy making makes sense for NGOs and voluntary organizations?

The strategy making that is now essential must evolve from a particular kind of learning: learning forged from experience and honed by dialogue, reflection, and debate. It must distil individual and organizational experience gained through failure and success, through conflict and engagement with the world. Such learning is a process of building new knowledge, of transformation.

What is strategy?

Strategy is the basic *how*, the principal method of accomplishing the mission. It embeds the fundamental choices made to govern the use of resources and day-to-day actions. Business literature emphasizes that the purpose of strategy is to gain competitive advantage. NGOs may or may not be trying to obtain competitive advantage, but they still need to be able to demonstrate that they deserve the support of partners, funders, volunteers, and staff – that public funds and human energy are being well spent.

The word "strategy" has many meanings. The following section describes the two aspects of strategy as we understand the term.

First, strategy embodies the notion of *positioning*. In the private sector, position refers to market niche. In the public sector, it refers to the service or expertise that your organization is qualified to offer; it defines what you do. Thus, an international-development NGO may be positioned to support the development of co-operatives, or to advocate for more environmental safeguards, or to monitor human rights.

Strategy also includes considerations of *perspective*.[2] Perspective involves the choice of a particular set of values and ways of operating that creates an organization's "way of being." Perspective comes from our experience, what we have learned from our work. It is the knowledge we have created in an ongoing dialogue of action and reflection. Perspective is the amalgam of what we learn with others. When we put our perspective into practice, we are setting limits around the work we will do and how we will do it; we are making strategic, and in many cases ethical, choices.

For example, a public-health department reviewed its mission and its performance in meeting it. As a result of considerable reflection, it decided to devote more resources to prevention and education, and to cut back on public-health nursing. This

Strategy is the basic *how*, the principal method of accomplishing the mission. It embeds the fundamental choices made to govern the use of resources and day-to-day actions.

Strategy embodies the notion of positioning and perspective. **Position** refers to the service or expertise your organization has to offer. **Perspective** involves values and ways of operating which come from experience, knowledge, and dialogue.

decision reflects a change in their position. It required a similar change in perspective. They needed to view themselves as more directly connected, and accountable, to the community. As a result, the department has set up regional health councils, has decentralized many of its operations, and has restructured the department into multi-disciplinary teams.

Strategic Planning and Strategic Management

Every organization has a strategy, whether explicit or implicit. Implicit strategies can be observed in the way an organization defines its activities, in its budget decisions, and by looking at how people spend their time.

Strategic Planning

Strategic planning is a set of formal analytic procedures used to develop a "plan."

Strategic planning is a set of formal analytic procedures used to develop a "plan." There are many such systems, but most include the following steps:

1. Analysing the internal capabilities – strengths, weaknesses

2. Analysing the external environment for threats and opportunities; looking at competitors and the needs of customers, or clients

3. Analysing the future possibilities and current activities

4. Developing a mission, vision, or statement of principles

5. Establishing a strategy (embodying position and perspective)

6. Setting organizational goals within that strategy

7. Discussing with and communicating the plan to the various parts of the organization to develop commitment

8. Developing a set of subordinate goals for each part of the organization

9. Aligning the budget with the plan

10. Monitoring performance

Well, it all looks good, but does it help an organization do a better job? In the past several years there has been growing criticism of the underlying assumptions and some of the practices of strategic planning. In a recent book on strategic planning, Henry Mintzberg, a McGill University management professor, reviews current research on the effectiveness of strategic planning and finds that strategic planning does not seem to create more effective performance.[3] J. A. Pearce, summing up seventeen years of research on this issue, is quoted by Mintzberg as saying, "at best it may have some suitability in some contexts, such as larger organizations, those in mass production, etc."[4]

A formal planning structure does have some benefits: it enforces a break in the action to let us think, and it focuses attention on strategy.

So why hasn't strategic planning worked as it was supposed to? We believe that one answer lies in its formal logic, its detachment from the field, and its inflexibility. It encourages small additions to the existing plan, and discourages "start-from-scratch" thinking. It relies on a rationality that manipulates and sifts information to fit specified objectives. This sifting process can eliminate important sources of learning – the deeper and more implicit, sometimes intuitive, knowledge of our experience and feelings about our work. This experience is as much about our relationships with partner organizations, staff, members, and donors as it is about traditional development programming. Strategic planning, therefore, can impede responsiveness and openness to important ways of understanding.[5]

Strategic planning is often a centralizing as well as a co-ordinating process. In many larger organizations, responsibility for planning rests with head-office specialists in the belief that the head office has an overview of the whole organization. Although there is a certain logic to this division of labour, it erodes the opportunity for experiential learning that is such a rich source of knowledge for strategy making. A centralized and rational process also precludes or ignores other ways of making decisions.

Decision making is not always the result of a rational-analytic process. Researchers document what we all know so well: that decisions are often forged from multiple and competing goals, through political coalition building, compromises, hunches, and late-night resolutions. In fact, the strategic action of most organizations is often outside the planning system. After years of research and consulting, James Quinn, a management writer, concluded,

> For good reasons, strategies ... tend to emerge in ways that differ quite markedly from the usually prescribed textbook methodologies.... The processes used to arrive at the total strategy are usually fragmented, evolutionary and largely intuitive.... In well run organizations, managers proactively guide these streams of actions and events toward conscious strategies.... Far from being an abrogation of good management practice, [this approach] probably provides the best normative model for strategic decision-making.[6]

This is not to suggest that we can dismiss strategic planning as just another fad. On the contrary, many NGOs and voluntary organizations have found that an explicit, more open, strategy-making process has taken them in directions they did not foresee. The effectiveness lies in the approach to planning.

Strategic Management

Strategic management is an orientation to managing not bounded by deadlines in the way that planning exercises are;

it is a more holistic approach. Those who manage strategically are plugged in to their working environment at many different levels: listening, watching, and thinking all the time about what they see and hear; constantly wondering about alternatives, about how to do this better, and about whether the work is focused on what is most important. In other words, strategic management, unlike strategic planning, happens all year around.

Strategic management is an orientation to managing not bounded by deadlines in the way that planning exercises are; it is a more holistic approach.

Many NGOs we have worked with have profitably invested considerable time in strategic-management activities. Some of the benefits have included:

- Finding a new way forward in a rapidly changing set of circumstances

- Focusing scarce resources on priority areas

- Engaging the board to deepen understanding of what the organization is about and provide fuller, better informed leadership

- Clarifying and resolving conflicts or contradictions that had been growing over the years; building greater organizational coherence

- Energizing the organization through questioning, learning, and harnessing creative energy

How should NGOs think about strategic management? These guiding criteria can ensure strategy making that is effective:

Criteria for strategic management

1. Strategy making should focus the board, management, and programming staff on the big questions: why the organization exists, who it serves and where, how this service is expected to happen, and whether or not the current strategy is successful.

2. It should balance thoughtful analysis with intuitive and emerging understandings.

3. It should make the best possible use of all forms of information and knowledge built on the experience of partners, front-line staff, and managers.

4. It should combine the thoughtfulness of periodic retreats with the immediacy of day-to-day practicalities.

5. Attention should be paid to the political process and dynamics of the organization so that various perspectives can be reconciled. Participation and commitment are critical.

6. The strategic control required in a well-structured manufacturing company is not possible or desirable in many NGOs. The level of specificity of plans needs to take this into account.

7. The process needs to be sufficiently loose and dynamic to respond to changing situations. Having a strategic plan is not enough: implementing the plan, responding to changing events, and updating the plan are essential aspects of strategy making.

How should NGOs do it?

Strategy making should be seen as a great opportunity for organizational learning and renewal. For international-development NGOs, it should bring people together from across cultures, national boundaries, and all levels in the organization. The process matters! A strategy that breathes with the organization demands broad participation, not mere token consultation.

Although much has been written on strategic management, it can be seen essentially as four interrelated activities. (See diagram below.)

These four activities are not necessarily carried out in a particular order. In most organizations, the mission, values, and vision remain in place for some years, while other aspects of strategy may be revised in response to the environment and

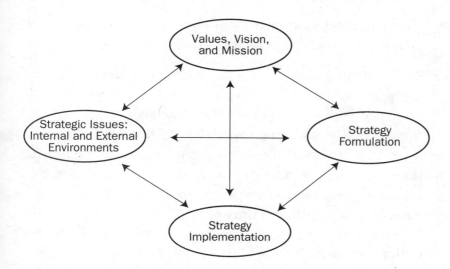

the realities of implementing the strategy in the field. The arrows indicate that all four activities are related, and that changing one can necessitate or cause changes in the others.

Boards need to be involved in each of the four aspects of strategic management, although management and staff must have a central role.

Strategic Issues

Defining strategic issues might be thought of as looking for key dilemmas that have the power to fundamentally enhance or threaten an organization. These are the critical policy choices that an organization must face. They have both practical and ethical dimensions. Bringing these dilemmas and choices to the surface in a way that allows them to be managed and acted on is the work of strategic-issue management.

These issues might include:

- Dependence: Overdependence on a particular source of income has become a major strategic issue of survival. Recent cuts in Canadian government funding for some

Strategic Issues: key dilemmas that have the power to fundamentally enhance or threaten an organization.

international-development work has highlighted one of the dilemmas of the NGO-state relationship.

- Ethics of fundraising: NGOs are sometimes faced with the problem that their fund raising appeals are at odds with their deeper values, or with the changing nature of their programs. For example, many international-development NGOs have rejected the depiction of starving children in their fund-raising appeals because these images, while effective, feed the stereotype of people in the South as vulnerable and helpless victims rather than showing them to be people with courage, dignity, and resourcefulness. This ethical decision, however, can result in a loss of income. Lower income has resulted in less funding for overseas programs. How does an NGO deal with these competing values and needs?

- Policy advocacy: Many international NGOs are aware of the importance of being involved in the policy process. But governments in the North have less and less influence on international and national economic activity. What then are the strategic options for NGOs?

- Programming ethics: International-development NGOs are frequently confronted with dilemmas that pit one set of values against another. The way these dilemmas are posed and understood can have serious implications for follow-up action. For example, an NGO working with women in South Asia discovered that 40 per cent of the income earned by the women in income-generation projects was being turned over to the male head of the family. The NGO faced a dilemma: should it intervene to ensure its primary objective of increasing women's equality and economic status, or should it respect the traditional practices of the community? What impact would intervention have on the women? Is this a dilemma to be defined in terms of community values or as power differentials and inequality?

Identifying and acting on strategic issues needs to be an ongoing process to be effective. The most important role of senior managers is to ensure that strategic issues are being identified, considered, and managed.

Vision, Values, and Mission

This work sets out what the organization cares most about, who it works with, and how it accomplishes its goals, not merely what programs might be undertaken in the coming year. Such overarching and fundamental statements set out to capture the essence of why the organization exists and where it is heading. Searching for the answer to these questions must be a process of collective reflection, visioning, and analysis that involves the people who work with or relate to the organization. This might be the beginning of the strategy-making process that draws on many sources of information, experiences, and perspectives to examine what is happening in the world, the strengths and weaknesses of the organization, the effectiveness of current programs, and the values the organization holds dear. Questions of the relationship to the state, to constituents and to donors, the voluntary character of the organization, and the role and accountability of the board should be considered. As a planning document from one NGO described this stage: "... it is a search to find out who we are and where we as individuals are morally positioned within the context of our global home."

The process might involve activities with staff, board, members, and partners, including surveys, workshops, search conferences, debates, and electronic conferences.

Vision, Values, and Mission: what the organization cares most about.

One NGO developed a thorough mission exercise led by a committee of staff and board executives, along with a team of external consultants. This committee carried out a survey on values, held a seminar with trusted outsiders to discuss trends and possible strategies, held a series of regional membership meetings, and set up a "correspondents' network," which debated via letter issues facing the organization. All this work was synthesized into a three-paragraph statement by the planning committee, and was then debated and accepted by the board.

Strategy Formulation

This element involves specifying *how* the organization will accomplish the mission, given the strategic issues it faces.

Strategy Formulation: how the organization will accomplish the mission.

After the broad policy choices or dilemmas have been enunciated, other decisions need to be made, or confirmed, about the organization's position, perspective, and strategic directions or goals, as well as how these will be accomplished. How will the organization know that it is getting where it wants to go? What are the indicators of success, including those that cannot be quantified?

Formulating strategy promotes ever-greater clarity about one's work, and about *the reason it deserves the support of its partners funders, staff, and volunteers.* This is the context for considering again the "who," "where," "how," and "what" of the work – the specifics. For example, an organization with a mission statement that specifies a commitment to gender and racial equality might formulate its strategy as "We are a feminist organization working in southern Africa to support poor rural women." This statement goes beyond the mission statement by specifying a perspective (feminism) and a group of people the organization will work with (poor, rural women). The strategy should also specify the kinds of women's organizations that the organization wishes to work with – co-operatives, legal clinics, training programs, small businesses – and how these will be supported. Do they send funds for core operations or to invest in businesses or revolving-loan schemes; do they send trainers or other technical support? The strategy statement may also specify goals for the next one to three years.

There are no perfect or packaged strategies. Each organization has to develop strategy that responds to the issues facing it and that is congruent with its history, values, and abilities. Strategies change in response to changing issues and to learning acquired in implementing the strategy.

This said, there are some generic "strategy families" that emerge when we look at the strategies NGOs pursue:[7]

• Volunteer sending/technical support: sending volunteers

to work with southern organizations, both to bring needed expertise and to learn

- Relief: sending food and other material goods to countries suffering shortages because of war or natural disasters

- Institution building: funding and supporting the development of local organizations that pursue development goals

- Policy/advocacy: developing an analysis of the effects of government policy, and advocating for change in the North

- Human rights/good governance: working with NGOs and government agencies to strengthen democratic practices and advocacy for human rights

- Implementation of local self-help projects

The following are some criteria or questions for evaluating strategy:

- Was the strategy formed in relationship with partners in the south – through genuine dialogue?

- Does it build on the core capacities of the organization?

- Does it show understanding of what will work?

- Does it respond to the strategic issues facing the organization?

- Does it have the commitment of the people implementing it?

- Is it amenable to evaluation so it can be altered?

- Does it anticipate the learning requirements of those who will implement it?

Strategy Implementation

This is the task of focusing the day-to-day work on the accomplishment of the mission. Once the board has agreed on a

Strategy Implementation: focusing the day-to-day work on accomplishing the mission.

The crucial dynamic is that of flexibility and control – especially for NGOs working in a complex social, political, and cultural environment with many other organizations.

mission statement and a strategy, each level and/or region of the organization needs to work within this framework – building their own analysis of strategic issues, position, and the implementation plan.

The crucial dynamic is that of flexibility and control – especially for NGOs working in a complex social, political, and cultural environment with many other organizations. How does the organization define and value expertise, and where is it to be found? Whose experience counts? What value is placed on partner and client experience and perspectives, and how are these integrated into the strategy formulation and implementation? What type and amount of dissonance is tolerated? To what degree are local solutions tolerated? What latitude do field programming staff and managers have to formulate their own plans within the organization's overall strategy?

These questions are not simple ones, for they aim at the nature of the complex relationships between northern and southern NGOs, especially those that are not implementing agencies. They pose powerful political and ethical questions about the work we do and how we do it. In this situation, who "owns" the outcome? Who is responsible for results?

What should NGOs and voluntary organizations do about strategic control? Funders and donors are demanding greater accountability and, as the researchers M. Goold and J. J. Quinn found, the planning literature is unanimous on the importance of monitoring and controlling the implementation of strategy. Yet in their survey of the two hundred largest organizations in England, Goold and Quinn found that fewer than 11 per cent had a full-fledged control system.[8]

How do we ensure a measure of control when there are multiple accountabilities? When programmers are working in different parts of the organization, in different organizations, and in different countries? How closely managed should it be?

This needs to be worked out in each situation, based on the

level of co-ordination needed, and on a realistic assessment of those things one can influence, as well as on more traditional considerations, such as the level of professionalism required. Overcontrol has its hazards – inflexibility, low responsiveness to local needs, bureaucratic reporting requirements, and control struggles between head office and regions. Too much flexibility results in no accountability, little co-ordination, few opportunities for synergy, and most important, little organizational learning about the effectiveness of the strategy.

The decisions about control should be made in response to particular circumstances. These decisions do not need to be made in deference to a private-sector literature that is not followed even by private-sector firms.

Formulating and implementing strategy requires an organizational approach committed to learning, understanding, achievement, and to the fundamental values that motivate action. Such a strategic management approach risks conflict and unpredictable outcomes but can be infinitely more rewarding.

LINK INTERNATIONAL: Strategy As Learning

Case Study

Humble Beginnings

Link International (Link)[*] is a small church-based international-development organization that started work in Canada in the late 1970s. In the early years, Link was run by a volunteer board appointed by its sponsoring church in the United States. Its original mission was to raise funds for church-related community-development and aid projects overseas.

During the 1980s, Link grew steadily from a one-person office to a six-person office with a budget of over $1 million,

[*] Link International is not the name of the agency used as the example in this case.

raised from individual donors, from other Canadian NGOs, and through matching grants from the Canadian government.

Over time, the executive director, who has been with the organization almost from the beginning, was able to articulate a vision of development that emphasized the partnership relationship: to be responsive to what he heard from partners, and respect their way of working and thinking. He was deeply influenced by the experience and learning of southern-development NGOs, especially in Southeast Asia and Central America. Everything was built on trust between the partners and on a strong, guiding spiritual commitment. In time, a more ecumenical programming orientation emerged.

There was no written statement or plan, and no particular thematic or sectoral specialization. The choice of partners was made by the executive director based on his judgement and experience in the six or seven countries where Link projects were based. The new organization was clearly focused on development work with a strong "entrepreneurial" approach – responding to opportunities with a minimum of red tape. The church, for its part, was interested in charitable giving and in aid and relief, motivated by sense of Christian concern. Link International, however, was following a different path, moving away from its American counterpart and the approach it had inherited. The result was a growing divide between church work and the development work of Link.

Outside Scrutiny Helps Trigger Change

In 1990, the Canadian International Development Agency (CIDA) commissioned an institutional evaluation of Link International as part of the conditions of funding. It was the first time that external evaluators had scrutinized the work of the organization. The evaluation was positive about Link's work and recommended that Link write a mission statement and do a strategic plan, and that it be more proactive in setting program goals. The executive director stated that strategic planning was never considered until it was raised by CIDA. In retrospect, it is clear that this recommendation for greater clarity set in motion a chain of events that shook up the staff and began a process of questioning and experimentation that took Link into areas it had never anticipated.

The executive director describes the beginning of the process:

> *We agreed to write the mission down – and made some attempts in 1991. But after a year it still was not done. It just wasn't that much of a priority. The board felt comfortable because the church was on top of things. The bishop was on the board, so people were quite relaxed about the organization. Some board members did not appreciate how difficult this exercise could be, or saw it as too confusing. It took a whole weekend in December 1992 – a weekend to write a paragraph! The bishop simply couldn't believe we could spend so much time and money on this exercise. But this was the key to getting the board involved.*

A board member described the outcome:

> *The result was that people got to know one another better, and there is more valuing of different points of view. Everything came out on the table. This has established a new norm of getting things out, talking them through, and figuring out what lies underneath. We've established focus, guiding principles, rather than just focusing on the balance sheet. One upshot is that there has been some self-sorting-out among people – some have left when they see things going in a new direction.*

The writing of the mission statement in 1992 set the tone for an extended strategic-planning exercise, which opened up a number of strategic issues about how Link International was working.

Link's Strategic Issues

- Questions about the role of overseas voices and non-church people in strategic decision making: if Link was so responsive to, and respectful of, its partners, then why was the board so solidly white and Canadian? The issue of participation has resulted in changes in the composition of the board. (Canadians born in programming countries have been recruited onto the board.)

- The question of the work being congruent with the values and mission has taken Link International out from under the control of the church, although the relationship is close and cordial. Many partners are secular. The criteria for support are based on principles of community, development, and participation, not on connections with the church.

- Questions about the kind of expertise and experience needed to staff the organization: for many years staff had been church people – well-meaning and committed friends, but not trained for or experienced in this kind of work. New staff are hired for their skills and experience.

- Questions about the explicit values and principles that guided the board and staff came up in thinking about whether Link practised what it preached, how it raised funds, how it could be more accountable to Canadian supporters and partners.

- Questions about the role of supporters in shaping organizational policy, as they do not vote for board members: what level of accountability was acceptable? Could Link become more democratic in shaping organizational policy? How much control could be ceded to supporters, especially as they grew beyond the confines of the church? The board has begun to experiment with several carefully considered processes to tap in to supporters' views: some would guide the board, and others would be binding on the board. They have considered surveys and polls. The board remains, however, self-appointing.

- The way the board works was completely overhauled. It meets for longer periods of time, clusters its agenda into business items (to be voted on without much debate, on the assumption that all members have read and understood the issue), and governance items (important policy and strategic issues that require consensus).

The process of change has been both invigorating and stressful. As issues came to the surface, they shook loose a number of organizational blocks to change. Some board members and all the older staff, except for the executive director, have left the organization, sometimes under duress. Staffing conflicts were especially difficult, given that it was such a small organization with active links to a relatively small church community. However, new faces around the boardroom table and in the office are bringing fresh perspectives from both inside and outside the church. "All this is very very new to everyone," says one board member. "What we are doing is trying to change thinking and the way of action. All stakeholders need to be brought in – donors, partners, members."

The executive director describes the outcome:

The board used to be more head-strong; now it is more heart-strong. Why? because people really support the work and believe in it. There is no other reason to be on the board. Spending time on the process has encouraged us to look – to really look – at what we are doing; are our ideals leading us anywhere? Now we are working together to be more coherent and tied into our mission. It was our partners who really called us, who got us thinking about our values, about our way of making decisions. The move to consensus building came out of discussions with them.

This short case demonstrates clearly that entering a strategic-planning exercise can bring to the surface issues and new directions previously not considered or not seen. It can shake loose assumptions about the way things should be done. Some risk taking and openness to new approaches has both enriched and challenged the organization. It did not, in the case of Link, lead to over-control of the staff by the board.

Link International is still in the strategy-making process: it has reiterated its commitment to its mission and brought to the surface fundamental values that must guide its work; it has identified some of the strategic issues requiring attention, debate, and resolution – issues related to accountability, participation, inclusion, the ethics of fund raising, and decision making; it has formulated a strategy for its work, and put it on paper as a program plan; and it is working through the implementation issues. The vision and energy of the new staff, especially of the executive director, are now more closely matched with the skills and commitment of the board. One can foresee that over time, a more democratic and open policy-making orientation will bring new pressures for change. The strategic-planning exercise, imposed from the outside, became an opportunity for important organizational learning.

This chapter has argued that strategic management is an important tool for surviving the perils of a rapidly changing environment. Many NGOs have carried out strategic-planning exercises, but strategic planning needs to be adapted in order to be successful in NGOs and voluntary organizations. The corporate model described in the business literature can be too formal, rational, and controlling to be of help to NGOs. In fact, the evidence is that it is of only limited help to private companies.

When strategic management is seen as learning, it focuses the board, staff, and management on the core questions: why do we exist, what do we face, whom do we serve, how do we do it? This dialogue is ongoing and uses the best intuitive understanding as well as the best logical judgement.

References

1. A. Wildavsky, *Speaking Truth to Power: The Art and Craft of Policy Analysis* (Toronto: Little, Brown & Co., 1979), quoted in H. Mintzberg, *The Rise and Fall of Strategic Planning* (New York: The Free Press, 1994), 189.

2. H. Mintzberg, op. cit.

3. Ibid.

4. J. A. Pearce et al., "The Tenuous Link between Formal Strategic Planning and Financial Performance," *Academy of Management Review*, XII, no. 4, (1987), quoted in Mintzberg, op. cit., 97.

5. R. D. Stacey, *Managing the Unknowable: Strategic Boundaries between Order and Chaos in Organizations* (San Francisco: Jossey-Bass, 1992).

6. J. B. Quinn, *Strategies for Change, Logical Incrementalism* (Homewood: Irwin, 1980).

7. T. Brodhead, B. Herbert-Copley, and A.-M. Lambert, *Bridges of Hope? Canadian Voluntary Agencies and the Third World* (Ottawa: North-South Institute, 1988) and D. Korten, *Getting to the 21st Century: Voluntary Action and the Global Agenda* (West Hartford: Kumarian, 1990).

8. M. Goold and J. J. Quinn, "The Paradox of Strategic Controls," *Strategic Management Journal* 11, 1990, quoted in Mintzberg, op. cit.

Structure and Organizational Design

5

"You can restructure any which way, but if you don't deal with people's real needs and conflicts, the restructuring won't help. The old problems will re-emerge."

– *Executive director, "Link International"*

THIS CHAPTER DESCRIBES THE PROCESS OF ORGANIZATIONAL design, the task of aligning structure, management practices, and people with strategy and culture. Very often we equate organizational change with restructuring, or more recently with downsizing. Structural considerations are an important element, but far from the whole picture, as we have seen. By "structure" we mean the formal pattern of relationships in the workplace – both lateral and vertical; the division of labour among functions and departments; the distribution of power and authority; and various co-ordination functions.

Structure:
By "structure" we mean the formal pattern of relationships in the workplace – both lateral and vertical; the division of labour among functions and departments; the distribution of power and authority; and various coordination functions.

Structural change is time-consuming and disruptive, so why would leaders want to undertake it?

Often enough the motivation originates outside the organization, in a crisis or changed environment that alters the demands placed on the organization. Competition or falling revenues, for example, might indicate a need for more efficient systems or information flows. A changed strategy or a new leader might also be an impetus. Whatever the cause, ongoing organizational redesign is a fact of life for many NGOs and voluntary organizations. This chapter will discuss how different designs suit the particular needs of an organization.

Imagine that you are on the board of a medium-sized NGO with anticipated financial problems, and a new strategic plan that has made major changes to programming priorities. You don't know much about restructuring, but the board has set out some criteria for the change. The new structure needs to be:

- More efficient and perhaps smaller

- More directly accountable to partners, members, and the public, in addition to funders

- Clearly focused on the mission and strategy

- More flexible and responsive to uncertain and changing times

- Sensitive to the culture of the organization

- Gender equitable, as well as equitable to other underrepresented groups

Let's look at the design options that you might consider in order to meet these criteria. The options must consider the staff side of the structure, the board, and the relationship between the two.

Design Criteria

1. More Efficient and Smaller

An organization that is smaller and more efficient will look at ways to reduce hierarchy. In recent downsizing in the private and public sectors, clerical and managerial positions have been cut before program positions. Most organizations hope to compensate for the lost human capacity with improved information systems and technology. Some organizations contract out work formerly done in house, creating a network of service providers.

2. More Accountable

Accountability has typically focused on one of three areas: financial accountability with stronger central control systems; greater board accountability to a membership or other constituency; and greater managerial accountability by reporting up the hierarchy for specific productivity or planning objectives. The legal requirements of voluntary organizations include having a formal membership that elects the members of the board. (Definitions of membership vary among organizations.)

Board accountability is a growing issue among NGOs in Canada. There must be effective mechanisms for boards to be accountable to organizational members, to partners, and to donors and funders. The election of board members is one form of accountability, but it is not without problems, especially if membership requirements are vague or if members are not active and/or are widely dispersed. There are two levels of accountability: collective (the board is accountable to its stakeholders for the overall health and operations), and individual (each board member undertakes to be responsible for a particular area of work or to represent a particular constituency). Whatever its structure, each organization needs to consider an optimum level of participation, representation, and feedback to its constituency, balancing the need for participation against the need for coherence or consistency over time. For example, the board of Link International, described in Chapter 4, has decided against elections but is now experimenting with other forms of direct supporter participation in policy development. Link also encourages board members to participate in field trips to meet partners face to face. This approach has built up a core of highly motivated and involved board members.

3. Focused on the Mission and Strategy

The issue here is whether the structure should be organized by function, by program, or by geographic region. A "functional" structure gives priority to professional or service functions such as communications, policy, operations, finance, revenue generation, and so on. A structure that is program ("product") oriented is organized along programming lines such as agriculture, refugee support, or perhaps by issue. The choice of functional versus program structure depends on the nature of the work, strategic priorities, and culture. A functional structure reflects a preference for professional skills; a regionalized structure may reflect the need to be responsive to different local needs, in a more decentralized organization.

Functional Structure: A functional structure is built on common activities that are grouped together.

Regional Structure: A regional structure is more decentralized and responsive to local needs.

The choice of structure will determine the flow of information, reporting relationships, and the way decisions are made. For example, an organization based on functions might value high-quality research and would structure its co-ordinating mechanisms (such as committees, working groups, or task forces) around performance in this area. In a regional structure, work units and decisions are likely to coalesce around the needs of local regions.

The structure of the board – its committees and composition – should enhance its strategic leadership capabilities. This is easiest if the board and staff structures are aligned, or similarly defined, around a function or programming division. Board positions might be defined according to particular areas of expertise required to support a policy area; or positions might be allotted along regional lines, if the organization has a geographically based membership. This kind of alignment ensures a better flow of information to the board from all areas of the organization and keeps the board focused on organizational objectives.

4. Flexible and Responsive

We have noted that NGOs and voluntary organizations are caught in a turbulent present and are facing an uncertain future. Survival depends on being able to gather, process, and act on information quickly and effectively. This has not been a strength of many NGOs in the past. Such responsiveness is "organic" rather than mechanistic or rule bound. Responsive, flexible organizations are more oriented to their clientele or constituency, have fewer supervisory levels, and give front-line staff more latitude than traditional bureaucratic or hierarchical organizations.[1]

Obtaining and processing information is only the first step, however; organizations must also act on it. This is more difficult in the public sector, given its multiple accountabilities and its service orientation.

5. Fit with the Culture

As we now know, organizational culture encompasses values, beliefs, and norms of behaviour. Organizational structure must be congruent with existing values or set out to change them. One helpful way to think about values in organizations was developed by an American management professor, James O'Toole. He clusters them along two continua, as follows. The vertical continuum describes the principles of reward and recognition. The horizontal dimension defines the overall orientation of an organization toward people or production.[2]

Organizations that value merit base their reward systems on individual performance. These organizations often encourage friendly competition – in sales, for example – and have wide disparities in pay, perks, and status. This value is not strong in

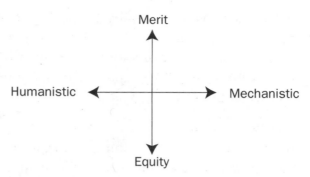

voluntary organizations, although experience and competence are rewarded by paying managers more than programming and administrative staff. The merit principle, however, is gaining ground in some NGOs as a way of attracting people with specialized skills, in particular fund raising.

Organizations that value equity, at the other end of the continuum, minimize status and pay differences. The resources available for staff are shared more equally and are not tied to traditional criteria such as job role, age, gender, or experience. Teamwork emphasizes the contribution of all and the importance of sharing opportunities for experience and learning. An agency at the equity end of this continuum would pay any staff the same base wage perhaps with a supplement for dependents. Staff would handle their own administration, and roles such as office manager or reception might be shared or rotated. Smaller NGOs tend to be the ones committed to this principle. Most organizations that subscribe to an equity approach have some pay differentiation, but downplay status symbols such as better offices or free parking for executive members. Recognition for excellent work comes from peer feedback as well as formal performance reviews.

O'Toole's second continuum describes the overall orientation as being toward "people" (humanistic) or "procedures" (mechanistic). The mechanistic organization carefully prescribes the nature of the work – valuing efficiency, productivity, and consistency. The prototypical example is a fast-food restaurant chain, in which a formula is carefully set out and then followed exactly. Many voluntary organizations have worked out systems for certain aspects of their endeavours that require routine approaches. BRAC, a large Bangladeshi NGO, has well-developed systems for ensuring that its credit-provision program is managed in exactly the same way in all of its six hundred area offices.

In a more humanistic organization, the emphasis is on learning and flexibility, giving people scope to interpret and innovate. The underlying assumption is that the nature of the work requires less structure and procedure than face-to-face communication, training, and individual and team innovation. Performance might be merit or equity oriented. Prototypical humanistic organizations might be small consulting firms, research departments, or some software-development companies. Many voluntary and not-for-profit organizations value a humanistic culture because it fits their overall mission. The need for quality control and accountability to government funders, however, helps ensure a healthy balance between humanistic and mechanistic ends; and indeed, few organizations are at the extreme of either continuum.

6. Gender Equitable

This aspect of organizational structure has been given the least attention by organizational designers; both organizational theory and design have been largely gender blind.[3] What are the structural aspects of a gender-equitable organization? One is accessibility that results from procedures, policies, and attitudes ensuring that women and other underrepresented groups are recruited, selected, and promoted, especially to senior positions on staff and the board. Feminist theorists have demonstrated, however, that there are many ways beyond representation, that organizational structures benefit men over women and other groups experiencing systemic discrimination. For example, an organization that distributes rewards, interesting projects, and opportunities to people who can travel and work long hours and weekends discriminates against women, who are still primarily responsible for child care and other domestic tasks. More equitable organizations use flexible working arrangements: adjustable schedules, time out for child rearing, parental leave for men and women, job sharing, and working from home. While important, such policies are not enough. Women (and men as well) who take up these options are still subjected to subtle negative assumptions about their "commitment" to their careers. A more profound and long-term change in attitudes about work and family is needed. This is a societal challenge that is bigger than any one organization.

Another way that organizations advantage men is in the way work itself is designed. If women are successful in obtaining the job, some may find that they face serious difficulties because of their gender: international travel may require taking certain drugs and inoculations that are inappropriate for pregnant women. In some countries, indigenous female staff cannot travel alone or with the same ease as men, or cannot travel in the company of males who are not family members.

Certain forms of organizational structure are more amenable to women's way of working. Sally Helgesen identified what she saw as a women's style of management, which was significantly different from that favoured by men:

> In the process of devising ways to lead that made sense to them, the women I studied had built profoundly integrated and organic organizations, in which the focus was on nurturing good relationships; in which the niceties of hierarchical rank and distinction played little part; and in which lines of communication were multiplicitous, open and diffuse. I noted that the women tended to put themselves at the centres of their organizations rather than the top, thus emphasizing both accessibility and equality, and that they laboured constantly to include people in decision-making.[4]

This is a controversial finding. In a paper on gender and administration, Anne-Marie Goetz quotes a number of studies that show that:

- Flat, decentralized organizations may actually contribute to the invisibility of gender issues, as on the surface they appear more equitable; however, forms of systemic discrimination discussed above still exist

- Collectivist organizational forms are not necessarily related to feminist attitudes and outcomes, if gender issues are not openly addressed

- The extra time required to function in an understructured organization is resented by many women employees with child-care responsibilities, which set limits on the length of the working day [5]

An inclusive organization with multiple communication channels might prove to be a gender-equitable structure in some settings; other situations may require different approaches. (Like all nostrums of organizational design, local dynamics are important.)

In summary, an organization wishing to be more gender equitable, would ensure that women were well represented in leadership positions on staff and the board; facilitate a better work-family balance, assuring that the structure of the work is equally possible for men and women, and that decision making is inclusive.

Configurations of Organizational Design

There are four broad approaches to managing and organizing work.[6] The first, hierarchy, is the oldest structure and the one most people are familiar with. The other three are not "pure" types but are usually found grafted on to a hierarchy of some kind. These four approaches are sketched below.

Hierarchy Structures

Hierarchy:
Hierarchies favour clear reporting channels, a small span of control, and efficient systems.

In a hierarchy, managers are assumed to be knowledgeable and in control.

A hierarchical structure can be "taller" or "flatter," more or less patriarchal, authoritarian, or friendly, but the assumptions are the same: a reasonably small management span of control (i.e, fewer work units or staff under each manager's supervision), and work controlled by managers appointed on merit. Efficiency is highly valued and achieved by the predesign of tasks grouped into specialized units. Managers are assumed to be knowledgeable, in control, and able to discipline and to encourage co-operation and compliance. The organization looks like a pyramid. It is likely to be directive in management style but may permit considerable participation. Reporting is linear from bottom to top.

A hierarchical NGO might have the structure that appears on page 93.

Let's look at this hierarchy in terms of the criteria for a new structure discussed earlier:

HIERARCHY

1. More Efficient and Smaller

In theory, hierarchies are considered to be efficient because of a clear division of labour and responsibility. More layers of reporting and decision making, however, often take time rather than save it, especially as unpredictability increases.

2. More Accountable

A hierarchy is generally thought to be highly accountable. Each staff person is clearly accountable for her or his work and is responsible to one boss. In practice, however, many bosses avoid accountability measures, sometimes because they are more interested in programming issues than in traditional management, and sometimes out of reticence to give negative feedback regarding employee performance.

3. Focused on the Mission and Strategy

A hierarchical structure is inherently no worse or better

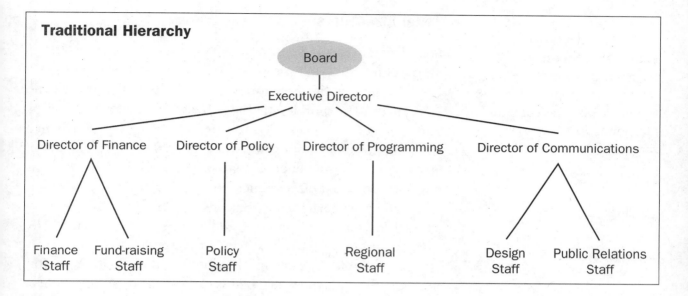

Traditional Hierarchy

than other structures in focusing on the mission. Any organization can go off track if internal structures are not appropriate for current work needs. A functional hierarchy may have worked well for years, under particular conditions, but may need to be restructured when conditions change.

4. Flexible and Responsive

Hierarchy is not a good form for building responsiveness. Hierarchies are slow at processing information and generally staff are allowed less latitude than other forms. Hierarchies were in fact designed to inhibit flexibility; nevertheless, a decentralized hierarchy can allow considerable latitude to local or regional units.

5. Fit with the Culture

Some NGO cultures are compatible with hierarchies, and others are not.

6. Gender Equitable

Hierarchies can be made more amenable to flexible work, and other gender sensitive processes, but have not been organized with this in mind.

Team Structures

Team Structures:
are more likely to be
"organic" or participatory,
valuing horizontal commu-
nication across the organization.

In a team structure, man-
agers function as facilitator.

Social scientists have found that people in organizations
aren't controlled only, or even primarily, by the formal hierarchy as much as by their informal group relationships in the
workplace. Thus, understanding these informal relationships
and their effect on workplace behaviour and performance
has become more important when considering organizational design. A core belief is that organizational effectiveness
and interpersonal effectiveness are linked. In an organization
concerned primarily with relationships and motivation, managers function as facilitators and group leaders: being supportive and more participatory. In this model, the manager is
still responsible for setting objectives and evaluating performance, although there are many variations (including collec-
tives in which these functions are shared by the group).
Control is focused on the accomplishment of objectives and
accountability to the team as well as to the leader. Team-
structured organizations usually involve some hierarchy but
are likely to be more "organic" or participatory than classical
hierarchies. Organic structures focus on people and their
learning as well as on tasks, de-emphasize the hierarchy, are
concerned with shared norms, beliefs and values, and believe
in self-control and mutual adjustment.

An example of a team structure is shown below. The organization is made up of several teams: program, communications, and fund-raising, each led by a manager. The managers
make up a fourth team. Temporary teams are built to deal
with particular issues.

TEAM

1. More Efficient and Smaller

True team structures use self-managed teams, which
reduce the number of management staff needed. This efficiency is somewhat mitigated by increased time needed in
meetings and the cost of the transition, as staff learn new

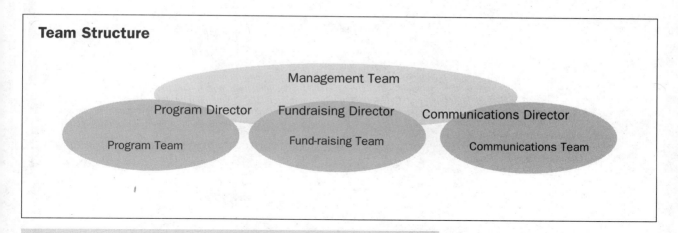

Team Structure

skills of group decision making and conflict resolution.

2. More Accountable

Teams, team leaders, and individuals can be held accountable to a manager, to the executive director, or to the board of directors, although team structures lack the clear-cut accountability of hierarchy.

3. Focused on the Mission and Strategy

Team-based organizations can focus effectively on the mission and particular strategy, whether the teams are permanent or temporary. The main thing is to be sure the task is defined against the mission, and that each team has a program to realize.

4. Flexible and Responsive

Team organizations can be highly responsive if they have the mandate, scope, and resources to do the job. Without these, a team can spin its wheels, like any other committee.

5. Fit with the Culture

Once again, this depends on the organization, but quite often the move from a hierarchical to a team organization is a difficult cultural change. Staff need to learn new skills of team management and greater self-reliance.

6. Gender Equitable

Team structures may be more equitable and supportive, as team members are interdependent. A "team" by definition values all members. But teamwork can demand a considerable time commitment. It may not be well suited to the administrative staff – often women – whose work tends to be more structured. Team structures, therefore, may need to be modified and customized for each organization and type of work.

Matrix Structures

Matrix Structures:
In a matrix structure, staff have dual responsibilities, and formal accountability to more than one manager.

Matrix structures combine hierarchical and team approaches to organizational structure; however, a matrix structure differs in that many people have dual responsibilities and formal accountability to more than one manager. For example, a finance officer may be responsible both to the director of finance and to the director of a regional program. (Often the performance appraisal is done by both managers.) The matrix blends functional expertise – administration, human resources, communications, and so on – with programming expertise (sectoral, regional, and others). It is a structural response to highly unstable external environments requiring high levels of responsiveness, innovation, and co-ordination.

The key difficulty with matrix structures is that complex lines of authority and responsibility can generate interpersonal conflict and increased meeting time. Relations between headquarters and local or regional operations can become very fraught and energy sapping. Matrix structures seem to work best in mid-size organizations, or in a division of a larger organization.

INGO, described in Chapter 3, created a matrix in the programming departments when it restructured the head office in 1992. (The structure is shown below.) The matrix was built around regional programs – each staffed by a regional "team" made up of program staff, policy staff, sectoral experts, and

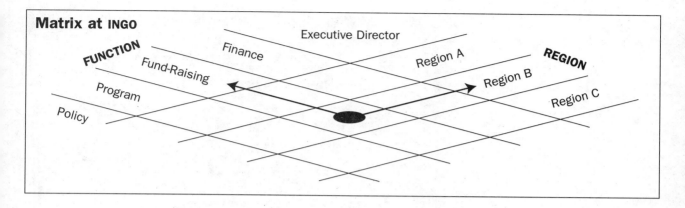

Matrix at INGO

finance and fund-raising staff who were based in their own departments. The fund-raising staff on the regional teams also met as a fund-raising team, and were therefore in a good position to integrate fund-raising plans across regions. Matrix structures are complex, mirroring the complexity of the world. They enhance organizational integration and coordination.

How do matrix structures measure up to our design criteria?

MATRIX

1. More Efficient and Smaller

Matrix structures are not necessarily more efficient, given the high meeting time, but they can prevent duplication, where lack of communication between departments is a problem.

2. More Accountable

Accountability is more complex with matrices. Staff may have two or three supervisors. However, a matrix is designed to enhance the sense of joint responsibility.

3. Focused on the Mission and Strategy

This is one of the main attractions of the matrix form. It is possible to build multi-disciplinary teams that focus directly on key aspects of the mission and strategy. The team members are then accountable to the team leader, and the unit head. For example, a matrix could support a "Sustainable

Agriculture Project Team" that included agricultural specialists, program staff from the region where the program is based, a fundraiser, and a communications person.

4. Flexible and Responsive

Because of the lateral flow of information through multi-sectoral and functional teams, the matrix should be able to adapt quickly to changing needs. Decisions are taken within the programming team as much as possible, which also increases adaptability; however, it can block individual initiative of staff used to lobbying their manager with an idea. The structure enforces a certain amount of team involvement and consensus decision making, although a clear understanding of who is empowered to make decisions is critical.

5. Fit with the Culture

Matrix structures are far from such conventional expectations as "Everyone is responsible to one boss," "Meetings are not work," "Career advancement means moving up," and "We can't agree, so the boss will resolve it." For many organizations considerable time and cultural change are required to function well in a matrix.

6. Gender Equitable

Matrix and team structures need to value the participation of all members, whether program, administrative, or functional staff. This valuing can go a long way to breaking down gender stereotypes and blocks to participation. The structure alone, though, is not enough to counter any patriarchal attitudes staff may bring with them.

Network Structures

A network is a loose affiliation among autonomous or semi-autonomous organizations. It facilitates the exchange of data and information, and works on joint projects, under various contractual agreements.

Networks of organizations have existed for many years in the international-development field. The Red Cross and the International Council of YMCAs are examples of semi-autonomous units linked under one name and approach to work. In both, national bodies are not controlled from the international centre, but both organizations have a set of principles that guide the work worldwide.

Structuring one organization as a network is a newer phenomenon that is gaining ground in private- and public-sector organizations. A tough and competitive environment has led to drastic cuts in core infrastructure in many organizations. Sophisticated and accessible information technologies have encouraged new ways of getting the work done with fewer resources. There is now considerable interest in the "virtual" organization that exists as a web of relationships rather than as a place where people go to work.[7]

Network Structure:
A network organization is as much a web of relationships, as a place where people go to work. It is comprised of highly autonomous program units and a relatively small core infrastructure.

A "network organization" implies considerable autonomy among its functional and programming units. The core of the organization might consist of a very small infrastructure that provides certain services. Around the core might be programming units that implement the mission. These units are highly responsive and fluid. They might be staffed almost entirely by contract staff, hired for their expertise to carry out a particular program. It is not up to headquarters to direct or co-ordinate the relations between units – they co-ordinate with one another as needed. The organization is defined increasingly by such webs of relationships with other organizations, partners, and alliances – all of which are essential to carrying out its mission. Decisions are made within a web of strategic alliances with partners and temporary project staff.

In a network organization program units are highly responsive and fluid. They may be staffed by a variety of people contracted for their expertise.

As the writer Kevin Kelly explains it, "The metaphor for the corporation is shifting from a tightly coupled, tightly bounded organism to a loosely coupled, loosely bounded ecosystem."[8]

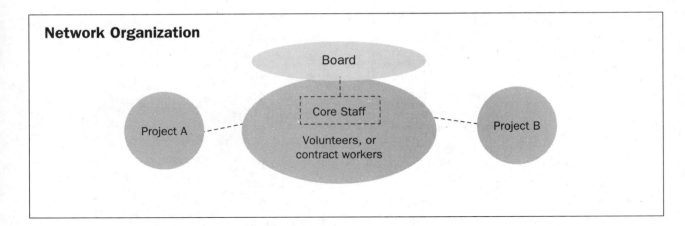

There are a number of variations on this model. As Cumming and Singleton have noted, some NGOs have adopted management structures and approaches from the private sector, and are setting up arm's-length profit centres or fee-for-service arrangements among their various programming or regional units.[9] Other NGOs are negotiating formal mergers that combine complementary programs and resources in an effort to be more cost effective.

What would the board of a networked organization look like? Would board positions be open to persons from other organizations in the network? To representatives of the membership, client, or partner groups? Membership on the board might come from "advisory committees" mandated to work on particular programming matters. The board structure might also be much looser, with different levels and forms of involvement, some focused on program and on the traditional role of board as trustee. All are evolving as organizations seek innovative ways to respond to organizational crises.

Case Example

A Networked Community NGO for Youth Employment

A local NGO in the Ottawa-Carleton region is experimenting with a form of networked structure. The organization was set up several years ago to provide job training for unemployed young people. Cutbacks in government funding have since pushed the organization to explore more innovative ways of supporting the program by drawing on community resources and expertise.

The organization is guided by a "core board" elected by members at an annual general meeting. The board oversees the operations of the organization. In response to the funding crisis, it has recently set up two more specialized entities, each of which has its own separate board of directors reporting to the core board.

One of these is a not-for-profit fund-raising corporation responsible for revenue generation. This board attracts "money-minded" persons who share the values and goals of the organization but are less interested in being directly involved in the programs. The fund-raising corporation is involved in a wide variety of schemes – raffles, dances, bingos – and has plans for many more.

The second entity is a profit-making corporation to set up small businesses that will eventually raise funds for the organization and provide employment opportunities for youth trainees. Their first project is a catering business to involve unemployed young people in setting up and running the business. The trainees will receive a salary and a share of the profits.

Both of these subsidiary boards have considerable autonomy from the core board and will evolve in different ways. Different people are recruited for each, with different skills and interests. The volunteers involved in program delivery are seldom involved in fund-raising, and vice versa. The structure is thus a network of individuals tied together by a common objective. The cultures of the three boards reflect these differences: the core board works much like a traditional NGO board, while the "for-profit" corporation board is much more focused on the bottom line.

The executive director sits on all three boards and has a strong co-ordinating role. She supervises a small staff that relates to each of the boards and subcommittees.

The essence of this organization is innovative energy which is channeled by a strong executive director. A small core staff supports a wide-ranging, largely volunteer organization led by a board that has considerable community support. The volunteers on the board and committees are skilled and caring people who enjoy their contribution. Each part of the organization has sufficient autonomy to allow people to focus on their task and not on the whole structure.

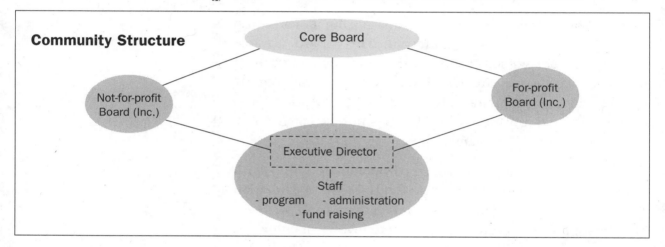

Community Structure

Core Board

Not-for-profit Board (Inc.)

For-profit Board (Inc.)

Executive Director

Staff
- program   - administration
- fund raising

How might the network structure accomplish the goals we have been discussing in this chapter?

NETWORK

1. More Efficient and Smaller
The core-staff complement can be very small, although the total number of people involved can be much larger.

2. More Accountable
The board remains accountable to the membership. Staff are accountable as teams for accomplishment; individual staff are accountable to other team members and one or

more managers. Some organizations introduce a "market accountability" with some units providing service to other parts of the organization on a cost-recovery basis. Organizational "customers" are free to go outside the organization for services if they find other service providers who are more dependable, cost effective, or deliver higher quality.

3. Focused on the Mission and Strategy

This structure can be clearly focused on the mission and strategy. The strategy may be realized as a series of projects with people contracted to carry them out under the "supervision" of core staff.

4. Flexible and Responsive

A network should be a very flexible structure. It needs coordinating mechanisms and basic operating agreements but should not be overly regulated. It is not as tied to fixed infrastructure and staffing costs.

5. Fit with the Culture

Network forms may or may not fit with the current organizational culture, but the transition to a network can be difficult even for the most decentralized organization. It is based on non-traditional working assumptions and requires a very particular set of skills and orientations for core staff.

6. Gender Equitable

Because of its organic nature, networks are possibly most amenable to flexible work arrangements and bounded work assignments, which could be easier for women and men to balance with family requirements. Nevertheless, staffing and contracting practices still need to be compatible with a commitment to equity for women and minority groups.

Inter-Organizational Networks

The current highly insecure environment in which NGOs must function is encouraging new collaborative strategies and more radical organizational forms. Collaboration among organizations is nothing new, as the many professional associations, trade councils, and umbrella groups demonstrate; and this trend is likely to continue. In the 1980s, a number of Canadian NGO consortia and coalitions were set up to jointly administer government and NGO funds, generally in one region of the world.

What is newer, at least among international-co-operation NGOs in Canada, are efforts to develop joint strategies for action that would be binding on individual organizations. The following case describes one such effort, which is still in process but which raises several important questions for future efforts.*

Case Study

The Provincial Council: Joint Strategy Making in an NGO Network

The Provincial Council is an association of international NGOs based in one province of Canada. It has spent most of the past decade attempting to build greater inter-agency co-operation. It has been a major challenge to find common ground in terms of values, ideology, and public profile, and to balance needs for agency autonomy with needs for increased public and policy impact. The strains among the members threatened progress on more than one occasion.

The council was formed in the 1970s. With the assistance of federal and provincial government grants, a small staffed secretariat co-ordinated the work of the association. Its early mission was to increase members' collective and individual impact in the province, primarily through member education and joint public-education campaigns. This goal was impeded

---

* In the Canadian federal budget of February 1995, all international-development education grants were eliminated, as well as federal funding for provincial councils of international-development NGOs. Many organizations have closed or have downsized operations while devising new strategies for their work.

by two co-existing political perspectives: that of the smaller educational and solidarity NGOs, and of the larger development NGOs with programs overseas. The development-education NGOs tended to be more critical of the status quo, and more vocal in advocating structural change; certain development NGOs shared this approach but several were satisfied to work within the current structures and system, as development professionals.

In 1985, an external evaluation revealed this serious lack of cohesion and political tensions in the council. Partly to resolve these issues, the council undertook a strategic-planning process in 1986 with the aim of reaching agreement on the mission, objectives, membership, and areas for joint learning: education, policy development, communications, funding.

The outcome of this exercise was not entirely satisfactory. It put a number of initiatives in place but failed to resolve the nature of this umbrella organization. Could the council be greater than the sum of its parts? Could it be more than a meeting place for individual members to share and exchange, and then leave?

The strategic-planning work did produce an important breakthrough, however; after considerable debate among members, a "development charter" was adopted in 1987. The final document represented a political compromise acceptable to every member, an ideological compromise. The charter defined a set of agreed principles, but did not set out common strategies.

With the charter, the council adopted an explicit mission and ceased being simply an association of groups working in the same field. It provided a vision of its mandate, principles, and direction: the association was to be a crossroads for reflection and the development of joint positions on crucial development issues, such as: women in development, human rights, third world debt, structural adjustment, provincial government policies on international development, etc. Joint reflection, however, was far easier than creating the basis for joint action and advocacy that would require a deeper commitment to consensus, collective action, and the resolution of issues of self versus collective interests of the members.

The membership was finally galvanized by budget cuts to federal government grants, and by the rapidly changing external world, as the postwar political and economic structures fell apart. The NGO community in the province needed to rethink its strategic stance on development issues. In 1992, the council initiated a process aimed at revising its priorities.

Inter-Agency Strategy Making

In early 1992, the program committee – a joint body of board and staff – mounted a major consultation on the council's priorities. The consultation revealed that many members were ready for joint action, especially on advocating policy. CCIC's foreign policy review had also helped to build common strategies but the consultation raised a number of issues that tested the comfort levels of individual members on questions of agency visibility on political issues, external communications, and differing policy perspectives.

The ensuing plan was a major achievement that built an innovative co-ordinating structure of work groups and committees, which has engaged the energies of the NGO community.

Despite the success of this process to date, a number of reservations remain about the strength of this new strategic alliance, and the level of commitment of individual agencies. The experience demonstrates the difficulty in bringing together a diverse group of organizations with different political agendas, missions, and programming approaches.

Case Study Analysis

Important as all the careful and participatory planning activities have been, the association was not able to come to terms with several essential organizational issues. First, the association still does not have the political authority to make certain decisions with implications for individual members. Persons representing their organizations on the board of directors do not come with a mandate to act on their organization's behalf. Second, council members do not easily accept the need for other members to provide feedback on their work. There is no culture of self-critique. This is an important lack. It means the council cannot fully control its work.

What can be learned from this experience to date?

- The process of reaching political consensus on a common strategy requires an extended learning process that respects members' differences, and that brings to the surface shared values and needs. This was accomplished by the council over time, beginning with the development charter, through a process of debate, reflection, and joint activities.

- The approach to change must be incremental, building common ground and inter-agency trust.

After much effort, however, the council is not able to hold its members accountable for successful completion of agreed tasks. Perhaps it never will, beyond an agreement on a charter of principles or a code of ethics. It could be that the trade-off of organizational autonomy for collective impact is too great. Each NGO would need to cede some of its control in exchange for reduced vulnerability overall, and a more focused and coherent community effort.

Elements of Successful Inter-agency Collaboration

One should not conclude from this that inter-agency collaboration is unrealistic. There are many examples of effectively functioning, if less ambitious, inter-agency partnerships and joint initiatives. Canadian NGOs have collaborated among themselves in developing and delivering shared programming in Central America, Southern Africa, and other parts of the world. Development NGOs similarly collaborate in many other countries to deliver joint programs, public campaigns, or education programs.

Such collaborative efforts seem to work best where agencies negotiate their respective roles and levels of decision-making autonomy in clearly defined areas.

Successful Collaboration Criteria and Lessons

The following points suggest some of the characteristics of successful collaborations:

- Agencies choose to work together – i.e., the collaboration is not a by-product of joining a larger association
- There are shared values and approaches to the work
- There is shared responsibility, and clear roles for each agency
- The collaboration is bounded and finite
- The shared work is central, rather than marginal, to the core program of the participating agencies

In the above case example, the Provincial Council is an association open to all development NGOs in the province, with goals that are general and open-ended. The creation of strategic and binding program collaborations is thus more difficult and longer term. The process requires some level of change in all participating organizations, as well as in the council itself.

There are several lessons for networks of all types:

1. Inter-organizational relationships are best formed around specific, program-related initiatives that are considered central by participating members.

2. The collaboration must add value or solve pressing dilemmas of the participating organizations – the sum must be greater than the parts.

3. The absence of traditional structures highlights the importance of strong leadership capable of building and maintaining the network of relationships.

4. The work of the partnership must have resources dedicated to implementation and to the collaborative process itself. Meetings, information exchange, joint research, and reporting all take staff time from individual members. The collaborative work needs to be recognized in work plans, or must have sufficient funding to contract program staff.

This chapter has reviewed four different structural options and measured them against six criteria for an effective organization in today's turbulent environment.

The table below summarizes this discussion.

In any restructuring activity, the leadership of an organization – staff and board – needs to be clear about the criteria for change and ensure a process that will meet them. A decisive factor in the success of restructuring is that staff be fully involved, that the change not be planned behind closed doors. The process of making decisions about a new structure should be seen as an opportunity for staff to develop ownership of and commitment to the change, and for conflicts and confusion to be addressed head-on.

It may be that the challenge of the future is not solely in the structures of individual organizations but in the design of a

Performance of Organization Models Against Criteria				
Criteria	**Hierarchy**	**Team**	**Matrix**	**Network**
Efficient and smaller	low/med	med	med	high
Accountable	high	med	med	high
Focus on mission and strategy	med	high	high	high
Flexible and responsive	low	med	high	high
Fit with the Culture	depends on the organization			
Gender Equity	low	med	med	high

variety of new forms of inter-organizational partnership. Networks offer the possibility of greater impact and innovative programming but must deal with the basic human issues that underlie all partnerships – trust, respect, and recognition of the value of different approaches. Although many of our colleagues see new collaborative forms as essential to work in the future, the case of the Provincial Council is a reminder that these relationships are far from easy.

References

1. J. Galbraith, E. Lawler & Associates, *Organizing for the Future: The New Logic for Managing Complex Organizations* (San Francisco: Jossey-Bass, 1993).

2. J. O'Toole, *Vanguard Management: Re-designing the Corporate Future* (New York: Doubleday, 1985).

3. A. Mills, and P. Tancred, eds., *Gendering Organizational Analysis* (Newbury Park: Sage, 1992).

4. S. Helgesen, *The Web of Inclusion* (New York: Currency/Doubleday, 1995), 10.

5. A.-M. Goetz, "Gender & Administration," *IDS Bulletin* 23, no. 4, 1992.

6. D. Limerick, and B. Cunningham, *Managing the New Organization: A Blueprint for Networks and Strategic Alliances* (San Francisco: Jossey-Bass, 1993); S. Rahnema, *Organization Structure: A Systemic Approach* (Toronto: McGraw-Hill Ryerson, 1992); C. Handy, *The Empty Raincoat: Making Sense of the Future* (London: Hutchison, 1994).

7. D. Limerick and B. Cunningham, op. cit.

8. K. Kelly, *Out of Control: The Rise of Neo-Biological Civilization* (Reading: Addison-Wesley, 1994), 88.

9. L. Cumming with B. Singleton, "Organizational Sustainability: An End of the Century Challenge for Canadian Voluntary International Development Organizations," presented to the Eleventh Annual Conference of the Canadian Association for the Study of International Development, Université du Québec à Montreal, June 6, 1995.

PART III

Making It Happen: Process and Tools

The first two parts of this book concentrated on what is happening to NGOs and voluntary organizations and *what* they need to change. We have said that NGOs are facing uncertain financial futures, and in some cases a crisis of relevance. We have discussed particularly pressing problems, such as accountability, staff morale, and the quality of strategic leadership. We have considered the bureaucratic approach to organizing work and have looked at issues underlying bureaucracy, hierarchy, and patriarchy. We have proposed an approach that focuses on organizational learning and managing for change rather than on the status quo. And we have presented different ways of thinking about the three levers for change - culture, strategy, and structure.

The question remaining is *how* to make these changes? The next two chapters describe the change process itself. Chapter 6 concerns how change happens in these organizations and the three steps or phases of change: start-up, transition, and resolution.

Chapter 7 describes specific tools that have proved helpful in participatory change processes. Finally, a concluding chapter speculates about the future, and summarizes the capabilities, orientations, and "attitudes" that will be needed to manoeuvre through the waves without capsizing.

Organizational Change: The Process

"We don't have a process for change. We just do it all the time."

– an NGO Executive Director

THIS CHAPTER IS ABOUT "DOING CHANGE" – THE PROCESS OR phases of change. You can muddle through without a process, as the above NGO manager boasted, relying on intuition and good will. Or you can be more deliberate.

Scope and Depth of Change

There are several distinctions to be made about the nature of change in organizations. The first distinction concerns the *scope* of change. Local change may affect a region, an office, or even a person's job, but it does not change all regions, or all jobs. The second kind of change – the kind that affects the entire organization – is the primary object of our focus.

"First-order" change happens within the existing paradigm.

"Second-order" change affects the core organizational principles, the very definition of the mission.

A more fundamental distinction concerns the *depth* of change.[1] "First-order" changes happen within the existing paradigm. Take, for example, a newly elected government – new people in, old ones out, individual lives changed. At a deeper level, though, it's business as usual: the system of distribution of income is the same, the role of the military continues unchanged, the ruling elite continues to control the assets of the country. In other words, change has happened but within the existing paradigm.

"Second-order" change affects the core organizational principles, the very definition of the mission. For example, an international-co-operation NGO may have started out as a relief agency, raising funds to send supplies to poor countries. Over time, some of the field staff come to realize that the problem isn't poverty alone but the powerlessness of poor people. This insight eventually results in a complete reorientation of the organization – new board members, new staff, a new strategy focused on political change, a culture built on ideas of political equity, new partners committed to similar goals, and a new organizational structure.[2]

Second-order change is not always better than first-order change; indeed, organizations, societies, and individuals usually learn and change at the first level. Occasionally situations demand second-order change.

This chapter will describe three types of change process that emerge from these distinctions of local versus organizational-level change, and first-order versus second-order change:
- Innovation
- Organizational Improvement
- Organizational Rebuilding

Innovation

Innovation is the development of new programs, new processes, even new structures that improve the functioning of the organization. Innovation often begins as the work of one person in the normal context of her or his job, but it usually requires a number of people to develop, build support, and implement.

Innovation is change within the existing paradigm, and it generally tends to be localized. Some examples might include a new method of reconciling bank statements, developing a new program in a particular region, and developing different fund-raising events such as the Human Rights Now! campaign built around a worldwide series of rock concerts.

Innovation might be administrative, such as using E-mail to update field staff on organizational news, or instituting a meeting to deal with staff morale issues. All these grow out of the ongoing work and responsibilities of individual staff people and are driven by their energy and creativity.

These changes are not intended to threaten the overall way of being of the organization but are generally localized in their effects.

An environment that supports innovation must have:

- Lots of lateral communication within the organization

- Wide latitude for staff decision making

- Pressure for learning: a sense of a need to keep changing to remain relevant and effective; and challenging expectations of managers and board members to encourage a flow of innovative solutions to organizational problems

- Solid connections between staff and outside colleagues, partners and funders

- Resources that support learning in all its forms

- An environment that rewards learning with increased status, access to information, and opportunities for more interesting challenges[3]

Organizational Innovation:
Innovation is change within the existing paradigm, and it generally tends to be localized.

Resources for Change

- Research budgets
- Staff time
- External consultants
- Courses
- Pilots
- Field visits
- Workshops and other participatory forums
- Evaluations

Innovation may not be enough. Extensive change may be needed to come to grips with more fundamental problems.

Organizational Improvement

Organizational Improvement:
"Improvement" processes aim at organization-wide change within the operating paradigm of the organization.

"Improvement" processes aim at organization-wide change within the operating paradigm of the organization (although they may go beyond the current paradigm). Ideally, identification of improvements flows from a strategy-making process, and is part of a pattern of response to strategic issues. Improvements might include policy changes, such as the development of a gender policy, a new strategic plan, or a new decision-making structure and practice. Organizational-improvement efforts are distinguished from innovation by their effect on large parts of the organization's functioning, thereby going beyond the job responsibilities of any one person or group. Instead, the task is given to some cross-departmental task force or committee.

Steps in Organizational Improvement

The steps of the process are generally like the following, although it may be abandoned at any stage or downgraded to an innovation.

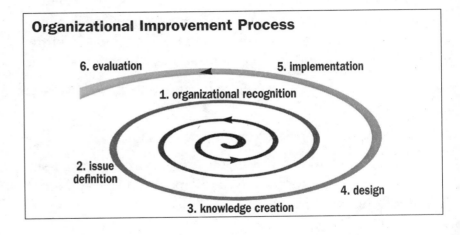

Organizational Improvement Process

6. evaluation

5. implementation

1. organizational recognition

2. issue definition

3. knowledge creation

4. design

Organizational improvement begins with **organizational recognition**: from among all the possibilities for organizational improvement, the leadership decides that a particular improvement is required. Recognition is followed by a period of **issue definition**, when decisions about the resources to be invested and the improvement team to be assembled are made. The team generally begins with a process of issue identification, research, and information collection – **knowledge creation**. This knowledge is used to **design** the improvement; the design is then negotiated and discussed within the organization. This is a significant step: the improvement will probably change the way of working as well as the relationships and agendas of many people. It is therefore important to shape the improvement so that it meets the needs and gains the support of a wide range of organization members and leaders. If this support is generated, the improvement is **implemented.** During implementation, it emerges that things are a little more complicated than anticipated, and some redesign is required. This spiral of action and redesign can continue indefinitely or be completed quite soon, depending on the complexity of the improvement.

A good example of the organizational-improvement process is the gender training program of the large South Asian NGO described in Chapter 2. Here is how the process worked:

Gender Training in an Asian NGO

1. Organizational Recognition

The executive director had for a number of years felt that gender and development were important, and although his organization worked largely with women, he felt that it needed to improve the quality of gender relations within the organization. Donors had also been pushing for more focus on gender issues. The organization had attempted a number of

Case Example

innovations, such as hiring more women and setting up a women's committee, with unsatisfactory results. At a conference, the executive director attended a presentation on gender, which he found very helpful. He asked the presenter if she would do some work with his group. He consulted other managers in the organization to see if there would be support for work on gender issues. This coming together of problem, pressure, person, and a feeling that the time was right encouraged him to go ahead.

2. Issue Definition, Resources, Team Selection

Once it was accepted that something would happen, discussion of the issue and how to proceed began. Goals for the program were developed, and two key decisions were made. The first was to view this as more than a training problem, to see it as a problem of organizational culture and process. There were a number of ways that women's participation in the organization was limited, although not always deliberately. In other words, the intent was not just to hire more women but to make the organization a place where women would wish to stay, be promoted, and make a contribution.

The second decision was that the team be made up of insiders and outsiders. The insiders would bring organizational knowledge, and the outsiders technical expertise and different perspectives. The outsiders would be gender trainers but would also offer organizational-development expertise.

After these decisions were made, sufficient funding was secured to make a serious change effort possible.

3. Information Collection and Knowledge Building

When the team started work, it was evident that what was meant by terms such as "gender" and "women's empowerment" was very unclear. To guide their work and to build the necessary joint understanding, the team began a process of clarifying what was meant by these and other terms. Eventually they developed a framework, which they then tested with a variety of groups including senior managers. These discussions led to further development of the framework, which was then used as the basis of needs assessment and gender discussions throughout the organization. The results of the assessment discussions were assembled and discussed with the managers in a two-day workshop.

What emerged from these discussions were three broad programming goals for women's empowerment:

a) To increase women's ability to be economically self-sufficient

b) To increase women's confidence and ability to understand and negotiate their rights in the household and community

c) To increase women's control over their own bodies, time, and movement, including freedom from violence

With respect to transforming gender relations, the following strategies emerged from the analysis:

a) Increasing men's and women's ability to analyse and reshape gender relationships (i.e., power relationships) in order to transform them

b) Equitable access and control over both public and private resources

c) Equitable participation in household, community, and national life

d) Reshaping of social institutions and organizations to include different gender perspectives, to the benefit of both sexes

An essential requirement for the successful completion of this stage is the creation of "shared knowledge." It is not enough that the change team have a good understanding of the issues, their importance and what, in general, is a reasonable strategy for change. These also must be understood by managers and others in the organization.

In the above NGO, the team leader followed up the planning

Key Assumptions about Change:

1. Start with stated goals for gender equity and women's empowerment

2. Define these two terms in language relevant to the organization

3. Mix pressure from senior management with a supportive, participatory field-level process.

workshop with a series of one-on-one meetings with managers to continue the knowledge-creation process. Managers were also considering the issue in their own meetings. When there was sufficient consensus, the design process began.

4. Design

In general, design builds on the understanding of what to do and creates a detailed intervention plan. As directions become more clear and detailed, old agreements often need to be renegotiated as people realize the potential impact of the intervention. In this example, the Gender Team designed an "action-learning" process to train staff on site in office teams. The office teams would implement small-scale gender improvement projects that aimed to bring to consciousness and to challenge unspoken assumptions about the division of labour and resources between men and women. When managers realized that the training would be quite different from previous training in the organization, they once more became involved to shape the design so that it was feasible, given other aspects of the work.

5. Implementation

In this phase, the risks and the resistance are highest. Training trainers, managing scheduling and logistics, and dealing with the inevitable unexpected outcomes make this phase very demanding. It is also the time when the process moves out of the hands of the proponents and designers and into the larger sphere, where it is susceptible to misunderstanding, subversion, and error. All this points to careful monitoring, regular meetings with key players, and a willingness to keep shaping the process as more knowledge is gained.

6. Evaluation

As this is being written, the evaluation is being developed for the gender program. Evaluation is not only to assess the impact of the intervention but to understand it well enough to redesign and recycle it so that it becomes a sustained effort, in this case to change gender relations.

Factors Crucial to Organizational Improvement

The conditions that support successful organizational improvements are similar to those supporting innovation but with some important additions. Because organizational improvement has the potential to affect the work of far more people than does innovation, two important elements are required:

1. The work teams should be made up of persons with different backgrounds and perspectives in order to ensure a full understanding. The team must be skilled in analytic techniques and have an ability to build knowledge *together*.

2. The solutions designed by the team must meet the requirements – sometimes contradictory – of the range of stakeholders. This means the team must be capable of negotiating, consulting, and "shaping" a solution that meets many different demands.

The team, then, must have extremely good links to the rest of the organization and maintain communication with all the players.

We have noted earlier that organizational improvement is generally a first-order change, i.e., that it does not affect the core ways of doing things in the organization. A new strategic plan, for example, may affirm old values, work with many of the same partners but in different ways, or set more ambitious goals. None of these turn the organization upside down. Occasionally, however, an organizational-improvement effort tips the organization into a much more profound process of rebuilding.

Organizational Rebuilding

One NGO started an "It's Broken" committee. Another had a "Should We Be Alive in 2000?" committee. Both grew out of the leadership's realization that circumstances demanded a

Organizational rebuilding requires a rethinking of the basic premises.

rethinking of many of the basic premises of the organization. The impetus is almost always a crisis that cannot be resolved by tinkering, a crisis sufficiently compelling to require radical change – what in the private sector is called "re-engineering."

When an organization engages in this level of change, it usually involves a change of strategy, structure, and culture. It is generally experienced as alternately frightening and exhilarating, demanding and liberating. Perhaps its most dominant feature is its chaotic "busyness". Leaders need to juggle many tasks at once, all of them underdefined, most urgent, and many vexed.

It is because of the difficulty of standing back from this chaotic busyness and seeing the flow that leaders need a model of the process in order to do more than merely respond to events. The remainder of this chapter will discuss a model of organizational rebuilding that has been developed out of work with numerous non-profit domestic and international organizations.

The Organizational Rebuilding Process

It is possible to see the change process as having three stages:

1. Start-up

This translates a sense of concern and a recognition of organizational difficulties into a set of engaging activities. People need to understand why the change is necessary, determine the personal relevance of the change, and build agreement on the process. This stage is one of "unfreezing," which brings with it distinct discomfort and disorientation, as the search for answers begins. The unfreezing is the result of a powerful, even traumatic event or events that propels change, as happened to INGO in Chapter 3, when the board of directors voted down the cutback plan of management. Once unfreezing occurs, there is no turning back.

2. Transition

When an organization starts to "live" and design its new

approach while still caught in old ways of acting, it is beginning the transition phase. This is often a time of conflict, discouragement, and excitement as the new organization struggles to be born. In many ways the organization feels schizophrenic as it is operating under two sets of principles and values – the old and the emerging. Acting on new priorities and modelling new ways of behaving can be intensely difficult for organizational leaders and staff.

The main tasks are to design the details of the change in a way that engages and makes owners of all the stakeholders while at the same time, discontinuing outmoded operational work processes.

3. Resolution

This is the work of implementing and managing the strategy so that the new ways of being eventually become the normal processes of the organization.

Although there are three distinct phases, the work often unfolds in a cyclical manner: the start-up leads to a transition and a resolution, which in turn leads to a start-up at a different level, and to another transition, and so on.

In each of these phases, there are three tasks: building **support**,

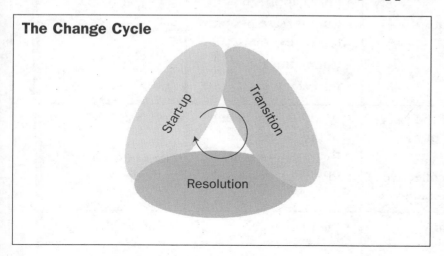

The Change Cycle

Start-up

Transition

Resolution

developing **clarity**, and taking **action**. When the three phases are combined with the three tasks we get the table below.

This table shows the activities required at each phase of the process. It also reminds us that at any given time in the process it is important to be thinking about a number of things at once. For example, at the start-up phase, the leaders must be thinking about building a change team, collecting information, identifying the issues, and so on.

Phase One: Start-up

Looking more closely at the table, we see that the start-up phase is devoted to assessing whether the organization is ready for change, and whether people will work on it and support it. The other task is to begin to collect information

	START-UP	TRANSITION	RESOLUTION
SUPPORT	• Assess/build readiness • Build a change team • Agree on process • Undertake organizational and external analysis • Communicate • Educate	• Build a joint team for detailed planning • Training • Deal with conflict and grieving • Board approval • Compensate people for losses • Communicate • Educate	• Maintain momentum • Get feedback • Launch new change initiatives • Communicate • Educate
CLARITY	• Understand the issues and "whys" of the change • Develop a collective vision and strategy	• Work out the details of the strategy and the organizational options	• Smooth out the rough parts • Set new targets for change
ACTION	• Act differently	• Pilot key ideas	• Full implementation

and ideas so that the issues are made clearer and the emerging sense of vision – the general idea of what you want to accomplish after analysing the critical factors in the environment and in the organization – is grounded in the needs of a broad range of people. Vision is critical, as it is the *emotional catalyst* as well as the preferred future state.

What is also important is that the behaviour of the leaders begin to reflect the change they are trying to lead. If, for example, the change is related to an improvement in democratic functioning, then everything related to the project needs to reflect that value.

Start-up Tasks:

In each phase, there are tasks to accomplish related to support, clarity, and action, as shown in the above table.

Support

At this first phase, there are six main support tasks:

1. Assess readiness

Is there a pattern of pressures that have the attention of board and staff? Is there at least a direction for change that has some support? Are there the resources (energy, time, money, expertise) available? Is a critical mass of the leadership committed to a serious change effort that could take two to three years at least?

One NGO invested in a number of board/staff retreats to build the readiness and relationships required for change. They set up the "Committee to Plan the Plan," which recognized that a rift between board, staff, and management needed to be healed and trust needed to be built before significant change could get under way.

2. Agree on Process

It is essential that there be a description of the nature of the process at the beginning, and that this be widely shared and discussed: the purpose of the change, how people will be involved, how information will be collected, how it will be analysed, expected programming areas to be involved, and a description of how and when organizational members will make decisions.

3. Build a Change Team

A large-scale change requires people to manage it. The team should include people with different perspectives and representing different interests. The team members must have wide legitimacy in the organization. This does not mean that every unit should have direct representation; generally, four or five people representing different parts of the staff and board is an appropriate team. The team members must be able to work well together.

4. Build Shared Knowledge

Involve a broad group in an analysis of the situation. There is more on analysis below, but the most important point is that the process must build shared knowledge across the organization so that the understanding of the need for change grows.

5. Communication

There will never be enough information about what is happening, but it is crucial to develop a variety of ways of keeping people informed; otherwise, fantasy and rumour will fuel people's worst fears. All NGOs we have worked with have used a variety of briefing meetings and staff discussion. One set up the "Friday Fax," in which the executive director wrote to all the offices and board members about the events of that week. Other NGOs set up special newsletters to keep staff, members, and board abreast of what was happening and, from time to time, to publish key documents.

6. Education

Staff and board will need to understand the requirements of the process and to develop skills to carry it out. Some NGOs do board briefings on the change process, send leaders to residential seminars, and undertake training programs for staff to build their discussion, analysis, or conflict-resolution skills.

<u>Clarity</u>

The key tasks here are to develop an analysis of both the inside and the outside of the organization, and a "vision" of what will respond to the situation. Such visions are rarely specific but summarize the elements of a solution that responds to the issues and has the support of the leadership, staff, and members.

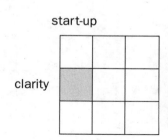

This task may be structured as a strategic-planning exercise, or it may be a loosely organized series of processes that analyse the situation and build clarity.

Some techniques that organizations have used (detailed in Chapter 7) have included:

- A search conference: A three-day meeting bringing together people from the organization as well as important stakeholders to do a series of structured activities leading to a jointly held analysis and understanding of the direction of change.

- An organizational-capacities-and-vulnerabilities analysis (see Chapter 7): Built on the four fields described in Chapter 2, this analysis can be done by a board or staff group in a short period of time (two or three hours).[4] In one NGO, the entire staff of eighty people did this analysis in groups of people from different departments. Each group was led by a staff member trained to facilitate this analysis. The change team then assembled the analyses of each of the groups and fed back the results at a staff meeting.

- An organizational mirror: One organization invited six outside people who knew the organization well to describe what they saw to be the organization's strengths and weaknesses. The meeting was videotaped and later shown to other staff and the board.

Key factors for success at this stage are wide involvement, good information, and focusing on finding common ground rather than highlighting ideological differences.

start-up

action

Action

Even at the start-up phase, action is important. The most important action is for change leaders to behave differently, to "start now." If you want the organization to be more democratic, start being more democratic, and make sure that the change process itself gives people the information and power to be truly involved. If you want to be more strategic, make the change process more strategic. It is only by acting in a manner congruent with the emerging goals of the change that people will trust the change; and it is only by beginning to act that you will learn your way to a new situation. For example, a change project used a multi-regional team to co-ordinate the change process. After they had done some work, the executive director realized that this group would be a good ongoing program-co-ordination body in line with one of the emerging change goals: better inter-regional co-ordination.

Phase Two: Transition

Once it is clear that there will be change and the broad outlines of the change have been described, there is a time of confusion. This transition period is a time of conflict, when emerging details about the change reveal that certain ways of being will be no longer. It is also a time of excitement, as a new organization struggles to be born.[5]

It is unrealistic to assume that things will go smoothly in the transition stage. As Rosabeth Moss Kantor put it, "Every innovation is a failure in the middle."[6] The important thing is to learn from the experience and keep redesigning until a workable solution emerges.

The transition phase is devoted to working with a broadly

based team that can develop the details of the plan. The main task is to translate the general idea into a detailed program that works in a given setting.

Transition Tasks:

Again, the tasks at this phase can be thought of in terms of support, clarity, and action.

<u>Support</u>

When people feel coerced into major change, they react either with nostalgia for the past or cynicism about the present, or both.[7] Neither is helpful in the midst of organizational rebuilding. What is needed is support both in working relationships and at the personal, emotional level. (One NGO held sessions for the staff to discuss their feelings about staying in an organization that many staff had left.) This means involving people directly in the change and allowing for emotions and conflicts to emerge. Conflict is an important indication of stress and grieving. It must be addressed openly, not suppressed in the hope that it will simply go away. (This is easier said than done, especially when conflicts are historic and entrenched.) Resolving conflicts can help move the process forward and give people a real opportunity to influence the direction of the change.

The transition phase is a time of high stress for staff; a high workload is compounded by the possibility that they or their co-workers may be leaving the organization as staff requirements change. Many NGOs we have worked with, and in, have supported the staff with special measures: stress-reduction seminars, job search, and financial-planning seminars.

These are important, but more is needed. If an organization is to move through the transition phase, its members and staff must feel that the change process is fair and honourable, that it values all the people who work for the organization – those

transition

support

"Change is too often seen as a negative thing, partly because there is a lot of conflict. You need to see personal conflicts in light of other things which are important to people; for example the fear of letting people and the mission down."

– Executive Director, "Link International"

who are staying, and those who are leaving. Fair financial compensation for those leaving is an important aspect of this.

Participation and the emotional elements of change are important, but they must be balanced by a determination to keep the purpose of the change – the content – in clear focus.

Clarity

The task at this point is to design the details of the change worked out in general terms in the start-up phase. Typical issues facing designers are:

transition

clarity

- Making the vision operational: What does the vision mean in terms of the actual work being done? ("Vision" is the general sense of what you want to accomplish after analysing the pertinent factors in the environment and in the organization. Vision is the *emotional catalyst* as well as the preferred future state.) What work must be discontinued? What is the new flow of work? Who does it? Will this change succeed, given the cultural values and norms of the organization? Will values and "old" behavioural norms need to be modified?

- The structure: What is the best way of structuring the organization in order to accomplish the vision?

- Governance: What are the implications of the vision for the board? What changes are needed to its role and/or structure?

This designing needs to be done *together*. Needed are mechanisms that allow a number of people to be involved in what used to be thought of as a solitary activity.

In one NGO, staff designed a new structure and new work processes built on a vision that had been developed by the board and membership. The staff held three workshops in which they used graphic tools to map out the work and isolate priority goals and directions. Smaller groups worked on particular issues, such as structure and co-ordination. The effort was led by a small team made up of management, program and clerical staff.

Action

The transition is the time to get changes happening on the ground: to build pilot projects so you can learn from experience; if possible, try out one part of the change to learn from it before implementing it across the organization. For example, one regional organization implemented a new structure and program in one region, evaluated it after six months, and then implemented it, with changes, in the other regions.

Phase Three: Resolution

Resolution is a little like spring. There is no one day that is obviously the end of winter, but one day you realize that there are more warm days than cold ones. Resolution is concerned with implementing the strategy, maintaining the momentum, and setting new targets for change. By this stage, new staffing arrangements are in place, there is less conflict, and now that you are working something approaching a normal work week, it feels like half time.

It is essential that the leaders continue to solicit feedback and continue to change in response to it, as there will be a tendency to retrench and return to old patterns. This period too can be managed by tasks defined in terms of support, clarity, and action.

Resolution Tasks:

Support

The key to continuing to build support at this stage is listening carefully to what is happening as the changes are being implemented, fine-tuned, and debugged. Inevitably things won't turn out quite as expected, but being blind to problems or dismissing them as mere "resistance to change" risks the success of the entire process.

Clarity

Evaluate the effects of the change to redesign and to start the next round of, it is hoped, smaller changes.

It is very difficult to find the time (or money) for effective evaluation in the busyness of implementation; for that reason, many NGOs plan in advance to carry out an evaluation at a specified future time.

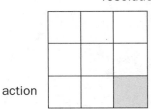

Action

To a certain extent, implementation builds on successes at earlier stages – in involving staff, creating good design, and so on. However, the implementation phase has several key success factors:

1. Careful planning, specifying who is responsible for each element on each schedule.

2. Providing sufficient time for meetings, training, and reorganizing, as staff will be performing new roles. Some NGOs plan to be less productive during this time and scale back activities accordingly.

3. Widespread discussion of the unanticipated results of the change. Leaders should take such information not as criticism of the change but as necessary to its proper implementation.

4. High-profile leadership that ties the pieces together and models the behaviour expected of staff and members.

What are the main messages of this chapter? Change is pervasive, but it is important to be aware of the different levels of change. Sometimes local innovation, such as an improved program in one region, is enough. Often a wider process that changes the way the whole organization functions, such as a strategic program review, is required. Occasionally the organization needs to rethink its fundamental operating principles and undertake a rebuilding process. Many of the principles are the same at each level; but the more pervasive the change, the more need there is for equitable, competent ways to involve large groups of people in jointly creating a more effective organization.

References

1. P. Watzlawick, J. Weakland, and R. Fisch, *Change, Principles of Problem Formation and Problem Resolution* (New York: Norton, 1974).

2. D. Korten, *Getting to the 21st Century: Voluntary Action and the Global Agenda* (West Hartford: Kumarian, 1990).

3. S. Mohrman, and A. Mohrman, "Organizational Change and Learning" in Galbraith et al., *Organizing for the Future: The New Logic for Managing Complex Organizations* (San Francisco: Jossey-Bass, 1993).

4. M. Anderson, and P. Woodrow, *Rising from the Ashes: Development Strategies in Times of Disaster* (Westview Press, 1989); R. Quinn, *Beyond Rational Management* (San Francisco: Jossey-Bass, 1988).

5. W. Bridges, *Managing Transitions: Making the Most of Change* (Reading: Addison-Wesley, 1991).

6. R. M. Kanter, *The Change Masters: Innovation for Productivity in the American Corporation* (New York: Simon and Schuster, 1984).

7. P. Marris, *Loss and Change* (London: Routledge, Kegan, Paul, 1974).

Tools for Organizational Learning

7

THIS CHAPTER DESCRIBES A NUMBER OF TOOLS TO AID THE collaborative search for learning and accomplishing the goals we have discussed. These are, first and foremost, tools for learning together – ways of involving groups of people in the task of understanding, planning, and taking action. This is not an exhaustive compendium, but rather those tools that we have found to be helpful in our work with NGOs and voluntary organizations.

A word of caution: we have all taken part in workshops that were exciting and full of promise but quickly faded to a dim memory as we once again became overwhelmed by day-to-day concerns and the pressure of the status quo. After all, buying a box of good chisels doesn't create the lovely cabinet. The effectiveness of these tools depends on the energy, good will and skill of the people using them, and the commitment to follow through.

Each tool is presented in a complete, ready-to-use format. The material can be reproduced from the book and used as is with a group. In order to make each tool complete in itself, some text is taken from earlier chapters or from other tools.

This chapter is divided into three sections:

Section I: Tools for Assessment
    Tool 1: CCIC Organizational-Assessment Tool
    Tool 2: Organizational Mirror
    Tool 3: Assessing Readiness for Change
    Tool 4: Images, Feelings, and Stories
    Tool 5: Mid-Course Assessment
Section II: Strategy Making
    Tool 6: Search Conference
Section III: People and Relationships
    Tool 7: Team Building
    Tool 8: Perspectives Analysis
    Tool 9: Cause Maps
    Tool 10: "Fishbowl" Exercise
Section IV: Planning Large-Scale Organizational Change
    Tool 11: Organizational-Change Planning Guide

Section I: Tools for Assessment

Assessment tools are generally used at the beginning of a change process to build a base of information that will enable the organization's leaders to map out a process of change. The tools are based on a participatory approach to understanding that assumes that people in different parts of the organization (board, managers, program staff, clerical staff) have very different perspectives on what is happening.

A participatory assessment is a powerful tool for change and can release considerable energy. Before embarking on an assessment, leaders should ask themselves if the organization is ready and has the capacity for change. Raising people's expectations without being able to follow through makes it very difficult to do such an assessment in the future.

Section II: Strategy Making

As discussed in Chapter 4, strategy making is not done in a weekend workshop; it is the ongoing preoccupation of the leadership. Periodically, however, it may be important to rethink the basic strategy of the organization and to quickly involve a large number of stakeholders in the discussion. Search conferences are the most effective tool we know of to develop strategy and commitment in a reasonably short period of time.

Section III: People and Relationships

Marvin Weisbord describes teamwork as "the quintessential achievement of a society grounded in individual accomplishment."[*] However lofty the achievement, teamwork, collaboration, and joint effort of all sorts are important to today's organizations, necessitating periodic team-building sessions, which depart from the usual routine to focus on team issues.

Team building is a social technology that has evolved from sessions focusing exclusively on interpersonal relationships. These sessions were generally held in a retreat setting and could last up to two weeks. The term "team building" now includes any meetings or processes that try to enhance working relationships. Examples include outdoor-survival programs designed to build trust and reliance on other team members; team-learning sessions that focus on building skills of joint inquiry and the relationships that can support coordination and unity;[**] planning sessions designed to build

---

[*] M. Weisbord, cited in B. Reedy, K. Jamison, *Team Building: Blueprints for Productivity and Satisfaction* (Alexandria, Virginia: NTL Institute for Applied Behaviour Science, 1988).

[**] P. Senge et al, *The Fifth Discipline Fieldbook* (New York: Doubleday, 1994).

consensus on future action; and conflict-resolution sessions to deal with work-related conflicts that block the accomplishment of goals.[*]

Section IV: Planning Large-Scale Organizational Change

The planning guide in this section is to help change leaders think about "second-order change" (see Chapter 6). It was developed a number of years ago by David Kelleher and has been used in a wide variety of organizations.

Second-order change will affect the core values and ways of working of the organization. Generally such change is disruptive, demands learning on everyone's part, and can involve considerable conflict. Good planning won't avoid conflict, but a factor in the success of organizational change is an agreement on the nature of the process: How will it unfold? Who will be involved? When will decisions be made?

---

[*] B. Reddy, and K. Jamison, op. cit.

Tool 1: Organizational-Assessment Guide
Canadian Council for International Co-operation

This guide is intended to help you assess key dimensions of your organization as a preparation for developing a change path. It was originally developed by CCIC as the first step in the "Tiger" workshops.

This assessment focuses on two areas:

A. Strategic Management

B. Organizational Capabilities and Vulnerabilities

Process

1. Ensure that the organization is committed to a serious assessment *and* to following up on the findings of the assessment.

2. Decide on who should be involved in this assessment – staff, board, partners, union, and others. This is an important decision. Should the assessors be good analysts? Should they be representatives of various groups? Should all voices be heard? In most cases it makes sense to include as many perspectives as possible and not to be afraid to build a picture that includes contradictory findings. To be effective, the process should include at least two groups (board and staff, for example).

3. Have participants complete the Assessment Guide individually to prepare for the meeting with other assessors.

4. Convene a meeting of the assessors and work through each item in the guide. The process of the meeting depends on the number present but should look generally like the following. Each person presents her/his response to each item. Record the responses on a flip chart. After hearing all the responses to an item, look for major areas of agreement and discuss major differences. Don't worry at this stage about resolving differences. Allow them to stand, recording the various points of view. This meeting generally takes at least a day.

5. Following the assessment meeting, write up the findings, distribute them to those at the meeting, and schedule time for planning action.

Getting Started

Before beginning the assessment, we would like you to focus on what you value in this organization.

What first attracted you to this organization? What were your initial impressions when you joined? What was exciting for you?

What things really matter to you about this organization? What achievements have you been happiest about in the recent past? What aspects of this organization are you most proud of?

A. Strategic Management

We would like to begin with a "visioning" approach to strategy. We will then turn to a more systematic approach to understanding strategic management in your NGO.

What is your positive vision of this organization three years from now? Imagine that you are looking at your organization in the future and it has been doing really well. Describe what's happening. What's the organization doing? Who is it doing it for? How is it doing it? What's the unique contribution it is making? What new directions has it established? What old directions did it keep? What obstacles were overcome in order to attain this successful state? What new constraints is it facing?

How is this "vision" different from the current situation?

Strategic management can be seen as four interrelated activities.

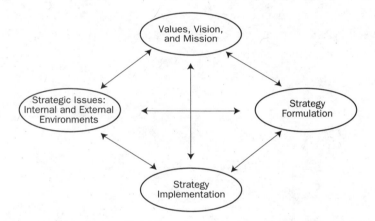

The **vision, values, and mission** outline what the organization cares about, its raison d'être, whom it serves, whom it works with, and how it will accomplish its goals.

The **strategic issues** summarize the crucial policy choices affecting the organization as a result of key factors in the environment (in Canada, the South, and other parts of the world) and in the organization (its capabilities, history, and other factors.)

Strategy formulation is the process of specifying how the organization will accomplish the mission, given the strategic issues it faces. Strategy includes goals, objectives, key success factors, and indicators of success.

Implementing strategy is the task of focusing the day-to-day work on the accomplishment of the mission. It means co-ordinating the work of the different parts of the organization to carry out on the strategy and monitor performance.

These four activities are not necessarily carried out sequentially. In most organizations, the mission, values, and vision remain in place for some years, but other aspects of strategy may be revised each year in response to the environment and the realities of implementing the strategy in the field.

Values, Vision, and Mission

Do you have a mission statement or a statement of organizational values? Does it adequately express your identity as an organization? Is there broad agreement on the values underlying it? How is it used in planning and priority setting?

Strategic Issues

What aspects of the external environment are currently most critical to your organization? For example:

1. Partners and their context
2. Funders
3. Your constituency in Canada
4. Others (list individually)

What aspects of your *internal* organizational environment are currently most important? (See also Capabilities and Vulnerabilities Analysis)

Process note: This discussion can get quite abstract. It is important to focus the discussion on those issues that have major impact on your organization. Differentiate between issues that will affect you strongly and issues that will affect you less strongly. Differentiate also between issues that will affect you immediately and those that will affect you over the longer term.

Strategy

What is your strategy to respond to the critical issues you have just identified?

Strategy Implementation

Does your organization have a strategic plan, or some statement about direction, and strategy? Is the plan well understood and accepted in the organization? How is it used to guide decision making and set priorities? How do you use it to focus resources on priority areas? How do you assess success?

B. Organizational Capabilities and Vulnerabilities

The following analysis looks at your organization by reference to a particular model of organizational effectiveness. The essential idea is that every organization needs to take care of four fields represented in the diagram below. (For more information on this framework, see Chapter 2.)[*]

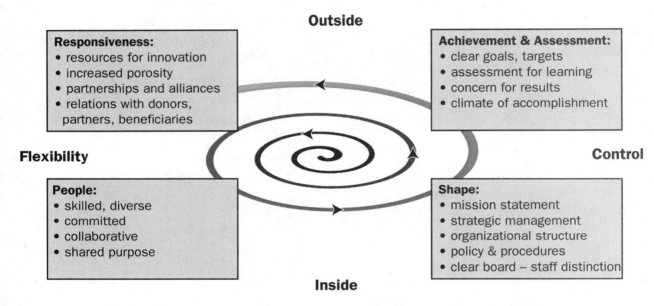

Outside

Responsiveness:
- resources for innovation
- increased porosity
- partnerships and alliances
- relations with donors, partners, beneficiaries

Achievement & Assessment:
- clear goals, targets
- assessment for learning
- concern for results
- climate of accomplishment

Flexibility

Control

People:
- skilled, diverse
- committed
- collaborative
- shared purpose

Shape:
- mission statement
- strategic management
- organizational structure
- policy & procedures
- clear board – staff distinction

Inside

Look first at the ***people*** field:

1. Do you have the right individuals – staff, board, and volunteers – committed to the organization, open to learning, capable of working together, and with a capacity for their own learning?

---

[*] M. Anderson, P. Woodrow, *Rising From the Ashes: Development Strategies in Times of Disaster* (Westview Press, 1989); R. Quinn, *Beyond Rational Management* (San Francisco: Jossey-Bass, 1988).

2. Can this diverse group work together? Will the relationships withstand the pressures and conflict of collaborative learning? Will the climate of the organization allow people to bring the best of themselves to the task?

3. Are the perspectives of women and minorities honoured?

4. Is there a climate of excitement that can unleash the energies of creative people?

5. Is there a sense of shared beliefs, a shared understanding of the purpose of the organization and its core values?

Looking back over your responses, what are your people capabilities? What are your vulnerabilities?

The second field is *responsiveness* – the organization's adaptability and ability to acquire outside support.

1. Is the organization in touch with the needs of its partners and donors?

2. Are donors and partners involved in the strategy-making process?

3. Does the organization have the capacity to evaluate economic and political trends?

4. Is it capable of formulating and carrying out changes such as joint ventures in response to that analysis?

5. Does it devote resources to innovation and to ensuring responses to changing circumstances?

What are your capabilities and vulnerabilities in this field?

Shape concerns building the vessel that can contain and channel the energy unleashed in the work described above. Does your organization have:

1. A clearly understood partnership between staff and board as to their respective responsibilities?

2. A mission statement or statement of purpose and values?

3. A set of policies and procedures that stimulate both individual and organizational learning, such as team assessments, a research policy, program and institutional evaluations, and project visits?

What are your capabilities and vulnerabilities in this field?

The fourth field is *Achievement and Assessment.*

1. Is your organization clear about what it is trying to do and for whom?

2. Is there a climate of achievement?

3. Are people focused on results?

4. Are there regular assessments of progress against targets?

What are your capabilities and vulnerabilities in this area?

Summarize your findings in the space below.

Tool 2: Organizational Mirror

This activity is designed to help an organization learn how others see it. Outsiders can see things insiders cannot and they often bring fresh perspectives. The core of the activity is to find a small group of people whose opinion you respect and who know your organization well, and to ask them to tell you what they think about your work.

One organization assembled a small group of clients, colleagues, and ex-staff people and asked them to think about a series of questions related to how the organization responded to clients, how innovative it was, how competent it was, how likely it was to move quickly on important issues. It asked them to find examples to support their assessment. This group was then asked to answer these questions in a panel discussion in front of the staff of the organization. All panelists made their comments, then the meeting was opened to questions from the floor. A facilitator ensured that staff listened as well as they were able. The session was videotaped and shown to staff in other offices.

Key success factors in the Organizational Mirror:

1. The outsiders must be credible, knowledgeable, and willing to tell the truth as they see it. They shouldn't necessarily agree with the main directions of the organization and they shouldn't just be friends of the leaders.

2. The questions must be within the competence of the outsiders.

3. The meeting must focus on understanding what the panelists have to say, not on defending the organization.

Tool 3: Assessing Readiness for Change: The Snapshot
Developed by David Kelleher and Bob Wiele

The first step in planning change is to analyse how ready your board, group, and/or organization is to change. It is also important to assess the chances of success of the change you are attempting.

Procedure:

1. Convene a meeting of representatives of board and staff to work on this question.

2. Complete your responses to the questionnaire. Be as accurate and specific as possible. Provide enough detail for a snapshot, but avoid a feature-length film!

3. Discuss your responses with your colleagues.

TIP: There are at least two ways of proceeding:

1. Each person completes the responses on his/her own, and the group then discusses the results together.

2. Complete the task in discussion as a group.

Six aspects of readiness are reviewed in this tool:

1. Difficulties in the organization

2. Vision

3. Resources

4. History

5. Politics

6. Leadership

A. Assessing the Readiness:

1. Difficulties in the Organization

a) Is the organization facing difficulty that is attracting the attention of staff, clients, board, or funders?

b) Are key members of the organization expressing their dissatisfaction?

2. Vision

a) Is there a vision or clear picture of how the difficulty facing the organization might be dealt with or resolved (a new structure, a new program, a new way of working, or other options)?

b) Does this vision have powerful advocates? Does the leadership hold this vision?

3. Resources

a) Are there qualified people prepared to work to bring about change?

b) Are board and committee members prepared to invest the time required?

c) Does the organization have the money and/or energy for the change (travel, meetings, consultants, training, and so on)?

4. History

a) Does the organization have a successful history of operations and of adaptation to changing situations?

b) Does the organization's history colour people's view of the likelihood of change? Can you influence that?

5. Politics

a) Has the board or executive committee authorized work on improving the current situation to bring about change?

b) Does the possibility of change fit with the self-interests of the powerful members of the system?

6. Leadership

a) Does the need for change have the support of powerful people in the organization?

b) To what extent do you in your role meet the following criteria of a successful inside-change agent?

LEADERSHIP FACTORS	LOW	MED	HIGH
1. Knowledge of the organization, its people, its politics			
2. Good reputation and credibility within the organization			
3. Good relationships with staff and key volunteers			
4. Willingness to consider changes to own work style			
5. Commitment to the change project and to the organization			
6. Prior experience in managing change			
7. Ability to make things happen			
8. Position or role in the organization			
9. Time available for the project			

B. Analysis

1. Look over your responses. Some areas will look better than others. List those areas that pose the greatest problem.

2. What is the main message you are receiving about your organization's readiness to change?

C. Strategy

Note any good ideas you have about what you might do to enhance the possibility of change by dealing with each of the areas you listed as problems.

Tool 4: Images, Feelings, and Stories

The following exercises allow participants to use their more creative, less linear faculties to discover what they may feel about an issue or the organization itself.

1. Collages

A collage is a collection of paper or other materials mounted on a surface such as a large piece of paper or card. Participants are given a stack of magazines and newspapers, markers, and glue. They are asked to make a collage expressing a particular theme. For example, they may be asked to express the future of the organization, its current state, the contribution they want to make, or any other aspect.

Each participant makes a collage that expresses her or his understanding of the theme. Participants leaf through the magazines and newspapers looking for images or words that fit their collage. (It is preferable to rely more heavily on images.) When they have collected enough of these, the participants paste them on a large piece of paper in any way they see fit. When everyone is finished, each person discusses his or her collage and what it is trying to say. Other participants may contribute by describing what they see in the collage.

2. Photo Stories*

Participants either take photos or are given photos of a particular locale. It may be the office, it may be a neighbourhood in which the organization is working, it may be a country where the organization has a program, or another place.

Each participant selects a number of photographs and then arranges them to tell a story. Participants tell the stories and then reflect on the themes in the stories and the images in the photos. After the discussion of the meaning of the stories, participants discuss the action they can take.

This activity was undertaken by clerical workers in a municipal government. A photographer took photos throughout the office. The clerical workers then met to create stories with the photos. After they had told one another the stories, it became evident that certain themes were important for them: relations with their supervisor, respect from the male inspectors who worked in the office, and the chaos of the current reorganization. A smaller group then worked with management on these issues.

* D. Barnt, F. Crystal, and d. marino, *Getting There: Producing Photostories with Immigrant Women* (Toronto: Between the Lines, 1982).

Tool 5: Mid-Course Assessment

Effective organizational change is sustained by a continuous flow of reliable feedback. In the middle of a change process, it can be very difficult to sort out rumour, fact, opinion, and trend. All forms of feedback are important, including gossip and rumour. Feedback-gathering efforts can range from the very informal to carefully designed information-collection activities.

A number of mid-term assessments are possible:

1. The change process should be evaluated after six months to one year to see if it is achieving its goals and to assess implications for more widespread implementation.

2. Because some staff or board members are going to be much more vocal than others, it is important to develop a means of providing a balanced picture. In a large organization, a questionnaire can be used, perhaps in conjunction with focus groups. In a smaller organization, meetings of groups of staff and board, perhaps led by an outsider, can develop a comprehensive picture of how people are experiencing the change.

3. Some organizations have held a mid-term workshop to take stock and to celebrate achievements.

4. Identify as liaison people human "sensors" who can collect information, formally and informally, from particular parts of the organization. These people must be trusted by the groups they interact with.

Mid-term assessments provide information, increased ownership, and a chance to celebrate. Unfortunately, they are needed just when everyone is their busiest, but it is important to commit to the mid-term assessment as part of the original agreement about the process.

Tool 6: Search Conference

Although the search conference originated in England more than forty years ago, its methodology has been developed around the world.[*] Lately such conferences have become increasingly popular as organizations realize that they need mechanisms for involving many stakeholders in learning, planning, and envisioning the future together. This section includes a brief description of search conferences and describes a recent search conference led by David Kelleher.

Search conferences have grown out of the work of many people:

1. Eric Trist and Fred Emery worked with British industry to get away from decision making by experts in favour of developing a decision-making conference that involved people in the process.

2. The work of Ron Lippit and Eva Schindler-Raiman[*], who discovered that problem-solving meetings resulted in long lists of problems, depressed participants, and solutions that were short-term and focused on anxiety reduction. They developed conferences in which participants envisioned "images of potentiality" and planned by working back from a desired future.

3. Community land-use planners, who have to build agreement among stakeholders, many of whom have contradictory requirements for a given piece of land.

Search conferences are now held all over the world and take many forms. The search conference described below is based on the following key assumptions:

1. Participation matters. It is not only important to get all the key people into a room together, but it is also important to design the discussion to ensure that there is high-quality participation on the part of those attending.

2. The best strategy comes from having people look at the past, present, and future and to use the future as a basis on which to plan a new present.

[*] M. Weisbord, *Building Common Ground* (San Francisco: Berret-Kohler, 1993).

In designing a search conference, consider some important questions:

1. Who should be there? Generally, you want as broad a range as possible: partners, funders, allies, staff, board, etc. It is important that there be sufficient diversity to develop new and different ideas, and that those who will be affected by the new directions are part of creating them. Search conferences can be run with as many as eighty people and as few as twenty-five.

2. Ideally, the conference should last about two and one-half days, including evening sessions. This gives time not only for meeting activities but also for private thought, informal discussions, and community building. (The conference described below took one evening and a very long day. It felt terribly rushed but worked.)

3. Where should it be held? This kind of a conference should be held in a place where people can stay overnight. It needs a large room big enough for all participants to break into small groups. Windows and natural light are important; these meetings are hard work and the energy from the light makes a difference. Finally, the room needs lots of wall space for hanging up the flip-chart sheets summarizing the work of the various groups.

Case Example: Relief International Canada (RIC)[*]

Relief International Canada (RIC) is the Canadian branch of an international organization with a head office in Europe and branches in many other northern countries. RIC was engaged in a review of its work and a search for new directions. The work was occasioned in part by serious financial problems but also by new program ideas being developed at the international head office. RIC was clearly embarked on a major renovation of their strategy and structure, but they were unsure how to proceed. The leaders realized that they needed to involve a broad cross section of the leadership, staff, and membership in the discussion in order to find directions that would not only ensure the future of RIC but would also be supported by a committed membership.

---

[*] RIC is a pseudonym for the organization.

They decided to hold a forum, to involve members and staff in a face-to-face discussion of where they were going.

RIC began by developing a large-scale survey of members, donors, and others interested in the organization's work, such as other development experts, media people, and government foreign-affairs staff. This data was analysed by a group of staff and board members and developed into a report.

The forum was held (during one evening and one full day) using the search-conference approach. Fifty staff, board members, and overseas guests participated. A synthesis committee drawn from the participants worked during the second evening to pull together a draft vision statement.

It declared that RIC held seven core values, which would be the basis for its future operation. After some further consultation, the vision was adopted by the board.

Because this statement was developed in such a democratic forum, it had real credibility, which was a key to the later success of the change process. In the inevitable conflict of organizational change, the leaders could always come back to the vision as a basis for action.

In order to help the reader understand the functioning of search conferences, we have attached the materials from the RIC search conference. They include:

1. The agenda for the conference

2. The design developed by the facilitator

3. The three worksheets used to give direction to the participants

RELIEF INTERNATIONAL CANADA FORUM – AGENDA

Friday

7:30   Welcome, getting organized and getting started, introductions
Scan Exercise: A look at critical events, trends, and developments
in the world, in the international movement of RI and in RI Canada
Wine and Cheese

Saturday

9:00   Analysis of information generated Friday evening

10:15 Refreshment break

10:40 RIC capabilities and vulnerabilities
Trends facing RIC

12:00 LUNCH

1:00   Implications of the capabilities,
vulnerabilities, and trends

1:30   Consideration of survey data

2:30   Synthesis – big ideas so far

3:00   Refreshment break

3:20   RIC at the millennium.
Development of a vision of our future

6:00   Selection of representatives from each group to
synthesis committee

6:15   Close

Conference Design

Relief International Canada Forum

Participants arrive at the hotel sometime Friday afternoon or early evening. As people register at the hotel, they should receive a package with a welcome letter from the steering committee, including an agenda for the forum, a copy of the letter from the president and the executive director outlining the financial situation, the report of the survey findings, a two-page piece on the financial situation (graph of fund-raising targets and actual income over the past three years, along with two paras from the annual report that describe the shortfall and what has been done), a one-page summary (graph?) on the decline in local group membership over the past three years.

Registration table outside the room, which will open at 7:00 P.M. (coffee?) to welcome people, give non-hotel guests their packages, and provide name tags for all (colour-coded for group).

The room needs to be set up in circles of five chairs (approx. nine groups). Each group is to have an easel, flip chart, and a marker for each person in the group.

7:30 Welcome from steering committee, and introduction of the facilitator. Some introductory remarks about the *purpose* and the process of the forum, where it fits in the overall process. Review of the agenda. Statement of the importance of finding common ground, the egalitarian nature of the conference, keeping on time, and the nature of the task confronting us. Also a word about speaking up; we really want to bring all our perspectives to bear on this. Introductions at the table – where are you from, your hopes for the forum.

8:00 Scan exercise: Explanation of the purpose – to build the first basis for a vision by focusing our attention *outside*, on the broader context. Individually, participants list the major events, trends, and important changes affecting RI Canada in each of the following categories: the world, Relief International (the movement) and RI Canada. List these events in three decades: the 70s, the 80s, the 90s. (See Worksheet #1.) When you have finished your list, write these events on the paper on the wall. We will analyse the data tomorrow, but in the meantime it will be up for us to look at.

8:45   A word on tomorrow's agenda: remind people that we are starting at 9:00 and invite them to stay for wine and cheese. The meeting room will be open for quiet reading and coffee at 8:30.

Saturday

9:00   Welcome. The task is for small groups to analyse the data on the walls. Different groups will be responsible for different parts. What are the events, trends etc.? Three groups look at WORLD, discuss what they see, what patterns etc., then develop a list of the most important trends, directions, in terms of relief work. Three other groups look at RELIEF INTERNATIONAL, discuss patterns they see and then what are the main implications of the events, trends in the movement for RIC. Three groups look at RIC, discuss the trends and patterns and develop two lists – PROBABLE FUTURE if we continue as we are, and IDEAL FUTURE they would like to see. Groups allow members to scan the wall, brainstorm, hearing from each member, and then decide which are the seven most important points. Make a flip chart and post this. (See Worksheet #2.)

Participants read other groups' analyses on the wall.

Short plenary discussion

10:15   Coffee

10:40   RIC capabilities and vulnerabilities analysis. Four small groups use the following matrix to do an analysis of RI Canada. (See Worksheet #3.)

Groups divide the flip chart into quadrants and list the strengths and weaknesses of RI Canada in each quadrant. They then "vote" on the most crucial in each quadrant and post their matrices.

Working As a Coherent Movement	Attracting Support from the Public
Being well organized	Accomplishing goals

The other four groups will work in a "sub-plenary" to develop a trends mindmap.* (This is a large graphic developed together that "maps" key trends.)

11:30   Participants examine mind map and capabilities and vulnerabilities matrices and indicate most critical items.

12:00   LUNCH

1:00   Panel: How RIC is seen from the outside, how it might move. (Possible panelists: foreign affairs expert, NGO leader, media person.)

---

* T. Buzan, *The Mind Map Book.* (London: BBC Books, 1993).

1:30 Consideration of the survey data: Small groups discuss; no conclusion is required at this time. Small groups focus on core questions or whatever is provocative and interesting. Post on wall paper.

2:30 Big ideas so far: Plenary. Short presentation from the facilitator to summarize, and comments from the floor.

3:00 Coffee break

3:20 Vision session: RIC at the millennium. A creative task – small groups think in new directions. What we are trying to do is describe the RIC we want in the year 2000 and beyond. This vision should take into account the capacities, history, vulnerabilities, etc. that we have been developing all day. The vision could describe what RIC is, how it is working, who is involved, how big is RIC, who is it serving ... Another approach would be to ask the strategy question – what is RIC's unique advantage in doing relief work? What opportunities do we have that build on our strengths and position as members in Canada?

The current choice as the method for this session is to ask each member of the small groups to write ideas on index cards of what they would like to see at the millennium. These cards are sorted in small groups into themes, and the group develops a coherent vision using the themes.

The group then develops a presentation to the plenary to describe their vision.

4:30 Group Presentations: Groups summarize their vision on a flip chart and present it in any fashion they like – could be a skit, a song, a body sculpture...

Presentations to be ten minutes maximum.

6:00 Discussion of common themes, hands-up voting for big ideas, election of representatives to synthesis committee (one from each group). Emphasize that this is not a decision-making group.

6:30 Last words; next steps in the process; thanks to all; close.

7:30 Meeting of the synthesis group to pull together the nine presentations into two or three alternative visions. This group made up of one rep from each group plus the facilitator.

Worksheet # 1 – Focus on Past[*]

Purpose: An appreciation of changes we have experienced, and what our past means, in order to sketch the relevant environment.

1. Individually, list memorable events, trends, and developments in each era

1970s	WORLD	RELIEF INTERNATIONAL	RI CANADA
1980s			
1990s			

2. Use a marker to transfer your items to the sheets on the walls.

---

[*] These materials are based on those developed by M. Wiesbord for a session at the Cape Cod Institute, August 1992.

Worksheet # 2 – What We See, What It Means

(40 minutes)

Groups pick recorder and discussion leader who also acts as timer. (Rotate these roles.)

Recorder: Writes on flip chart, using speaker's words. Asks people to restate ideas succinctly.

Discussion leader: Makes sure everybody has a chance to speak, keeps the group on track, and makes sure the group finishes on time.

Groups black, brown, orange focus on THE WORLD.

1. Look at the sheets, what trends, patterns, key trends do you see? Discuss.

2. List on the flip chart key implications for relief work into the 21st century. Narrow the list to seven items and post your flip chart.

Groups yellow, purple, blue focus on RELIEF INTERNATIONAL.

1. Look at the sheets. What key trends, directions, or patterns do you see?

2. List on the flip chart the implications of these directions for the work of RI Canada into the 21st century. Narrow this list to a maximum of seven. Post your flip chart.

Groups red, green and double blue focus on RIC.

1. Look at the lists. Discuss the main trends, patterns.

2. Draw a line down the middle of the flip chart. On one side, list the PROBABLE FUTURE (what will happen if the current trends continue.) On the other side of the line list the IDEAL FUTURE you would like to see. Post your flip chart.

Worksheet # 3 – Capabilities and Vulnerabilities Analysis

Decide on a discussion leader and a recorder.

Use the matrix below to analyse the current capabilities and vulnerabilities of RIC. Divide the flip chart into quadrants and list capabilities with a + and the vulnerabilities with a – sign. At the end of your discussion, each person should select the five most important items and make a mark beside these items to indicate the items most critical to RIC into the 21st century.

(Note: this is a variation on the four fields framework in chapter 2.)

Working As a Coherent Movement	**Attracting Support from the Public**
• Commonly held understandings of values, mandate, and strategy • Strong leadership and committed membership, professional staff • Sense of belonging • Ability to build organizational consensus • Capable of recruiting new members and providing opportunities for learning • Sense of member and staff empowerment	• High public profile • Attracts the respect of governments and other relief organizations • Capable of raising money, works well with donors • Capable of evaluating current trends and developing new and innovative program
Being Well Organized	**Accomplishing Goals**
• Stable organization • Clear written policy • Measurement • Good financial and other internal information systems • Clear statements of roles of board and staff • Efficient use of resources	• Clear about direction and intention of program • Capable of assessing results and taking action to insure accomplishment of goals • climate of goal-oriented accomplishment

Tool 7: Team Building

Team-building sessions are often a combination of elements, but the goals should be:

1. To develop a basic level of knowledge of one another: Who are these people? What have they done with their lives before they came here? What do they care about? What do they want to accomplish?

2. To understand the beliefs and mental models that each member carries regarding important aspects of the work and how it gets done.

3. To discuss conflicts hindering the accomplishment of goals or depleting the energy of group members.

4. To develop with the participation of all members, the clear direction of the team.

Teamwork is hard, especially for North Americans, who are trained to value individual accomplishment. Often our need for power overcomes our desire to collaborate, and our ability to work as peers is often badly underdeveloped.

This section will describe some team-building activities that mitigate some of these tendencies.

1. Check-In

At the beginning of a meeting, each person is given a few minutes to talk about what he or she is thinking or feeling. This may be an update on recent important personal events, feelings about something happening in the organization, hopes for this meeting, or other matters. The group merely listens; people may comment but not challenge.

2. Team Analysis

This activity may be the basis of an entire session (three hours to three days, depending on the need), or it can be undertaken after the completion of another task, such as an organizational plan. Using a framework for analysing teamwork, each member rates the performance of the team. The ratings are then shared in discussion. The team may use a very simple framework, such as:

a) Do I feel like a contributing member of this team?

b) Am I pleased with our productivity?

If the team wants more detail, they may consider other team issues, such as:

a) The level of trust in this group: low, medium, or high?

b) The clarity and joint ownership of goals: low, medium, or high?

c) The distribution of power and influence in the group.

d) The quality of our relationships to other teams: low, medium, or high?

e) Our ability to make decisions: low, medium, or high?

f) Our ability to learn from one another.

g) Our ability to develop innovative responses to situations facing the team.

Tool 8: Perspectives Analysis

This technique is a means of learning from a program that has run into trouble. The key to this technique is to get beyond blaming, to realize that everyone has acted in ways that made sense at the time and that there are many perspectives and realities.

The exercise is done in a meeting that includes the people who were involved in the management of the program, as well as knowledgeable others. The first step is to map the experience. Using sheets of newsprint taped to the wall, begin by marking down the dates to recreate the time line. Then note the events and how people felt about them, on the time line, in chronological order. What is important is that *everyone's* experience be incorporated. If, for example, two people have conflicting understandings of a particular event, both understandings go into the time line with no effort to decide who is "right." The finished "map" should express the events and the feelings of all participants.

At that point, call a break to allow participants to walk around and read the various pieces of the map. Then reconvene (in small groups or in the large group) to discuss the map in terms that will help the group learn from the experience. The focus is not on the past, and it is certainly not on assigning individual blame or deciding who was right or wrong. The purpose is to use the experience for team learning. Questions such as the following can help focus the discussion:

- What does this experience reveal about our teamwork?

- What does this experience reveal about our relations with other groups?

- What are the implications of this for other programs we are involved in?

This exercise usually leads to new ways of working, defuses conflict related to the program, and brings to the surface different understandings and feelings related to the program.

Tool 9: Cause Maps

This is an excellent planning activity that helps a team to understand individuals' assumptions about work and to identify - and avoid – potential pitfalls in a program.

The exercise begins by specifying the goal of a particular piece of work and then asking what is required in order to accomplish that goal. When the group has answered by saying, "We must do..." then the discussion leader writes these on the board with arrows leading to the goal. She or he then asks what is required to accomplish these new requirements. Eventually there is a map of everything that needs to get done and how the various actions relate to one another.

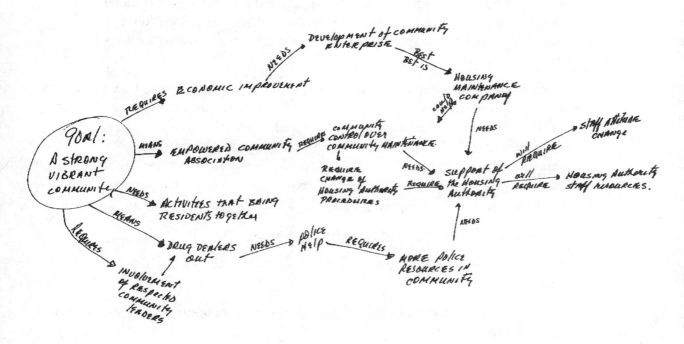

The map above was devised by a team planning a community-development project in a public-housing community. It appeared in about one hour, and it had two notable results. First, it allowed a new project team to understand another's beliefs about how community development would happen in this setting; and second, it revealed a number of central issues that previous planning hadn't considered.

For example, it became very clear that economic development was an intrinsic part of this project and that the proposed solution – a housing-maintenance company that would train residents to look after the maintenance in the community – was going to require a lot more negotiation with the Public Housing Authority than was originally thought. It was then observed that many of the arrows led to a box entitled "Support of the housing authority." This in turn raised the questions, What was required to get that support, and how feasible was it? The team was able to reapportion their time to spend more of it than they had anticipated with the Public Housing Authority.

Tool 10: Fishbowl Exercise

This is a group exercise that can be used to break out of a polarized discussion when participants seem to be making no progress. It gives people space to hear the different perspectives in a more impersonal way, and then to work through the issues that emerge. It also provides a break in the action.

Process

The idea is to restage the debate by asking several participants to replay the key points in a "fishbowl" at the front or the middle of the room. Participants are asked to represent the positions they previously opposed while others observe. A facilitator is needed to watch the time, then to work with the group to discover what has been learned.

The volunteers for the fishbowl put their chairs in a semi-circle, with the rest of the group seated around them as the audience. The audience does not intervene until the end of the discussion. The group should agree on a length of time for the fishbowl. The debate begins with each person making a summary of the position. Then a discussion among the fishbowl participants follows. The discussion must attempt to get at the contentious issues.

When the discussion is over, the facilitator asks the fishbowl participants what they can now agree on. This list becomes the basis for a new discussion with the larger group. What often emerges is that areas of agreement are much larger than they had seen earlier and disagreements feel less important than previously. If serious disagreements persist, they should be recognized and fed into the larger change process.

Tool 11: Organizational Change Planning Guide

This guide, which grows from the material in Chapter 6, is intended to help leaders of NGOs develop a clear understanding of how they can manage medium- to large- scale organizational-change projects. The guide presents a model of organizational change and then asks a series of questions related to the model.

The Organizational-Change Process

The change process can be seen as having three stages:

1. Start-up
A sense of concern and a recognition of organizational difficulties is translated to a set of activities that begins to engage people.

2. Transition
The period in which the organization is trying to "live" its new approach, as well as to design it while caught in old ways of acting. This is often a time of conflict, discouragement, and excitement, as the new organization struggles to be born.

3. Resolution
Implementing and managing the strategy so that the new ways of being become the norm for the organization and its partners.

In each of these phases, there are three tasks: building **support**, developing **clarity** and understanding, and taking **action**.

When the three phases are combined with the three tasks, we get the table on the following page.

This matrix again shows the various activities required at each stage of the process. The diagram reminds us that at any given point in the process it is important to be thinking about a number of things at once. For example, at the start-up stage, the leaders must be thinking about building a change team, collecting information, identifying the issues, and so on.

Looking more closely at the matrix, we see that the start-up stage is devoted to assessing whether the organization is ready for change, and if so, whether or not there are people who will work on it and support it. The other task is to begin to collect information and ideas so that the issues

	START-UP	TRANSITION	RESOLUTION
SUPPORT	• Assess/build readiness • Build a change team • Agree on process • Undertake organizational and external analysis • Communicate • Educate	• Build a joint team for detailed planning • Training • Deal with conflict and grieving • Board approval • Compensate people for losses • Communicate • Educate	• Maintain momentum • Get feedback • Launch new change initiatives • Communicate • Educate
CLARITY	• Understand the issues and the "whys" of the change • Develop a collective vision and strategy	• Work out the details of the strategy and the organizational options	• Smooth out the rough parts • Set new targets for change
ACTION	• Act differently	• Pilot key ideas	• Full implementation

become clearer and the emerging sense of vision is grounded in the needs of a broad group of people.

It is also important that the behaviour of the leaders reflect the change they are trying to bring about. If, for example, the change is related to an improvement in democratic functioning, then everything related to the project should reflect that value.

In the transition stage, a broadly based team develops the details of the plan. The main task is to translate the general vision into a detailed program that works in *a given setting*. This is often the time of considerable confusion and conflict. It is also important at this stage to begin to try things out in order to learn from them.

It is unrealistic to assume that things will go smoothly in the transition stage. The important thing is to learn from the experience.[*]

[*] W. Bridges, *Managing Organizational Transitions: Making the Most of Change*. (Reading: Addison-Wesley, 1991); and R. M. Kanter, *The Change Masters: Innovation for Productivity in the American Corporation*. (New York: Simon and Schuster, 1984).

Resolution comprises implementing the strategy, maintaining momentum, and setting targets for new change. The leaders must continue to solicit feedback and change in response to the changing situation. This is a tricky stage, as the organization will have a tendency to retrench and return to old patterns.

Planning Guide

1. What is the nature of the change you wish to implement?

2. What is causing you to contemplate this change?

3. How significant a change do you expect this to be? Who will it affect? How much will their lives change as a result of this change? Who will benefit? Who will lose?

4. After reading over the material on the Organizational-Change Process in the previous pages, where would you situate yourself? Which aspects of the process have you accomplished? What remains to be done?

The planning guide is organized to give you information and raise questions relevant to the stage you are at. For example, if you are working at the transition stage, turn to the Transition section. There you will be asked about participation, conflict, and detailed design.

Start Up

1. Have you analysed the readiness of various parts of your organization to accept and participate in the change you envision? To work on this issue, turn to Tool 3: Assessing Readiness for Change.

2. Have you analysed your personal readiness for this change? How could the change affect you?

3. Have you developed an approach to the change that specifies the goals of the change, how information will be collected, who will lead the process, how people will participate, and how decisions will be made?

4. Have you developed this approach unilaterally or with the involvement of stakeholders?

5. Have you built a team capable of leading the change process? It should be small enough to meet often; enjoy the support of the various constituencies in the organization (union, management, board, etc.); have superior process skills (organizational analysis, meetings, writing, etc.); and include at least one member of the senior management group. It must also be a team capable of working together.

6. Have you conducted a process of organizational analysis? This could focus on mission, program, strategy, or various organizational capabilities and vulnerabilities. For help here refer to the questions in the Assessment Guide (Tool 1).

    Have you conducted an analysis of the "environment" that affects your organization? This could include macro political/economic considerations, issues related to expectations and situations of partners, issues related to donors, etc. Think in terms of the immediate "task" environment of your program, as well as the macro environment.

7. Have you built a vision or a strategy for change? This may be at a general level, such as "integrating our program in Canada and overseas," "developing and implementing a strategic plan," "merging with a similar organization", "focusing our program and functioning with 75 percent of our current budget," etc.

8. Have you built this vision unilaterally or with the involvement of stakeholders?

9. Have you identified the roadblocks as well as the potential leverage points that will determine the accomplishment of the vision?

10. Is your own behaviour as a change leader congruent with the new world you are trying to build? For example, if you want the organization to be more strategic, the change process itself must exemplify that; if you want the organization to be more democratic, the process should also be a model for how the organization could function more democratically.

11. What is your plan for board involvement and approval?

Transition

At this stage, the organization is designing the details of the change and beginning to live differently. This is a time of intense feeling – ambivalence, anger, excitement. The change leaders need to ensure the organization that the process for designing the details is participatory and allows staff and members intense debate and, if necessary, conflict. Recognize that this will be a difficult time and build in supports. Expect leaders and staff to be experiencing considerable stress.

1. Is there a team in place to design the details of the change? These details include a clear, specific, concrete understanding of the change, the implications for staffing, and organizational structure and budgets.

2. Is there a process in place for staff to participate in the emerging design that will channel and use conflict for the improvement of the change?

3. Have you developed training programs to enable staff to create and deal with the new reality?

4. Have you a communications plan in place that will keep all organization members up to date?

5. Have you a plan for compensating those who lost in the change?

6. What parts of the change could serve as a pilot project? Can you find a particularly supportive yet realistic set of circumstances in which to nurture the pilot?

Resolution

This stage centres on implementation, maintaining momentum, monitoring the change, and redesigning in response to feedback. This stage will also outline the next change that the organization requires.

1. Is there a clear implementation plan that specifies who, how, when, etc.? Is there a communication strategy for the implementation plan?

2. Is there an educational plan that provides for the ongoing learning and skill building required for the new reality?

3. Are you ready for the reality that others in the organization will misunderstand, be ambivalent, and not be as enthusiastic about the change as the leaders?

4. Is there a monitoring mechanism that will tell the change leaders what is going well and what needs redesign?

5. Is there an understanding that the change process is not over?

6. Are there ways to celebrate successes and reward effort?

Plan Summary

Where we are in the change process is:

What we need to do in the medium term (nine months to a year) is:

What we need to do immediately (in the next two weeks) is:

What success looks like organizationally is:

What success looks like personally is:

Facing the Future

8

THIS BOOK HAS BEEN A JOURNEY THAT HAS INVOLVED THE AUTHORS in conversations with some very thoughtful and engaged people. We have held focus groups, met with a committee of peer advisers, listened to readers of unfinished drafts, discussed the ideas in the "Tiger" workshops and with clients; and debated the ideas among ourselves. Where does this exploration leave us? What are the ideas we carry forward into our own practice?

When we started this project, we knew about the changes facing NGOs; in the past year, however, the pace of change has accelerated and the changes are both deeper and more pervasive. Voluntary and public-sector organizations in Canada and around the world are facing change so profound that it is impossible to predict the full impact.

For some of our colleagues, the key issue is funding. They foresee the end of government funding to much development aid and domestic social development. If non-governmental and voluntary organizations have a fraction of their former resources to spend, they face a major challenge to their existence. What do they do? Where is their legitimacy? What is their role as donors in a "post-donor" world?

Others have asked how NGOs can contribute to the social and political challenges facing us at the millennium. Perhaps a role for Northern NGOs is to use the knowledge gained from North and South to mobilize for social change in the north. This would require a very different relationship with organizations in the South and a new way of working with constituencies in the North. Currently, most of our organizations do not know how to do these things.

Many of our colleagues are concerned about the strength of right-wing ideologies in the West and how social and international relations are governed increasingly by considerations of the global market economy. This is a challenge to once deeply held beliefs about government responsibility for the well-being of its less well off citizens in addition to the peoples of other countries.

This and more adds up to a time of transition. Many NGOs and voluntary organizations will be closed, and some will find new roles or new ways of supporting their work. New ways of organizing will emerge where older ones have failed. These new organizations will be sustainable in very different ways.

What will these new organizations look like?

The new world will favour collaborative strategies both inside and outside the organization. This does not mean merely expanding electronic communication networks and information sharing; it means creating both physical and psychological space for people to think and learn together, what David Schrage calls "shared creativity."[1] This is not an area in which NGOs have done well. On the contrary, organizational chauvinism, or protectionism, is at the root of many failed attempts at more strategic inter-agency collaboration.

Organizational conflict is a companion of change. A stable external and internal environment is unlikely to produce high

"The question is not whether individual organizations will survive. The question is what will come into being to replace them."
– An NGO observer

levels of conflict. The way an organization deals with conflict says a lot about how it will cope with ongoing organizational turbulence. Conflict-averse organizations are not well disposed to dealing with the messier aspects of the change process. Organizations that prize high levels of unity and peace can inadvertently cut off dissenting voices and ideas that should be heard. Conflict should not be ignored or silenced, or let drift into the recesses of the organization where it can eat away at legitimate processes. Instead, it should be harnessed to meet creative ends. New visions and strategies often rub against the old. Organizations capable of surviving need their rebels and critical thinkers. Sometimes unpopular ideas come directly from field experience – from partners, field workers, and volunteers who live with the program. Being open to all these voices is at the centre of the learning process.

Traditional ideas about organizational structure need to change, and are changing. In the environment we face, we need structures that are more fluid than the top-heavy, overly formal organizations of the past. What should replace them? Now is the time to experiment, to design staffing structures and decision-making processes in a way that responds more directly and quickly to the needs of our programs. A number of organizations are discovering that this means keeping a small core staff to carry out certain agreed functions, but building around the core a larger "amoeba-like" set of relationships with experts or program staff who work on a program for a particular period of time. The organization is defined by a variety of negotiated working arrangements held together by a commitment to programming goals, and by sophisticated information technologies.

This approach has many obvious advantages, but it also has some equally obvious disadvantages. Such flexible working arrangements do not benefit all workers equally. This kind of structure is most amenable to the "knowledge workers" – those with the education, experience, and skill to be portable; or people who are temperamentally, or financially, prepared to live with high levels of risk and instability. This is often easier for people without major family commitments. As organizations shed some of their employed labour force, more people are making the decision, whether voluntarily or not, to work as contract employees. Over time, this parallel workforce is growing in size.

As state funding for domestic and international NGOs is cut back, NGOs are competing for private funds. Traditional fund-raising activities such as direct mail and special events are not sufficient for many. Entrepreneurial approaches are gaining ground as NGOs seek greater revenues in the private sector. Some NGOs are creating profit centres and joint ventures with private business to deliver a service people will pay for. Others are bidding, like private-sector firms, for government contracts overseas. Although these approaches are often creative and energetic, they raise ethical questions about organizational values and principles. Whatever the strategy, NGOs continually need to measure their actions against their values and core principles, not only to ensure that they remain compatible but to ensure that they remain relevant, that the original impetus for the work is not sacrificed by the need for organizational sustainability.[2]

Can people live this way? The stress of increasing demands, fewer resources, and high levels of insecurity are taking their toll on the people who lead and work in voluntary organizations. Many organizational leaders and programming staff are asking what kind of personal cost they must pay to ensure the relevance and survival of their organizations into the twenty-first century. It is clear that just as we need to reconceive the process of social transformation, we need to create a new understanding of the personal and spiritual transformation that will be necessary to thrive in these organizations in the future.

Lessons Learned in Managing Change

Collectively we have learned that there are no guaranteed formulas for managing change. We understand that simple, one-factor approaches are eventually found wanting: visionary leadership, strategic planning, teams, total quality management – each has risen and fallen away. Yet each has worked in one place at one time or other. Each has contributed to our growing understanding of the complex entities we know as organizations.

What can we conclude from this experience? We can conclude that the right approach must be contextual, must be conditioned by the particular situation an organization is facing, and by the accumulated best judgement of the persons involved with the organization. As conditions change, approaches and strategies must be reinvented. This reinvention is aided by certain organizational capabilities and orientations.

Our experience over the years has taught us that NGO's organizational process must be congruent with the participation they espouse in their program and mission. It is important not to give in to panic in the face of strong external pressure for budget cuts or a quick fix that may or may not have worked in the private sector or in large public institutions.

Organizational Capabilities for Change

1. The ability to analyse, interpret, and build a shared understanding of one's organizational context and dynamics – outside and inside; this includes anticipating the likely reactions of persons inside and outside the organization who will interpret the change in terms of their own legitimate needs: for status, security, satisfaction, or influence.

2. A preference for closer relationships with, and higher levels of accountability to, members, volunteers, partners, funders, and donors, and ways to nurture these relationships.

3. A willingness to look beyond rational, planned approaches for new insights found in stories, hunches, and indigenous forms of knowledge.

4. An ability to manage the power dynamics and conflict that go hand-in-hand with organizational change, and to view conflict as a potential for learning as well as a stressor.

5. An understanding that leadership energy for major change may not come exclusively from the top of the organization: senior staff and board need to facilitate and make the space for change initiatives to evolve out of other structures and relationships.

6. The willingness to commit time and resources to a process with deadlines but without a predictable end.

7. Maintenance of a positive attitude to change; attitudes toward change are more likely to be supportive rather than skeptical where there are high levels of trust and openness.

8. Keeping a clear focus on the results of what we are doing: our theories of social transformation have lagged behind the evolution of the global crises we are dealing with, but a vigilant eye on the impact of our work is central to our change process and the evolution of our understanding.

Organizations that survive, and the new ones that develop, will succeed because they are relevant, nimble, worthy of public and private support, and because they understand the basic ingredients of working with change.

References

1. M. Schrage, *Shared Minds: The New Technologies of Collaboration* (New York: Random House, 1990).

2. L. Cumming with B. Singleton, "Organizational Sustainability – An End of the Century Challenge for Canadian Voluntary International Development Organizations." Paper presented to the Eleventh Annual Conference of the Canadian Association for the Study of International Development, Université à Montréal, June 6, 1995.

Bibliography

ACORD. "Operationality in Turbulence: The Need for Change," Draft discussion paper, November 1992.

Agocs, C., C. Burr, and F. Somerset. *Employment Equity: Co-operative Strategies for Organizational Change*. Scarborough: Prentice Hall, 1992.

Anderson, M., and P. Woodrow. *Rising from the Ashes: Development Strategies in Times of Disaster*. Westview Press, 1989.

Arnold, R., Burke, B., *Le processus de pacification en Amérique centrale : une étude des options des ONG canadiennes*, Ottawa, CCCI, 1989.

Barndt, D., F. Cristall, and d. marino. *Getting There: Producing Photostories with Immigrant Women*. Toronto: Between the Lines, 1982.

Bateson, G. *Steps to an Ecology of Mind*. New York: Ballantine, 1972.

———— *Mind and Nature: A Necessary Unity*. New York: Dutton, 1979.

Beaudoux, E., *Cheminement d'une action de développement : de l'identification à l'évaluation*, Paris, L'Harmattan, 1992.

Beckhard, R., *La gestion du changement dans les organisations, un outil pour gérer la transition*, Éditions du renouveau pédagogique, Montréal, 1991.

Benayoun, R., *Entreprises en éveil, technique et cas de maîtrise du changement*, Entreprise moderne d'édition, Paris, 1979.

Bridges, W. *Managing Transitions: Making the Most of Change*. Reading: Addison-Wesley, 1991.

Brodhead, T., B. Herbert-Copley, and A. M. Lambert. *Bridges of Hope: Canadian Voluntary Agencies and the Third World*. Ottawa: North-South Institute, 1988.

Bryson, J. *Strategic Planning for Public and Non-Profit Organizations: A Guide to Strengthening and Sustaining Organizational Achievement*. London: Jossey-Bass, 1988.

Buzan, T. *The Mind Map Book*. London: BBC Books, 1993.

Cameron, K., R. Sutten, and D. Whetten. *Readings in Organizational Decline: Frameworks, Research and Prescriptions*. Cambridge: Ballinger, 1988.

Carver, J. *Boards That Make a Difference*. San Francisco: Jossey-Bass, 1988.

Chambers, R. *Rural Development: Putting the Last First*. London: Longman, 1983.

Clark, J. *Democratising Development: The Role of Voluntary Organizations*. London: Earthscan, 1991.

Coalition des organisations nationales volontaires, *Taking Voluntarism to the Year 2015*, Ottawa, 1994.

Coalition of National Voluntary Organizations. *Taking Voluntarism to the Year 2015*. Ottawa, 1994.

Collerette, P., *Pouvoir, leadership et autorité dans les organisations*, Presses de l'Université du Québec, Sillery, 1991.

Collerette, P., et Delisle, G., *Le changement planifié : une approche pour intervenir dans les systèmes organisationnels*, Éditions Agence d'Arc; c1982.

Cooper, C.L., and I. Mangham. *T-Groups: A Survey of Research*. Toronto: Wiley, 1971.

Cumming, L. with B. Singleton, "Organizational Sustainability - An End of the Century Challenge for Voluntary International Development Organizations." Paper presented to Annual Conference of the Canadian Association for the Study of International Development, Montreal, 1995.

Dinnerstein, D. *The Mermaid and the Minotaur: Sexual Arrangements and Human Malaise*. New York: Harper, 1976.

Drucker, P. *Managing Non-Profit Organizations: Principles and Practices*. New York: Harper, 1990.

École nationale d'administration, Groupe d'étude, de recherche et de formation inernationales, "Réussir une campagne de levée de fonds : séminaire organisé par le GERFI, Québec, ENAP, 1992.

Faure, G., *Structure, organisation et efficacité de l'entreprise*, Dunod, Paris, 1991.

Galbraith, J., and E. Lawler & Associates. *Organizing for the Future: The New Logic for Managing Complex Organizations*. San Francisco: Jossey-Bass, 1993.

Gillen, M. "Religious Women in Transition: A Qualitative Study of Personal Growth and Organizational Change." Ph.D. thesis, University of Toronto, (OISE), 1980.

Goetz, A. "Gender and Administration." *IDS Bulletin* 23, no. 4 (1992).

Goold M., and J. J. Quinn. "The Paradox of Strategic Controls." *Strategic Management Journal* 11 (1990).

Greiner, L., and V. Schein. *Power and Organizational Development: Mobilizing Power to Implement Change.* Reading: Addison-Wesley, 1988.

Habana-Hafner, S. and H. Reed. *Partnerships for Community Development.* Amherst: Centre for Organizational and Community Development, University of Massachusetts, 1989.

Handy, C. *The Gods of Management.* London: Souvenir Press, 1978.

——— *Understanding Voluntary Organizations.* London: Pelican, 1988.

——— *The Empty Raincoat.* London: Hutchison, 1994.

Hampden-Turner, C. *Charting the Corporate Mind.* New York: Free Press, 1990.

——— *Creating Corporate Culture: From Discord to Harmony.* Reading: Addison-Wesley, 1990.

Harrison, M. *Diagnosing Organizations: Methods, Models and Processes.* 2d ed. Thousand Oaks: Sage, 1994.

Harrison, R. "Understanding Your Organization's Character." *Harvard Business Review,* May-June 1972.

Helgesen, S. *The Web of Inclusion.* New York: Currency/Doubleday, 1995.

Howard, R. *The Learning Imperative: Managing People for Continuous Innovation.* Boston: Harvard Business Review Books, 1993.

Huberman, M., and M. Miles. *Innovation Up Close.* New York: Plenum, 1984.

Hurst, D. "Of Bubbles, Boxes and Effective Management." *Harvard Business Review.* May–June 1984.

Kanter, R. *The Change Masters: Innovation for Productivity in the American Corporation.* New York: Simon and Schuster, 1984.

Kaufman, H. *Time, Change and Organizations: Natural Selection in a Perilous Environment.* 2d Ed. Chatham: Chatham House, 1991.

Kaye, K. *Workplace Wars and How to End Them.* New York: American Management Association, 1994.

Kelleher, D., P. Finestone, and A. Lowy. "Managerial Learning, First Notes from an Unstudied Frontier." *Group and Organizational Studies.* September, 1986.

Kelly, K.. *Out of Control: The Rise of Neo-Biological Civilization*. Reading: Addison-Wesley, 1994.

Kofman, F., and P. Senge. "Communities of Commitment, The Heart of Learning Organizations." *Organizational Dynamics*, Fall 1993.

Korten, D. *Getting to the 21st Century: Voluntary Action and the Global Agenda*. West Hartford: Kumarian, 1990.

Kotter, J. *A Force for Change: How Leadership Differs from Management*. New York: The Free Press, 1990.

Kotter, J. *Power and Influence*. New York: The Free Press, 1985.

Lafleur, G., "Les organismes de coopération internationale : des ponts de l'espoir?" Nouvelles pratiques sociales, vol. 4, n° 1, printemps 1990.

Lidener, R. "Stretching the Boundaries of Liberal Feminism: Democratic Innovation in a Feminist Organization." *Signs* 16, no. 2: 263–289. 1991.

Limerick D., and B. Cunningham. *Managing the New Organization: A Blueprint for Networks and Strategic Alliances*. San Francisco: Jossey-Bass, 1993.

Marquardt, R. "The Voluntary Sector and the Federal Government: A Perspective in the Aftermath of the 1995 Federal Budget." Discussion paper prepared for the CCIC Annual Meeting, May 1995.

Miller, D. *The Icarus Paradox*. New York: Harper, 1990.

Mills, A., and P. Tancred, eds. *Gendering Organizational Analysis*. Newbury Park: Sage, 1992.

Mintzberg, H. *The Rise and Fall of Strategic Planning*. New York: Free Press, 1994.

Mohrman, S., and A. Mohrman. "Organizational Change and Learning" in Galbraith et al., *Organizing for the Future: The New Logic for Managing Complex Organizations*. San Francisco, Jossey-Bass, 1993.

Morgan, G. *Images of Organization*. Beverly Hills: Sage, 1986.

Murphy, B. "Canadian NGOs and the Politics of Participation." In Swift, J., and B. Tomlinson. *Conflicts of Interest: Canada and the Third World*. Toronto: Between the Lines, 1991.

Narayan, U. "Working Together Across Difference: Some Considerations on Emotions and Political Practice." *Hypatia* 3, no. 2 (1988).

Noer, D. *Healing the Wounds*. San Francisco: Jossey-Bass, 1993.

O'Toole, J. *Vanguard Management: Re-designing the Corporate Future*. New York: Doubleday, 1985.

Pascale, R., *Les risques de l'excellence : la stratégie des conflits constructifs*, InterÉditions, Paris, 1992.

Pascale, R. *Managing on the Edge*. New York: Simon and Schuster, 1990.

Pearce, J., et al. "The Tenuous Link Between Formal Strategic Planning and Financial Performance." *Academy of Mananagement Review* 12, no. 4 (1987).

Pfeiffer, W., L. Goodstein, and T. Nolan. *Applied Strategic Planning: A How to Do it Guide*. San Diego: University Associates, 1986.

Phillips, S. "Of Visions and Revisions: The Voluntary Sector Beyond 2000." *Bulletin of the Coalition of National Voluntary Organizations* 12, no. 3, (Winter 1993).

Porter, M. *Competitive Strategy: Techniques for Analysing Industries and Competitors*. New York: The Free Press, 1980.

Prince, G. "Creativity and Learning as Skills, not Talents." *The Phillips Exeter Bulletin* June–July and September–October, 1980.

Quinn, J. *Strategies for Change: Logical Incrementalism*. Homewood: Irwin, 1980.

Quinn, R. *Beyond Rational Management*. San Francisco: Jossey-Bass, 1988.

Rashford, N., and D. Coghlan. *The Dynamics of Organizational Levels*. Reading: Addison-Wesley, 1994.

Rahnema, S. *Organization Structure: A Systemic Approach*. Toronto: McGraw-Hill Ryerson, 1992.

Reddy, B., and K. Jamison. *Team Building: Blueprints for Productivity and Satisfaction*. Alexandria: NTL Institute for Applied Behavioural Science, 1988.

Rossum, C., ed. *How to Assess Your Non-Profit Organization with Peter Drucker's Five Most Important Questions*. San Francisco: Jossey-Bass, 1993.

Rothschild, J., and J. Whitt. *The Co-operative Workplace*. ASA Rose Monograph Series. Cambridge: Cambridge University Press, 1986.

Sackmann, S. *Cultural Knowledge in Organizations: Exploring the Collective Mind*. Beverly Hills: Sage, 1991.

Saxby, J. "Who Owns the Private Aid Agencies? Mythology ...and Some Awkward Questions." Draft chapter for Transnational Institute publication, Amsterdam, 1995.

Schein, E. *Organizational Culture and Leadership*. 2d ed. San Francisco: Jossey-Bass, 1992.

Schrage, M. *Shared Minds: The New Technologies of Collaboration*. New York: Random House, 1990.

Schutz, W. "The Effects of a T-Group Laboratory on Interpersonal Behaviour." *Journal of Applied Behavioural Science* 2 (1966).

Senge, P, et al. *The Fifth Discipline Fieldbook*. New York: Doubleday, 1994.

Singer, M., and J. Yankey. "Organizational Metamorphosis: A Study of Eighteen Non-Profit Mergers, Acquisitions, and Consolidations." *Non-Profit Mananagement and Leadership* 1, no. 4 (Summer, 1991).

Smillie, I., "Le temps est venu de promouvoir de nouvelles formes de coopération entre les ONG et l'ACDI", Ottawa, CCCI, 1991.

Smillie, I., and H. Helmich, eds. *Non-Governmental Organizations: Stakeholders for Development*. Paris: Development Centre of the OECD, 1993.

Sow, O., Coulibaly, D., Lankouanade, S., Dounbia, A., Sharp, R., *Réseaux de l'environnement et du développement dans quatre pays du Sahel : Burkina Faso, Mali, Sénégal et Niger*, Londres, IIED, 1992.

Stacey, R. *Managing the Unknowable: Strategic Boundaries Between Order and Chaos in Organizations*. San Francisco: Jossey-Bass, 1992.

Tannen, D. *Talking From 9 to 5*. New York: Morrow, 1994.

Tjosvold, D. *The Conflict-Positive Organization*. Reading: Addison-Wesley, 1991.

Wallace, T., and C. March, eds. *Changing Perceptions: Writings on Gender and Development*. Oxford: Oxfam, 1991.

Watzlawick, P., J. Weakland, and R. Fisch. *Change, Principles of Problem Formation and Problem Resolution*. New York: Norton, 1974.

Weisbord, M. *Building Common Ground*. San Francisco: Berret-Koehler, 1993.

Wheatley, M. *Leadership and the New Science*. San Francisco: Berret-Koehler, 1992.

Wildavsky, A. *Speaking Truth to Power: The Art and Craft of Policy Analysis*. Toronto: Little Brown & Co., 1979.

Index

First Responder
Your First Response in Emergency Care

Student Workbook

JONES AND BARTLETT PUBLISHERS

Sudbury, Massachusetts

BOSTON   TORONTO   LONDON   SINGAPORE

Jones and Bartlett Publishers

World Headquarters
40 Tall Pine Drive, Sudbury, MA 01776
info@jbpub.com
www.jbpub.com

Jones and Bartlett Publishers Canada
6339 Ormindale Way
Mississauga, Ontario L5V 1J2
Canada

Jones and Bartlett Publishers International
Barb House, Barb Mews
London W6 7PA
United Kingdom

Jones and Bartlett's books and products are available through most bookstores and online booksellers. To contact Jones and Bartlett Publishers directly, call 800-832-0034, fax 978-443-8000, or visit our website www.jbpub.com.

Substantial discounts on bulk quantities of Jones and Bartlett's publications are available to corporations, professional associations, and other qualified organizations. For details and specific discount information, contact the special sales department at Jones and Bartlett via the above contact information or send an email to specialsales@jbpub.com.

AAOS
AMERICAN ASSOCIATION OF
ORTHOPAEDIC SURGEONS

Production Credits

Chief Executive Officer: Clayton Jones
Chief Operating Officer: Donald W. Jones, Jr.
President, Higher Education and Professional Publishing: Robert Holland
V.P., Sales and Marketing: William J. Kane
V.P., Production and Design: Anne Spencer
V.P., Manufacturing and Inventory Control: Therese Connell
Publisher, Public Safety Group: Kimberly Brophy
Acquisitions Editor, EMS: Christine Emerton
Associate Managing Editor: Robyn Schafer
Production Editor: Jenny L. Corriveau
Photo Research Manager/Photographer: Kimberly Potvin
Director of Marketing: Alisha Weisman

Cover Design: Kristin Ohlin
Interior Design: Anne Spencer
Composition: Cape Cod Compositors, Inc.
Text Printing and Binding: Courier, Inc.
Cover Printing: Courier, Inc.

Editorial Credits

Authors:
Major Ray Burton
J. Hudson Garrett, Jr.
Lynn Henley, NREMT-P

CONTENTS

CHAPTER

1 Introduction to the EMS System

Matching

Match each of the items in the left column to the appropriate description in the right column.

_____ **1.** Paramedic

_____ **2.** Emergency medical technician-basic (EMT-B)

_____ **3.** Emergency services dispatch center

_____ **4.** Appropriate medical facility

_____ **5.** Basic life support (BLS)

_____ **6.** Advanced life support (ALS)

_____ **7.** Defibrillation

A. Use of specialized equipment to stabilize patients

B. Emergency lifesaving procedures used to stabilize patients

C. Provides continuing care to patients transported by first responders

D. Delivery of an electric current

E. Receives and dispatches requests for emergency care

F. Trained to provide ALS

G. Trained to provide BLS and perform other noninvasive procedures

Multiple Choice

Read each item carefully, then select the best response.

_____ **1.** Medical control provided by a physician who is in contact with prehospital providers is known as:
  A. indirect.
  B. offline.
  C. two-way.
  D. online.

_____ **2.** A physician who directs training courses, helps set medical policies, and ensures quality management of the EMS system is known as:
  A. online medical control.
  B. indirect medical control.
  C. direct medical control.
  D. unnecessary medical control.

_____ **3.** The roles and responsibilities of first responders include:
  A. protecting themselves.
  B. summoning appropriate assistance.
  C. performing patient assessments.
  D. all of the above.

_____ **4.** A first responder needs to have skills that include:

    A. the ability to control airway, breathing, and circulation.

    B. treating wounds and shock.

    C. splinting injuries to stabilize extremities.

    D. all of the above.

_____ **5.** The EMS system was developed to:

    A. give patients a greater chance of survival.

    B. eliminate unnecessary hospital treatment.

    C. reduce the time spent waiting for hospital treatment.

    D. make better use of physicians' time and energy.

_____ **6.** A person who is trained and certified to provide advanced life support and other medical procedures is called a/an:

    A. first responder.

    B. BLS.

    C. paramedic.

    D. ALS.

_____ **7.** A BLS unit consists of:

    A. a properly equipped vehicle and EMTs.

    B. a precise measurement of blood volume.

    C. the equipment needed to treat a burn patient.

    D. a portable device for communicating with the hospital.

_____ **8.** EMS systems are evaluated by the:

    A. National Highway Traffic Safety Administration.

    B. American Academy of Orthopaedic Surgeons.

    C. American Red Cross.

    D. state agencies designated by each state.

_____ **9.** Evaluation of an EMS system includes evaluation of all of the following EXCEPT:

    A. public information and education programs.

    B. transportation system and equipment.

    C. fatality rates.

    D. medical direction.

_____ **10.** The need for transport (as opposed to rapid or prompt transport) means that:

    A. the patient's condition requires care by medical professionals.

    B. speed of transport is of great importance.

    C. the patient's life is in danger.

    D. specialized medical attention is needed.

_____ **11.** Prompt transport to an appropriate medical facility means that the:

    A. injury is not life threatening.

    B. patient's condition is stable.

    C. patient's condition may worsen without treatment.

    D. patient is unconscious.

_____ **12.** Rapid transport to an appropriate medical facility means that:

    A. EMS personnel cannot give adequate care in the field.

    B. traffic patterns are prohibiting transport of the patient.

    C. the patient's condition is stable.

    D. the patient has requested a facility by name.

_____ **13.** Which is not a responsibility of first responders?
  A. To gain access to the patient
  B. To seek help from bystanders
  C. To protect themselves
  D. To notify the patient's family

_____ **14.** When EMTs or paramedics arrive, the first responder should:
  A. leave the scene as quickly as possible.
  B. get statements from bystanders.
  C. assist the EMTs or paramedics.
  D. all of the above.

_____ **15.** Which of the following needs to be documented by the first responder?
  A. Condition of the patient when found
  B. Vital signs
  C. Agency and personnel who took over treatment
  D. All of the above

_____ **16.** Direct or online medical control:
  A. can be accessed by an 800 number.
  B. gives information regarding a physician's training and certification.
  C. is usually done by two-way radio or wireless telephone.
  D. helps to eliminate negligence lawsuits.

_____ **17.** First responders are a critical component of an EMS system because they are:
  A. trained in traffic control.
  B. responsible for reporting emergencies.
  C. the first medically trained personnel to arrive on the scene.
  D. able to provide both basic and advanced life support.

Fill-in-the-Blanks

Read each item carefully, then complete the statement by filling in the missing word(s).

1. As a first responder, your primary goal is to provide _____ for a sick or injured patient.

2. Medical information about a patient is _____ and should be shared only with other medical personnel who are involved in the care of that patient.

3. The four basic goals of first responder training are to know what not to do, know how to use the first responder life support kit, know how to _____, and know how to _____ other EMS providers.

4. Fire fighters or _____ personnel are most likely to be the first responders in most emergencies.

5. Ambulances were first used to remove wounded patients from the battlefield during the _____ War.

True/False

For each statement, write the letter "T" if you believe it to be more true than false, or write the letter "F" if you believe it to be more false than true.

_____ **1.** First responders can sometimes play a critical role in life-or-death situations.
_____ **2.** Once EMTs or paramedics arrive on the scene, a first responder's role in an emergency situation is over.
_____ **3.** Bandaging and dressing equipment should be included in a first responder life support kit.
_____ **4.** A first responder's actions can prevent a minor situation from becoming serious.

_____ **5.** Reporting and dispatch procedures are the same in every community.

_____ **6.** EMTs are more highly trained than paramedics.

_____ **7.** First responders should provide emergency medical care to patients even if more highly trained medical personnel are on the way.

_____ **8.** The overall leader of the EMS system is the physician or medical director.

_____ **9.** As long as you provide adequate medical care, your behavior and appearance are of little importance.

_____ **10.** In cases where large numbers of people are injured, physicians may respond to the scene of the incident.

_____ **11.** Patient care should be based on the patient's socioeconomic status and cultural background.

_____ **12.** The first medically trained person present at the scene of sudden illness or injury is called an EMT.

_____ **13.** A well-prepared first responder will have all emergency medical equipment that may possibly be needed available for use.

_____ **14.** Everyday articles found at the scene should never be used in treatment because of the danger of contamination and the spread of infectious disease.

_____ **15.** The report of an emergency incident is the first step in the EMS system.

_____ **16.** The enhanced 9-1-1 system is not considered part of the emergency services dispatch center.

_____ **17.** Fire fighters and/or law enforcement personnel should not be dispatched to a medical emergency.

_____ **18.** In a well-managed community, EMTs and paramedics will outnumber fire fighters and law enforcement officials.

_____ **19.** First responders are responsible for determining hazards at the scene of an emergency.

_____ **20.** Documentation serves as a legal record of your treatment and may be required in the event of a lawsuit.

Short Answer

Write a brief response to each of the following questions.

1. What are the seven elements of the EMS system?

2. What are the three points of patient contact with the EMS system?

3. Name three things that should be included in proper documentation.

4. What are the four major goals of first responder training?

5. Why is it important to have medical oversight?

_____

_____

_____

6. List three criteria used to evaluate the administration of an EMS system.

_____

_____

_____

7. Name any five items that should be included in a first responder life support kit.

_____

_____

_____

You Make the Call

The following scenario provides an opportunity to explore the concerns associated with patient management. Read the scenario, then describe the best way to handle the situation.

You are dispatched to an emergency scene and gain access to the patient. You complete the initial patient assessment and stabilize the patient, then paramedics arrive on the scene to assist. What should you do?

CHAPTER

2 The Well-Being of the First Responder

Matching

Match each of the items in the left column to the appropriate description in the right column.

_____ **1.** Denial

_____ **2.** Anger

_____ **3.** Bargaining

_____ **4.** Depression

_____ **5.** Acceptance

A. Recognition of the finality of the grief-causing event

B. "Why me?"

C. Trying to make a deal to postpone death and dying

D. Disbelief or rejection

E. Characterized by sadness or despair

Multiple Choice

Read each item carefully, then select the best response.

_____ **1.** Techniques that can be used to prevent stress include all of the following EXCEPT:

    A. drinking an adequate amount of healthy fluids.

    B. eating a well-balanced diet.

    C. focusing on stressful events and what should have been done differently.

    D. trying to create a stress-reducing environment away from work.

_____ **2.** Hepatitis B:

    A. is a disease that is easily treated.

    B. poses no risk to the first responder.

    C. cannot be prevented.

    D. is spread by direct contact with infected blood.

_____ **3.** Critical incident stress debriefings (CISDs) are usually held:

    A. during an incident.

    B. 10 to 20 days after an incident.

    C. 24 to 72 hours after an incident.

    D. because they are mandatory.

_____ **4.** Which of the following is true of tuberculosis?

    A. It is spread by blood-to-blood contact.

    B. There are treatment-resistant strains.

    C. Health care workers face a low risk of exposure.

    D. Skin tests should be performed every month.

_____ **5.** The stage of the grief process in which the finality of death is recognized is called:

    A. depression.

    B. comprehension.

    C. conclusion.

    D. acceptance.

_____ **6.** Which is not a sign of stress?

    A. Difficulty sleeping

    B. Increased efficiency

    C. Loss of appetite

    D. Inability to concentrate

_____ **7.** The first step in managing stress is to:

    A. get more sleep.

    B. recognize the signs and symptoms.

    C. change jobs.

    D. change eating habits.

_____ **8.** When you feel angry about an emergency situation that you have experienced and you discuss your anger with others, you are:

    A. showing that you are not capable.

    B. breaking the confidentiality laws.

    C. causing additional stress for others.

    D. avoiding unhealthy physical symptoms caused by bottling up your emotions.

_____ **9.** The stage of the grief process that involves trying to negotiate a postponement of death is called:

    A. bargaining.

    B. acceptance.

    C. contracts.

    D. denial.

_____ **10.** Which of the following is not usually a sign of depression?

    A. Quiet or silent behavior

    B. Laughing at inappropriate situations

    C. Being out of touch with one's surroundings

    D. Feeling sadness and despair

_____ **11.** In the grief process, a normal reaction is one of disbelief, which protects those who are experiencing the situation. This stage is called:

    A. preservation.

    B. denial.

    C. depression.

    D. skepticism.

_____ **12.** HIV stands for:

    A. human immunization virus.

    B. histamine immune vaccine.

    C. hyperinspiration vaporization.

    D. human immunodeficiency virus.

_____ **13.** Two examples of bloodborne pathogens are:

    A. HIV and HBV.

    B. AIDS and BSI.

    C. HEPA and HBV.

    D. PASG and CISD.

_____ **14.** HIV is transmitted by direct contact with infected:

    A. blood and/or semen.

    B. blood and/or vomitus.

    C. semen and/or sputum.

    D. saliva and/or tears.

_____ **15.** Tuberculosis is spread by contact with contaminated:

    A. blood.

    B. feces.

    C. air.

    D. all of the above.

_____ **16.** Universal precautions give guidelines for safe procedures for:

    A. transporting patients.

    B. sexual relations.

    C. responding to major natural disasters.

    D. minimizing the spread of pathogens.

_____ **17.** The universal precautions recommended by the Centers for Disease Control and Prevention (CDC) call for the use of:

    A. equipment with the OSHA seal.

    B. reflective vests and hard hats or helmets.

    C. supplies manufactured in the United States.

    D. medical gloves, protective eyewear, and a face shield or pocket mask.

_____ **18.** An emergency medical care provider should have a:

    A. hepatitis B vaccine.

    B. tetanus prophylaxis.

    C. tuberculin skin test.

    D. all of the above.

_____ **19.** The most important consideration at the scene of an accident is to:

    A. protect the emergency scene from further accidents.

    B. make sure your vehicle is visible.

    C. park your vehicle as close as possible to victims.

    D. have your vehicle facing the flow of traffic.

_____ **20.** Hazardous materials situations that require special attention may occur:

    A. with vehicles marked with specific placards.

    B. in homes.

    C. at industrial sites.

    D. all of the above.

Fill-in-the-Blanks

Read each item carefully, then complete the statement by filling in the missing word(s).

1. Stress management consists of recognizing, preventing, and _____ critical incident stress.

2. Scientific studies show that most people need about _____ hours of uninterrupted sleep per night.

3. _____ stress education provides information about the stresses that you will encounter and the reactions you may experience.

4. On-scene _____ support and disaster support services provide aid on the scene of especially stressful incidents.

5. A _____ is used to alleviate the stress reactions caused by high-stress emergency situations.

True/False

For each statement, write the letter "T" if you believe it to be more true than false, or write the letter "F" if you believe it to be more false than true.

_____ 1. Providing emergency medical care as a first responder is stressful only if you are unsure of what you are doing.

_____ 2. Stress can be eliminated if you learn proper techniques.

_____ 3. A healthy, well-balanced diet contributes to the prevention and reduction of stress.

_____ 4. You should utilize CISD personnel only when you can no longer cope with your stress.

_____ 5. Caffeine is a drug that causes an increase in blood pressure and an increase in your stress level.

_____ 6. Alcoholic beverages are encouraged in small quantities because they help reduce your ability to deal with stress.

_____ 7. First responders working rotating shifts or 24-hour shifts may suffer from disruption of normal sleep patterns.

_____ 8. Gowns and aprons should be worn on all first responder calls.

_____ 9. Medical gloves are adequate protection for first responders, and there is little need to wash hands if they are worn.

_____ 10. There is substantial evidence that HIV can be spread by direct contact with patient saliva or urine.

_____ 11. You should never enter an emergency situation that is unsafe unless you have the proper training and equipment.

_____ 12. If a person has adequate training and is competent, the services of a mental health care professional will not be needed.

_____ 13. A health care worker in an emergency situation should decide by visual examination whether or not protective equipment for bloodborne pathogens is necessary.

_____ 14. Receiving the hepatitis vaccine may help to protect you against hepatitis B.

_____ 15. Testing for the presence of tuberculosis is not recommended for first responders unless there is a family history of the disease.

_____ 16. To minimize exposure to tuberculosis, a first responder should use a HEPA respirator, oxygen mask, and/or face mask.

_____ 17. A health care worker should assume that all patients are potential carriers of bloodborne pathogens.

_____ 18. A used hypodermic needle needs to be cut or bent to ensure that it will not be reused.

_____ 19. At the scene of a crime, your responsibilities are only medical in nature and do not involve any responsibility for criminal evidence.

_____ 20. There are situations in which the first responder should wait for law enforcement personnel before approaching the scene.

Short Answer

Write a brief response to each of the following questions.

1. List three types of calls that can create a higher level of stress.

_____

_____

_____

2. List five signs or symptoms of stress.

_____

_____

_____

3. Describe the five universal precautions recommended by the CDC.

_____

_____

_____

4. List three things you should keep in mind when parking your vehicle at an emergency scene.

_____

_____

_____

5. What four special rescue situations require special safety considerations, training, or equipment?

_____

_____

_____

6. List five hazards that may be present at an accident scene and would need to be considered by the first responder.

_____

_____

_____

7. Name the five stages of the grief process.

_____

_____

_____

You Make the Call

The following scenario provides an opportunity to explore the concerns associated with patient management. Read the scenario, then describe the best way to handle the situation.

At 4:00 A.M. you are dispatched to a shooting at a residence. As you approach, two police cars leave the scene of the crime with their lights and sirens on, and dispatch informs you that law enforcement personnel believe the shooter has left the scene. What should you do?

CHAPTER

3 Medical, Legal, and Ethical Issues

Matching
Match each of the items in the left column to the appropriate description in the right column.

_____ **1.** Expressed consent

_____ **2.** Implied consent

_____ **3.** Consent for a minor

_____ **4.** Consent of the mentally ill

_____ **5.** Patient refusal

A. Type of consent given by a parent or guardian for treatment of an individual under age 18 years

B. Type of consent when a patient is unconscious or when a serious threat to life exists

C. Right of a person who is mentally in control to choose not to be treated in an emergency setting

D. Permission for treatment given to the first responder by the patient

E. Treatment that can be rendered if the patient is out of touch with reality

Multiple Choice
Read each item carefully, then select the best response.

_____ **1.** At the crime scene, your first priority should be to:
  A. avoid touching anything that could be used as evidence.
  B. provide patient care as long as your own safety is not at risk.
  C. ask the patient for information about the crime.
  D. make sure no witnesses leave the scene.

_____ **2.** Which of the following patients can refuse medical treatment?
  A. 9-year-old girl with a broken leg
  B. 12-year-old girl who is unconscious
  C. 21-year-old man with a broken nose
  D. 86-year-old woman with Alzheimer's disease

_____ **3.** For negligence to occur, four conditions must be present, including all of the following EXCEPT:
  A. duty to act.
  B. breech of duty.
  C. proximate cause.
  D. death of the patient.

_____ **4.** Abandonment occurs when:

    A. patient care is terminated before another first responder or more highly trained person assumes care.

    B. you turn over patient care to a paramedic.

    C. you turn the patient over to another first responder.

    D. the patient refuses treatment by a first responder.

_____ **5.** To comply with the standard of care you must:

    A. treat the patient to the best of your ability.

    B. provide care that a reasonable, prudent person with similar training would provide under similar circumstances.

    C. know what the local standards of care are and what statutes pertain to your community.

    D. all of the above.

_____ **6.** As a first responder you are responsible for:

    A. staying up-to-date on skills.

    B. evaluating your response times.

    C. reviewing your performance.

    D. all of the above.

_____ **7.** Dependent lividity:

    A. is the red or purple color that occurs several hours after death.

    B. may be confused with signs of an assault, especially in the small child or infant.

    C. occurs on the parts of the patient's body that are closest to the ground.

    D. all of the above.

_____ **8.** Rigor mortis is:

    A. a sign that you should begin CPR.

    B. proper protocol for caring for deceased patients.

    C. an indication that the patient cannot be resuscitated.

    D. none of the above.

_____ **9.** As a first responder on the scene of an emergency, the first legal principle you need to consider is:

    A. the confidentiality of patient information.

    B. obtaining consent for treatment.

    C. if your training qualifies you to give treatment.

    D. duty to act.

_____ **10.** Responsibilities that concern a first responder include:

    A. professional standards of conduct.

    B. honesty.

    C. competence.

    D. all of the above.

_____ **11.** If you have made a mistake while treating a patient, you should:

    A. gather evidence to show why you were justified.

    B. not put anything in writing.

    C. document the incident.

    D. file a claim with an attorney.

_____ **12.** Consent means:

    A. approval or permission.

    B. ethical responsibility.

    C. to confine or restrict movement.

    D. a soft-tissue injury.

_____ **13.** If a patient understands who you are and agrees to treatment, this is called:

    A. expressed consent.

    B. implied consent.

    C. assumed consent.

    D. durable power.

_____ **14.** A patient who does not refuse emergency care can be treated under the principle of:

    A. expressed consent.

    B. implied consent.

    C. protective custody.

    D. durable power.

_____ **15.** Minors:

    A. are those who are not of legal age as designated by the state.

    B. are considered to be incapable of speaking for themselves with regard to medical decisions.

    C. can be given emergency medical treatment in the field without expressed consent.

    D. all of the above.

_____ **16.** If a patient is a danger to self or to others and refuses help, a first responder may:

    A. call for help from law enforcement agencies.

    B. conduct field testing to determine mental condition.

    C. safely leave the scene.

    D. transport the patient to the nearest appropriate treatment facility.

_____ **17.** A first responder must honor refusal of treatment if the patient:

    A. is competent.

    B. has an order of protective custody.

    C. is incompetent.

    D. is a minor.

_____ **18.** A legal document with specific instructions that the patient does not want to be resuscitated or kept alive by mechanical support is known as:

    A. protective custody.

    B. a living will.

    C. abandonment.

    D. all of the above.

_____ **19.** A living will:

    A. is a legal document drawn up by a patient, physician, and lawyer.

    B. is similar to an advance directive.

    C. may contain do-not-resuscitate (DNR) orders.

    D. all of the above.

_____ **20.** The failure of the first responder to continue emergency medical treatment until another qualified person assumes care is called:

    A. advance directive.

    B. incompetency.

    C. abandonment.

    D. dependent lividity.

_____ **21.** The red or purple color that occurs on the parts of the patient's body that are closest to the ground is:

    A. dependent lividity.

    B. common several days after death.

    C. a sign of severe trauma.

    D. rigor mortis.

_____ **22.** Deviation from the accepted standard of care resulting in further injury to the patient is known as:
   A. redirection.
   B. improvisation.
   C. abandonment.
   D. negligence.

_____ **23.** Which is not a condition of negligence?
   A. Duty to act
   B. Breech of duty
   C. Resulting injuries
   D. Advance directive

_____ **24.** Failure to provide care according to the level of your training could constitute:
   A. duty to act.
   B. breech of duty.
   C. abandonment.
   D. proximal cause.

_____ **25.** In crime scene operations, a first responder's first consideration should be:
   A. patient care.
   B. safety of bystanders.
   C. evidence of the crime.
   D. personal safety.

Fill-in-the-Blanks

Read each item carefully, then complete the statement by filling in the missing word(s).

1. A/an _____ is a written legal document giving specific instructions that the patient does not want to be resuscitated or kept alive by mechanical support systems.

2. Injuries caused by improper care can be found to be a situation of _____.

3. In order for the Good Samaritan law to provide any protection from civil liability, you must act in good _____ to provide care to the level of your training and to the best of your ability.

4. One who is able to make rational decisions about personal well-being is said to be _____.

5. _____ consent is based on the assumption that the patient has the right to determine what will be done to his or her body.

True/False

For each statement, write the letter "T" if you believe it to be more true than false, or write the letter "F" if you believe it to be more false than true.

_____ **1.** To comply with the standard of care, you must treat the patient to the best of your ability.

_____ **2.** As a first responder, it is principally the responsibility of your state or agency to make sure that you maintain up-to-date skills.

_____ **3.** You have a legal duty to provide emergency care as a first responder if your agency dispatches you to a scene.

_____ **4.** Good Samaritan laws provide complete legal protection for people who provide emergency medical care.

_____ **5.** Even if a patient is unable to communicate, the principles of law do not assume consent for treatment.

_____ **6.** First responders should provide emergency medical care to minors even if parents or guardians are not at the scene to give permission.

_____ **7.** In some states, Good Samaritan laws do not apply to first responders.

_____ **8.** Documentation should not include any unusual details regarding the case if they do not relate to the patient's condition or the treatment provided.

_____ **9.** Expectations concerning the standard of care may be different in different communities, cities, or counties.

_____ **10.** If a patient is not conscious, permission for treatment needs to be obtained from a family member.

_____ **11.** A rational adult can legally refuse treatment.

_____ **12.** A first responder must determine whether a living will exists before beginning lifesaving procedures.

_____ **13.** Some information about a patient's care may be classified as public information.

_____ **14.** Dog bites are classified as a reportable crime.

_____ **15.** At a crime scene, a patient cannot be moved until law enforcement officials have arrived and approved movement.

Short Answer

Write a brief response to each of the following questions.

1. What agency developed the National Curriculum for First Responders?

2. What is the purpose of Good Samaritan laws?

3. What four conditions can be used to reliably determine that a patient is dead?

4. Name three crimes that are reportable.

5. Name three factors that should be included in documentation.

You Make the Call

The following scenario provides an opportunity to explore the concerns associated with patient management. Read the scenario, then describe the best way to handle the situation.

You are called to the scene of a fight in a bar where a patron reportedly has been stabbed, and you consider it a potential crime scene. What should you do?

CHAPTER

4 The Human Body

Matching

Match each of the items in the left column to the appropriate description in the right column.

_____ 1. Cervical spine   **A.** Base of the spine

_____ 2. Thoracic spine   **B.** Upper back

_____ 3. Lumbar spine   **C.** Neck

_____ 4. Sacrum   **D.** Tail bone

_____ 5. Coccyx   **E.** Lower back

Multiple Choice

Read each item carefully, then select the best response.

_____ 1. The pancreas has several functions, including the production of:

     A. bile.

     B. insulin.

     C. plasma.

     D. platelets.

_____ 2. The removal of waste products from the body begins with which organ of the genitourinary system?

     A. Liver

     B. Urethra

     C. Kidneys

     D. Fallopian tubes

_____ 3. The heart consists of _____ chambers.

     A. one

     B. two

     C. three

     D. four

_____ 4. The bones that make up the spine are called the:

     A. ribs.

     B. xiphoid.

     C. vertebrae.

     D. sternum.

_____   **5.** The sternum is located:
  A. in the middle of the back.
  B. superior to the ribs.
  C. in the front of the chest.
  D. in the shoulder girdle.

_____   **6.** Oxygen is transported throughout the body by means of the:
  A. blood.
  B. lungs.
  C. nerves.
  D. diaphragm.

_____   **7.** Which of the following statements best describes how the circulatory system works?
  A. The heart pumps blood to the lungs to receive carbon dioxide.
  B. Blood picks up oxygen in the lungs and is then pumped by the heart to the rest of the body.
  C. Blood releases oxygen in the lungs and is then pumped by the heart back to the cells.
  D. Blood picks up oxygen in the lungs and then releases it in the heart before being pumped to the rest of the body.

_____   **8.** The large muscle that forms the bottom of the chest cavity is the:
  A. epiglottis.
  B. trachea.
  C. diaphragm.
  D. vena cava.

_____   **9.** The exchange of carbon dioxide for oxygen in the body normally occurs _____ times per minute.
  A. 8 to10
  B. 12 to16
  C. 18 to 22
  D. 24 to 28

_____   **10.** Which is not part of the genitourinary system?
  A. Uterus
  B. Kidneys
  C. Rectum
  D. Urethra

_____   **11.** Which is not a function of skin?
  A. Receiving information from the outside environment
  B. Protecting the body from the environment
  C. Eliminating excess waste products
  D. Regulating the body temperature

_____   **12.** Cardiac muscle:
  A. is found only in the heart.
  B. can live only a few minutes without an adequate supply of oxygen.
  C. is adapted to working all the time.
  D. all of the above.

_____   **13.** The brain:
  A. is part of the nervous system.
  B. may be called the body's central computer.
  C. controls the functions of thinking, voluntary actions, and involuntary functions.
  D. all of the above.

_____ **14.** Muscles that provide support and movement and are attached to bones by tendons are _____ muscles.

    A. cardiac

    B. skeletal

    C. smooth

    D. thoracic

_____ **15.** The muscles that carry out many of the automatic functions of the body are:

    A. responsible for propelling food through the digestive system.

    B. involuntary muscles.

    C. smooth muscles.

    D. all of the above.

_____ **16.** The closed, bony ring that serves as the link between the body and the lower extremities is the:

    A. femur.

    B. patella.

    C. coccyx.

    D. pelvis.

_____ **17.** The reproductive organs are protected by the:

    A. vertebrae.

    B. pelvis.

    C. intestines.

    D. xiphoid process.

_____ **18.** The longest and strongest bone in the body is the:

    A. femur.

    B. tibia.

    C. fibula.

    D. humerus.

_____ **19.** The xiphoid process is:

    A. followed at the scene of a major disaster.

    B. used to determine the competency of a patient.

    C. used when a patient is in the last stages of labor.

    D. the pointed structure at the bottom of the sternum.

_____ **20.** The rib cage:

    A. consists of 13 sets of ribs.

    B. protects the kidneys and lungs.

    C. includes the ulna and radius bones.

    D. includes the sternum, xiphoid process, and ribs.

_____ **21.** The bones of the head, collectively, are known as the:

    A. spine.

    B. skull.

    C. the jaw bones.

    D. stoma.

_____ **22.** Each of the 33 bones of the spinal column is known as a:

    A. lumbar spine.

    B. sacrum.

    C. thoracic.

    D. vertebra.

_____ **23.** The tough, ropelike cords of fibrous tissue that attach muscles to bones are called:
  A. tendons.
  B. ligaments.
  C. sternum.
  D. cartilage.

_____ **24.** The fibrous bands that connect bones to bones and support and strengthen joints are called:
  A. tendons.
  B. ligaments.
  C. sternum.
  D. cartilage.

_____ **25.** The shoulder girdles consist of the:
  A. thoracic spine, clavicle, and scapula.
  B. clavicle, scapula, and humerus.
  C. vertebrae, humerus, and ulna.
  D. clavicle, humerus, and thoracic spine.

_____ **26.** Capillaries are the:
  A. lower chambers of the heart.
  B. smallest pipes in the circulatory system.
  C. small airway branches of the lungs.
  D. fluid part of the blood.

_____ **27.** Blood is returned to the heart by:
  A. veins.
  B. arteries.
  C. platelets.
  D. the aorta.

_____ **28.** The function of the skeletal system is:
  A. to manufacture red blood cells.
  B. to protect vital structures.
  C. to support the body.
  D. all of the above.

_____ **29.** Blood is carried away from the heart by the:
  A. ventricles.
  B. atriums.
  C. veins.
  D. arteries.

_____ **30.** When describing a location on a body, anterior means:
  A. front.
  B. back.
  C. close.
  D. distant.

_____ **31.** When describing a location on a body, posterior means:
  A. front.
  B. back.
  C. close.
  D. distant.

_____ **32.** The term used to describe a location on the body close to the point where an arm or leg is attached is:
   A. anterior.
   B. posterior.
   C. proximal.
   D. distal.

_____ **33.** The term used to describe a location on the body that is not close to the point where an arm or leg is attached is:
   A. anterior.
   B. posterior.
   C. proximal.
   D. distal.

_____ **34.** A term to describe a body location closer to the head is:
   A. lateral.
   B. medial.
   C. superior.
   D. inferior.

_____ **35.** A term to describe a body location closer to the feet is:
   A. lateral.
   B. medial.
   C. superior.
   D. inferior.

_____ **36.** All the structures of the body that contribute to normal breathing make up which system?
   A. Respiratory
   B. Circulatory
   C. Genitourinary
   D. Digestive

_____ **37.** Which is not part of the respiratory system?
   A. Trachea
   B. Nose
   C. Kidneys
   D. Mouth

Fill-in-the-Blanks

Read each item carefully, then complete the statement by filling in the missing word(s).

1. _____ sets of ribs protect the heart, lungs, liver, and spleen.

2. The spine is the second area of the skeletal system and consists of 33 separate bones called _____.

3. The _____ is a group of nerves that carry messages to and from the brain.

4. The bones of the head include the skull and the lower _____.

5. The 11th and 12th rib sets are not attached to the sternum in any way and are called _____ ribs.

6. The lower leg has two bones, the tibia and _____.

7. Where two bones come in contact with each other, a/an _____ is formed.

8. Cardiac muscle is found only in the _____.

9. The major organs of the digestive system are located in the _____.

10. The digestive track begins at the _____.

True/False

For each statement, write the letter "T" if you believe it to be more true than false, or write the letter "F" if you believe it to be more false than true.

_____ **1.** The brain controls only voluntary actions such as speaking and moving.

_____ **2.** The spinal cord is an important part of the two-way communication system between the brain and the rest of the body.

_____ **3.** Blood is pumped away from the heart through the veins.

_____ **4.** Blood reverses the direction of its flow after delivering oxygen and nutrients to the cells.

_____ **5.** Blood cells and tissue cells exchange oxygen and carbon dioxide when the blood reaches the capillaries.

_____ **6.** A person in the standard anatomic position is standing in front of you, facing you, with hands extended over the head.

_____ **7.** Left and right, when used to describe an injury, refer to the patient's left and right.

_____ **8.** The term midline refers to an imaginary vertical line drawn from head to toe that separates the body into a left half and a right half.

_____ **9.** The term *lateral* refers to a wound that resembles a straight line.

_____ **10.** The term *medial* means closer to the midline of the body.

_____ **11.** The epiglottis helps to regulate the rate of breathing.

_____ **12.** A patient's pulse can be measured at the neck, the groin, or the wrist because of the location of veins.

_____ **13.** The upper extremity area of the skeletal system consists of the humerus, ulna, radius, wrist, and hand.

_____ **14.** Floating ribs are ribs that have been broken from the spine and/or sternum and are no longer attached by the ligaments.

_____ **15.** There are four different kinds of muscles.

_____ **16.** Cardiac muscle, like skeletal muscle, is found throughout the body.

_____ **17.** The skeletal and muscular systems can be considered together and called the musculoskeletal system.

_____ **18.** The organs of reproduction, together with the organs involved in the production and excretion of urine, are known as the genitourinary system.

_____ **19.** The digestive system includes the stomach, intestines, liver, rectum, bladder, and kidneys.

_____ **20.** The nervous system includes the brain, spinal cord, and individual nerves.

Short Answer

Write a brief response to each of the following questions.

1. Name the six parts of the airway.

_____

_____

_____

2. List the three major functions of the skin.

_____

_____

_____

3. Name the three major functions of the skeletal system.

_____

_____

_____

4. Name the two actions of muscles that cause movement.

_____

_____

_____

5. Name the five sections of the spine.

_____

_____

_____

6. Name the eight parts of the digestive tract.

_____

_____

_____

7. What are the differences between the respiratory system of an adult and that of an infant?

_____

_____

_____

8. List the seven areas of the skeletal system.

_____

_____

_____

Word Fun

The following crossword puzzle is an activity provided to reinforce correct spelling and understanding of terminology associated with emergency care and the first responder. Use the clues in the column to complete the puzzle.

Across

3. Toward the front
5. System that supports the body
6. Toward the midline
7. Closer to the trunk
9. System made up of a pump and pipes
11. System that governs the body's functioning
12. Distant from the midline

Down

1. Toward the back
2. System with elements that are skeletal, smooth, and cardiac
4. Closer to the feet
8. Away from the midline
10. Regulates temperature

Labeling

Label the following diagrams with the correct terms.

1. Label the parts of the respiratory system.

A. _____

B. _____

C. _____

D. _____

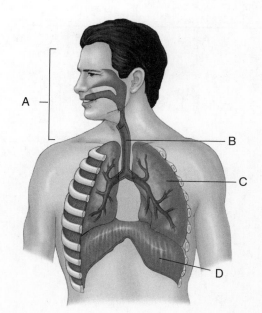

2. Label the parts of the airway.

A. _____

B. _____

C. _____

D. _____

E. _____

F. _____

G. _____

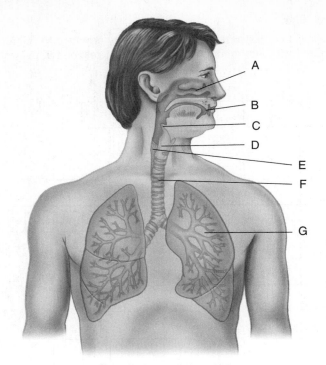

3. Label the parts of the circulatory system.

A. _____

B. _____

C. _____

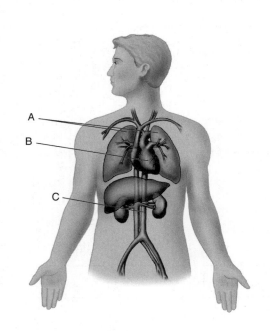

4. Label the sections of the rib cage.

A. _____

B. _____

C. _____

D. _____

5. Label the parts of the digestive system.

A. _____

B. _____

C. _____

D. _____

E. _____

F. _____

G. _____

H. _____

I. _____

J. _____

K. _____

You Make the Call

The following scenario provides an opportunity to explore the concerns associated with patient management. Read the scenario, then describe the best way to handle the situation.

You arrive at a scene where you are told that a 14-year-old boy has fallen about 10 feet and is lying semiconscious underneath the bleachers at a football field. You determine that you will need to check the three major pulse points. What should you do?

CHAPTER

5 # Lifting and Moving Patients

Matching

Match each of the items in the left column to the appropriate description in the right column.

_____ **1.** Arm-to-arm drag

_____ **2.** Blanket drag

_____ **3.** Clothes drag

_____ **4.** Fire fighter drag

_____ **5.** Emergency drag

_____ **6.** Two-rescuer drag

A. Used when the patient is heavier than the rescuer; involves tying the patient's wrists around the rescuer's neck and crawling to safety

B. Used if a patient is not dressed or is dressed in clothing that could easily tear

C. Allows a rescuer to move the patient by carrying the weight of the upper body and letting the lower trunk and legs drag

D. Simplest way to move the patient in an emergency

E. Drag that provides the most support for the patient's head and neck

F. Used when one rescuer needs to remove a patient from a vehicle

Multiple Choice

Read each item carefully, then select the best response.

_____ **1.** A man who is lying on the ground next to his automobile must be moved. To protect the patient's spine, you should move him longways with the:

A. arm-to-arm drag.

B. clothes or blanket drag.

C. leg drag.

D. fire fighter drag.

_____ **2.** Which of the following can be used successfully to move a patient who is too heavy for a rescuer to lift or carry?

A. Clothes or blanket drag

B. Arm-to-arm drag

C. Fire fighter drag

D. All of the above

_____ **3.** Which drag provides some protection for the patient's head and neck?
   A. Clothes drag
   B. Blanket drag
   C. Arm-to-arm drag
   D. All of the above

_____ **4.** In order to perform a fire fighter drag:
   A. place the patient on a blanket or rug.
   B. tie the patient's hands around your neck.
   C. the patient must be wearing clothes that will not easily tear.
   D. all of the above.

_____ **5.** Moving a patient onto a long backboard:
   A. requires a team of four rescuers.
   B. can be performed with the use of log rolling.
   C. can be performed with the use of a straddle lift.
   D. all of the above.

_____ **6.** Log rolling a patient safely requires:
   A. a team of four rescuers.
   B. a long backboard.
   C. verbal commands.
   D. all of the above.

_____ **7.** The head and neck of a patient on a backboard:
   A. do not need further immobilization.
   B. may be immobilized with a short backboard.
   C. may be immobilized with foam blocks or a blanket roll.
   D. all of the above.

_____ **8.** A patient who is in a sitting position and has suffered possible head or spine injuries will probably need a:
   A. long backboard.
   B. short backboard device.
   C. scoop stretcher.
   D. stair chair.

_____ **9.** A scoop stretcher:
   A. is also called an orthopedic stretcher.
   B. separates into halves.
   C. should not be used when there are head or spinal injuries.
   D. all of the above.

_____ **10.** A patient should be transported on a backboard:
   A. in a face-up position.
   B. with the head and neck turned to one side.
   C. when unconscious.
   D. all of the above.

_____ **11.** Transfer of a patient from a bed to a stretcher:
   A. requires coordinated commands.
   B. requires three rescuers.
   C. should be used only when a patient is unconscious.
   D. all of the above.

_____ **12.** The two-person extremity carry:
    A. makes use of the patient's arms and legs.
    B. requires the use of equipment.
    C. allows the two rescuers to see each other.
    D. all of the above.

_____ **13.** The two-person seat carry:
    A. is used only for unconscious patients.
    B. requires the use of equipment.
    C. allows the two rescuers to see each other.
    D. all of the above.

_____ **14.** The cradle-in-arms carry:
    A. requires no equipment.
    B. can be used by one rescuer.
    C. is used to carry a child.
    D. all of the above.

_____ **15.** The two-person chair carry:
    A. requires the use of a folding chair.
    B. requires close attention to the patient's airway.
    C. should not be used on stairways.
    D. all of the above.

_____ **16.** The pack-strap carry:
    A. requires the use of equipment.
    B. requires two rescuers.
    C. may use straps that are improvised.
    D. is a one-person carry.

_____ **17.** A small portable device used for transporting patients in a sitting position is a:
    A. pack-strap.
    B. portable stretcher.
    C. stair chair.
    D. reclining stretcher.

Fill-in-the-Blanks

Read each item carefully, then complete the statement by filling in the missing word(s).

1. The primary technique used to move patients onto a long backboard is _____.

2. The main purpose of backboards is to _____ the spine.

3. _____ are used to prevent excess movement of the neck and head.

4. A/an _____ stretcher or orthopedic stretcher is a rigid device that is helpful in moving patients out of small spaces.

5. _____ cervical collars do not provide sufficient support for trauma patients.

6. The rescuer holding the patient's _____ should always give the commands to move the patient.

7. Because the log-rolling maneuver requires sufficient space for _____ rescuers, it is not always possible to perform it correctly.

8. Carefully monitor all immobilized patients for _____ problems.

True/False

For each statement, write the letter "T" if you believe it to be more true than false, or write the letter "F" if you believe it to be more false than true.

_____ **1.** One rescuer alone should not attempt to remove a patient from any wrecked car.

_____ **2.** The use of the direct ground lift is to be discouraged because of the danger of back injuries to the rescuers.

_____ **3.** The direct ground lift is an appropriate lift for patients who have traumatic injuries.

_____ **4.** The direct ground lift requires the coordination of two rescuers.

_____ **5.** Walking assists for ambulatory patients should always involve two rescuers.

_____ **6.** The two rescuers completely support the patient when the two-person walking assist is used.

_____ **7.** Wheeled ambulance stretchers are also called cots.

_____ **8.** Wheeled ambulance stretchers require four persons for safe transport.

_____ **9.** A portable stretcher may be required in areas that do not have adequate space for a wheeled ambulance stretcher.

_____ **10.** The frame of a portable stretcher is of lighter weight than that of a wheeled ambulance stretcher.

_____ **11.** A stair chair is used to transport trauma patients up or down stairways.

_____ **12.** A long backboard is used for lifting or moving patients who have suffered trauma, especially back or neck injuries.

_____ **13.** Scoop stretchers are also called orthopedic stretchers because they are used in cases of spinal injuries.

_____ **14.** Improper initial treatment of patients who have suffered head or spine injuries can lead to paralysis.

_____ **15.** When used correctly, cervical collars will prevent all head and neck movement.

_____ **16.** A blanket roll or foam blocks may be used to immobilize the head and neck only if a cervical collar is not available.

_____ **17.** Hard and soft cervical collars both provide sufficient support for trauma patients.

_____ **18.** A patient should be placed on a long backboard before a cervical collar is applied.

_____ **19.** A short backboard is used instead of a long backboard when a patient is more comfortable in a sitting position.

_____ **20.** It is the responsibility of the first responder to apply the short backboard before other medical personnel arrive at the scene of an accident.

_____ **21.** In confined spaces, the straddle lift can be used instead of the log-rolling technique.

_____ **22.** In a straddle slide, the patient is slid onto the backboard.

_____ **23.** A patient on a backboard should be strapped on at the shoulders, hips, and ankles to avoid sliding off the backboard.

_____ **24.** If a blanket roll is used to immobilize a patient's head and neck on a backboard, the roll should be secured with one of the straps found on the backboard.

_____ **25.** Immobilizing a patient on a long backboard ensures that the airway will remain open during transport.

_____ **26.** If you have to move a patient, you should try to move the patient as little as possible and in a way that will not cause further harm.

_____ **27.** If possible, you should wait to move a patient until additional help arrives on the scene.

_____ **28.** If you must move a patient, you should move the patient first and then begin treatment.

_____ **29.** As a first responder, you should concentrate on treatment and let EMS personnel explain to the patient what is happening and move the patient if necessary.

_____ **30.** You must decide if there is enough room to perform CPR properly on a patient in cardiac arrest and move the patient if there is not.

_____ **31.** When you are alone, you should avoid moving a patient from a vehicle to prevent further neck or spinal injuries, even if the patient is in cardiac arrest.

_____ **32.** There is no way to prevent some movement to the neck when removing a patient from a vehicle by yourself.

_____ **33.** The best way to move a patient from a vehicle when you are alone is to grasp the patient under the arms and cradle the head between your arms.

_____ **34.** If two rescuers are at the scene of a motor vehicle crash, the first rescuer can best help by supporting the patient's head and preventing excess movement of the neck while the second rescuer moves the patient by lifting under the arms.

_____ **35.** Proper lifting requires the back to be as straight as possible and having the leg muscles do the work.

Short Answer

Write a brief response to each of the following questions.

1. Name the two most common reasons why you would move a patient.

_____

_____

_____

2. What should you do if you suspect that the patient has suffered trauma to the head or spine?

_____

_____

_____

3. Why is the recovery position used for an unconscious patient?

_____

_____

_____

4. Describe three situations that require moving a patient before emergency medical care is provided.

_____

_____

_____

5. Name three pieces of equipment that EMS providers commonly use for lifting and moving patients.

_____

_____

_____

Labeling

Write the name of each type of carry or drag below the appropriate picture.

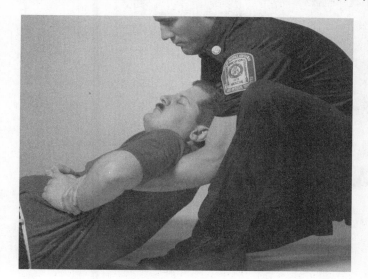

1. _____

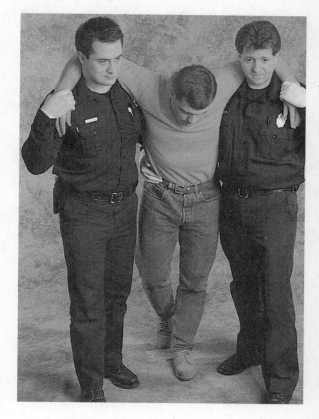

2. _____

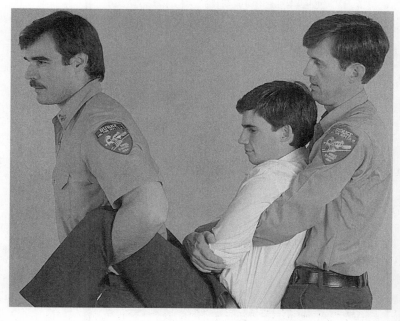

3. _____

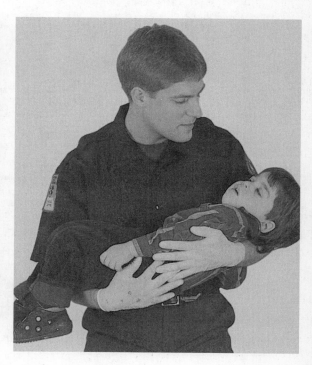

4. _____

5. _____

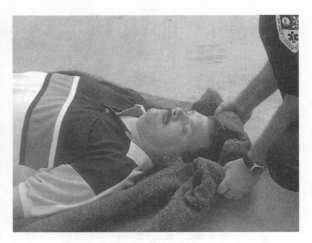

6. _____

7. _____

8. _____

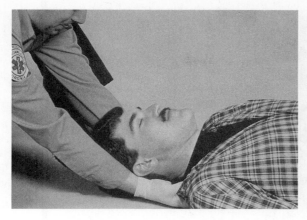

9. _____

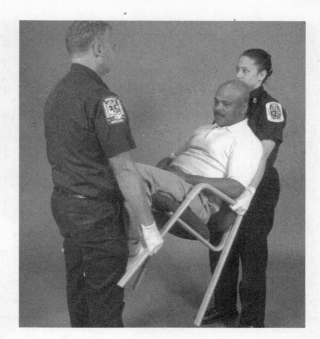

10. _____

11. _____

Skill Drills

Test your knowledge by filling in the correct words in the photo captions.

A. Four-Person Log Roll

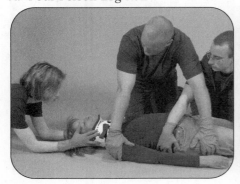

1. Get in position to _____ the patient.

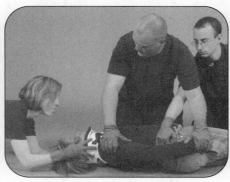

2. Roll the patient onto his or her _____.

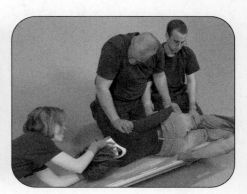

3. The fourth person slides the _____ toward the patient.

4. _____ the patient onto the backboard.

5. Center the patient on the backboard and _____ the patient before moving.

B. Applying the Blanket Roll to Stabilize the Patient's Head and Neck

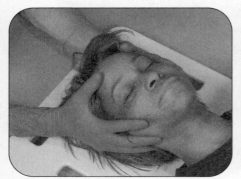

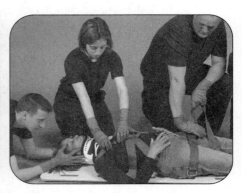

1. _____ the head.

2. Apply a _____.

3. Place the _____ around the backboard and patient.

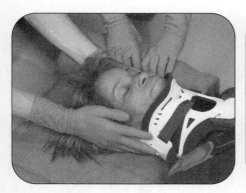

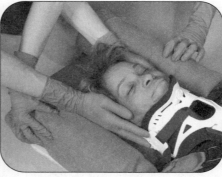

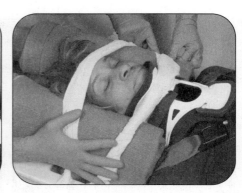

4. Insert the _____.

5. Roll the blanket snugly against the _____ and shoulders.

6. Tie two _____ around the blanket roll and around the backboard.

You Make the Call

The following scenario provides an opportunity to explore the concerns associated with patient management. Read the scenario, then describe the best way to handle the situation.

You and your partner are directed to an elderly man who lives in a house near a major fire. He says that he has a heart condition and gets out of breath after walking a few steps. What should you do?

CHAPTER

6 Airway Management

Matching
Match each of the items in the left column to the appropriate description in the right column.

_____ **1.** Oropharynx

_____ **2.** Trachea

_____ **3.** Alveoli

_____ **4.** Nasopharynx

_____ **5.** Aspirator

A. Suction device

B. Windpipe

C. Posterior part of the nose

D. Posterior part of the mouth

E. Air sacs of the lungs where the exchange of oxygen and carbon dioxide takes place

Multiple Choice
Read each item carefully, then select the best response.

_____ **1.** The correct way to open the airway of an unconscious adult with no suspected spinal injury is to use the:

    A. head tilt–chin lift.

    B. head lift–chin tilt.

    C. head tilt–jaw lift.

    D. head lift–jaw lift.

_____ **2.** If a patient has suffered a head or neck injury, you should use the _____ technique to open the patient's airway.

    A. head tilt–chin lift

    B. chin thrust–jaw lift

    C. tongue–jaw lift

    D. jaw-thrust

_____ **3.** Finger sweeps:

    A. require special equipment.

    B. are done only as a last resort.

    C. should not be done by first responders.

    D. should only be performed while wearing medical gloves.

_____ **4.** Mechanical suctioning of an adult should not last more than _____ seconds.

    A. 5

    B. 10

    C. 15

    D. 20

_____ **5.** Mechanical suctioning of an infant should not last more than _____ seconds.

    A. 5

    B. 10

    C. 15

    D. 20

_____ **6.** To select the proper size of a nasal airway, measure:

    A. from the bottom of the nose to the top of the ear.

    B. from the earlobe to the tip of the nose.

    C. from the bottom of the nose to the bottom of the ear.

    D. from the tip of the nose to the top of the ear.

_____ **7.** Coat the nasal airway with:

    A. petroleum-based lubricant.

    B. water.

    C. water-soluble lubricant.

    D. nothing; no lubricant is needed.

_____ **8.** If an unconscious person is lying on his or her back, the passage of air into the lungs may be blocked by the:

    A. larynx.

    B. tongue.

    C. epiglottis.

    D. relaxed diaphragm.

_____ **9.** Oxygen enters the respiratory system through the mouth and/or nose and then:

    A. enters the body via the contractions of the lungs.

    B. fills the upper airway until the epiglottis flaps open.

    C. passes through the throat and trachea into the lungs, where it enters the bloodstream.

    D. passes through the throat and esophagus into the lungs, where it converts into carbon dioxide.

_____ **10.** If your assessment shows that a person is not breathing, you should immediately:

    A. begin rescue breathing.

    B. check for signs of injury.

    C. ask bystanders for help.

    D. assume the person is dead.

_____ **11.** You should check for breathing by looking, listening, and feeling for at least _____ seconds.

    A. 3 to 5

    B. 10 to 15

    C. 30 to 45

    D. 60 to 90

_____ **12.** If a patient is breathing, you should:

    A. begin rescue breathing.

    B. begin external chest compressions.

    C. check for the odor of alcohol and, if present, let the patient sleep.

    D. check the rate and depth of the breathing and continue to maintain the airway during your assessment.

_____ **13.** When performing rescue breathing, you should remember to:
  A. blow gently enough so that the chest does not rise.
  B. pause as little as possible between breaths so the patient's chest does not have time to deflate.
  C. continue the head tilt–chin lift or jaw-thrust technique.
  D. maintain an open airway so that the tongue does not fall back into the throat and block your efforts.

_____ **14.** When ventilating an adult patient, each rescue breath should last for _____ second(s).
  A. 1
  B. 2
  C. $2^1/_2$
  D. 3

_____ **15.** Which of the following techniques should you first use to open the airway of an unconscious infant?
  A. Jaw-thrust
  B. Finger sweep
  C. Head tilt only
  D. Head tilt–chin lift

_____ **16.** The head of an infant should be tilted back only slightly, if at all, because:
  A. no pressure should be placed on the back of an infant's head.
  B. tilting the head back could block the airway.
  C. the infant's mouth and nose will close if you tilt the head too far.
  D. this will place too much pressure on the forehead.

_____ **17.** Another difference between infant and adult rescue breathing is that infants need:
  A. smaller, more frequent breaths.
  B. smaller, less frequent breaths.
  C. larger, more frequent breaths.
  D. larger, less frequent breaths.

_____ **18.** You know you are blowing hard enough while performing rescue breathing when:
  A. the patient revives.
  B. the patient's chest rises slightly.
  C. you begin to feel lightheaded.
  D. you feel slightly out of breath.

_____ **19.** You are eating in a restaurant when a woman at the next table begins coughing violently. When you ask her if she is choking, she nods and continues to cough. You should:
  A. perform the Heimlich maneuver.
  B. encourage her to cough and wait for her to become unconscious before performing the Heimlich maneuver.
  C. encourage her to cough, monitor her carefully, and arrange for transport to a hospital.
  D. demand that she answer your question out loud so you can determine whether or not her airway is completely blocked.

_____ **20.** The woman suddenly stops coughing and grabs at her throat. You tell her to cough and she shakes her head violently from side to side. You should:
  A. try to convince the woman that she should still cough.
  B. perform the Heimlich maneuver if she loses consciousness.
  C. perform the Heimlich maneuver until the object is expelled or the woman loses consciousness.
  D. alert the EMS system that rapid transport is now required.

_____ **21.** In performing the Heimlich maneuver, your fist should be placed between the person's:

    A. navel and pubis.

    B. navel and xiphoid process.

    C. heart and xiphoid process.

    D. sternum and xiphoid process.

_____ **22.** When checking for signs of circulation, coughing and movement may indicate:

    A. the presence of a pulse.

    B. heart fibrillation.

    C. a seizure.

    D. a heart attack.

_____ **23.** A mouth-to-mask ventilation device will be most effective if you:

    A. use the device only on a patient with a stoma.

    B. seal the device over the patient's mouth so that no infectious diseases are transmitted.

    C. maintain both proper head position and an airtight seal of the mask at the same time.

    D. remember that a patient will not get as much air through the mask as with mouth-to-mouth breathing.

_____ **24.** The posterior part of the mouth used in breathing is the:

    A. oropharynx.

    B. nasopharynx.

    C. trachea.

    D. none of the above.

_____ **25.** The posterior part of the nose used in breathing is the:

    A. oropharynx.

    B. nasopharynx.

    C. trachea.

    D. all of the above.

_____ **26.** Parts of the body used in breathing include the:

    A. oropharynx and nasopharynx.

    B. trachea and chest muscles.

    C. lungs and diaphragm.

    D. all of the above.

_____ **27.** The air sacs of the lungs where the exchange of oxygen and carbon dioxide takes place are:

    A. bronchi.

    B. alveoli.

    C. tracheae.

    D. none of the above.

_____ **28.** The first step in assessing a patient's airway is to:

    A. place the patient on his or her back.

    B. look and listen for signs of breathing.

    C. check for responsiveness.

    D. use the head tilt–chin lift technique.

_____ **29.** A patient's airway may be cleared with:

    A. manual suction devices.

    B. finger sweeps.

    C. aspirators.

    D. all of the above.

_____ **30.** A mechanical suction device:

    A. should be used until the patient arrives at a medical facility.

    B. usually has two different tips.

    C. is used in the same way for all nonbreathing patients.

    D. all of the above.

_____ **31.** Signs of inadequate breathing include:

    A. wheezing or gurgling.

    B. pale or blue skin.

    C. rapid or gasping respirations.

    D. all of the above.

_____ **32.** Respiratory arrest can be caused by:

    A. poisoning.

    B. drug overdose.

    C. severe loss of blood.

    D. all of the above.

_____ **33.** The recovery position may help keep the airway open:

    A. if the patient has not suffered trauma.

    B. by allowing secretions to drain out of the mouth.

    C. because gravity will help keep the patient's tongue and lower jaw from blocking the airway.

    D. all of the above.

_____ **34.** An oral airway:

    A. should not be used in any unconscious patient.

    B. can serve as the pathway through which you can suction a patient.

    C. cannot be used with mechanical breathing devices.

    D. all of the above.

_____ **35.** Rescue breathing for adult patients:

    A. uses a rate of 10 to 12 breaths a minute.

    B. may involve a mouth-to-mask device or a barrier device.

    C. may be performed without any equipment.

    D. all of the above.

_____ **36.** Mouth-to-mask rescue breathing allows the rescuer to:

    A. add the use of supplemental oxygen.

    B. perform rescue breathing without mouth-to-mouth contact.

    C. reduce his or her risk of transmitting infectious diseases.

    D. all of the above.

_____ **37.** To perform mouth-to-mask rescue breathing:

    A. follow steps similar to those used for mouth-to-mouth rescue breathing.

    B. you need two rescuers.

    C. the rescuer must have supplemental oxygen.

    D. all of the above.

_____ **38.** Mouth-to-barrier rescue breathing:

    A. provides a barrier between patient and rescuer.

    B. requires an additional device.

    C. provides variable degrees of infection control.

    D. all of the above.

_____ **39.** Mild and severe obstruction of the respiratory passages:
   A. may be caused by food, vomitus, or objects.
   B. cannot cause unconsciousness.
   C. require the Heimlich maneuver.
   D. all of the above.

_____ **40.** A series of manual thrusts to the abdomen:
   A. may relieve upper airway obstruction.
   B. is called the xiphoid process.
   C. should be delivered to a patient with partial airway obstruction.
   D. all of the above.

Fill-in-the-Blanks

Read each item carefully, then complete the statement by filling in the missing word(s).

1. Two types of suction devices are _____ and _____.

2. If a patient is breathing adequately, you can keep the airway open by placing the patient in the _____ position.

3. The major signs of respiratory arrest are no chest movement, no breath sounds, no air movement, and _____.

4. The most critical sign of inadequate breathing is _____.

5. To check if a person is _____ adequately, you should place the side of your face to the patient's nose and mouth and watch the patient's chest.

True/False

For each statement, write the letter "T" if you believe it to be more true than false, or write the letter "F" if you believe it to be more false than true.

_____ **1.** Brain cells are the most sensitive cells in the human body.

_____ **2.** Without oxygen, the brain will die in 4 to 6 minutes.

_____ **3.** If a foreign object completely blocks the airway, a patient will lose consciousness in 3 to 4 minutes.

_____ **4.** If the Heimlich maneuver is successful in removing a foreign object from a person's airway, medical care is considered complete.

_____ **5.** In an unconscious victim, the head tilt–chin lift or jaw-thrust techniques are effective in opening an airway obstructed by a foreign object.

_____ **6.** If a person is coughing or gagging, you can assume the airway is only partially obstructed.

_____ **7.** Coughing is the most effective way for a person to bring up a foreign object partially blocking the airway.

_____ **8.** Air that cannot be exhaled but that remains in the lungs can pop an object out when the air is compressed by properly administered abdominal thrusts.

_____ **9.** A stoma is an opening in the neck.

_____ **10.** If a patient's chest rises during mouth-to-stoma breathing, you should seal the mouth and nose with one hand.

_____ 11. A stoma may have to be cleared of mucus before mouth-to-stoma breathing is begun.

_____ 12. The patient's airway is the pipeline that transports carbon dioxide from the lungs.

_____ 13. Always insert the manual suction device just beyond where you can see.

_____ 14. Suctioning the airway is a lifesaving technique.

_____ 15. Unconscious patients will not be able to keep their airways open.

_____ 16. Usually a patient will tolerate a nasal airway better than an oral airway.

_____ 17. A normal breathing rate in an adult is 12 to 20 breaths per minute.

_____ 18. A mouth-to-mask ventilator device consists of a mask that fits your mouth and a mouthpiece.

_____ 19. Mouth-to-mouth rescue breathing should be your first method of delivering rescue breaths.

_____ 20. The recovery position helps to maintain an open airway in an unconscious patient.

_____ 21. The artificial circulation of the blood and movement of air into and out of the lungs in a pulseless, nonbreathing person is called cardiopulmonary resuscitation (CPR).

_____ 22. The lower jaw is called the mandible.

_____ 23. Strong muscles are an important part of healthy lungs.

_____ 24. Children and infants are less likely than adults to have their airways blocked by their tongues.

_____ 25. Key words in caring for a patient's airway are "check" and "correct."

_____ 26. The decision to use the head tilt–chin lift technique or the jaw-thrust technique should be made after determining the type of blockage found in the patient's airway.

_____ 27. Use of the head tilt–chin lift technique on a patient who has neck injuries may cause further damage.

_____ 28. The jaw-thrust maneuver should never be attempted on a patient who may have injuries to the neck.

_____ 29. After a patient's airway has been opened with the head tilt–chin lift or the jaw-thrust technique, the next step is to check for blockage of the airway.

_____ 30. The recovery position can be used to keep the airway open once a patient is breathing adequately.

_____ 31. If an unconscious patient is breathing adequately, the airway can be kept open with the use of an oral or nasal airway.

_____ 32. Before insertion of an oral airway, the proper size must be determined by measuring from the patient's earlobe to the corner of the mouth.

_____ 33. An oral airway is used to open the patient's airway.

_____ 34. Nasal airways can be used in both conscious and unconscious patients.

_____ 35. In cases of severe head trauma, a nasal airway may cause further brain damage.

_____ 36. The proper size nasal airway is determined by measuring from the tip of the patient's nose to the bottom of the ear.

_____ 37. Adequate breathing in a patient can be determined by looking, listening, and feeling.

_____ 38. If no signs of breathing are detected by the look, listen, and feel test, medical personnel should begin rescue breathing.

_____ 39. The first step in the airway assessment is to check the mouth for secretions, vomitus, or solid objects that may cause blockage.

_____ 40. External cardiac compressions are usually required when rescue breathing is necessary.

_____ 41. Mouth-to-mouth rescue breathing puts the rescuer at higher risk of contracting disease.

_____ 42. A child should receive 1 minute of rescue breathing before a single rescuer leaves to call for additional help.

_____ 43. In performing rescue breathing for an infant, you must extend the head back as far as possible.

_____ 44. Rescue breathing for children is done at a slightly slower rate than for adults.

_____ 45. Rescue breathing for infants does not use the look, listen, and feel sequence.

_____ 46. The nose does not need to be pinched shut when rescue breathing is being administered to an infant.

_____ 47. The most common foreign object that causes airway obstruction is food.

_____ 48. A common cause of airway obstruction is the tongue.

_____ 49. If a patient can speak or cough, the airway is only partially obstructed.

_____ **50.** If it has been determined that a patient's airway is partially obstructed, the patient should be instructed not to cough.

_____ **51.** Partial obstruction of an airway can become complete obstruction.

_____ **52.** Treatment of complete airway obstruction should remain the same whether the patient is conscious or unconscious.

_____ **53.** Chest thrusts may be the appropriate treatment for airway obstruction in some cases.

_____ **54.** Talking to the patient is an important step in the sequence of assisting a patient with an airway obstruction.

_____ **55.** Crying in an infant is an indication that there is no severe airway obstruction.

_____ **56.** Airway obstruction in a conscious infant may require a combination of back slaps and chest thrusts.

Short Answer

Write a brief response to each of the following questions.

1. List at least three special respiratory considerations for infants and children.

_____

_____

_____

2. List at least three things that may block a person's airway.

_____

_____

_____

3. Name the two primary purposes of an oral airway.

_____

_____

_____

4. List the steps involved in inserting an oral airway.

_____

_____

_____

5. List the steps involved in inserting a nasal airway.

_____

_____

_____

6. List the steps involved in ventilating a patient with a mouth-to-mask device.

_____

_____

_____

7. Name two signs of inadequate breathing.

_____

_____

_____

8. Name two types of airway obstructions.

_____

_____

_____

9. Describe how to place a patient in the recovery position.

_____

_____

_____

Word Fun

The following crossword puzzle is an activity provided to reinforce correct spelling and understanding of terminology associated with emergency care and the first responder. Use the clues in the column to complete the puzzle.

Across

2. Posterior part of the mouth
3. Lower jaw
6. Air sacs
8. Posterior part of the nose
10. Food tube
11. Voice box

Down

1. Very small blood vessels
4. Windpipe
5. Two large tubes that divide the airway
7. Organs located on either side of the heart
9. Keeps cells alive

Labeling

Label the following diagrams with the correct terms.

1. Label the parts of the respiratory system.

A. _____

B. _____

C. _____

D. _____

E. _____

F. _____

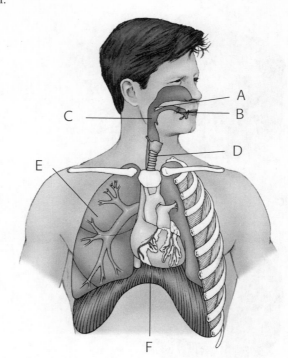

2. Label these airway management devices.

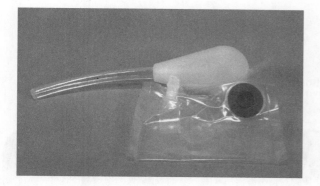

A. _____

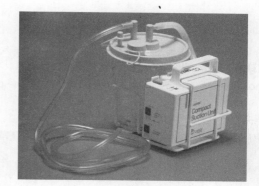

B. _____

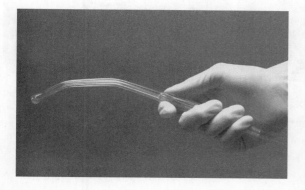

C. _____

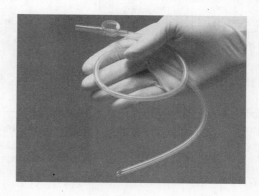

D. _____

3. Label these common causes of airway obstruction.

A

Obstruction

B

Obstruction

C

Obstruction

D

Obstruction

A. _____

B. _____

C. _____

D. _____

Skill Drills

Test your knowledge by filling in the correct words in the photo captions.

A. Inserting an Oral Airway

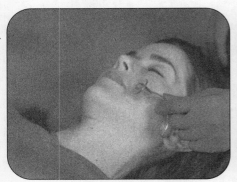 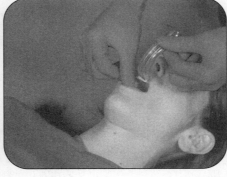 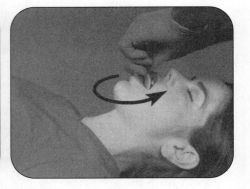

1. Size the airway by measuring from the patient's _____ to the corner of the mouth.

2. Insert the _____ upside down along the roof of the patient's mouth until you feel resistance.

3. Rotate the airway _____ until the flange comes to rest on the patient's lips or teeth.

B. Inserting a Nasal Airway

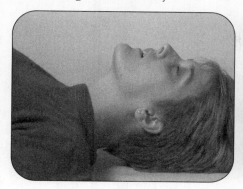 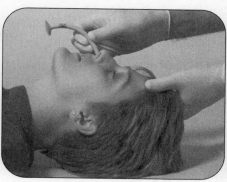 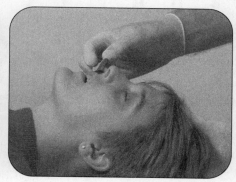

1. Size the _____ by measuring from the tip of the patient's nose to the patient's earlobe.

2. Insert the lubricated airway into the _____ nostril.

3. Advance the airway until the flange rests against the _____.

You Make the Call
The following scenario provides an opportunity to explore the concerns associated with patient management. Read the scenario, then describe the best way to handle the situation.

You are called to a scene where an unconscious 18-year-old has choked on a piece of food and has a severe airway obstruction. You treat this patient by performing CPR. What should you have done differently if this patient had been conscious when you arrived?

CHAPTER

7 Patient Assessment

Matching

Match each of the items in the left column to the appropriate description in the right column.

_____ **1.** Carotid   **A.** Weak pulse

_____ **2.** Thready   **B.** Wrist pulse

_____ **3.** Posterior tibial   **C.** Ankle pulse

_____ **4.** Bounding   **D.** Strong pulse

_____ **5.** Radial   **E.** Neck pulse

_____ **6.** Brachial   **F.** Arm pulse

Multiple Choice

Read each item carefully, then select the best response.

_____ **1.** When assessing for scene safety, you should scan for:

     A. the number of injured patients.

     B. your own safety.

     C. presence of hazards.

     D. all of the above.

_____ **2.** With patients appearing to be unconscious, you should:

     A. shout at them until they respond.

     B. shake them vigorously until they respond.

     C. call to them in a loud tone, and if you receive no response, gently touch or shake their shoulder.

     D. begin CPR immediately.

_____ **3.** If you cannot find a pulse within 5 to 10 seconds, you should:

     A. try another location.

     B. ask your partner to check.

     C. begin CPR.

     D. check the patient's color; if it is good, assume there is a pulse.

_____   **4.** Once an airway is open, you should do all of the following EXCEPT:

     A. immediately begin rescue breathing.

     B. clear the airway if necessary.

     C. insert an airway adjunct if necessary.

     D. check the airway for foreign bodies.

_____   **5.** When assessing respiration, you should:

     A. determine rate and quality of respiration.

     B. determine rate by checking inhalation for 30 seconds.

     C. determine quality by placing your hand over the patient's face.

     D. tell the patient you are counting respirations and to breathe normally.

_____   **6.** Capillary refill is:

     A. tested on the patient's face.

     B. not present in children.

     C. always accurate if done correctly.

     D. the ability of the circulatory system to return blood to the capillary vessels after the blood has been squeezed out.

_____   **7.** The normal adult heart rate is _____ beats per minute.

     A. 40 to 60

     B. 60 to 100

     C. 100 to 120

     D. 120 to 180

_____   **8.** The normal pulse rate for children is _____ beats per minute.

     A. 30 to 50

     B. 50 to 70

     C. 70 to 150

     D. 150 to 200

_____   **9.** During the physical examination, you should try to avoid moving which of the following parts of the body, especially in an unresponsive or injured patient?

     A. legs.

     B. arms.

     C. neck.

     D. pelvis.

_____   **10.** What is the proper order of steps in examining the extremities?

     A. Assess the circulatory status, observe the extremities, check for movement and sensation, and examine for tenderness.

     B. Assess the circulatory status, check for movement, observe the extremities, examine for tenderness, and check for sensation.

     C. Observe the extremities, examine for tenderness, check for movement and sensation, and assess the circulatory status.

     D. Observe the extremities, assess the circulatory status, check for sensation, examine for tenderness, and check for movement.

_____   **11.** The initial patient assessment includes:

     A. a medical history.

     B. a SAMPLE history.

     C. a physical examination.

     D. forming a general impression.

_____ **12.** The initial patient assessment includes:
  A. assessing the patient's responsiveness.
  B. acknowledging the patient's primary complaint.
  C. checking ABCs.
  D. all of the above.

_____ **13.** The AVPU scale is a four-level scale used for:
  A. communicating the patient's vital signs to the hospital.
  B. describing a patient's level of consciousness.
  C. determining how rapidly you will need to transport the patient.
  D. all of the above.

_____ **14.** To check breathing:
  A. see if the chest rises and falls with each breath.
  B. place the side of your face next to the patient's nose and mouth.
  C. listen for air exchange.
  D. all of the above.

_____ **15.** To check for the brachial pulse:
  A. use the index and middle fingers.
  B. you need to remove the patient's shoes.
  C. you must find the patient's larynx.
  D. all of the above.

_____ **16.** The brachial pulse:
  A. is used for infants.
  B. is found on the inside of the arm.
  C. should be checked for 5 to 10 seconds.
  D. all of the above.

_____ **17.** The carotid pulse is located on the:
  A. neck.
  B. ankle.
  C. wrist.
  D. foot.

_____ **18.** The first step used to control severe bleeding is to:
  A. elevate the body part.
  B. bandage the wound.
  C. apply direct pressure.
  D. apply pressure to a pressure point.

_____ **19.** Your dispatcher should have obtained information about the:
  A. safety level of the scene.
  B. number of people involved in the incident.
  C. location of the incident.
  D. all of the above.

_____ **20.** If you can determine the mechanism of injury, you can sometimes:
  A. eliminate the need for a complete head-to-toe examination.
  B. predict the patient's injuries.
  C. help law enforcement officers deal with vehicle removal.
  D. all of the above.

_____ **21.** If your patient was in an automobile accident and you notice that the windshield is broken, you should pay particular attention to the possibility of:

    A. head and spine injuries.

    B. inclement weather.

    C. chest injuries.

    D. all of the above.

_____ **22.** Yellowish skin may indicate:

    A. shock.

    B. fever or sunburn.

    C. lack of oxygen.

    D. liver problems.

_____ **23.** A blue skin tone often indicates:

    A. shock.

    B. fever or sunburn.

    C. lack of oxygen.

    D. liver problems.

_____ **24.** Flushed reddish skin often indicates:

    A. shock.

    B. fever or sunburn.

    C. lack of oxygen.

    D. liver problems.

_____ **25.** Pale skin often indicates:

    A. shock.

    B. fever or sunburn.

    C. lack of oxygen.

    D. liver problems.

_____ **26.** When updating responding EMS units, you should include which of the following in your report?

    A. Age and sex of the patient

    B. The chief complaint

    C. Status of the airway

    D. All of the above

_____ **27.** A normal resting respiratory rate in an adult is between _____ breaths per minute.

    A. 8 and10

    B. 12 and 20

    C. 20 and 25

    D. none of the above

_____ **28.** When you check a patient's respiration rate:

    A. count one complete cycle of inhaling and exhaling.

    B. count for one minute.

    C. don't tell the patient you are counting respirations.

    D. all of the above.

_____ **29.** The capillary refill test should not be used in a cold environment because:

    A. it can delay transport.

    B. there is a higher risk of frostbite.

    C. refill will be delayed.

    D. all of the above.

_____ **30.** The patient's skin condition should be checked for:

    A. color.

    B. temperature.

    C. moisture.

    D. all of the above.

_____ **31.** Unequal pupils may be an indication of:

    A. stroke.

    B. cardiac arrest.

    C. diabetes.

    D. all of the above.

_____ **32.** Dilated pupils may be an indication of:

    A. cardiac arrest.

    B. the use of barbiturates.

    C. head injuries.

    D. all of the above.

_____ **33.** Pupils that remain constricted may be an indication of:

    A. cardiac arrest or head injury.

    B. stroke or brain damage.

    C. use of narcotics or central nervous system disease.

    D. none of the above.

_____ **34.** All of the following are vital signs EXCEPT:

    A. capillary refill.

    B. pulse.

    C. respiration rate.

    D. body temperature.

_____ **35.** A neck breather is a person who:

    A. has distended carotid veins upon exertion.

    B. has wheezing sounds when breathing.

    C. has a stoma.

    D. none of the above.

_____ **36.** Flail chest can result from:

    A. inadequate oxygen supply.

    B. multiple rib fractures.

    C. internal bleeding.

    D. all of the above.

_____ **37.** Examination of the extremities may include:

    A. asking the patient to move the extremity.

    B. touching the patient's bare skin.

    C. looking for bleeding.

    D. all of the above.

_____ **38.** Your patient is conscious, and you detect no radial pulse. The patient may:

    A. be in shock.

    B. have blood vessel damage.

    C. have an ulnar pulse.

    D. all of the above.

_____ **39.** The patient assessment sequence should be completed in about _____ minute(s).
   A. 1
   B. 5
   C. 2
   D. 10

_____ **40.** When dealing with a patient who has suffered from an illness, you should:
   A. use the same patient assessment sequence you use for trauma patients.
   B. obtain the patient's medical history before performing the head-to-toe examination.
   C. skip the scene size-up.
   D. not perform an ongoing assessment.

Fill-in-the-Blanks

Read each item carefully, then complete the statement by filling in the missing word(s).

1. The first thing you should do when determining a patient's responsiveness is to _____.

2. When there is no response to verbal or painful stimuli, a patient's condition is described as _____.

3. The method for opening the airway of an unresponsive patient is the _____.

4. If a patient is responsive, assess the _____ and _____ of the patient's breathing.

5. The third part of the initial assessment is to check the _____.

6. Anything a patient tells you about his or her condition is known as a/an _____.

7. Anything you see or feel concerning the patient's condition is known as a/an _____.

8. A slow pulse may indicate _____.

9. A fast pulse may indicate _____.

10. To assess a pulse, you should determine _____, _____, and _____.

11. Normal body temperature is _____.

12. The first step of the physical exam is to determine vital signs, which consist of _____, _____, and _____.

13. Initial assessment consists of the following six steps. Arrange them in the proper order.

_____ **A.** Assess the patient's breathing.
_____ **B.** Assess the patient's responsiveness and stabilize the spine if necessary.
_____ **C.** Form a general impression of the patient.
_____ **D.** Assess the patient's circulation, including the presence of severe bleeding.
_____ **E.** Acknowledge the patient's chief complaint.
_____ **F.** Assess the patient's airway.
_____ **G.** Update responding EMS units.

True/False

For each statement, write the letter "T" if you believe it to be more true than false, or write the letter "F" if you believe it to be more false than true.

_____ **1.** Your scene size-up begins before you arrive at the emergency scene.

_____ **2.** During the scene size-up, you should try to anticipate what equipment you need to ensure good body substance isolation.

_____ **3.** Hazards on the scene may be visible or invisible.

_____ **4.** Upon arriving at the scene, you should park your vehicle to block all traffic.

_____ **5.** The purpose of determining the mechanism of injury is to help predict patient injury.

_____ **6.** The mechanism of injury can be useful in determining all injuries that are present.

_____ **7.** AVPU is a scale used to determine level of consciousness.

_____ **8.** If patients are unconscious, it is not necessary to speak with them because they cannot hear anyway.

_____ **9.** When determining level of consciousness in infants or children, it is best to assess how they interact with their caregivers.

_____ **10.** You should always check the patient's pulse by using your thumb or index finger.

_____ **11.** The injury most readily apparent to the patient is usually the most severe injury.

_____ **12.** The head-to-toe physical exam will help you get a better picture of the patient's overall condition.

_____ **13.** You should perform the patient assessment before asking family or bystanders for information.

_____ **14.** The initial patient assessment is performed immediately after the scene size-up.

_____ **15.** You should take a patient's medical history before you update responding EMS units.

_____ **16.** First impressions of a patient's condition are often misleading and should therefore not be considered valuable information.

_____ **17.** One effective tool for determining a patient's responsiveness is to introduce yourself to the patient.

_____ **18.** The initial patient assessment is your first opportunity to check the patient's ABCs.

_____ **19.** Introducing yourself to an unconscious patient is often considered disrespectful by bystanders.

_____ **20.** If a patient is not responsive to verbal stimuli, you must assume that the airway is closed.

_____ **21.** If a patient has suffered trauma and is unconscious, use the head tilt-chin lift method to open the airway.

_____ **22.** If an unconscious patient has a medical problem and has not suffered trauma, use the head tilt-chin lift method to open the airway.

_____ **23.** If an adult patient is conscious, you should measure the radial pulse.

_____ **24.** If an adult patient is unconscious, you should measure the carotid pulse.

_____ **25.** The patient's chief complaint may be misleading but should be acknowledged anyway.

_____ **26.** Downed electrical wires can be assumed safe if the electric company is on the scene when you arrive.

_____ **27.** The head-to-toe physical examination is done to assess life-threatening conditions.

_____ **28.** A sign is something about the patient you can see or feel for yourself.

_____ **29.** A symptom is something the patient tells you about his or her condition.

_____ **30.** The respiratory rate is the speed at which the patient is breathing.

_____ **31.** The pulse indicates the speed and force with which the heart is beating.

_____ **32.** The pulse can be felt anywhere on the body where an artery passes over a hard structure such as a bone.

_____ **33.** The brachial pulse is used to assess the circulatory status of a leg.

_____ **34.** A weak pulse is often called a threatened pulse.

_____ **35.** A strong pulse is often called a bounding pulse.

_____ **36.** The normal reaction of a pupil to light is to expand.

_____ **37.** Swollen (distended) neck veins are usually an indication of heart problems.

_____ **38.** If you suspect fractured ribs, you should avoid pushing down on the chest.

_____ **39.** Rigidity is often a sign of abdominal injury.

_____ **40.** If a conscious patient cannot move the foot or toes, the limb is seriously injured or paralyzed.

Short Answer

Write a brief response to each of the following questions.

1. Name the five steps of patient assessment.

_____

_____

_____

2. List three pieces of information a dispatcher should obtain prior to your arrival on the scene.

_____

_____

_____

3. List the five components of scene size-up.

_____

_____

_____

4. List four types of hazards that may be found at any emergency scene.

_____

_____

_____

5. List three signs to look for when determining the mechanism of injury to a patient.

_____

_____

_____

6. What does the acronym AVPU stand for?

_____

_____

_____

7. What is the best way to check an unresponsive patient's breathing?

_____

_____

_____

8. Name at least one condition that could cause a person's skin to turn the following colors:

    A. Pale

    B. Flushed

    C. Blue

    D. Yellow

_____

_____

_____

9. What does the acronym DOTS stand for?

_____

_____

_____

10. Describe the three pulses you will most often check, where each is located, and when each one should be used.

_____

_____

_____

11. Describe the method for checking capillary refill.

_____

_____

_____

12. What does the acronym SAMPLE stand for?

_____

_____

_____

13. Describe the proper sequence of body areas to check in the physical examination of a patient.

_____

_____

_____

14. List three places to look for skin color changes in patients with deeply pigmented skin.

_____

_____

_____

Word Fun

The following crossword puzzle is an activity provided to reinforce correct spelling and understanding of terminology associated with emergency care and the first responder. Use the clues in the column to complete the puzzle.

Across

3. Abbreviation for body substance isolation
5. _____ pulse, found in the neck
7. Abbreviation for airway, breathing, circulation
10. _____ rate, indicates how fast the patient is breathing
12. Format for obtaining medical history
15. Abbreviation for level of consciousness

Down

1. Initial patient _____
2. Something you observe in a patient
4. _____ of injury
5. Term for blue skin color
6. _____ refill
8. _____ pulse, pulse found in the arm
9. Something the patient describes to you
11. _____ pulse, pulse found in the wrist
13. Scale used to measure level of consciousness
14. Head-to-toe assessment
16. Abbreviation for chief complaint

Labeling

Label the following diagram with the correct terms.

1. Label the type of pupils shown.

A. _____

B. _____

C. _____

A

B

C

You Make the Call

The following scenario provides an opportunity to explore the concerns associated with patient management. Read the scenario, then describe the best way to handle the situation.

You are dispatched to a residence for an 83-year-old woman who is reportedly unconscious. As you arrive, the woman's husband tells you he thinks she has had a stroke. What should you do?

CHAPTER

8 Communications and Documentation

Matching

Match each of the items in the left column to the appropriate description in the right column.

_____ **1.** Base station	**A.** Communications systems used to send voice or text messages to radio receivers
_____ **2.** Repeater	**B.** Radio system that automatically transmits a radio signal on a different frequency
_____ **3.** Telemetry	
_____ **4.** Mobile data terminal	**C.** Process by which electronic signals are transmitted and received by radio or telephone
_____ **5.** Paging systems	**D.** Vehicle computer terminal that sends and receives data through radio communication
	E. Powerful two-way radio permanently mounted in a communications center

Multiple Choice

Read each item carefully, then select the best response.

_____ **1.** After you have turned over the care of the patient to other EMS providers, you need to report this status to:

    A. your supervisor.

    B. your partner.

    C. the communications center.

    D. medical dispatch at the hospital.

_____ **2.** When EMTs or paramedics arrive, it is important to provide them with the:

    A. age and sex of the patient.

    B. hand-off report.

    C. complete diagnosis.

    D. care you have provided.

_____ **3.** Which one of the following is not part of the hand-off report?

    A. Postrun activity

    B. History of the incident

    C. Intervention provided

    D. Level of responsiveness

_____ **4.** In effective communication, the receiver needs to communicate that the message has been received and understood. This is called:

    A. formal communication.

    B. informal communication.

    C. nonverbal communication.

    D. feedback.

_____ **5.** Don't rush when speaking to the patient. By slowing down and speaking distinctly, you can avoid:

    A. long explanations.

    B. indirect communication.

    C. having to repeat questions or explanations.

    D. writing things down.

_____ **6.** Because body language is an important part of communication, you should try to avoid:

    A. kneeling next to a patient on the ground.

    B. standing relatively near to the patient.

    C. crossing your arms in front of your chest.

    D. making eye contact.

_____ **7.** First responders should speak to and treat all patients as if they were:

    A. seriously ill or injured.

    B. family members.

    C. non-English speakers.

    D. potentially dangerous.

_____ **8.** Patients who are temporarily deaf will not usually:

    A. be cooperative.

    B. be able to read lips.

    C. sit still or settle down.

    D. communicate through written language.

_____ **9.** If the deaf patient is with a young hearing child, resist:

    A. the urge to use the child as an interpreter.

    B. speaking to the child in front of the parent.

    C. using sign language.

    D. giving treatment with the child present.

_____ **10.** Radio-use protocols are important; they provide a standard format that:

    A. reduces liability.

    B. guarantees quality communication.

    C. reduces miscommunication.

    D. documents each call.

Fill-in-the-Blanks

Read each item carefully, then complete the statement by filling in the missing word(s).

1. A fax machine is a device used to send or receive _____ or _____ text documents or images over a telephone or radio system.

2. A two-way radio mounted in a vehicle is a/an _____ radio.

3. For effective communication, first responders should always designate _____ provider(s) to talk with the patient.

4. Radio communications are regulated by the FCC, which stands for _____.

5. When communicating with non-English speakers, you may be able to adapt some techniques generally used to communicate with _____ patients.

True/False

For each statement, write the letter "T" if you believe it to be more true than false, or write the letter "F" if you believe it to be more false than true.

_____ 1. In addition to radio and oral communications, first responders must have excellent person-to-person communication skills.

_____ 2. Along with your radio report and oral report, you must also complete a formal hand-off report for other EMS professionals at the scene.

_____ 3. You should familiarize yourself with one communication method, such as two-way radio communications, mobile radios, or handheld portable radios.

_____ 4. Written documentation is important in the event of a court case because it will prevent you from being sued.

_____ 5. Certain infectious diseases are reportable. It is important that you learn how this process is handled in your agency and what responsibilities you have in these situations.

_____ 6. Disruptive behavior can present a danger to the patient and others and can cause delays in treatment.

_____ 7. When dealing with young children, it is not necessary to tell them the truth about their injury or illness.

_____ 8. If you encounter a deaf patient with whom you cannot communicate, you should rely on writing and gestures to communicate.

_____ 9. When communicating with developmentally disabled patients, you should avoid touching the patient if touching is unnecessary.

_____ 10. When communicating with children, you should speak in a professional manner.

Short Answer

Write a brief response to each of the following questions.

1. What is the difference between a base station and a mobile radio?

_____

_____

_____

2. What are the two categories of communications systems?

_____

_____

_____

3. A portable radio is designed to be carried by rescuers. What do these self-contained units incorporate?

_____

_____

_____

4. List the three types of data systems used by first responders.

_____

_____

_____

5. How is telemetry used by advanced life support providers?

_____

_____

_____

6. Why is it important to introduce yourself by name and title?

_____

_____

_____

7. Why is it important to avoid using technical medical terms when talking to a patient?

_____

_____

_____

You Make the Call

The following scenario provides an opportunity to explore the concerns associated with patient management. Read the scenario, then describe the best way to handle the situation.

Additional EMS personnel and paramedics arrive on the scene to care for the patient after you have completed your assessment. You need to provide them with a hand-off report. What should it include?

CHAPTER

9 Professional Rescuer CPR

Matching
Match each of the items in the left column to the appropriate description in the right column.

_____ **1.** Early defibrillation

_____ **2.** Complications of CPR

_____ **3.** 2

_____ **4.** 100

_____ **5.** Causes of cardiac arrest

_____ **6.** Establish responsiveness

_____ **7.** 4

_____ **8.** Brachial artery

_____ **9.** Infant

_____ **10.** Child

A. Heart attack, stroke, respiratory arrest, medical emergencies, drowning, suffocation, trauma, and shock

B. Number of major arteries

C. Third link in the Cardiac Chain of Survival

D. Person under 1 year of age

E. Person between 1 year of age and the onset of puberty

F. First step in one-rescuer adult CPR

G. Rate per minute for external chest compressions

H. Site where infant pulse is checked

 I. Broken ribs, gastric distention, and regurgitation

J. Number of minutes in five cycles of adult CPR

Multiple Choice
Read each item carefully, then select the best response.

_____ **1.** A woman who collapses on the beach is unresponsive and is not breathing when you arrive. She has no pulse and appears dead. You should:

A. begin CPR.

B. perform a primary survey.

C. search her purse for identification.

D. check her arms and legs for sting marks.

_____ **2.** Which of the following are components of blood?

A. Plasma

B. Platelets

C. Red and white blood cells

D. All of the above

_____ **3.** What part of your hand should you place on an adult's sternum to deliver chest compressions?
A. Thumb
B. First three fingers
C. Heel of the hand
D. Back of the hand in a fisted position

_____ **4.** Signs of cardiac arrest in children are _____ those of an adult.
A. completely different from
B. the same as
C. more easily observed than
D. less easily observed than

_____ **5.** If you are alone with an adult patient who needs CPR, you should:
A. perform CPR for 1 minute before activating the EMS system.
B. perform CPR for 3 minutes before activating the EMS system.
C. perform CPR for 5 minutes before activating the EMS system.
D. activate the EMS system before beginning CPR.

_____ **6.** What is the ratio of chest compressions to ventilations in adult one-rescuer CPR?
A. 5 to 2
B. 10 to 2
C. 15 to 2
D. 30 to 2

_____ **7.** What is the ratio of chest compressions to ventilations in adult two-rescuer CPR?
A. 5 to 2
B. 10 to 2
C. 15 to 2
D. 30 to 2

_____ **8.** In adult one-rescuer CPR, each set of chest compressions should be delivered within _____ seconds.
A. 10
B. 15
C. 20
D. 30

_____ **9.** After giving chest compressions and ventilations for 2 minutes, you should:
A. turn the patient.
B. check the carotid pulse.
C. check the eyes.
D. stop CPR to see if the patient has responded.

_____ **10.** You should use _____ finger(s) to deliver chest compressions to an infant.
A. 1
B. 2
C. 3
D. 4

_____ **11.** An alternative method for doing chest compressions on an infant is:
A. three-finger compressions.
B. two-finger/encircling hands technique.
C. one-thumb compression technique.
D. two-thumb/encircling hands technique.

_____ **12.** An infant's chest should be compressed:

    A. 0 to 1 inches.

    B. 1 to 1½ inches.

    C. 1½ to 2 inches.

    D. ½ to ⅓ the depth of the chest.

_____ **13.** A child's chest should be compressed:

    A. 0 to 1 inches.

    B. 1 to 1½ inches.

    C. 1½ to 2 inches.

    D. ½ to ⅓ the depth of the chest.

_____ **14.** In two-rescuer CPR, the ratio of chest compressions to ventilations for both infants and children should be:

    A. 5 to 1.

    B. 5 to 2.

    C. 10 to 1.

    D. 15 to 2.

_____ **15.** You should place an infant in what position to deliver effective CPR?

    A. Lying on a firm surface

    B. Lying on pillows

    C. Lying in your arms

    D. Upright in your arms

_____ **16.** If you hear a cracking sound as you are performing CPR, you should:

    A. stop CPR and wait for additional help to arrive.

    B. stop CPR until you can determine whether the patient's ribs are broken.

    C. continue CPR but check and/or adjust the position of your hands.

    D. continue CPR without stopping because ribs sometimes break even when CPR is performed properly.

_____ **17.** You can relieve gastric distention in a patient by:

    A. delivering back blows.

    B. placing the patient in a sitting position to encourage burping.

    C. stopping CPR to allow the air to be released on its own.

    D. turning the patient on one side and pressing the upper abdomen.

_____ **18.** Two rescuers find an unconscious woman lying on the ground next to her automobile. There are no bystanders or other rescue personnel at the scene. It would be most appropriate for:

    A. one rescuer to activate the EMS system but only if the patient needs CPR.

    B. one rescuer to activate the EMS system while the other examines the patient and begins CPR, if necessary.

    C. both rescuers to perform two-rescuer CPR for several minutes and activate the EMS system only if the patient does not respond.

    D. both rescuers to perform two-rescuer CPR for 1 minute and then switch to one-rescuer CPR while the second rescuer activates the EMS system.

_____ **19.** What is the ratio of chest compressions to ventilations for infants and children in two-rescuer CPR?

    A. 5 to 1

    B. 5 to 2

    C. 10 to 1

    D. 15 to 2

_____ **20.** During two-rescuer CPR, _____ compressions per minute should be delivered to a patient.

    A. 50 to 60

    B. 60 to 70

    C. 70 to 80

    D. 80 to 100

_____ **21.** When performing rescue breathing on an adult patient, each rescue breath should be given over a period of _____ second(s).

    A. 1

    B. 1½

    C. 2

    D. 3

_____ **22.** An automated external defibrillator (AED) will do all of the following EXCEPT:

    A. analyze the patient's heart rhythm.

    B. deliver a shock to the patient.

    C. check the patient's pulse.

    D. recommend a shock.

_____ **23.** You should discontinue CPR when:

    A. there are reliable criteria for death.

    B. you are too exhausted to continue.

    C. a physician assumes responsibility for the patient.

    D. all of the above.

_____ **24.** Chest compression:

    A. mimics the squeezing and relaxation cycles of a normal heart.

    B. should be used if there is no carotid pulse.

    C. requires a firm horizontal surface.

    D. all of the above.

_____ **25.** The three parts of CPR can be remembered with the letters:

    A. SAMPLE.

    B. ABC.

    C. AVPU.

    D. DNR.

_____ **26.** Which is not a link in the American Heart Association's Chain of Survival?

    A. Early CPR

    B. Early access to EMS system

    C. Early diagnosis of cause

    D. Early advanced care by paramedics and hospital personnel

_____ **27.** Signs of effective CPR include which of the following?

    A. Patient's skin color improves

    B. Patient gasps

    C. Carotid pulse is present during chest compression

    D. All of the above

_____ **28.** Gastric distention:

    A. may cause vomiting.

    B. requires a change in CPR technique.

    C. may signal a partially obstructed airway.

    D. all of the above.

_____ **29.** Cardiac arrest means that:

    A. the heart suddenly stops functioning.

    B. oxygen is not getting to the body's organs.

    C. a patient is unconscious and not breathing.

    D. all of the above.

_____ **30.** CPR consists of three major components:

    A. assessment, blood pressure, and compressions.

    B. airway, breathing, and circulation.

    C. acknowledgment, behavior, and care.

    D. administration, best treatment, and conclusion.

_____ **31.** The exchange of air between the lungs and the air of the environment is:

    A. ventilation.

    B. defibrillation.

    C. compression.

    D. all of the above.

Fill-in-the-Blanks

Read each item carefully, then complete the statement by filling in the missing word(s).

1. An infant should receive _____ chest compressions per minute during CPR.

2. An infant's pulse should be checked at the _____ artery.

3. Mark a "V" in the blanks for tasks that should be performed by the ventilator in two-rescuer CPR and a "C" for tasks that should be performed by the compressor.

_____ **A.** Check the carotid pulse periodically during CPR.

_____ **B.** Open the patient's airway.

_____ **C.** Count aloud during CPR.

_____ **D.** Check for breathing.

_____ **E.** Check the pulse when a switch is made.

_____ **F.** Decide when a switch should be made.

4. The circulatory system acts like a city water system with a/an _____ and a network of pipes.

5. The heart acts as a large pump and is made up of _____ chambers.

6. The left side of the heart receives blood from the _____.

True/False

For each statement, write the letter "T" if you believe it to be more true than false, or write the letter "F" if you believe it to be more false than true.

_____ **1.** "Phone first" means you should call for help before starting CPR on an adult patient if you are by yourself.

_____ **2.** If a valid DNR (do not resuscitate) order is present, you can withhold CPR.

_____ **3.** You should practice delivering chest compressions on a manikin until you can compress the chest smoothly and rhythmically.

_____ **4.** If you are delivering chest compressions properly, your downward pushes should be smooth and rhythmic.

_____ **5.** By interlocking your fingers during chest compressions, you will avoid digging into (and potentially hurting) the patient with your fingers.

_____ **6.** To be sure you are relaxing chest compressions completely, you should lift your hand off the patient's chest after each compression.

_____ **7.** Relieving gastric distention may cause vomiting.

_____ **8.** Both your fingers and a clean cloth can be used to clear a patient's mouth of vomitus.

_____ **9.** A patient should not be moved or turned simply to clear the mouth of vomitus.

_____ **10.** If a patient regurgitates while you are performing CPR, you must clear away the vomitus before resuming CPR.

_____ **11.** If a patient's heart has stopped, rescue breathing alone will not save the patient.

_____ **12.** When done properly, chest compressions circulate a patient's blood as effectively as the heart.

_____ **13.** An adult heart is about the size of a fist.

_____ **14.** Between chest compressions, the heart relaxes and refills with blood automatically.

_____ **15.** Chest compressions should be done on patients whose hearts have not yet stopped.

_____ **16.** Chest compressions should be done along with rescue breathing for oxygen to travel throughout the body.

_____ **17.** One-rescuer CPR is more effective than two-rescuer CPR.

_____ **18.** Because two-rescuer CPR is less tiring than one-rescuer CPR, rescuers are generally able to perform it for a longer period of time.

_____ **19.** The two rescuers should be on the same side of a patient during two-rescuer CPR.

_____ **20.** In two-rescuer CPR, the compressor should give the ventilator enough time to fully ventilate the patient after each 10th compression.

_____ **21.** In two-rescuer CPR, the ventilator provides the oxygen that the compressor is trying to keep circulating through the patient's body.

_____ **22.** During two-rescuer CPR, if the two rescuers have practiced together before, the compressor may count compressions silently.

_____ **23.** If a patient vomits during CPR, it is unpleasant for the rescuer, but it creates no danger to the patient.

_____ **24.** Before beginning CPR, rescuers should consider the amount of space needed to administer CPR.

_____ **25.** A first responder needs to know about any living wills or advance directives a patient may have before starting CPR.

_____ **26.** To perform chest compressions effectively, you should straddle the patient.

_____ **27.** To perform chest compressions effectively, the location of the hands in relation to the sternum is of critical importance.

_____ **28.** When performing chest compressions, improper placement of the rescuer's hands can cause damage to the patient's lungs, ribs, or liver.

_____ **29.** Chest compressions on an adult should be at the rate of 100 compressions per minute.

_____ **30.** Before beginning chest compressions on an infant, rescuers should check for the presence of circulation by feeling for the radial artery on the wrist.

_____ **31.** Chest compressions on an infant require the use of the heel of only one hand.

_____ **32.** An infant can be cradled in the arm of the rescuer during chest compressions.

_____ **33.** Chest compressions on a child may require the use of the heel of only one hand.

_____ **34.** If there are signs of dependent lividity, CPR should not be started.

_____ **35.** In two-rescuer CPR, one rescuer is positioned on one side of the patient and delivers ventilations.

_____ **36.** The sequence of steps for one-person CPR must be different from the sequence for two-person CPR.

_____ **37.** The ratio of chest compressions to ventilations remains the same whether there are one or two rescuers.

_____ **38.** If rescuers are available, two-person CPR is always more successful than one-person CPR.

_____ **39.** It is possible, and may be necessary, to switch the positions of the rescuers while doing two-person CPR.

_____ **40.** When performing CPR on an infant, the techniques for establishing responsiveness, opening the airway, assessing breathing, checking for circulation, and administering chest compressions will all be different from the techniques used for adults.

_____ **41.** Cardiac arrest may be caused by epilepsy, diabetes, poisoning, or trauma.

_____ **42.** The cause of cardiac arrest should be determined before beginning treatment.

_____ **43.** If a rescuer is alone, he or she should perform one-person CPR for 5 minutes, then leave the patient briefly to call for additional help.

Short Answer

Write a brief response to each of the following questions.

1. If you are using only one hand to deliver chest compressions to a child, what should you do with your other hand?

_____

_____

_____

2. Where along the sternum should you place your fingers to deliver chest compressions to an infant?

_____

_____

_____

3. Name two causes of gastric distention during CPR.

_____

_____

_____

4. Name the four major arteries.

_____

_____

_____

5. What are the four reliable signs of death?

_____

_____

_____

Labeling

Label the following diagram with the correct terms.

1. Label each body part and the pulse located there.

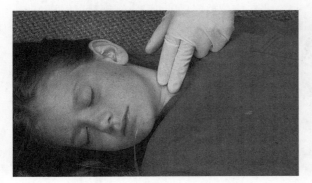

A. _____

B. _____

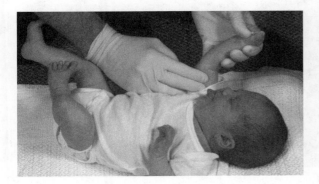

C. _____

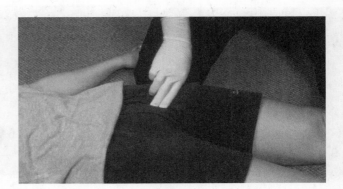

D. _____

Skill Drills

Test your knowledge by filling in the correct words in the photo captions.

A. Performing Chest Compressions

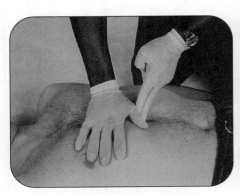

1. Locate the top and bottom of the

_____.

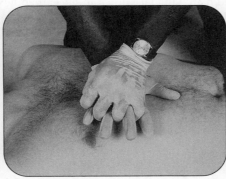

2. Place the heel of your hand in the

_____ of the chest.

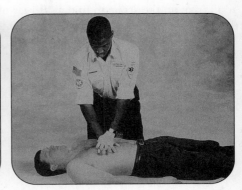

3. Place your other hand on top of your

first hand and _____

your fingers.

B. One-Rescuer Adult CPR

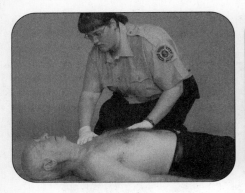

1. Establish _____.

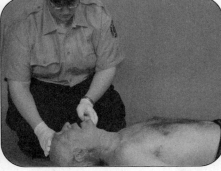

2. Open the _____.

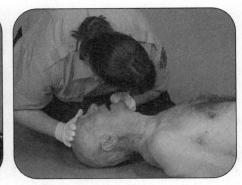

3. Check for _____.

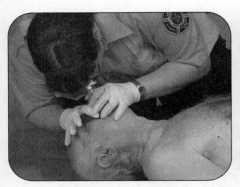

4. Perform _____.

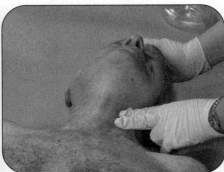

5. Check for _____.

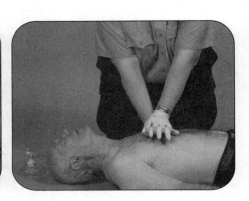

6. Perform _____.

You Make the Call

The following scenario provides an opportunity to explore the concerns associated with patient management. Read the scenario, then describe the best way to handle the situation.

You arrive on the scene to find a 58-year-old man lying face down in his garden next to the tiller he has been operating. He does not respond to you as you approach. In fact, you think he looks dead. What should you do?

CHAPTER

10 Medical Emergencies

Matching

Match each of the items in the left column to the appropriate description in the right column.

_____ **1.** Diabetic coma

_____ **2.** Bronchitis

_____ **3.** Hypothermia

_____ **4.** AVPU scale

_____ **5.** Acute abdomen

_____ **6.** Dyspnea

_____ **7.** Insulin shock

_____ **8.** Heatstroke

_____ **9.** Chronic obstructive pulmonary disease (COPD)

_____ **10.** Angina pectoris

A. Caused by inadequate flow of blood to heart muscle

B. Inflammation of the airways in lungs

C. Caused by chronic bronchial obstruction (emphysema)

D. Difficulty or pain with breathing

E. Sudden onset of abdominal pain caused by disease or trauma

F. Used to assess altered mental status

G. Occurs when a person's body is not able to produce enough energy to keep the body temperature at a satisfactory level

H. Occurs when the body has too much blood sugar and not enough insulin

I. Occurs if the body has enough insulin but not enough blood sugar

J. Occurs when a person has been in a hot environment for a long period of time

Multiple Choice

Read each item carefully, then select the best response.

_____ **1.** An acute abdomen is:

A. irritated or infected.

B. attractive.

C. caused by overeating.

D. large.

_____ **2.** Which of the following heart conditions rarely lasts more than 5 minutes and is usually relieved when the patient takes a nitroglycerin pill?

A. Heart attack

B. Cardiac arrest

C. Angina pectoris

D. Congestive heart failure

_____ **3.** If the heart becomes weak and does not pump properly, the patient will most likely experience:

A. cardiac arrest.

B. crushing chest pain.

C. congestion of blood in the heart, which causes the heart to stop pumping.

D. congestion of the blood vessels of the lungs, which causes breathing difficulties.

_____ **4.** Complete blockage of an artery in the heart by a blood clot or a buildup of fatty deposits will result in:

A. chest pain.

B. heart attack.

C. atherosclerosis.

D. breathing difficulties.

_____ **5.** The first step in caring for a patient who has chest pain should be to:

A. begin CPR.

B. assist the patient in contacting a physician.

C. examine the patient for chest wounds.

D. summon additional help.

_____ **6.** A man who tells you that he feels as if something is sitting on, pressing on, or crushing his chest is most likely having a heart attack or:

A. stroke.

B. cardiac arrest.

C. an angina attack.

D. congestive heart failure.

_____ **7.** If you suspect or cannot tell whether a person is having a heart attack, your first concern should be to:

A. call for additional help.

B. make the person comfortable.

C. place the person on a hard surface.

D. try to relieve the person's emotional distress.

_____ **8.** Your second concern for a patient believed to be having a heart attack should be to:

A. call for additional help.

B. make the person comfortable.

C. place the person on a hard surface.

D. try to relieve the person's emotional distress.

_____ **9.** If a patient having a heart attack goes into cardiac arrest, you should first:

A. begin CPR.

B. give oxygen.

C. try to make the patient comfortable.

D. transport the patient to the hospital.

_____ **10.** The first step in caring for patients who are having difficulty breathing is to:

A. check for airway obstruction.

B. put them in a comfortable position to ease breathing.

C. ask them if they are being treated for a heart condition.

D. ask if they are experiencing chest pain.

_____ **11.** A patient who has dyspnea should always be checked first for:

A. pneumonia.

B. heart attack.

C. angina pectoris.

D. airway obstruction.

_____ **12.** The first priority in treating a stroke patient is to:

    A. give the patient emotional support.

    B. determine if the patient is paralyzed.

    C. maintain the airway and give oxygen, if possible.

    D. arrange for prompt transportation to the hospital.

_____ **13.** The second priority in treating a stroke patient is to:

    A. maintain the airway.

    B. watch for convulsions.

    C. provide emotional support.

    D. arrange for prompt transportation to the hospital.

_____ **14.** The Cincinnati Prehospital Stroke Scale measures which of the following?

    A. Facial droop, arm drift, abnormal speech

    B. Facial balance, arm strength, hearing

    C. All of the above

    D. None of the above

_____ **15.** Insulin is best described as:

    A. a substance similar to sugar.

    B. a chemical that is injected to counteract insulin shock.

    C. a chemical that allows sugar in the blood to be used as fuel in the body's cells.

    D. a diabetic medication for patients who cannot produce sugar in their blood.

_____ **16.** A person with diabetes has abnormally low levels of insulin in the body and, as a result, must:

    A. always wear a medic alert tag.

    B. eat more sugar than most.

    C. avoid eating sugar in any form.

    D. supplement insulin levels with insulin injections or oral medications.

_____ **17.** A person in insulin shock must receive:

    A. CPR.

    B. sugar.

    C. insulin.

    D. oxygen.

_____ **18.** The signs and symptoms of insulin shock should be considered:

    A. similar to those of other types of shock.

    B. more serious than those of diabetic coma.

    C. different from those of other types of shock.

    D. almost impossible to identify unless the person is wearing a medic alert tag.

_____ **19.** The first step in caring for a patient who has just had a seizure should be to:

    A. give the patient sugar.

    B. ask the patient what caused the seizure.

    C. make sure the airway is open and the patient is breathing adequately and make sure the mouth is clear of any secretions or blood.

    D. make sure the airway is open and give mouth-to-mouth breathing until the patient is no longer confused or sleepy.

_____ **20.** Immediate emergency medical care for a patient who has heatstroke should consist of:

    A. calling for help.

    B. arranging for rapid transport to the hospital.

    C. giving the patient a drink of cool water and then treating for shock.

    D. maintaining the patient's ABCs, then lowering the body temperature as quickly as possible.

_____ **21.** Treatment of mild shock caused by heat exhaustion differs from treatment of other types of shock in that:

    A. monitoring the ABCs is usually not necessary.

    B. the patient should be soaked in cold water.

    C. the patient's feet and legs should not be elevated.

    D. the patient, if conscious, should be given a drink of cool water.

_____ **22.** Which of the following signs and symptoms is associated with hypothermia?

    A. Agitation

    B. Sleepiness

    C. Bright red skin

    D. Elevated body temperature

_____ **23.** Your first step in caring for a patient with hypothermia should be to:

    A. treat the patient for shock.

    B. rewarm the patient as quickly as possible.

    C. help the patient walk around to produce more body heat.

    D. give the patient something to eat and drink.

_____ **24.** A patient who is suffering from hypothermia may become unconscious at what body core temperature?

    A. Less than 80°F

    B. 80° to 88°F

    C. 89° to 92°F

    D. 93° to 95°F

_____ **25.** The patient assessment sequence does not include the use of:

    A. ABCs.

    B. a physical examination.

    C. CPR.

    D. SAMPLE.

_____ **26.** If a patient is seizing on a hard surface, the first responder can:

    A. restrain the patient.

    B. keep the patient's airway open.

    C. assess the level of consciousness.

    D. place his or her feet under the patient's head.

_____ **27.** The letters in SAMPLE will help a first responder to remember the steps of:

    A. conducting a physical examination.

    B. collecting a medical history.

    C. assessing an accident scene.

    D. performing CPR.

_____ **28.** Once a seizure has stopped, the first action of the first responder is to:

    A. begin CPR.

    B. ensure an open airway.

    C. assess the patient's level of consciousness.

    D. gather information of medical history.

_____ **29.** The symptoms of dizziness, nausea, profuse sweating, normal body temperature, and cool, clammy skin indicate:

    A. heatstroke.

    B. heat exhaustion.

    C. hypothermia.

    D. none of the above.

_____ **30.** The symptoms of hot red skin, loss of consciousness, and high body temperature are indications of:

    A. heatstroke.

    B. heat exhaustion.

    C. hypothermia.

    D. none of the above.

_____ **31.** Which is not true of frostbite?

    A. It may occur on the face.

    B. It occurs only after an extended exposure to cold.

    C. Age, exhaustion, and hunger may increase susceptibility.

    D. Wind speed may be a factor.

_____ **32.** If a person's body is not able to produce enough energy to keep the core temperature at a satisfactory level, the person has:

    A. hypothermia.

    B. superficial frostbite.

    C. deep frostbite.

    D. heat exhaustion.

_____ **33.** A patient's symptoms include shivering, sleepiness, and feeling cold. These symptoms indicate:

    A. hypothermia.

    B. superficial frostbite.

    C. deep frostbite.

    D. heat deprivation.

_____ **34.** Layers of fat can coat the inner walls of the arteries, causing them to become narrower. This process:

    A. is called atherosclerosis.

    B. causes angina pectoris.

    C. causes heart attacks.

    D. all of the above.

_____ **35.** An angina attack:

    A. may cause fright and a sense of doom.

    B. may be treated with nitroglycerin.

    C. may cause pain in the arms, neck, or jaw.

    D. all of the above.

_____ **36.** Nitroglycerin should:

    A. not be taken at intervals of less than 10 minutes.

    B. be given by mouth or in aerosol form.

    C. ease the pain of a heart attack.

    D. all of the above.

_____ **37.** A heart attack:

    A. is known as a myocardial infarction.

    B. is caused by complete blockage of a coronary artery.

    C. causes part of the heart muscle to die.

    D. all of the above.

_____ **38.** A patient is short of breath, weak, sweating, nauseated, and complains of crushing pain from the chest to the left arm or jaw. The first responder should:

    A. call for additional help.

    B. talk to the patient to reassure and to establish a bond.

    C. help the patient find a comfortable position.

    D. all of the above.

_____ **39.** The heart is not pumping adequately and the circulatory system becomes unbalanced. Which of the following statements applies?

    A. The patient will be short of breath.

    B. The patient will complain of crushing chest pain.

    C. CPR should be provided.

    D. All of the above.

_____ **40.** Shortness of breath, rapid and shallow breathing, moist or gurgling respirations, profuse sweating, and swollen ankles are all signs and symptoms of:

    A. cardiac arrest.

    B. myocardial infarction.

    C. congestive heart failure.

    D. diabetic coma.

_____ **41.** Treatment of a patient with congestive heart failure includes:

    A. placing the legs lower than the rest of the body.

    B. administration of nitroglycerin.

    C. CPR.

    D. all of the above.

_____ **42.** A diabetic who has taken insulin but has not eaten enough food may:

    A. be suffering from insulin shock.

    B. be dizzy or confused.

    C. have pale, moist, cool skin and a rapid pulse.

    D. all of the above.

_____ **43.** A state of sickness that occurs when the body has too much sugar and not enough insulin is:

    A. diabetes.

    B. insulin shock.

    C. diabetic coma.

    D. none of the above.

_____ **44.** A disease in which the body is unable to use sugar normally because of a deficiency or total lack of insulin is:

    A. diabetes.

    B. insulin shock.

    C. diabetic coma.

    D. none of the above.

_____ **45.** Insulin shock can:

    A. be treated with sugar or glucose.

    B. occur quickly.

    C. be confused with drunkenness.

    D. all of the above.

_____ **46.** A rapid, weak pulse, deep and rapid breathing, and a history of diabetes are signs and symptoms of:

    A. a diabetic coma.

    B. too much blood sugar in the body.

    C. failure to take insulin over a period of days.

    D. all of the above.

Fill-in-the-Blanks

Read each item carefully, then complete the statement by filling in the missing word(s).

1. Altered _____ status is a sudden or gradual decrease in the patient's level of consciousness.

2. Identify each of the following signs associated with heat exhaustion or heatstroke by placing HE, HS, or both, in the blanks.

    _____ **A.** Low blood pressure

    _____ **B.** Lightheadedness or dizziness

    _____ **C.** Brain damage

    _____ **D.** Profuse sweating

    _____ **E.** Semiconsciousness or unconsciousness

    _____ **F.** Flushed, dry skin

    _____ **G.** Weak pulse

    _____ **H.** Nausea

    _____ **I.** High body temperature

3. Coronary arteries may narrow as a result of a disease process called _____, in which layers of fat coat the inner walls of the arteries.

4. _____ are caused by sudden episodes of uncontrolled electrical impulses in the brain.

5. Patients experiencing a/an _____ have great difficulty exhaling through partially obstructed air passages.

True/False

For each statement, write the letter "T" if you believe it to be more true than false, or write the letter "F" if you believe it to be more false than true.

_____ 1. The emergency medical care that first responders can provide to people who have heart attacks sometimes saves their lives.

_____ 2. One seizure typically lasts between 30 and 45 minutes.

_____ 3. If a person is having a seizure, you should attempt to apply restraints.

_____ 4. A person who is anxious or hostile after a seizure may be embarrassed and need privacy.

_____ 5. A person having a seizure should only be moved if he or she is in a dangerous location.

_____ 6. If a person is having a seizure, you should place a barrier between his or her teeth.

_____ 7. Some seizures may have serious underlying causes such as stroke or diabetic emergencies.

_____ 8. Patients are usually responsive during seizures.

_____ 9. You cannot adequately ventilate a nonbreathing patient during a seizure.

_____ 10. A person in diabetic coma needs insulin.

_____ 11. Even if you are unsure about whether a fully responsive patient is in diabetic coma or insulin shock, you can give sugar without harming the patient.

_____ 12. A person who has had a stroke may appear unresponsive yet still be able to hear you.

_____ 13. The only way for responders to care for stroke patients is by providing oxygen.

_____ 14. A blood clot or a rupture of a blood vessel anywhere in the body can cause a stroke.

_____ 15. Symptoms of a stroke can vary because different areas of the brain can be affected by a stroke.

_____ 16. Stroke victims are always unresponsive.

_____ 17. Unequal pupil size and difficulty in speaking are two common signs of stroke.

_____ 18. A person who has had a severe stroke may stop breathing.

_____ **19.** A patient with abdominal pain should be examined by a physician.

_____ **20.** The elderly and persons who are exhausted or hungry are more susceptible to frostbite.

_____ **21.** A person must be exposed to the cold for a long time to sustain frostbite injuries, even on very cold, windy days.

_____ **22.** In cases of frostbite, exposed body parts actually freeze.

_____ **23.** In the first stage of frostbite, the exposed body part becomes pale white.

_____ **24.** If a person with frostbite has been out in the cold for hours, you should arrange for transport to the hospital rather than try to rewarm the affected body parts yourself.

_____ **25.** As a first responder, your emergency medical care of frostbite will consist of rewarming the affected body parts and treating the patient for signs of shock.

_____ **26.** Although you should never rub a frostbitten area with snow or ice, rubbing the area with your hands or a cloth is a good way to rewarm the area.

_____ **27.** The core body temperature of a person with hypothermia is lower than normal.

_____ **28.** Hypothermia occurs only in conditions of extreme cold.

_____ **29.** You should remove all wet clothing from a person who has hypothermia.

_____ **30.** Left untreated, hypothermia is serious but rarely fatal.

_____ **31.** If a patient who has hypothermia is conscious, you should give the patient something warm to drink.

_____ **32.** If at all possible, you should move a patient who has hypothermia to a warmer place.

_____ **33.** If a patient goes into cardiac arrest as a result of hypothermia, you should immediately transport the patient to the hospital.

_____ **34.** A person with hypothermia who may have been considered dead for hours can be revived in the hospital.

_____ **35.** It is necessary to determine the exact cause of a medical problem before appropriate treatment can be administered.

_____ **36.** Heatstroke may cause brain damage or death.

_____ **37.** The most important step in treating heatstroke is rehydration.

_____ **38.** Frostbite and hypothermia may be encountered at any time of the year.

_____ **39.** Exercise, age, and medications may all be factors in heat-related illness.

_____ **40.** A patient showing indications of heat exhaustion should not be moved until ABCs are monitored and blood pressure is stabilized.

_____ **41.** During a seizure, if the patient stops breathing and turns blue, CPR should be administered.

_____ **42.** Many factors cause seizures, and the type of seizure will indicate the cause.

_____ **43.** The AVPU scale is used to assess a patient's mental status and may be used when there has been a head injury, poisoning, or an infection.

_____ **44.** A first responder must first determine the cause of the patient's altered level of consciousness and then begin appropriate treatment.

_____ **45.** It is important to categorize patients as medical patients or trauma patients in order to determine the best course of treatment.

_____ **46.** A patient with deep frostbite should be transported to a medical facility for treatment.

_____ **47.** If a patient who appears to have hypothermia stops shivering, it is safe to assume that the patient has recovered and needs no treatment.

_____ **48.** CPR should be used on hypothermic patients even if there are no vital signs to indicate life.

_____ **49.** Chest pain with squeezing or tightness in the chest may be a sign of angina pectoris.

_____ **50.** Exertion, emotion, or eating can contribute to angina attacks.

_____ **51.** Causes of dyspnea include angina pectoris, heart attack, congestive heart failure, chronic obstructive lung disease, emphysema, chronic bronchitis, and pneumonia.

_____ **52.** It is important to determine the cause of dyspnea in order to determine the appropriate treatment.

_____ **53.** Loosening any tight clothing and comfortably positioning the patient are steps in treatment for a patient with dyspnea.

_____ **54.** The first priority in treatment of a stroke patient is to maintain an open airway.

Short Answer

Write a brief response to each of the following questions.

1. Describe two medical emergencies that can occur as a result of diabetes.

_____

_____

_____

2. What three questions should you ask a person believed to be going into insulin shock?

_____

_____

_____

3. Name two substances with high concentrations of sugar that would be appropriate to give to a person in insulin shock.

_____

_____

_____

4. When assessing the patient's mental status, what two factors should be considered?

_____

_____

_____

5. List four conditions that may contribute to an altered level of consciousness.

_____

_____

_____

6. Name the four body parts most susceptible to frostbite.

_____

_____

_____

You Make the Call

The following scenario provides an opportunity to explore the concerns associated with patient management. Read the scenario, then describe the best way to handle the situation.

When you arrive at the grocery store, you are greeted by a young woman asking you to help her mother. As you are walking to the mother, the young woman explains that her mother, who is a diabetic, became confused and is now unresponsive. When you complete your AVPU assessment, you find she responds only to pain. What should you do?

CHAPTER

11 Poisoning and Substance Abuse

Matching

Match each of the items in the left column to the appropriate description in the right column.

_____ **1.** Carbon monoxide	**A.** Identified as "poisonous"
_____ **2.** Cocaine	**B.** State of consciousness from which the patient cannot be aroused
_____ **3.** Uppers	**C.** Includes the brain and spinal cord
_____ **4.** Hallucinogens	**D.** Chemical substance with a pH of less than 7.0 that can cause severe burns
_____ **5.** Central nervous system	**E.** Categorized as depressants; barbiturates
_____ **6.** Toxic	**F.** Powerful stimulant that induces an extreme state of euphoria
_____ **7.** Downers	**G.** Colorless, odorless, poisonous gas formed by incomplete combustion
_____ **8.** Hives	**H.** Allergic skin disorder marked by patches of swelling, redness, and intense itching
_____ **9.** Acid	**I.** Drugs that stimulate the central nervous system
_____ **10.** Coma	**J.** Chemicals that cause a person to see visions or hear sounds that are not real

Multiple Choice

Read each item carefully, then select the best response.

_____ **1.** More than _____ of all poisonings are caused by ingestion.

    A. 50%

    B. 80%

    C. 90%

    D. 65%

_____ **2.** Deaths from poisoning are highest in people _____ years of age.

    A. 0 to 4

    B. 4 to 10

    C. 11 to 25

    D. 25 to 44

_____ 3. Unconscious patients should be placed in the _____ position to keep their airway open.
  A. recovery
  B. reclining
  C. sitting
  D. shock

_____ 4. The first step in treating a patient who is suffering from inhalation of any poison gas is to:
  A. identify the gas that is present.
  B. remove the patient from the source of the gas.
  C. transport to the closest facility.
  D. call the poison control center for direction.

_____ 5. Your patient has been poisoned by absorption. You should first:
  A. administer supplementary oxygen.
  B. wash the affected area.
  C. treat for shock.
  D. have the patient remove his or her clothing, then brush off the dry chemical.

_____ 6. After removing chemicals absorbed into clothing, responders treating patients poisoned by absorption should:
  A. arrange for immediate transport to the hospital.
  B. wash the patient thoroughly with a hose or a shower.
  C. ask the patient to lie down and then elevate his or her legs.
  D. withhold any additional treatment unless the person feels dizzy.

_____ 7. When caring for a patient suffering from hallucinations, you should:
  A. tell the patient to stop talking.
  B. tell the patient that you believe he or she really sees or hears those things.
  C. ask the patient to describe the hallucination.
  D. try to convince the patient that what he or she is seeing or hearing is not real.

_____ 8. Which of the following substances can result in unconsciousness when inhaled?
  A. Gasoline and paint thinner
  B. Lacquers
  C. Aerosol can propellants
  D. All of the above

_____ 9. If poison enters the body through the mouth and is absorbed by the digestive system, it is called:
  A. inhalation.
  B. ingestion.
  C. injection.
  D. absorption.

_____ 10. If a poison enters the body through the mouth or nose and is absorbed by the mucous membranes lining the respiratory system, it is called:
  A. inhalation.
  B. ingestion.
  C. injection.
  D. absorption.

_____ 11. When poison enters the body through a small opening in the skin, it may then be spread by the circulatory system. This is known as:
  A. inhalation.
  B. ingestion.
  C. absorption.
  D. injection.

_____ 12. If poison enters the body through intact skin, it may then be spread by the circulatory system. This is known as:

   A. inhalation.

   B. ingestion.

   C. absorption.

   D. injection.

_____ 13. Signs and symptoms of poisoning by ingestion may include:

   A. abdominal pain and diarrhea.

   B. nausea and vomiting.

   C. unusual breath odors.

   D. all of the above.

_____ 14. The first step in treating a patient who has ingested a poison is to:

   A. induce vomiting.

   B. dilute the poison with water.

   C. administer activated charcoal.

   D. attempt to identify the poison.

_____ 15. Syrup of ipecac:

   A. will produce vomiting.

   B. requires a prescription.

   C. can be administered safely for any type of poisoning.

   D. all of the above.

_____ 16. If a toxic substance is breathed in and absorbed through the lungs, poisoning occurs by:

   A. ingestion.

   B. inhalation.

   C. injection.

   D. absorption.

_____ 17. Respiratory distress, cough, dizziness, headache, and confusion may be signs of poisoning by:

   A. ingestion.

   B. inhalation.

   C. injection.

   D. absorption.

_____ 18. If several members of one household are found at home, all with headache, nausea, disorientation, or unconsciousness, you should:

   A. remove everyone from the dwelling.

   B. suspect carbon monoxide poisoning.

   C. administer oxygen if available.

   D. all of the above.

_____ 19. Areas where poisonous gases are present:

   A. require self-contained breathing apparatus (SCBA).

   B. are usually easily detected using carbon monoxide detectors.

   C. should be evacuated for at least ten minutes until the gases dissipate.

   D. all of the above.

_____ 20. Anaphylactic shock:

   A. may cause itching, hives, and swelling.

   B. may cause hoarseness and chest pain.

   C. may cause unusual breath odors and abdominal pain.

   D. all of the above.

_____ **21.** Anaphylactic shock:

   A. can be helped by elevating the patient's legs.

   B. causes the patient's blood pressure to drop.

   C. requires rapid transport to a medical facility.

   D. all of the above.

_____ **22.** A person who has been poisoned by absorption:

   A. may have been in contact with insecticides or industrial chemicals.

   B. may have skin irritation.

   C. may exhibit signs and symptoms such as nausea, vomiting, dizziness, or shock.

   D. all of the above.

_____ **23.** Delirium tremens (DTs):

   A. are a common side effect of snake bite treatment.

   B. usually only occur in children and adolescents.

   C. are a serious and possibly fatal medical emergency.

   D. all of the above.

_____ **24.** Drugs that stimulate the nervous system:

   A. include PCP and LSD.

   B. include amphetamines and cocaine.

   C. include opiates and marijuana.

   D. all of the above.

_____ **25.** A first responder's responsibility in a situation of drug overdose includes:

   A. provide basic life support.

   B. keep the patient from hurting himself or herself and others.

   C. arrange for prompt transport to a medical facility.

   D. all of the above.

Fill-in-the-Blanks

Read each item carefully, then complete the statement by filling in the missing word(s).

1. Poisons may be ingested, inhaled, absorbed, or injected. For each of the findings, indicate which type of poisoning has occurred.

   _____ **A.** Stains around the mouth

   _____ **B.** Group of unconscious people in a house in the winter

   _____ **C.** Smell of bleach

   _____ **D.** Swelling with red streaks radiating from it

   _____ **E.** Empty pill bottles

   _____ **F.** Worker at a water treatment plant having difficulty breathing

   _____ **G.** Worker at a dry chemical plant who is dizzy

2. Many gases irritate the respiratory tract. Two of the most frequently encountered irritating gases are _____ and _____.

3. For each of the following terms or statements, identify whether it is associated with uppers (U), downers (D), or hallucinogens (H).

_____ **A.** PCP or mescaline

_____ **B.** Overdose symptoms include talkativeness and restlessness

_____ **C.** Amphetamines

_____ **D.** Tranquilizers

_____ **E.** Overdose symptoms include respiratory depression or respiratory arrest

_____ **F.** LSD or peyote

_____ **G.** Coke or crack

_____ **H.** Overdose symptoms include seeing or hearing things that are not real

4. The most popular drugs fall into four categories: uppers, downers, hallucinogens, and _____.

5. A patient who has attempted _____ needs both medical and psychological support.

True/False

For each statement, write the letter "T" if you believe it to be more true than false, or write the letter "F" if you believe it to be more false than true.

_____ **1.** Accidental poisoning is most common among teenagers.

_____ **2.** The survival of a person who has been poisoned can depend on how quickly you recognize that poisoning occurred.

_____ **3.** Only contact the poison control center if you can identify the exact substance a person has ingested.

_____ **4.** You should always dilute ingested poison by giving the patient water to drink.

_____ **5.** Treat the patient, then immediately attempt to identify the substance taken.

_____ **6.** Ipecac is a nonharmful drug and can be used as a treatment for all ingested poisons.

_____ **7.** The history of the patient and of the incident, as well as visual clues, are important in determining treatment of a patient who may have been poisoned.

_____ **8.** If poisoning is suspected, information about the method and type of poison must be obtained before treatment of the symptoms is begun.

_____ **9.** More than half of all poisoning cases are caused by injection.

_____ **10.** Ingestion is the most common method of poisoning.

_____ **11.** First responders should contact the dispatching center if the poison control center needs to be contacted for information.

_____ **12.** Most poisons can be diluted by giving the patient large quantities of water.

_____ **13.** Activated charcoal should be placed under the tongue of an unconscious patient who may have been poisoned.

_____ **14.** The first responder life support kit should contain the number of the poison control center.

_____ **15.** A tongue depressor should be used to induce vomiting in an unconscious patient who has been poisoned.

_____ **16.** If a patient shows signs and symptoms of poisoning but the poison cannot be identified easily, the safest treatment is to induce vomiting.

_____ **17.** A substance that causes poisoning by inhalation will always irritate the lungs and cause respiratory distress.

_____ **18.** A large quantity of carbon monoxide must be present for poisoning to occur.

_____ **19.** In agricultural settings, poisoning by chlorine gas is likely to occur and requires use of a proper encapsulating suit with a SCBA.

_____ **20.** Ammonia has a strong and irritating odor, can burn the skin, and requires use of a proper encapsulating suit with a SCBA.

_____ **21.** The first step in treating a patient who is suffering from inhalation of any poison gas is to remove him or her from the source of the gas.

_____ **22.** Poisoning by injection may occur accidentally or as a deliberate act by the patient.

_____ **23.** Animal stings and bites are one type of poisoning by injection.

_____ **24.** Poisoning by injection includes only the use of illegal drugs.

_____ **25.** Injected poisons may cause an anaphylactic reaction.

_____ **26.** Snakebite is the second leading cause of fatalities in rural areas of the United States.

_____ **27.** Permanent injury may result from snakebites.

_____ **28.** Shock, nausea, vomiting, sweating, and fainting may all be signs and symptoms of snakebite.

_____ **29.** Shock, dizziness, itching, burning, skin rash, and inflammation or redness of the skin may all be signs and symptoms of poisoning by absorption.

_____ **30.** Treatment of a patient who has absorbed a poisonous substance should begin by ensuring that the patient is no longer in contact with the toxic substance.

_____ **31.** Treatment of a patient who has absorbed a poisonous substance may require removal of the patient's clothes, followed immediately by a complete washing of the patient's body with large amounts of water.

_____ **32.** Dry chemicals should be brushed off a patient before any contact with water is made.

_____ **33.** In cases of absorbed chemicals, the patient should be treated for the symptoms, shock, and breathing difficulties if these are observed.

_____ **34.** Uppers such as amphetamines and cocaine are the most commonly abused drugs in our society.

_____ **35.** Auto accidents cause twice as many deaths as alcohol abuse.

_____ **36.** A well-trained and knowledgeable first responder will easily differentiate the symptoms of alcohol intoxication from those of insulin shock, diabetic coma, or other drug reactions.

_____ **37.** Users of hallucinogens may feel no pain and may be in danger of injuring themselves.

Short Answer

Write a brief response to each of the following questions.

1. Identify the most common method of poisoning.

_____

_____

_____

2. Name the result of administering syrup of ipecac to a patient who shows signs and symptoms of poisoning.

_____

_____

_____

3. Name five common signs of inhalation poisoning.

_____

_____

_____

_____

4. What should you do if several members of one household are found at home, all experiencing headache, nausea, disorientation, or unconsciousness?

_____

_____

_____

5. What is the first step in treating a patient who is suffering from inhalation of any poisonous gas?

_____

_____

6. What treatment does ammonia contamination require?

_____

_____

7. Name three commons signs or symptoms of anaphylactic shock.

_____

_____

_____

8. Name three commons signs or symptoms of poisoning by absorption.

_____

_____

_____

9. What are a first responder's responsibilities in a situation of drug overdose?

_____

_____

_____

10. In situations of poisoning by absorption, dry chemicals should be brushed off a patient before what step of care is taken?

_____

_____

_____

Word Fun

The following crossword puzzle is an activity provided to reinforce correct spelling and understanding of terminology associated with emergency care and the first responder. Use the clues in the column to complete the puzzle.

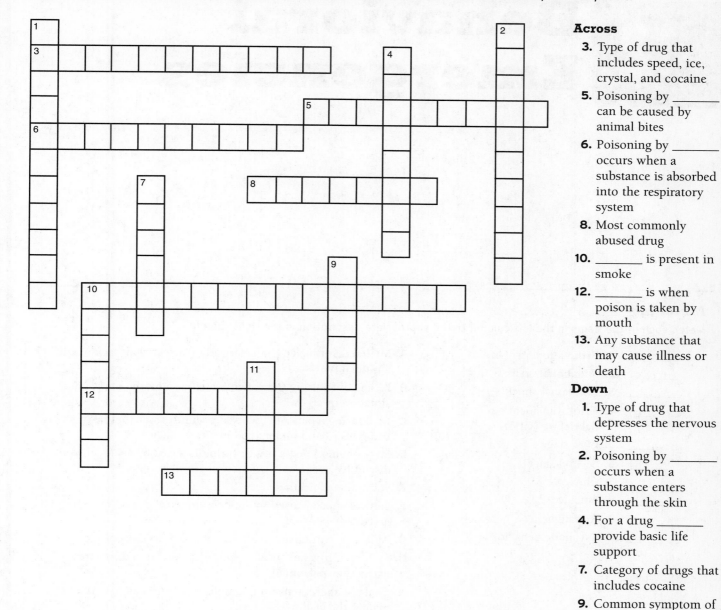

Across

3. Type of drug that includes speed, ice, crystal, and cocaine
5. Poisoning by _____ can be caused by animal bites
6. Poisoning by _____ occurs when a substance is absorbed into the respiratory system
8. Most commonly abused drug
10. _____ is present in smoke
12. _____ is when poison is taken by mouth
13. Any substance that may cause illness or death

Down

1. Type of drug that depresses the nervous system
2. Poisoning by _____ occurs when a substance enters through the skin
4. For a drug _____ provide basic life support
7. Category of drugs that includes cocaine
9. Common symptom of poisoning by inhalation
10. Coke
11. Allergic skin disorder

You Make the Call

The following scenario provides an opportunity to explore the concerns associated with patient management. Read the scenario, then describe the best way to handle the situation.

Your neighbor comes running to your home for help. She is sure her 3-year-old has taken several pills from the bathroom medicine cabinet, thinking they were candy. The child is becoming very sleepy by the time you arrive. What should you do?

CHAPTER

12 Behavioral Emergencies

Matching

Match each of the items in the left column to the appropriate description in the right column.

_____ 1. Redirection

_____ 2. Situational crisis

_____ 3. Emotional shock

_____ 4. Critical incident stress debriefing (CISD)

_____ 5. First stage

_____ 6. Second stage

_____ 7. Empathy

_____ 8. Suicide

_____ 9. Restatement

_____ 10. Psychotic behavior

A. Mental disturbance characterized by defective or lack of contact with reality

B. Means of focusing the patient's attention on the immediate situation or crisis

C. Rephrasing a patient's own statement to show that he or she is being heard and understood by the rescuer

D. State of emotional upset or turmoil caused by a sudden and disruptive event

E. Self-inflicted death

F. State of shock caused by sudden illness, accident, or death of a loved one

G. Ability to participate in another person's feelings or ideas

H. System of psychological support designed to reduce stress on emergency personnel

I. Cycle of abuse: tension (the abuser becomes angry and often blames the victim)

J. Cycle of abuse: explosive (most injuries to victims during this stage)

Multiple Choice

Read each item carefully, then select the best response.

_____ 1. Which of the following is not one of the phases of situational crisis?

A. Anger

B. Grief

C. Acceptance

D. Emotional shock

_____ **2.** You arrive at the scene of a motor vehicle crash and find a teenage girl staring at other emergency personnel caring for an older woman. She then says, "If I hadn't asked her to take me to the mall, this wouldn't have happened." What phase of a situational crisis is this girl probably experiencing?

    A. Grief

    B. Denial

    C. Remorse

    D. Emotional shock

_____ **3.** Which of the following should you not do when talking to a patient?

    A. Establish eye contact.

    B. Bring yourself to the patient's level.

    C. Talk in a calm, steady voice.

    D. Tell the patient that everything will be all right, if it will make the patient feel better.

_____ **4.** _____ responder(s) should attempt to talk to a potentially violent person.

    A. One

    B. Two

    C. No

    D. It doesn't matter

_____ **5.** Which is the correct order of phases in the domestic abuse cycle?

    A. Explosive, make up, tension

    B. Tension, make up, explosive

    C. Make up, tension, explosive

    D. Tension, explosive, make up

_____ **6.** A behavioral emergency:

    A. is a situation where a person behaves in an abnormal and unacceptable manner.

    B. may be caused by situational stress or physical trauma.

    C. calls for appropriate communication, especially body language.

    D. all of the above.

_____ **7.** Behavioral emergencies are caused by:

    A. mind-altering substances.

    B. situational stresses.

    C. uncontrolled diabetes or respiratory conditions.

    D. all of the above.

_____ **8.** A person experiencing a situational crisis may go through which emotional phases?

    A. Denial or anger

    B. Psychotic phase

    C. Anaphylactic shock

    D. All of the above

_____ **9.** A person who is experiencing high anxiety is likely to exhibit which characteristics?

    A. Loud or screaming voice

    B. Flushed face

    C. Rapid breathing and rapid speech

    D. All of the above

_____ **10.** Emotional shock may:

    A. cause the patient to turn pale.

    B. cause a strong, fast pulse.

    C. cause vomiting and nausea.

    D. all of the above.

_____ **11.** Rephrasing a patient's own statement to show understanding is called:
   A. empathy.
   B. redirection.
   C. restatement.
   D. all of the above.

_____ **12.** A means of focusing the patient's attention on the immediate situation or crisis is called:
   A. empathy.
   B. redirection.
   C. restatement.
   D. all of the above.

_____ **13.** The ability to participate in another person's feelings or ideas is called:
   A. empathy.
   B. redirection.
   C. restatement.
   D. all of the above.

_____ **14.** A first responder who is faced with treating an unarmed violent patient should:
   A. place the patient in a corner.
   B. get more help on the scene to deal with the patient.
   C. try to get the patient to stop talking.
   D. none of the above.

_____ **15.** Factors to be considered before applying force to restrain a patient include:
   A. the type of abnormal behavior exhibited.
   B. the size, strength, and sex of the patient.
   C. the type of restraint.
   D. all of the above.

_____ **16.** Management of a suicide crisis includes:
   A. treatment of injuries, if necessary.
   B. support of the patient's ABCs as needed.
   C. emotional support.
   D. all of the above.

_____ **17.** Signs and symptoms of extreme stress include:
   A. lack of interest in sleep.
   B. lack of interest in food.
   C. hyperactivity.
   D. all of the above.

Fill-in-the-Blanks

Read each item carefully, then complete the statement by filling in the missing word(s).

1. Every emergency creates some sort of a _____ for the patient and for those close to the patient.

2. _____ is one of the most important skills in working with a patient.

3. _____ can help focus the patient's attention on the immediate situation.

4. Trying to put yourself in the patient's shoes is known as _____.

5. Many suicide attempts are really _____.

True/False

For each statement, write the letter "T" if you believe it to be more true than false, or write the letter "F" if you believe it to be more false than true.

_____ **1.** In your role as a first responder, you should give psychological and emotional support to patients as well as emergency medical care.

_____ **2.** Sudden illness, injury, or death will almost always cause emotional upset or turmoil for those involved.

_____ **3.** When a person cannot cope with sudden or unexpected events, the person may act strange or even demonstrate dangerous behavior.

_____ **4.** As a first responder, you will rarely intervene in a situational crisis.

_____ **5.** Your honesty and concern for a person can be communicated by establishing eye contact.

_____ **6.** Even in serious situations, you can reassure a patient and still be honest by saying that everything possible is being done to help the patient.

_____ **7.** Standing above a patient with your hands on your hips assures the patient that you are a confident professional.

_____ **8.** Simple acts of kindness, such as offering a tissue or blanket, can often comfort a person who is emotionally upset and can sometimes lessen the severity of the crisis reaction.

_____ **9.** An appropriate sense of humor is important in emergency situations.

_____ **10.** A calm attitude on your part may help to calm a person who is in a crisis situation.

_____ **11.** If you have negative feelings about a patient, you should avoid caring for that patient.

_____ **12.** Loud, obscene, or bizarre speech may indicate emotional stability.

_____ **13.** The best way to avoid violence against first responders is prevention.

_____ **14.** The role of the first responder may include seeing to emotional and psychological needs as well as medical needs.

_____ **15.** Head injuries and shock may cause behavioral emergencies.

_____ **16.** High fevers and excess cold may cause behavioral emergencies.

_____ **17.** Psychotic behavior is characterized by defective or lost contact with reality.

_____ **18.** A state of emotional upset or turmoil caused by a sudden and disruptive event is called psychotic behavior.

_____ **19.** The majority of emergency calls will require only medical care and no psychological intervention.

_____ **20.** A person who is in emotional shock will not exhibit any of the physical signs of other types of shock.

_____ **21.** In a situational crisis, when a patient expresses denial, it is the responsibility of the first responder to quietly but firmly keep repeating the reality.

_____ **22.** During a situational crisis, a person begins screaming at you, calls you incompetent, and swears at you. You should immediately leave the scene and call your supervisor.

_____ **23.** Anger is difficult to handle objectively because it may seem to be directed at you personally.

_____ **24.** Treatment of a patient who is exhibiting abnormal behavior does not require the same steps of the patient assessment sequence as does treatment of other patients.

_____ **25.** If a patient is exhibiting abnormal behavior, the first responder should not try to communicate with him or her.

_____ **26.** Effective communication with a patient requires body language that exhibits empathy and interest.

_____ **27.** The best way to reassure patients is to tell them that everything is all right.

_____ **28.** Crisis intervention techniques include touching the patient.

_____ **29.** Crisis intervention techniques include good eye contact and a calm, steady voice.

_____ **30.** In crisis intervention, the most important factor is time.

_____ **31.** A good way to reassure a patient and to show that you understand is simply to say, "I know what you mean" or "I know how you feel."

_____ **32.** Empathy can best be expressed by telling the patient that you know exactly how he or she feels.

_____ **33.** The technique of redirection may call for movement of the patient.

_____ **34.** Redirection is an attempt to alleviate the patient's concerns and bring attention back to the immediate situation.

_____ **35.** Trying to understand the emotional and psychological trauma that a patient experiences is using the technique of empathy.

_____ **36.** If the presence of too many people is adding to a patient's anxiety, it is the responsibility of the first responder to ask them to move to another location.

_____ **37.** Crowds that may become hostile are the responsibility of law enforcement officers and not first responders.

_____ **38.** A first responder will identify himself or herself to the patient and give reassurance that he or she is there to help.

_____ **39.** A patient can identify a first responder by uniform, and no introduction should be necessary.

_____ **40.** Good communication skills for a first responder include the use of restatement and redirection.

_____ **41.** A patient's mental status can be assessed through the patient's appearance, activity, speech, and orientation to person, place, and time.

_____ **42.** The anxiety level of patients will be raised by informing them of what you are doing in order to assess their condition.

_____ **43.** A violent or potentially violent patient should be kept talking and encouraged to talk the situation out.

_____ **44.** A competent, well-trained first responder will be able to handle all violent patients without additional help.

_____ **45.** A competent, well-trained first responder will be able to handle a violent, armed patient without additional help.

_____ **46.** If you are confronted by an armed patient, you should immediately turn around and walk away.

_____ **47.** If a patient who appears to be disturbed refuses to accept treatment, you cannot legally transport the patient.

_____ **48.** If you have a reasonable belief that a disturbed patient would harm himself or herself or others, you may treat and/or transport that patient against his or her will.

_____ **49.** Assistance from law enforcement officials should be sought when considering the restraint of a disturbed patient.

_____ **50.** The sex of the disturbed patient and of the first responder are considerations when attempting to restrain a disturbed patient.

_____ **51.** A competent first responder can differentiate between a serious suicide attempt or threat and one that does not need to be taken seriously.

_____ **52.** The primary role of the first responder in a suicide crisis is to provide a caring attitude and good medical care.

_____ **53.** The sex of the first responder is a major consideration in the treatment of a victim of sexual assault.

_____ **54.** The first responsibility to the victim of sexual assault is to gather information that will help apprehend the criminal.

_____ **55.** How well a first responder can help a dying patient and the person's family depends greatly on the first responder's own feelings concerning death.

_____ **56.** Because dealing with death is a routine part of the job of a first responder, an experienced first responder will feel little emotion at the death of a patient.

_____ **57.** An emotionally stable first responder should not need any help or support in dealing with his or her job responsibilities.

Short Answer

Write a brief response to each of the following questions.

1. List the five main factors that can cause behavioral changes.

_____

_____

_____

2. What is the most important thing to remember when dealing with a person's anger?

_____

_____

_____

3. What is the proper patient assessment sequence for a patient with a behavioral emergency?

_____

_____

_____

4. When is it acceptable to provide care against the patient's will?

_____

_____

_____

5. Name three methods people use to attempt suicide.

_____

_____

_____

6. What are the three types of death that a first responder may encounter?

_____

_____

_____

7. List at least three signs and symptoms of stress.

_____

_____

_____

8. What is the purpose of CISD?

_____

_____

_____

9. Provide a response to each of the following statements using the technique of restatement. In addition to rephrasing the statement to show that you understand, try to add some reassuring or encouraging words to your restatement.

A. From a woman who has been hit by a car: "I can't stay here! I have to go home and start dinner for the kids!"

_____

_____

_____

B. From the driver of the car that hit the woman: "I didn't mean to hit her! She just ran out all of a sudden! What if she dies?"

_____

_____

_____

C. From one of the woman's children, who was with her but not struck by the car: "I want my mommy! Let me go to my mommy!"

_____

_____

_____

10. Provide a response to each of the statements above using the technique of redirection.

A. _____

_____

_____

B. _____

_____

_____

C. _____

_____

_____

You Make the Call

The following scenario provides an opportunity to explore the concerns associated with patient management. Read the scenario, then describe the best way to handle the situation.

When you arrive on the scene, you find the patient pacing the room and crying loudly. When you approach her, she pushes you away, saying, "I don't want your help; nobody can help me." She then turns her back to you and continues to pace. According to her friend, she and her boyfriend had a big fight and he just left. What should you do?

CHAPTER

13 Bleeding, Shock, and Soft-Tissue Injuries

Matching

Match each of the items in the left column to the appropriate description in the right column.

_____ **1.** Pulse
_____ **2.** Red blood cell
_____ **3.** Capillary
_____ **4.** Platelet
_____ **5.** White blood cell
_____ **6.** Vein
_____ **7.** Artery

A. Large, heavy-duty blood vessel that carries oxygenated blood away from the heart to the body

B. Blood cell that carries oxygen and carbon dioxide through the body

C. Blood cell that works with other substances to form blood clots

D. Pressure wave of blood that can be felt at various places along the main arteries of the body

E. Blood vessel that is so narrow that blood cells flow "single file"

F. Blood vessel that returns blood from the body back to the heart

G. Blood cell that helps the body fight infection

Multiple Choice

Read each item carefully, then select the best response.

_____ **1.** What is the greatest cause of death in trauma patients?
  A. Internal bleeding
  B. External wounds
  C. Shock
  D. Cardiac arrest

_____ **2.** Components of the circulatory system include all of the following, EXCEPT:
  A. pipes: arteries, capillaries, and veins.
  B. fluid: blood.
  C. pressure wave: pulse.
  D. pump: heart.

_____ **3.** The lower chambers of the heart:
  A. are smaller than the upper chambers.
  B. do most of the actual pumping.
  C. are called atria.
  D. all of the above.

_____ **4.** The upper chambers of the heart:
  A. serve as a reservoir for blood.
  B. are called atria.
  C. are less muscular than the lower chambers.
  D. all of the above.

_____ **5.** The red blood cells:
  A. have a search and destroy function.
  B. carry oxygen and carbon dioxide.
  C. interact with each other to form blood clots.
  D. all of the above.

_____ **6.** The white blood cells:
  A. consume bacteria and viruses.
  B. interact with each other to form blood clots.
  C. serve as a transporting medium for other parts of the blood.
  D. all of the above.

_____ **7.** A pulse is:
  A. the same as counting heartbeats.
  B. the pressure generated by the pumping action of the heart.
  C. caused by the blood being pushed into the main arteries.
  D. all of the above.

_____ **8.** Shock, or failure of the circulatory system, is caused by:
  A. pump failure.
  B. pipe failure.
  C. fluid loss.
  D. all of the above.

_____ **9.** If the heart is incapable of pumping enough blood to supply the needs of the body:
  A. blood can back up in the vessels of the lungs, causing congestive heart failure.
  B. cardiogenic shock may occur.
  C. the patient may have had a heart attack.
  D. all of the above.

_____ **10.** Shock as a result of capillary expansion may be caused by:
  A. spinal shock.
  B. fainting.
  C. anaphylactic shock.
  D. all of the above.

_____ **11.** Psychogenic shock:
  A. is the least serious type of shock caused by pipe failure.
  B. is known as fainting.
  C. will correct itself if the patient is placed in a horizontal position.
  D. all of the above.

_____ **12.** Anaphylactic shock:

    A. is caused by fluid loss.

    B. is usually caused by hemorrhage.

    C. may be accompanied by itching, rash, hives, or swelling of the face or tongue.

    D. all of the above.

_____ **13.** Shock caused by a temporary reduction in blood supply to the brain is called:

    A. anaphylactic shock.

    B. psychogenic shock.

    C. cardiogenic shock.

    D. all of the above.

_____ **14.** Shock caused by an allergic reaction to food, medicine, or insect stings is called:

    A. anaphylactic shock.

    B. psychogenic shock.

    C. cardiogenic shock.

    D. all of the above.

_____ **15.** Signs and symptoms of shock may include:

    A. nausea and vomiting.

    B. confusion, restlessness, or anxiety.

    C. thirst.

    D. all of the above.

_____ **16.** Which of the following is not a sign or symptom of shock?

    A. Rapid breathing

    B. Swollen feet or ankles

    C. Thirst

    D. All of the above

_____ **17.** General treatment for shock includes:

    A. giving the patient sips of water or other fluids.

    B. getting the patient to walk as soon as possible.

    C. maintaining the patient's ABCs.

    D. all of the above.

_____ **18.** Positioning a patient who shows signs of shock may include:

    A. placing a blanket under the patient.

    B. elevating the patient's legs.

    C. placing the patient flat on his or her back.

    D. all of the above.

_____ **19.** The first responder can treat a patient who exhibits signs and symptoms of shock by:

    A. treating the cause of shock.

    B. maintaining the body temperature of the patient.

    C. maintaining the patient's ABCs.

    D. all of the above.

_____ **20.** Upon arrival of BLS and/or ALS units, a patient who is in shock may be treated with:

    A. a pneumatic antishock garment (PASG).

    B. IV fluids.

    C. oxygen.

    D. all of the above.

_____ **21.** Treatment for shock caused by pump failure includes:
  A. giving the patient fluids by mouth.
  B. cooling the patient's temperature.
  C. maintaining the patient's ABCs.
  D. all of the above.

_____ **22.** Treatment for fainting includes which of the following?
  A. Elevation of the patient's legs
  B. Maintaining the patient's ABCs
  C. Examination of the patient for injuries
  D. All of the above

_____ **23.** Treatment of a patient with spinal shock includes:
  A. stabilization of the neck.
  B. maintaining the patient's ABCs and body temperature.
  C. placement of the patient on his or her back.
  D. all of the above.

_____ **24.** Which is not a part of the treatment for spinal shock?
  A. Giving a drink of water to the patient
  B. Elevating the patient's feet and legs
  C. Elevating the patient's head and shoulders
  D. All of the above

_____ **25.** Signs and symptoms of internal blood loss include:
  A. rectal and/or vaginal bleeding.
  B. coughing or vomiting of blood.
  C. abdominal tenderness, rigidity, or distention.
  D. all of the above.

_____ **26.** Treatment of shock caused by external blood loss includes which of the following steps?
  A. Providing glucose
  B. Elevating the head
  C. Applying direct pressure to the wound
  D. All of the above

_____ **27.** External bleeding can be controlled by:
  A. application of direct pressure.
  B. elevation of the body part.
  C. application of pressure at the pressure point.
  D. all of the above.

_____ **28.** In applying femoral pressure you should:
  A. kneel on the same side as the injury.
  B. position the patient on his or her side.
  C. be facing the patient.
  D. all of the above.

_____ **29.** A closed wound:
  A. is a bruise or contusion.
  B. is an injury of the soft tissue beneath the skin.
  C. causes discoloration and swelling.
  D. all of the above.

_____ **30.** An abrasion:

    A. is caused by a sharp object that penetrates the skin.

    B. is the tearing away of body tissue.

    C. may be called road rash or a rug burn.

    D. all of the above.

_____ **31.** Avulsion:

    A. is the most common type of open wound.

    B. is the tearing away of body tissue.

    C. may be caused by a sharp object penetrating the skin.

    D. all of the above.

_____ **32.** An occlusive dressing:

    A. is used for open chest wounds.

    B. is used to maintain air pressure in the lungs.

    C. can be plastic wrap or aluminum foil.

    D. all of the above.

_____ **33.** A burn that damages all layers of the skin:

    A. may not be accompanied by pain.

    B. may make the patient susceptible to shock and infection.

    C. is called a full-thickness or third-degree burn.

    D. all of the above.

_____ **34.** A respiratory burn:

    A. may cause breathing problems.

    B. will not cause any pain.

    C. will be visible immediately.

    D. all of the above.

_____ **35.** You are called to the scene where a 16-year-old boy has been beaten severely and is unresponsive. You should first feel for a pulse at which artery?

    A. Brachial

    B. Radial

    C. Carotid

    D. Temporal

_____ **36.** After a patient has fainted and has been placed in the correct position, you should check the patient's ABCs and then:

    A. shout at and shake the patient until he or she becomes responsive.

    B. make sure the patient is neither too hot nor too cold, and reassure the patient as he or she becomes responsive.

    C. call for help and keep the patient extra warm.

    D. call for help and watch for signs of responsiveness so you can immediately lower the patient's legs.

_____ **37.** Which of the following signs can develop quickly in a person who is in anaphylactic shock?

    A. Rash

    B. Pale skin

    C. Strong pulse

    D. High blood pressure

_____ **38.** After placing the patient in the correct position, what is the first thing you should do for a patient who is in shock?

    A. Give the patient some water

    B. Give the patient something to eat

    C. Check the patient's ABCs

    D. Begin one-person CPR

_____ **39.** A small boy has severe bleeding from a cut on the back of his head. He is sitting on the ground, sobbing and clinging to his mother. His mother tells you he was hit by a swing and begs you to do something before he "bleeds to death." The first step in providing care is to:

    A. reassure the mother that the boy will be fine.

    B. treat the boy immediately for shock from blood loss.

    C. apply direct pressure to the wound and then reassure the boy and his mother that you are trying to help.

    D. cover the wound and then bandage it loosely in case of skull fracture, even though no bone or bone chips are visible.

_____ **40.** You are called to a softball field where a young man has a scalp laceration after he is hit in the head with a ball. You check the man's airway and breathing and treat the wound. No brain tissue or bone chips are showing. You should next check for changes in:

    A. pulse.

    B. respirations.

    C. blood pressure.

    D. level of consciousness.

_____ **41.** Although a burn patient may have severe pain, the real danger of burns that damage or destroy the skin is the loss of:

    A. nerve endings that signal further injuries.

    B. body fluids from the dehydrating effect of the heat of the burns.

    C. the skin's ability to prevent infection-causing bacteria from entering the body and essential fluids from seeping out.

    D. the skin's ability to regulate body temperature.

_____ **42.** Thermal burns, if still warm, should be immediately cooled with:

    A. butter.

    B. grease.

    C. cold water.

    D. burn ointment.

_____ **43.** A man whose car battery exploded in his face is screaming and holding his hands over his eyes when you arrive. You grab a nearby garden hose to flush his eyes, but he will not remove his hands from his face. After you flush the man's eyes, you should:

    A. arrange for rapid transport to the hospital.

    B. allow the man to put his hands back over his eyes.

    C. tell the man to keep his hands away from his eyes and cover him with a burn sheet.

    D. cover his eyes with a loose gauze bandage and arrange for prompt transport to the hospital.

Fill-in-the-Blanks

Read each item carefully, then complete the statement by filling in the missing word(s).

  1. Using the Rule of Nines, fill in the percentage of the body that would be burned in each of the combinations listed.

    _____ **A.** Both legs

    _____ **B.** The groin, the front, and the head

    _____ **C.** One-half of the front of the body and one arm

    _____ **D.** Back of both arms and the back

    _____ **E.** Front of both legs and the groin

2. Identify each of the following signs or characteristics associated with first-, second-, or third-degree burns by placing the numbers 1, 2, and 3, alone or in combination, in the blanks provided below.

_____ **A.** May not require medical treatment

_____ **B.** All layers of skin damaged

_____ **C.** Moderate to severe pain

_____ **D.** Loss of large quantities of body fluids

_____ **E.** Reddened skin

_____ **F.** Pain sometimes absent

_____ **G.** Minor to moderate pain

_____ **H.** Presence of blisters

_____ **I.** Deepest layers of skin not damaged

_____ **J.** Greatest risk of shock and/or infection

True/False

For each statement, write the letter "T" if you believe it to be more true than false, or write the letter "F" if you believe it to be more false than true.

_____ **1.** Whenever a patient who may have suffered a soft-tissue injury is approached, the first responder must remember the body substance isolation (BSI) concepts and precautions.

_____ **2.** The heart serves as the circulatory system's pump for the human body.

_____ **3.** The heart is divided into top chambers, or ventricles, and bottom chambers, or atria.

_____ **4.** The ventricles of the heart are larger and do more of the actual pumping than the atria.

_____ **5.** The human body has five main types of blood vessels.

_____ **6.** The arteries return the blood to the heart and lungs for more oxygen.

_____ **7.** The capillaries are the smallest of the blood vessels.

_____ **8.** The veins are the smallest of the blood vessels and form a network that distributes blood to all parts of the body.

_____ **9.** In the lungs, the blood gives off carbon monoxide and takes on oxygen.

_____ **10.** The liquid part of blood is known as the platelets.

_____ **11.** Plasma serves as the transporting medium for the solid parts of the blood.

_____ **12.** The pulse is a reflection of the heart rate.

_____ **13.** Normally, you can feel a patient's radial and carotid pulses.

_____ **14.** If a patient is in shock, the carotid pulse may be impossible to find, and it will be necessary to find the radial pulse instead.

_____ **15.** The carotid pulse can be located and checked more easily than the radial pulse in a patient who is suffering from shock.

_____ **16.** The state of inadequate delivery of blood to the organs is known as shock.

_____ **17.** Capillaries may expand to three or four times their normal size and cause blood pressure to fall.

_____ **18.** Shock may be a result of blood pooling in the capillaries and causing the vital organs to be deprived of blood.

_____ **19.** Anaphylactic shock may develop very quickly and, without rapid treatment, death may occur.

_____ **20.** External bleeding or unchecked internal bleeding may cause shock and death.

_____ **21.** The loss of one pint of blood will most likely cause shock.

_____ **22.** As long as blood loss is not visible from a wound, the patient is not in danger of shock from fluid loss.

_____ **23.** The level of agitation or quietness in a patient can easily be used to assess shock.

_____ **24.** Skin color is an important factor in detecting shock in a patient.

_____ **25.** General treatment of shock should include proper positioning of the patient.

_____ **26.** General treatment of shock should include arranging for transport of the patient to an appropriate medical facility.

_____ **27.** A patient who has shown signs and symptoms of shock should have the ABCs checked every minute.

_____ **28.** First responders may be able to treat the cause of shock if it is external bleeding.

_____ **29.** Most often, the cause of shock must be treated in the hospital setting.

_____ **30.** Patients who are in shock usually recover after receiving treatment at the scene.

_____ **31.** Patients who are in shock because of pump failure are seldom in critical condition and therefore seldom require prompt or rapid transport.

_____ **32.** Anaphylactic shock patients usually recover without treatment at a medical facility.

_____ **33.** Treatment of a patient with anaphylactic shock includes prompt ambulance transport to an appropriate medical facility.

_____ **34.** Shock may be caused by internal or external blood loss.

_____ **35.** The most common cause of shock is allergic reactions.

_____ **36.** Excessive bleeding is the most common cause of shock.

_____ **37.** Surgery may be necessary to treat patients with internal blood loss.

_____ **38.** Venous bleeding has a steady flow and may be life threatening.

_____ **39.** The most serious type of bleeding is venous bleeding.

_____ **40.** Unchecked arterial bleeding can result in death in a short time.

_____ **41.** Elevation, in conjunction with direct pressure, will usually stop severe bleeding.

_____ **42.** The most important pressure points in the body are the brachial artery pressure point and the femoral artery pressure point.

_____ **43.** In applying pressure to the brachial artery, you should remember the words "slap, slide, and squeeze."

_____ **44.** The femoral artery pressure point is easier to locate and squeeze than the brachial artery.

_____ **45.** Tourniquets may frequently be required in cases of severe and uncontrolled bleeding.

_____ **46.** A puncture wound is easily recognized by its bleeding.

_____ **47.** An object that causes a puncture wound and remains sticking out of the skin is called an impaled object.

_____ **48.** Lacerations, a type of open wound, range in severity from minor to life threatening.

_____ **49.** Most bleeding from the scalp and face can be controlled by applying direct manual pressure.

_____ **50.** All neck injuries are to be considered serious because of the proximity of the trachea, esophagus, vertebrae, and spinal cord.

_____ **51.** If an abdominal wound causes the intestines to protrude from the abdomen, the intestines should be gently pushed into the opening before covering with a sterile dressing.

_____ **52.** There is little blood supply in the genital area, so injuries to the genitals will seldom be serious.

_____ **53.** Any injured extremities should be splinted because of the possibility of an underlying fracture.

_____ **54.** Superficial or first-degree burns do not necessarily require hospital treatment.

_____ **55.** Partial-thickness or second-degree burns damage the deepest layers of the skin.

_____ **56.** Thermal burns may be treated with cold water.

_____ **57.** Drain cleaner and battery acid may cause chemical burns.

_____ **58.** If a patient has been exposed to a substance that has caused a chemical burn, the initial treatment should be washing the area thoroughly with running water.

_____ **59.** If a patient is touching a live electrical power source, your first act should be to remove the person from that position.

_____ **60.** Shock is defined as failure of the circulatory system.

_____ **61.** Cardiogenic shock occurs when the heart cannot pump enough blood to meet the body's needs.

_____ **62.** Sudden expansion of the capillaries has little effect on the body's circulatory system because these blood vessels are so small.

_____ **63.** Sudden expansion of the capillaries may be caused by some allergic reactions, spinal cord injuries, or even severe psychological stress.

_____ **64.** Although anaphylactic shock is very serious, its symptoms develop slowly over time.

_____ **65.** Positioning a person who is experiencing shock includes placing the patient in a horizontal position with the legs elevated 12 to 18 inches off the floor.

_____ **66.** The more blood the body loses from external or internal hemorrhaging, the more ineffective circulation becomes.

_____ 67. With internal bleeding, blood leaves the circulatory system but remains inside the body.

_____ 68. A patient in shock will have a shorter capillary refill time.

_____ 69. At first, a patient in shock will have rapid, shallow breathing, but as the patient gets worse, the breathing will become deep.

_____ 70. A rapid, weak pulse is a common sign of shock.

_____ 71. Nausea, vomiting, and extreme thirst are common signs of shock.

_____ 72. A trauma patient who is agitated and vocal at first, but then becomes quiet, may be going into shock.

_____ 73. The most common type of external blood loss is blood loss from the capillaries.

_____ 74. Once you have a patient with a nosebleed in the correct position, you should pinch the nostrils together for at least 5 minutes.

_____ 75. A patient who has a nosebleed can often care for himself.

_____ 76. An impaled object should be removed and a dressing applied before the patient is sent to the hospital.

_____ 77. An occlusive dressing does not let any air pass through it.

_____ 78. Gunshot wounds to the neck or trunk are a major cause of spinal cord injuries.

_____ 79. Bruises of the legs and arms with tenderness and swelling should be splinted in case of an underlying fracture.

_____ 80. The first priority in caring for an open wound is to control the bleeding as quickly as possible.

_____ 81. With severe bleeding, you should only use a commercially prepared sterile bandage.

_____ 82. If a wound is contaminated, you should clean it before dressing and bandaging it.

_____ 83. Direct pressure can be applied to an open wound to stop bleeding even if no dressing is available.

_____ 84. If a dressing becomes soaked with blood, it should be removed and replaced with a clean one.

_____ 85. Dressings cover wounds, and bandages hold them in place.

_____ 86. Although roller gauze is easier to use and stays in place better, you may find that a triangular bandage is more useful in certain situations.

_____ 87. You can check whether a bandage is too tight by feeling for a pulse at a point farther away from the heart than the bandage.

_____ 88. You should wear protective medical gloves before touching blood or open wounds.

_____ 89. The first step in caring for a person who has a tissue-damaging chemical on the skin is to remove the chemical from the skin.

_____ 90. Flushing a patient's skin or eyes with water will relieve only the pain of chemical burns.

_____ 91. Any available water supply should be used to immediately flush damaging chemicals from the patient's skin or eyes.

_____ 92. It may be impossible to help someone who is being electrocuted if he or she is in contact with a live power source that you cannot disconnect or turn off.

_____ 93. A child who has burned his or her mouth after chewing on an electrical cord is likely to have injuries much worse than you can see.

_____ 94. Visible external electrical burns should be covered with a dry, sterile dressing.

_____ 95. If a downed power line is sitting on the hood of a car and the people inside seem uninjured, you should tell them to leave the car.

_____ 96. A person who is nearly hit by lightning can have severe internal damage from the electrical burns.

Short Answer

Write a brief response to each of the following questions.

1. Name the three primary parts of the circulatory system.

_____

_____

_____

2. Name the three primary causes of shock.

_____

_____

_____

3. Name three things you could use for an occlusive dressing.

_____

_____

_____

4. What are the three classifications of burns?

_____

_____

_____

5. What should you use to cover the area after a thermal burn has cooled?

_____

_____

_____

6. Name three signs and/or symptoms of respiratory burns.

_____

_____

_____

7. Describe the differences between capillary, venous, and arterial bleeding.

_____

_____

_____

8. What are the most important pressure points to know?

_____

_____

_____

9. List the four major principles of open wound treatment.

_____

_____

_____

Word Fun

The following crossword puzzle is an activity provided to reinforce correct spelling and understanding of terminology associated with emergency care and the first responder. Use the clues in the column to complete the puzzle.

Across

1. Cut

4. Burn caused by a strong substance

6. _____ wound, a wound where a bullet leaves the body

7. Scrape

8. Burn caused by heat

9. _____ wound, special type of puncture wound

11. _____ wound, a wound where skin remains intact

Down

2. Burn that causes major internal injuries

3. Wound from penetration

5. _____ object, an object sticking out from the skin

6. _____ wound, a wound where a bullet enters the body

7. Tearing away of body tissue

10. _____ wound, a wound where skin is disrupted

Labeling

Label the following diagrams with the correct terms.

1. Label the parts of the circulatory system.

A. _____

B. _____

C. _____

D. _____

E. _____

F. _____

G. _____

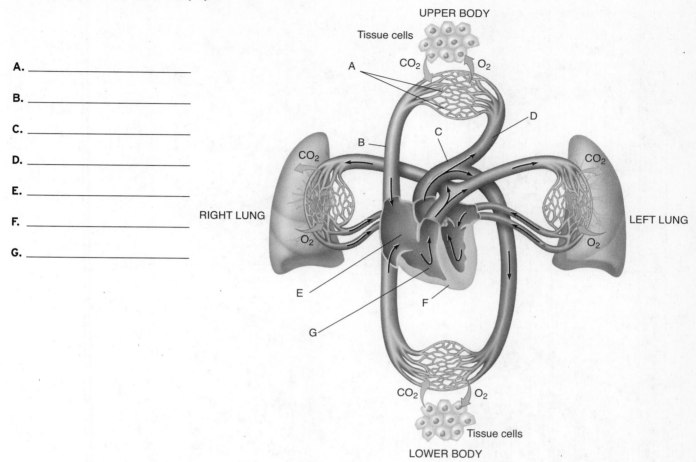

2. Label these three types of external bleeding.

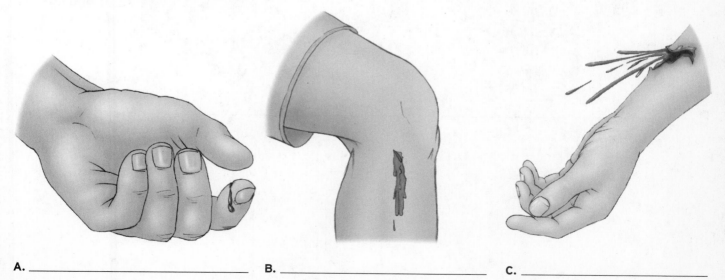

A. _____   B. _____   C. _____

3. Label these types of wounds.

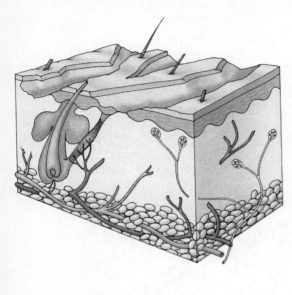

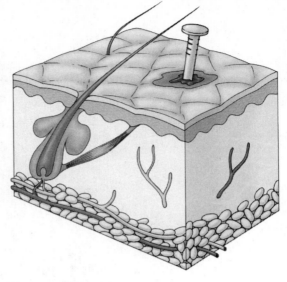

A. _____

B. _____

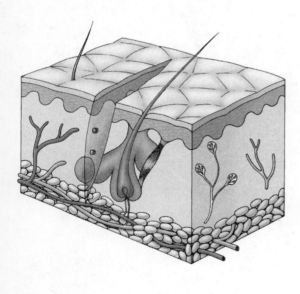

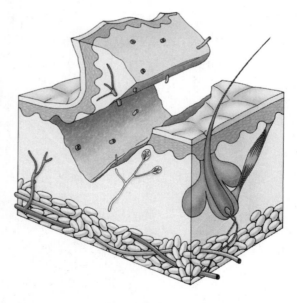

C. _____

D. _____

You Make the Call

The following scenarios provide an opportunity to explore the concerns associated with patient management. Read the scenarios, then describe the best way to handle the situation.

1. When you arrive at the scene, you find that your patient is a 6-year-old who was preparing breakfast to surprise her mother. She started the water boiling and when she attempted to pour it into a mug, the pan slipped and the boiling water burned her abdomen, the lower part of her left arm, and the front of both legs. Most of the burn area is covered with large blisters. Some of the blisters are intact, and others are broken with the skin peeling. What should you do?

2. You are dispatched to a local machine shop for the report of a man with an injured arm. You are on the scene in less than 1 minute because you are one block away. As you arrive, you are told that the patient got his arm caught in a lathe, and he has a severe laceration and damage to his lower arm. Upon examination, you note blood spurting from the patient's lower arm. What should you do?

CHAPTER

14 Injuries to Muscles and Bones

Matching
Match each of the items in the left column to the appropriate description in the right column.

_____ **1.** Mechanism of injury

_____ **2.** Closed fracture

_____ **3.** Sprain

_____ **4.** Dislocation

_____ **5.** Paralysis

_____ **6.** Joint

_____ **7.** Trauma

_____ **8.** Seizures

_____ **9.** Osteoporosis

_____ **10.** Cerebrospinal fluid

A. Sudden episodes of uncontrolled electrical activity in the brain

B. Place where two bones come in contact with each other

C. Means by which a traumatic injury occurs

D. Joint injury in which the joint is partially or temporarily dislocated and supporting ligaments are either stretched or torn

E. Wound or injury, either physical or psychological

F. Fracture in which the overlying skin has not been damaged

G. Clear, watery, straw-colored fluid that fills the space between the brain and spinal chord

H. Disruption of a joint so that the bone ends are not in alignment

I. Abnormal brittleness of the bones in older people

J. Inability of a conscious person to move voluntarily

Multiple Choice
Read each item carefully, then select the best response.

_____ **1.** Muscles of the body may be called:

  A. voluntary.

  B. involuntary.

  C. cardiac.

  D. all of the above.

_____ **2.** Muscles that can be contracted and relaxed by a person at will are called:

  A. voluntary.

  B. involuntary.

  C. cardiac.

  D. all of the above.

3. Muscles that are found in the inside of the digestive tract and other internal organs are called:
   A. voluntary.
   B. involuntary.
   C. cardiac.
   D. all of the above.

4. The mechanism of injury refers to:
   A. how to move an injured patient.
   B. whether a patient can move an injured limb.
   C. the means by which an injury has occurred.
   D. the type of transport needed for injuries.

5. Musculoskeletal injuries may be caused by:
   A. direct force.
   B. indirect force.
   C. twisting force.
   D. all of the above.

6. Terms used to describe musculoskeletal injuries include:
   A. fractures, dislocations, and sprains.
   B. closed and open fractures.
   C. painful, swollen, deformed extremity (PSDE).
   D. all of the above.

7. An injury that causes tears of the ligaments and separation of the bone ends is a/an:
   A. open fracture.
   B. sprain.
   C. dislocation.
   D. closed fracture.

8. An injury in which a joint is partially dislocated and there is excessive stretching of supporting ligaments is called a/an:
   A. open fracture.
   B. sprain.
   C. dislocation.
   D. closed fracture.

9. During examination of an injured limb, the first responder's best indicator of an underlying fracture, dislocation, or sprain is:
   A. an open wound.
   B. bruising.
   C. tenderness.
   D. swelling.

10. Signs that indicate an injury to the limb may include:
    A. deformity.
    B. swelling or bruising.
    C. tenderness or pain with motion.
    D. all of the above.

11. Use of the capillary refill test:
    A. will indicate a circulation problem.
    B. takes 2 to 3 minutes.
    C. gives an accurate indication under all circumstances.
    D. all of the above.

_____ **12.** General principles of splinting of limb injuries include which of the following?

   A. Do not splint joints unless injury is visible.

   B. Leave clothing in place.

   C. Splint the limb in the position it was found.

   D. All of the above.

_____ **13.** Splints made from wood, aluminum, or plastic are called:

   A. rigid splints.

   B. traction splints.

   C. improvised splints.

   D. all of the above.

_____ **14.** A clear plastic, inflatable splint is a type of:

   A. rigid splint.

   B. traction splint.

   C. soft splint.

   D. all of the above.

_____ **15.** A triangular bandage or similar material tied around the neck to support the weight of an injured upper extremity is called a/an:

   A. improvised splint.

   B. sling.

   C. traction sling.

   D. rigid splint.

_____ **16.** Head injuries may cause:

   A. bleeding and/or swelling within the skull.

   B. seepage of CSF.

   C. injury to the spine.

   D. all of the above.

_____ **17.** What is the first step for a first responder to take if there are signs or symptoms of head injury?

   A. Check and maintain the airway.

   B. Call for additional help.

   C. Immobilize the head and stabilize the neck.

   D. Check circulation and bleeding.

_____ **18.** When facial injuries are present:

   A. place the patient in the recovery position.

   B. bandage the entire head and face.

   C. stabilize the head in a neutral position.

   D. all of the above.

_____ **19.** Signs and symptoms of a spinal cord injury include which of the following?

   A. Tenderness over a point on the spine or neck

   B. Tingling in a part of the body below the neck

   C. Laceration or bruise to the head, neck, or spine

   D. All of the above

_____ **20.** If a patient with injuries to the chest exhibits a reversed movement of the chest during breathing:

   A. he or she may need oxygen.

   B. suspect flail chest.

   C. place a pillow on the patient's chest.

   D. all of the above.

_____ **21.** One way a dislocation differs from a sprain is that in a dislocation:

    A. fewer nerves are damaged.

    B. there is less pain.

    C. the supporting ligaments are torn from the joint.

    D. the bones always realign into their natural position in the joint.

_____ **22.** An injury in which the bone is broken but the skin remains intact is called a/an:

    A. bruise.

    B. contusion.

    C. closed fracture.

    D. open fracture.

_____ **23.** Which of the following statements best describes an open fracture?

    A. The ends of the bones at the break are aligned but are more than an inch apart.

    B. The risk of infection is high because dirt and bacteria often enter the wound.

    C. Bleeding is minimal because the bone end causes a puncture wound.

    D. To break the bone, a bullet or some sharp object must have broken the skin.

_____ **24.** To determine if a patient has adequate circulation in an injured arm, you should check the _____ pulse.

    A. carotid

    B. radial

    C. tibial

    D. femoral

_____ **25.** Emergency care of a patient who has no pulse or capillary refill in an injured limb should be to:

    A. encourage the patient to move the limb.

    B. briskly rub the limb to stimulate circulation.

    C. warm the limb to stimulate circulation.

    D. arrange for immediate transport to a hospital.

_____ **26.** A man who shows no sign of injury in his arm is unable to make a fist. He has most likely injured what structures in the arm?

    A. Nerves

    B. Muscles

    C. Bones

    D. Tendons and ligaments

_____ **27.** To test for sensation in an injured arm, you should touch the tips of the _____ fingers.

    A. index and middle

    B. index and little

    C. middle and little

    D. middle and ring

_____ **28.** To test for sensation in an injured leg, you should touch the tip of the big toe and the:

    A. heel.

    B. arch of the foot.

    C. top of the foot.

    D. side of the little toe.

_____ **29.** You should always inflate a soft splint with:

    A. water.

    B. your mouth (breath).

    C. an air pump.

    D. an air cylinder.

_____ **30.** Most splinting operations require two people; the first applies the splint and the second:

    A. inflates the splint.

    B. distracts the patient.

    C. supports the limb.

    D. makes sure the splint is applied properly.

_____ **31.** Emergency care of a patient who has a broken thighbone should include placing the patient in a comfortable position and:

    A. elevating the injured leg.

    B. bending the injured leg at the knee.

    C. treating the patient for shock.

    D. applying ice or cold compresses to the leg.

_____ **32.** You are in a remote rural area where a fire is burning near some farm equipment. You need to move a patient with a fractured thigh bone, but EMTs will not arrive for another 10 minutes. The best way to prevent additional injury would be to:

    A. wait for the EMTs to arrive.

    B. try to put the fire out.

    C. leave the patient and find help.

    D. secure the injured leg to the uninjured leg and then move the patient.

Fill-in-the-Blanks

Read each item carefully, then complete the statement by filling in the missing word(s).

1. Splinting of the cervical spine is accomplished with a/an _____ and a long or short spine board or backboard.

2. The primary danger in severe facial injuries is _____ of the airway.

3. How injuries occur is known as the _____ of injury.

4. A/An _____ is a disruption that tears the supporting ligaments of the joint.

5. One sign of a head injury, known as _____ sign, is a bruise behind one or both ears.

6. A spinal cord injury may paralyze respiratory muscles and cause the patient to breathe using only the diaphragm, which is known as _____ breathing.

7. Fracture of three or more ribs in at least two places causes a condition known as _____ chest.

8. _____ is the abnormal brittleness of the bones in older people caused by loss of calcium.

9. Do not move patients unless it is necessary to perform _____ or remove them from a dangerous situation.

10. The three basic types of splints are rigid, soft, and _____.

True/False

For each statement, write the letter "T" if you believe it to be more true than false, or write the letter "F" if you believe it to be more false than true.

_____ 1. The skeletal system is divided into seven areas.

_____ 2. The wrist and hand are considered part of the upper extremity.

_____ 3. The 12 sets of ribs provide protection for the heart and other organs and are attached to the spine and sternum.

_____ 4. Each of the essential organs of the body is encased in a protective bony structure.

_____ 5. The red blood cells are manufactured within the spaces inside the bone.

_____ 6. Muscles and bones work together and are often called the musculoskeletal system.

_____ 7. A first responder needs to be able to identify and name the signs and symptoms of an injury and to make an accurate diagnosis.

_____ 8. In a closed fracture, the end of the broken bone will be visible through the broken skin.

_____ 9. An open fracture will have more bleeding and more contamination than a closed fracture.

_____ 10. A sprain can be thought of as a partial dislocation.

_____ 11. Body substance isolation (BSI) techniques are usually not of great concern when examining and treating patients who have suffered musculoskeletal injuries.

_____ 12. Injuries to limbs do not usually require the general patient assessment sequence.

_____ 13. When examining a limb for injury, start at the top of the limb and move toward the distal aspect.

_____ 14. A thorough inspection and hands-on examination of an injured limb will not incorporate any information given by the patient verbally.

_____ 15. The pulse of an injured limb should be checked at a point distal to the injury.

_____ 16. The absence of a pulse or capillary refill in an injured limb indicates that the patient has been exposed to cold temperatures.

_____ 17. Any open wound, deformity, swelling, or bruising of a limb should be considered evidence of a possible limb injury.

_____ 18. Splinting of a limb injury is required only if the patient is unable to move it.

_____ 19. Splinting prevents closed fractures from becoming open fractures during movement or transport.

_____ 20. In a limb injury, notation of the pulse and sensation is not needed as long as the limb is splinted.

_____ 21. An inflatable clear plastic splint is inflated most easily and most effectively with a pump.

_____ 22. Acceptable splints for injured limbs can be fashioned from newspapers, magazines, towels, or belts.

_____ 23. A first responder should apply a traction splint if a fracture of the thighbone is suspected.

_____ 24. A competent, well-trained first responder can easily splint most injuries to limbs.

_____ 25. In the proper application of a sling, the elbow should be slightly higher than the wrist and hand.

_____ 26. Triangular bandages can effectively be used to immobilize and treat injuries to the arms, clavicle, and shoulders.

_____ 27. Common hip injuries such as dislocations and fractures may result from high-energy trauma.

_____ 28. Hip fractures are a break in the hip joint, most often occurring as a result of high-energy trauma.

_____ 29. A patient suspected of a hip fracture should be transported on a long backboard with splinting that uses pillows and/or blankets.

_____ 30. Securing the two lower extremities together will allow for quick removal of an injured patient from a dangerous environment.

_____ 31. A suspected fracture of the femur is effectively splinted with a traction splint.

_____ 32. Once the assessment of pulse, capillary refill, and nerve function have been checked and found to be within acceptable limits, it can be assumed that the patient with a limb injury is stable.

_____ 33. Once a knee injury is successfully splinted, the patient can safely be transported.

_____ 34. A well-trained first responder will be able to adequately splint most limb injuries alone.

_____ 35. One part of the human skull is the cranium, which protects the brain.

_____ 36. Spinal injury and head injury are usually not closely related.

_____ **37.** Brain injury is often caused by the brain striking the inside of the skull.

_____ **38.** All patients with head injuries should have the cervical spine splinted.

_____ **39.** The primary danger in severe facial injuries is obstruction of the airway.

_____ **40.** Any facial injuries with resulting profuse bleeding require treatment for life-threatening injuries.

_____ **41.** Abdominal breathing is a sign or symptom indicating spinal injury.

_____ **42.** If abdominal breathing is detected, oxygen should be administered when available.

_____ **43.** If spinal injury is suspected and there are breathing problems, the head tilt–chin lift technique should be used to open the airway.

_____ **44.** A long or short backboard and rigid collar are used to splint the cervical spine.

_____ **45.** In treating patients with neck injuries who are wearing motorcycle or football helmets, the helmet should be removed before proceeding with treatment.

_____ **46.** Rib fractures seldom cause interference with breathing or digestion.

_____ **47.** Rib fractures may cause internal injuries resulting in shock.

_____ **48.** A patient with a chest wound should always be transported in a sitting position.

_____ **49.** You should avoid cutting the patient's clothing to inspect an injured limb unless you are certain the patient has a serious wound.

_____ **50.** Part of your visual examination should include comparing the injured limb with the opposite, uninjured limb.

_____ **51.** Even if there are no signs of injury after a thorough visual examination of a limb, you should examine the limb by feeling it with your hands.

_____ **52.** Closed fractures, dislocations, and sprains are characterized by numbness or a slight tingling sensation at the injury site.

_____ **53.** Very few patients can tell where or whether their arms or legs are broken.

_____ **54.** In a hands-on examination of a limb, you should start where the limb joins the torso and then move to the hands or feet.

_____ **55.** Every part of a limb should be squeezed gently but firmly during a hands-on examination.

_____ **56.** You should always ask a patient to move the limb after your visual and hands-on examination.

_____ **57.** All limbs with open wounds should be splinted before the open wound is covered.

_____ **58.** You should always splint a limb injury before moving a patient unless you or the patient are in danger or if circumstances make it impossible to apply an effective splint.

_____ **59.** The only reason injured limbs are splinted in the field is to prevent further damage from occurring during transport.

_____ **60.** A splint should immobilize the bone above and below the wound, break, or dislocation.

_____ **61.** You should pad all rigid splints.

_____ **62.** You may move the limb as much as you want when applying a splint to ensure that the splint is applied correctly.

_____ **63.** If you are unsure about whether to splint a limb injury, you should splint it.

_____ **64.** Elderly people can break their hips by simply falling down.

_____ **65.** Hip dislocations are difficult to detect because there is little pain and no obvious deformity.

_____ **66.** A patient who has a fracture of the right hip will appear to have a shorter right leg.

_____ **67.** In hip fractures, the hip joint itself is broken.

_____ **68.** You should immobilize patients with hip injuries in the position in which you found them.

_____ **69.** Even if you see no obvious signs of injury, any elderly patient who has pain in the hip, thigh, or knee should be treated as if he or she has a hip fracture.

_____ **70.** You should quickly treat an open chest wound with a large pressure dressing.

Short Answer

Write a brief response to each of the following questions.

1. Name the four primary functions of the skeletal system.

_____

_____

_____

2. Name the three major types of injuries to the musculoskeletal system.

_____

_____

_____

3. Name four signs of injury you should look for during a visual examination of the limb.

_____

_____

_____

4. What two questions should you ask a patient who has a limb injury?

_____

_____

_____

5. Name two ways to check for adequate circulation in an injured limb.

_____

_____

_____

6. Name three key signs and symptoms of a spinal injury.

_____

_____

_____

7. Name three things you should always check on an injured limb both before and after splinting.

_____

_____

_____

8. Define mechanism of injury.

_____

_____

_____

9. Describe the three types of mechanism of injury and give an example of each type.

_____

_____

_____

10. List the seven areas of the skeletal system.

_____

_____

_____

11. Describe how you would splint an injury to the elbow.

_____

_____

_____

12. Describe four signs or symptoms of a head injury.

_____

_____

_____

13. Describe the treatment for a head injury.

_____

_____

_____

14. List three primary signs or symptoms of extremity injuries.

_____

_____

_____

Labeling

Label the following diagrams with the correct terms.

1.   Label the seven major areas of the human skeleton.

A. _____

B. _____

C. _____

D. _____

E. _____

F. _____

G. _____

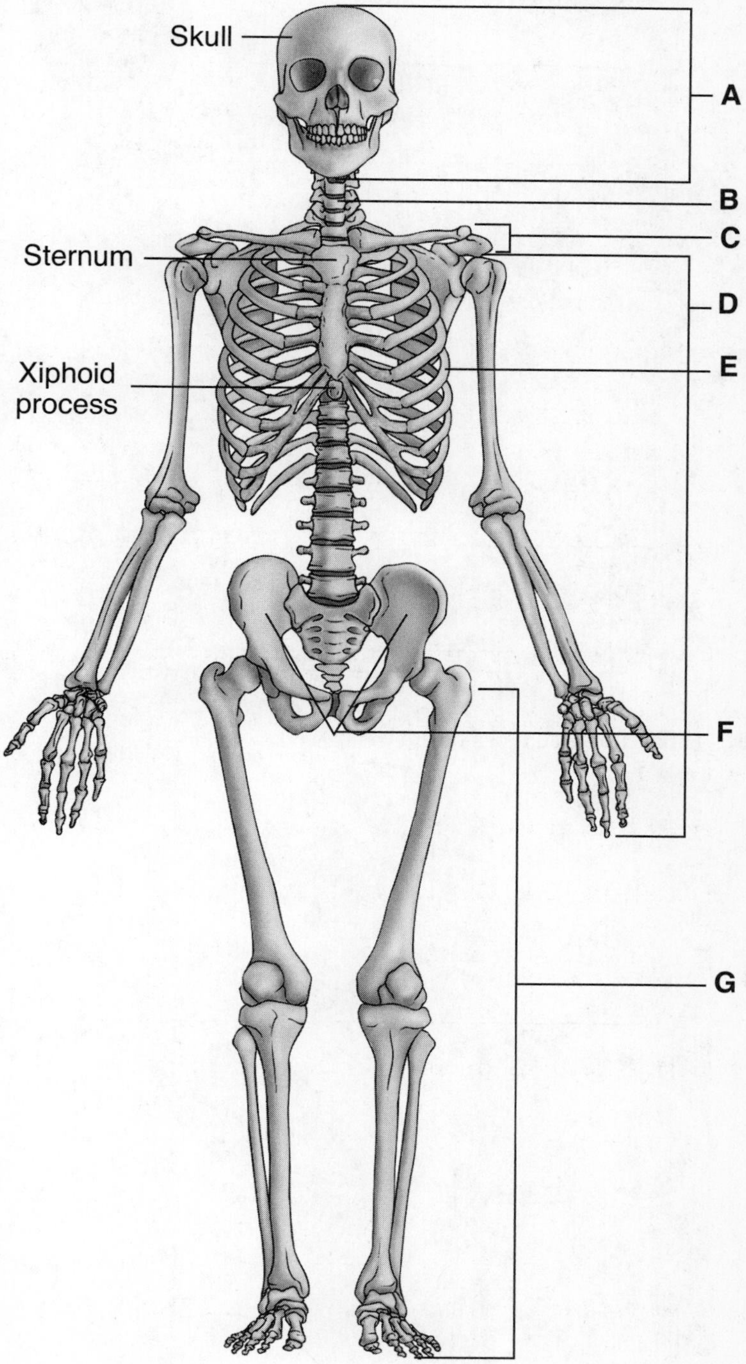

Skull

Sternum

Xiphoid
process

A

B

C

D

E

F

G

2. Label the five sections of the spine.

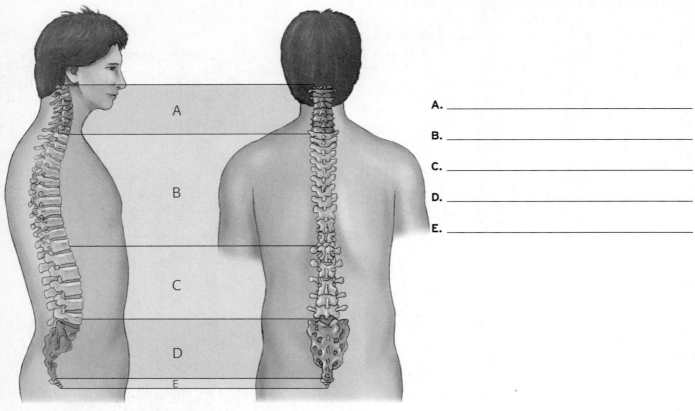

A. _____

B. _____

C. _____

D. _____

E. _____

3. Label the three types of muscle.

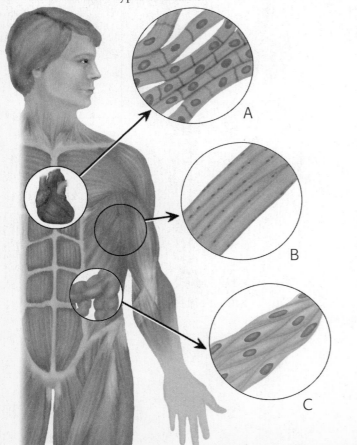

A. _____

B. _____

C. _____

Skill Drills

Test your knowledge by filling in the correct words in the photo captions.

A. Checking Circulation, Sensation, and Movement in an Injured Extremity

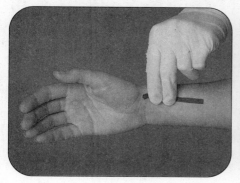 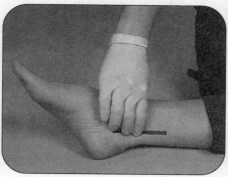 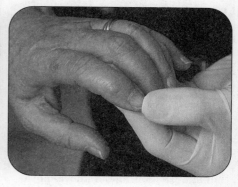

1. Check for circulation. If the injury is to an upper extremity, check the _____ pulse.

2. If the injury is to a lower extremity, check the _____ pulse.

3. Test _____ on a finger or toe of the injured limb.

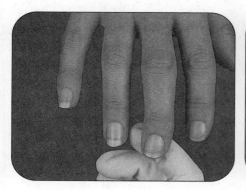  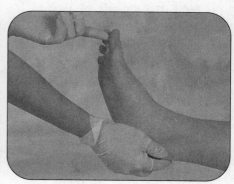

4. Release pressure. _____ color should return.

5. Check for _____ at fingertips.

6. Check for _____ at toes.

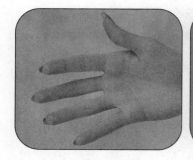 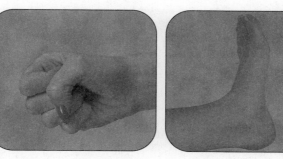

7. Check for _____ of the upper extremities by asking the patient to open and close the fist.

8. Check for _____ of the lower extremities by asking the patient to flex and extend the ankle.

B. Removing the Mask on a Sports Helmet

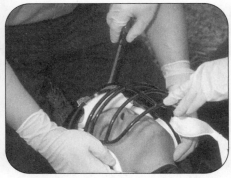

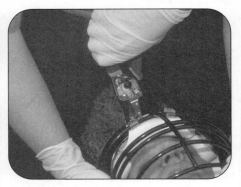

1. Stabilize the patient's head and helmet in a _____, in-line position. Then remove the mask in one of two ways.

2. Use a _____ to unscrew the retaining clips for the face mask, or perform step 3.

3. Use a _____ designed for cutting retainer clips.

A. Checking Circulation, Sensation, and Movement in an Injured Extremity

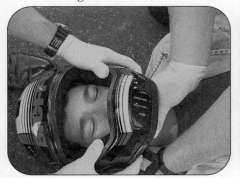

1. Kneel down at the patient's head and open the face shield to assess _____ and _____.

2. Stabilize the helmet by placing your hands on either side of it, ensuring that your fingers are on the patient's _____ to prevent movement of the head. Your partner can then loosen the strap.

3. Your partner should place one hand on the _____ and the other behind the _____ at the occiput.

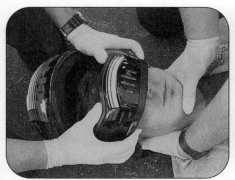

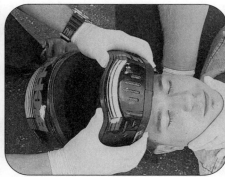

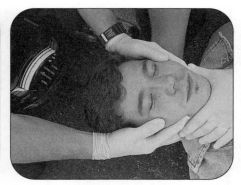

4. Gently slip the helmet off about _____ and then stop.

5. Your partner slides his or her hand from the occiput to the _____ of the head to prevent the head from snapping back once the helmet is removed.

6. With your partner's hand in place, remove the helmet and stabilize the _____. Apply a cervical collar and then secure the patient to a long backboard.

You Make the Call

The following scenario provides an opportunity to explore the concerns associated with patient management. Read the scenario, then describe the best way to handle the situation.

You are dispatched to the scene of a "long fall." When you arrive, you find a 26-year-old man lying on the snow next to a ladder leaning on the house and Christmas lights hanging from the front of the house. His right leg is deformed. What should you do?

CHAPTER

15 Childbirth

Matching

Match each of the items in the left column to the appropriate description in the right column.

_____ **1.** Placenta

_____ **2.** Bulb syringe

_____ **3.** Breech

_____ **4.** Bloody show

_____ **5.** Uterus

A. Muscular organ that holds and nourishes the developing baby

B. Bloody mucus plug that is discharged from the vagina when labor begins

C. Rubber or plastic device used for gentle suction in newborns and small infants

D. Presentation in which the baby's buttocks, arm, shoulder, or leg appear first, rather than the head

E. Life support system of the baby during its time inside the mother

Multiple Choice

Read each item carefully, then select the best response.

_____ **1.** If the baby's head is crowning, that means the baby will be born:

    A. breech.

    B. in a matter of minutes.

    C. with breathing difficulties.

    D. with a prolapsed cord.

_____ **2.** When you assess for crowning, you notice the umbilical cord protruding through the cervix. Your care should include all of the following EXCEPT:

    A. arranging for immediate transport.

    B. laying the mother on her right side.

    C. raising the mother's hips.

    D. administering oxygen.

_____ **3.** The first thing you must decide during a childbirth situation is whether you:

    A. are calm enough to handle the situation.

    B. have the proper equipment to deal with the situation.

    C. have time to transport the mother to the hospital before delivery.

    D. can rely on the mother to know enough about childbirth to help you with the delivery.

_____ **4.** A young mother in labor tells you that this is her first pregnancy, that she has been having contractions for the past 8 hours, and that her water broke some time ago. You should prepare to:

    A. deliver the baby because birth is imminent after 8 hours of labor.

    B. ask about discharge of bloody mucus because delivery will be a long time off unless this has also occurred.

    C. transport her immediately to the nearest hospital because the length of her labor indicates a serious problem with the pregnancy.

    D. time the contractions and check to see if the head is crowning before transporting her to a hospital.

_____ **5.** The mother's contractions are 4 minutes apart, and the baby's head is not crowning yet. In what stage of labor is the mother?

    A. First

    b. Second

    c. Third

    d. Between the second and the third

_____ **6.** A woman in labor is 30 minutes from the nearest hospital, and an ambulance has not yet been called when you arrive on the scene. You should:

    A. transport the mother immediately in your own vehicle.

    B. prepare for the delivery, given the mother's condition.

    C. call an ambulance but prepare for the delivery.

    D. call an ambulance, but transport the mother in your own vehicle if contractions start occurring closer together.

_____ **7.** The best way to detect crowning would be to:

    A. look at the vagina during a contraction.

    B. ask the mother if she feels the baby's head at her vagina.

    C. wait until a contraction has ended and then look at the vagina.

    D. use your gloved fingertips to feel gently for the baby's head at the vagina.

_____ **8.** To prevent the baby's head from emerging too rapidly, you should tell the mother to:

    A. stop pushing.

    B. hold her breath.

    C. push more slowly.

    D. relax her abdominal muscles.

_____ **9.** A mother in the second stage of labor says she has to move her bowels. You should:

    A. help her to the bathroom.

    B. find a container she can use as a bedpan.

    C. ask her if she is sure it is not just the pressure of the baby that she is feeling.

    D. tell her she is only feeling the pressure of the baby and should not try to relieve the feeling now.

_____ **10.** The only time you should actually handle the umbilical cord is when:

    A. it is caught in the vagina.

    B. it is wrapped around the baby's neck.

    C. delivery of the placenta is delayed.

    D. you pull on it to deliver the placenta.

_____ **11.** After a baby has been delivered, you should immediately:

    A. try to get it to cry.

    B. invert it.

    C. begin mouth-to-mouth resuscitation.

    D. clear its nose, mouth, and throat of secretions.

_____ **12.** If a baby is born with no signs of life and has an unpleasant odor, you should first:

    A. begin resuscitation efforts.

    B. try to keep the baby warm.

    C. tell the mother she has had a miscarriage.

    D. check the mother's vital signs.

_____ **13.** A mother tells you that she was pregnant for only 7 months with the baby you have just helped deliver. You should recognize that the baby will likely:

    A. require CPR.

    B. have bluish skin.

    C. need to be kept especially warm.

    D. have a larger head than a full-term baby.

_____ **14.** The muscular organ that holds and nourishes a developing baby is called the:

    A. placenta.

    B. vagina.

    C. uterus.

    D. fallopian tube.

_____ **15.** The process of delivering a baby is called:

    A. crowning.

    B. labor.

    C. contractions.

    D. fetus.

_____ **16.** During the first stage of labor:

    A. the bloody show occurs.

    B. the crowning of the baby's head occurs.

    C. the pregnant woman should not be transported.

    D. all of the above.

_____ **17.** You usually have time to transport a woman in labor when the contractions are more than how many minutes apart?

    A. 4

    B. 5

    C. 6

    D. 7

_____ **18.** The baby's head is beginning to emerge. Which of the following should occur?

    A. The woman should stop pushing.

    B. The woman should push harder.

    C. The woman should breathe rapidly.

    D. Both A and C.

_____ **19.** A newborn infant can be placed so that it can suck on the mother's breast. This action will help:

    A. stimulate the delivery of the placenta.

    B. the mother's uterus contract.

    C. stop any bleeding that may be occurring.

    D. all of the above.

_____ **20.** In the case of a breech birth:

    A. attempt to arrange for immediate transport to a medical facility.

    B. there will be no crowning of the baby's head.

    C. injury to the woman and to the baby is more likely.

    D. all of the above.

_____ **21.** If an infant does not begin breathing independently after delivery, the first responder may:

   A. suction the mouth and nose.

   B. tilt the infant's head down and to the side.

   C. gently stimulate the soles of the feet and/or back.

   D. all of the above.

Fill-in-the-Blanks

Read each item carefully, then complete the statement by filling in the missing word(s).

1. The _____, or afterbirth, draws nutrients from the wall of the mother's uterus.

2. Stage _____ of labor is when the mother's body prepares for birth.

3. To determine when the baby's head is _____, you must observe the vagina during a contraction.

4. Your primary purpose is to _____ in the delivery of the baby.

5. In a normal delivery, there is no need to cut the _____ cord.

6. In a/an _____ birth, some part of the baby other than the top of the head comes down the birth canal first.

7. A/An _____, also called a spontaneous abortion, is the delivery of an incomplete or underdeveloped fetus.

8. In the event of _____ births, another set of labor contractions will begin shortly after the delivery of the first baby.

9. Contractions should be timed from the _____ of one contraction to the beginning of the next contraction.

10. Any baby weighing less than 5.5 pounds or delivered before 37 weeks of pregnancy is considered _____.

True/False

For each statement, write the letter "T" if you believe it to be more true than false, or write the letter "F" if you believe it to be more false than true.

_____ **1.** Assisting in childbirth usually means no more than receiving the baby as it is delivered and making sure it begins to breathe.

_____ **2.** Wearing kitchen gloves for a delivery is better than wearing no gloves at all.

_____ **3.** You must pull the baby's body out of the mother after the head has emerged.

_____ **4.** If a baby turns to the side after the head emerges, you should try to correct its position.

_____ **5.** If instead of normal crowning, you see a breech presentation, you should prepare for immediate delivery.

_____ **6.** In the case of a breech birth, it may be necessary to gently pull the baby to assist with delivery.

_____ **7.** Prolapse of the umbilical cord means that the cord comes out of the vagina before the baby is born and needs to be pushed back into the vagina until delivery.

_____ **8.** If it looks like a woman has lost about 2 cups of blood during delivery, you should rapidly transport her to the hospital.

_____ **9.** If a miscarriage occurs, all of the tissues that have been passed from the vagina should be saved.

_____ **10.** A stillborn baby is one who does not begin breathing independently within 1 minute of delivery.

_____ **11.** Normal labor consists of five distinct stages.

_____ **12.** A pregnant woman in either of the first two stages of labor should be transported.

_____ **13.** In the second stage of labor, you will see the baby's head crowning during contractions.

_____ **14.** Stage three of labor involves delivery of the placenta.

_____ **15.** Contractions during labor are timed by calculating the amount of time between the end of one contraction and the beginning of the next.

_____ **16.** A woman who has previously had a baby will have more time to reach the hospital than a woman who is pregnant with her first baby.

_____ **17.** Transport of a pregnant woman in labor should not be attempted if the contractions are less than 3 minutes apart or if the baby's head is crowning.

_____ **18.** Newspapers, towels, aluminum foil, and shower curtains can be used as equipment during a home delivery.

_____ **19.** Face and eye protection are not necessary during delivery.

_____ **20.** Delivery of a baby should not be attempted unless a prepackaged delivery kit is available.

_____ **21.** In order to avoid contamination during delivery, a woman who is in labor should be encouraged to use the bathroom for bowel movements.

_____ **22.** It is important that the umbilical cord is cut as soon as the baby is breathing independently.

_____ **23.** Massaging the uterus will help it become firm and will help stop bleeding.

_____ **24.** If an infant does not breathe on its own within 1 minute after birth, CPR should be begun immediately.

_____ **25.** When a baby is born in an unbroken bag of waters, you should carefully break the bag, push it away from the baby's nose and mouth, and suction the baby's nose and mouth.

Short Answer

Write a brief response to each of the following questions.

1. Describe the three stages of labor.

_____

_____

_____

2. Describe the five steps in resuscitating a newborn infant.

_____

_____

_____

3. List the four phases of the second stage of labor.

_____

_____

_____

4. What is the appropriate procedure for putting on sterile gloves?

_____

_____

_____

5. Name three important steps of care after a miscarriage.

_____

_____

_____

Word Fun

Across

1. developing baby
2. transports nutrients to baby
4. _____ cord (hint: not umbilical)
5. encases baby
8. abnormal presentation during delivery
9. spontaneous abortion

Down

1. connect ovaries and uterus
3. vagina
6. appearance of the baby's head
7. holds fertilized egg

Labeling

Label the following diagrams with the correct terms.

1. Label the anatomy of a pregnant woman.

A. _____

B. _____

C. _____

D. _____

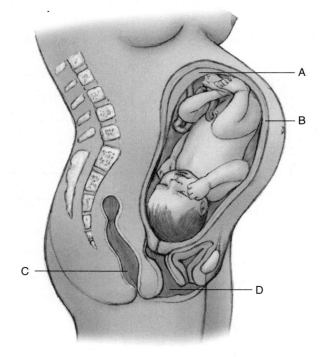

2. Label the phases of the second stage of labor.

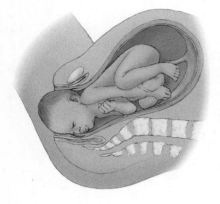

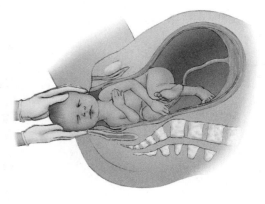

A. _____

B. _____

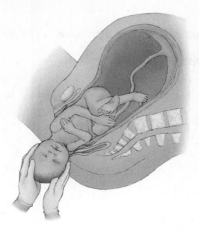 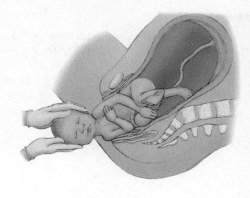

C. _____ D. _____

Skill Drills

Test your knowledge by filling in the correct words in the photo captions.

A. Resuscitating a Newborn Infant

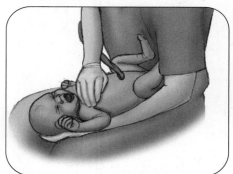 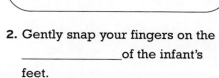 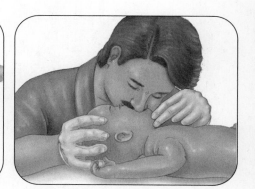

1. Tilt the infant so the _____ is down and to the side to clear the airway.

2. Gently snap your fingers on the _____ of the infant's feet.

3. Begin _____.

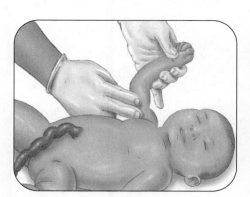 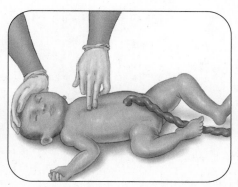

4. Check for a _____ pulse.

5. Begin _____, using the middle and ring fingers.

You Make the Call

The following scenario provides an opportunity to explore the concerns associated with patient management. Read the scenario, then describe the best way to handle the situation.

You arrive on the scene and find a 32-year-old woman who tells you she is 8½ months pregnant. This is her fifth pregnancy, and she's afraid she won't be able to make it to the hospital in time. She tells you her last labor lasted less than 2 hours. She is having frequent contractions. What should you do?

CHAPTER

16 Pediatric Emergencies

Matching

Match each of the items in the left column to the appropriate description in the right column.

_____ **1.** Drowning

_____ **2.** Mottling

_____ **3.** Suctioning

_____ **4.** Epilepsy

_____ **5.** Asthma

A. Aspirating fluid by mechanical means

B. Patchy skin discoloration caused by too little or too much circulation

C. Submersion in water that results in suffocation or respiratory impairment

D. Acute spasm of the smaller air passages marked by labored breathing and wheezing

E. Disease manifested by seizures; caused by abnormal focus of electrical activity in the brain

Multiple Choice

Read each item carefully, then select the best response.

_____ **1.** Although the technique used to open the airway of an infant is the same as that used for an adult, you should make sure that the infant's head is placed in what position?

A. Neutral

B. Extension

C. Hyperextension

D. Turned to the right side

_____ **2.** To remove a foreign object from an infant's airway, you should alternate chest thrusts with:

A. CPR.

B. back slaps.

C. rescue breathing.

D. the Heimlich maneuver.

_____ **3.** Rapid, shallow breathing and/or a rapid, weak pulse should immediately signal that a child is in:

A. shock.

B. a coma.

C. cardiac arrest.

D. the middle of a convulsion.

_____ **4.** You are called to the scene of a motor vehicle crash in which a man and a woman are killed, but their 6-month-old son is alive in a car seat in the back seat. You decide to remove the baby from the car because you smell gasoline. You should try to remove the baby:

A. after EMS personnel arrive.

B. while he is still in the car seat.

C. only after you take him out of the car seat.

D. only if you can place him on an infant backboard.

_____ **5.** Which of the following is not a sign or symptom of child abuse?

A. Multiple fractures

B. Human bites

C. Spider bite

D. Bruises in various stages of healing

_____ **6.** Which of the following is considered a medical emergency or sudden illness?

A. Drowning

B. Road rash

C. Headache

D. Coughing

_____ **7.** Noisy, whooping inhalations and a barking seal-like cough are symptoms of which of the following respiratory illnesses?

A. Asthma

B. Croup

C. Pneumonia

D. Allergies

_____ **8.** What are the essential basic life support skills required for pediatric emergencies?

A. CPR and rescue breathing

B. Use of a defibrillator

C. Opening the airway, basic life support, suctioning, and using airway adjuncts

D. Use of oxygen

_____ **9.** Which of the following is not a characteristic used for evaluating work of breathing?

A. Abnormal breath sounds

B. Facial color

C. Abnormal positioning

D. Flaring

_____ **10.** When caring for seriously ill or injured pediatric patients, it is important to check the vital signs every _____ minutes.

A. 2

B. 5

C. 10

D. 20

_____ **11.** Children lose relatively more heat than adults do because:

    A they tend to wear fewer outer garments.

    B. they use more energy.

    C. they have a greater surface area relative to the mass of their body.

    D. all of the above.

_____ **12.** When performing patient assessment on a child, you should pay special attention to:

    A. respirations.

    B. pulse rates.

    C. mental awareness.

    D. all of the above.

_____ **13.** High body temperatures in children are often accompanied by:

    A. wheezing and dry skin.

    B. unresponsiveness and lackluster appearance.

    C. flushed red skin and restlessness.

    D. decreased heart rate.

_____ **14.** The normal respiration rate for a newborn is _____ breaths per minute.

    A. 30 to 60

    B. 20 to 30

    C. 18 to 22

    D. 12 to 18

_____ **15.** The normal heart rate for a newborn is _____ breaths per minute.

    A. 90 to 180

    B. 140

    C. 120

    D. 100 to 160

_____ **16.** The normal respiration rate for a 10-year-old is _____ breaths per minute.

    A. 30 to 60

    B. 25 to 50

    C. 15 to 20

    D. 12 to 16

_____ **17.** A possible cause of cardiopulmonary arrest in a child is:

    A. infection of the airway, such as croup.

    B. sudden infant death syndrome.

    C. injuries around the head and neck.

    D. all of the above.

_____ **18.** To select the proper size of oral airway for a child or an infant, you should measure:

    A. from the earlobe to the jaw.

    B. from the earlobe to the nose.

    C. from the jaw to the corner of the mouth.

    D. from the earlobe to the corner of the mouth.

_____ **19.** For a severe airway obstruction in a conscious child:

    A. begin with blind finger sweeps.

    B. use the abdominal thrust maneuver.

    C. use the chest thrust maneuver.

    D. hyperextend the neck and recheck for breathing.

_____ **20.** For an airway obstruction in an unconscious infant:

   A. determine unresponsiveness by gently tapping the bottom of the child's foot.

   B. position the infant on a firm hard surface, supporting the head and neck.

   C. open the airway with the head tilt–chin lift.

   D. all of the above.

_____ **21.** A sign of respiratory distress in a child is:

   A. nasal flaring on each breath.

   B. retraction of the skin between the ribs and around the neck muscles.

   C. altered mental status.

   D. all of the above.

_____ **22.** A sign of respiratory failure in a child is:

   A. a respiratory rate of more than 30 breaths per minute.

   B. combativeness or restlessness.

   C. stridor, a high pitched sound on inspiration.

   D. limp muscle tone.

_____ **23.** Altered mental status in children can be caused by:

   A. head trauma.

   B. infection.

   C. low blood sugar.

   D. all of the above.

_____ **24.** The main signs of croup include all of the following EXCEPT:

   A. noisy, whooping inhalations.

   B. barking seal-like cough.

   C. fright or anxiety.

   D. history of a recent or current cold.

_____ **25.** Epiglottitis usually occurs in children from _____ of age.

   A. 3 to 6 months

   B. 3 to 6 years

   C. 1 to 3 months

   D. 1 to 3 years

_____ **26.** The signs and symptoms of epiglottitis include all of the following EXCEPT:

   A. drooling.

   B. inability to swallow.

   C. the child is lying down.

   D. anxiety and fright.

_____ **27.** If you encounter a child with a fever above 104°F, you should:

   A. fan the child to cool him or her down.

   B. attempt to reduce the temperature by undressing the child.

   C. protect the child during any seizure that might result.

   D. all of the above.

_____ **28.** Appropriate care for a child while he or she is having a seizure includes which of the following?

   A. Inserting an oral airway to keep the airway open

   B. Placing the child on a soft surface or bed to prevent injury

   C. Raising the child's legs to increase blood flow to the brain

   D. All of the above

_____ **29.** Appendicitis is most often seen in people between the ages of:
- **A.** 10 and 25 years.
- **B.** 5 and 10 years.
- **C.** 20 and 35 years.
- **D.** 35 and 50 years.

_____ **30.** Poisoning by absorption occurs when a poisonous substance enters the body through:
- **A.** the mouth.
- **B.** injection.
- **C.** the skin.
- **D.** the eyes.

_____ **31.** Poisoning by ingestion occurs when a poisonous substance enters the body through:
- **A.** the mouth.
- **B.** the skin.
- **C.** injection.
- **D.** the eyes.

_____ **32.** Typical injuries you should look for when a child has been hit by a car include:
- **A.** injuries to the femur.
- **B.** injuries to the chest.
- **C.** injuries to the head and neck.
- **D.** all of the above.

_____ **33.** Signs and symptoms of traumatic shock include all of the following EXCEPT:
- **A.** increased blood pressure.
- **B.** cool, clammy skin.
- **C.** rapid, weak pulse.
- **D.** rapid or shallow respirations.

Fill-in-the-Blanks

Read each item carefully, then complete the statement by filling in the missing word(s).

1. Sudden infant death syndrome (SIDS) usually occurs in infants between the ages of _____ and _____.

2. _____ is a characteristic of skin circulation that demonstrates white or pale skin or mucous membranes.

3. The _____ is an easy-to-remember tool for evaluating pediatric patients and incorporates appearance, work of breathing, and circulation into one model.

4. Normal vital signs for a newborn are a heart rate of _____ and respirations of _____.

5. The number one killer of children is _____.

True/False

For each statement, write the letter "T" if you believe it to be more true than false, or write the letter "F" if you believe it to be more false than true.

_____ **1.** Children's inability to explain what is wrong with them, especially when seriously ill or injured, can make even the most highly trained emergency worker feel inadequate.

_____ **2.** Calming a parent is sometimes the best way to calm a child.

_____ **3.** You should avoid telling a child when some parts of the treatment will be painful because the child will only become more nervous.

_____ **4.** When a child is poisoned, you should try to identify the poison and how much the child has swallowed to report to the doctor or the poison control center.

_____ **5.** The first step in caring for a child with chemical burns on the skin is to brush or flush the chemical off, then remove the child's clothing if necessary.

_____ **6.** You should always try to induce vomiting in a child who has swallowed poison.

_____ **7.** A child who has swallowed poison may require rescue breathing or even CPR.

_____ **8.** A high fever always means a child is seriously ill.

_____ **9.** A child who has signs of dehydration needs to be examined by a physician.

_____ **10.** A child with a high fever who is covered with blankets may actually go into convulsions.

_____ **11.** Even if you are able to reduce a high fever, the child must be seen by a physician.

_____ **12.** Trauma is the number one killer of children.

_____ **13.** A child shows signs of shock much sooner than an adult.

_____ **14.** You should always look for head and abdominal injuries in a child who has been struck by a car.

_____ **15.** You may skip a head-to-toe examination of a seriously injured child who is too young to understand or respond to your questions about his or her injuries.

_____ **16.** The only time you should attempt to remove an object that is partially blocking a child's airway is when you can see the object in the child's mouth and can remove it easily.

_____ **17.** If you are not sure whether you should remove an object partially blocking a child's airway or you cannot see the object, you should transport the child to the hospital as soon as possible without trying to remove the object.

_____ **18.** Talking and explaining what you are doing to a child who has a partially blocked airway is likely to make the child more anxious.

_____ **19.** You should constantly watch the breathing of a child who has a partially blocked airway until the object is removed.

_____ **20.** If a child's airway is completely blocked by a foreign object, you should immediately try to expel the object.

_____ **21.** Risks at home that can contribute to near-drowning include buckets of water, toilet bowls, wash bowls, and bathtubs.

_____ **22.** Children's airways are larger in relation to the rest of their body than adults' airways.

_____ **23.** Children have a greater surface area relative to the mass of their body than adults.

_____ **24.** Children are "nose breathers" from birth to about 6 months of age; they do not breathe through their mouths.

_____ **25.** The best place to take a child's pulse is the carotid artery.

_____ **26.** Children's heart rates become faster with each degree of body temperature increase.

_____ **27.** Three-year-olds have faster heart rates than newborns.

_____ **28.** Ten-year-olds have slower respiration rates than one-year-olds.

_____ **29.** Cardiopulmonary arrest in a child is usually caused by lack of oxygen produced by respiratory arrest.

_____ **30.** The head tilt–chin lift technique can be used for children who have suffered an injury to the neck or head.

_____ **31.** Use a bulb syringe to suction the nose of a child.

_____ **32.** Use a flexible catheter to suction the nose of an infant.

_____ **33.** Never perform a finger sweep on an infant or child unless the object blocking the airway is clearly visible and can be easily removed.

_____ **34.** Never transport a child in the arms of a parent because parents are too emotional and may excite the child.

_____ **35.** If you know that a child has swallowed an object, regardless of its size or shape, you should arrange for transport to an appropriate medical facility.

_____ **36.** Performing mouth-to-mask ventilations is an appropriate intervention for a child suffering from respiratory failure.

_____ **37.** Respiratory distress in a child often leads quickly to respiratory failure.

_____ **38.** It is important to determine the cause of a child's altered mental status before treating the symptoms.

_____ **39.** When experiencing an asthma attack, a child can exhale easily but has difficulty inhaling.

_____ **40.** When experiencing an asthma attack, a child should be placed in a sitting position.

_____ **41.** Croup is an infection of the upper airway that usually occurs in infants from 4 to 6 months of age.

_____ **42.** Epiglottitis is the most severe of the three major childhood respiratory problems.

_____ **43.** The epiglottis is a small flap that covers the trachea during swallowing.

_____ **44.** Epiglottitis usually occurs in children from 1 to 3 years of age.

_____ **45.** When a child has epiglottitis, you will usually find him or her in a prostrate position.

_____ **46.** Epiglottitis poses an immediate threat to life.

_____ **47.** If you suspect epiglottitis, you should avoid examining the child's throat.

_____ **48.** Although childhood seizures can be frightening, they are not usually dangerous.

_____ **49.** Prolonged vomiting can produce severe dehydration in a child.

_____ **50.** A patient suffering from appendicitis usually experiences pain originating in the belly button area of the stomach.

_____ **51.** SIDS is usually the result of chronic child abuse.

_____ **52.** The three components of the pediatric assessment triangle are appearance, work of breathing, and circulation to skin.

_____ **53.** By looking at the types of trauma a child has experienced, you can better anticipate the types of injuries a child may have suffered.

_____ **54.** Typical signs of child abuse include human bites, burns and scalds, multiple fractures, and bruises.

_____ **55.** In dealing with the parents of an abused child, you should conduct yourself in a judgmental manner to get them to confess.

Short Answer
Write a brief response to each of the following questions.

1. Name the three vital signs you should closely watch when performing your assessment on an infant or a young child.

_____

_____

_____

2. Name three objects a child might swallow that would have to be removed at the hospital.

_____

_____

_____

3. Name the three most important things you can do for a child who has traumatic injuries.

_____

_____

_____

4. Describe how you would care for a child who has heatstroke.

_____

_____

_____

5. Name four steps in caring for a child who has a high fever.

_____

_____

_____

6. What is the most important rule of thumb when responding to cases of abdominal pain in children?

_____

_____

_____

7. List five signs of possible child abuse.

_____

_____

_____

8. What should you do if you suspect that a child has been sexually or physically abused, but the parents refuse to allow you to arrange to have the child seen by a physician?

_____

_____

_____

9. Under what circumstances should you begin CPR on an infant who has been found dead for no apparent reason?

_____

_____

_____

You Make the Call

The following scenario provides an opportunity to explore the concerns associated with patient management. Read the scenario, then describe the best way to handle the situation.

As you are returning to your station, you notice a small child dart from the curb, right into the path of an oncoming car. The child is approximately 2 years old, and the car was moving at a speed of approximately 30 miles per hour. What should you do?

CHAPTER

17 Geriatric Emergencies

Matching

Match each of the items in the left column to the appropriate description in the right column.

_____ 1. Alzheimer's disease

_____ 2. Osteoporosis

_____ 3. Suicide

_____ 4. Hospice

_____ 5. Senile dementia

A. Intentionally causing one's own death

B. Chronic progressive dementia that accounts for 60% of all dementia

C. An interdisciplinary program designed to reduce or eliminate pain and address the physical, spiritual, social, and economic needs of terminally ill patients

D. Abnormal brittleness of the bones caused by loss of calcium; affected bones fracture easily

E. General term for dementia that occurs in older people

Multiple Choice

Read each item carefully, then select the best response.

_____ 1. An elderly man seems hesitant and unsure of himself when you ask him to walk from his bed to a nearby chair. You should:

    A. offer him your arm for support.

    B. prepare to move him yourself because he is probably senile.

    C. pull him gently in the direction you want him to go because he is probably hard of hearing.

    D. ask him again more slowly because, like other older people, he thinks more slowly.

_____ 2. Fractures are more common among the elderly because of a condition called:

    A. diabetes.

    B. senility.

    C. arthritis.

    D. osteoporosis.

_____ 3. As you begin to examine an elderly woman who is dressed in several layers of clothing, you should:

    A. take her vital signs only.

    B. remove her clothing only if you can move her to a warm place.

    C. remove as much of the clothing as you need to examine her properly.

    D. do a less than complete physical exam.

_____ **4.** A man who points at his ear and shakes his head "no" may be trying to tell you that:

     A. he is deaf.

     B. he is senile.

     C. he wants you to repeat what you said.

     D. you should not speak to him.

_____ **5.** The most important factor to consider when caring for a blind patient is that you will:

     A. have to watch the person's guide dog.

     B. have trouble reading the person's facial expressions.

     C. need to allow the patient to touch you more than a sighted patient would.

     D. need to explain more to the patient about what you are doing and what is happening.

_____ **6.** A geriatric patient is commonly defined as a patient who is more than _____ years of age.

     A. 50

     B. 55

     C. 60

     D. 65

_____ **7.** Special concerns for geriatric patients include:

     A. sensory changes such as hearing loss and vision impairment.

     B. changes in mobility.

     C. changes in medical conditions.

     D. all of the above.

_____ **8.** Which of the following can affect the natural aging process?

     A. Heredity

     B. Diet

     C. Stress level

     D. All of the above

_____ **9.** If an older patient loses his eyeglasses during an emergency and is anxious, you should:

     A. search and try to find them.

     B. explain what is going on for the patient who can no longer see.

     C. calm the patient and tell him not to worry about it.

     D. ask if the patient has the original prescription and try to obtain new eyeglasses.

_____ **10.** A common site for fractures is the:

     A. neck.

     B. ankle.

     C. wrist.

     D. knee.

Fill-in-the-Blanks

Read each item carefully, then complete the statement by filling in the missing word(s).

1. Elderly people often wear _____ clothing than younger people, even during warmer months.

2. Loss of bowel and _____ control occurs frequently in the geriatric population.

3. _____ is an invisible disability.

4. _____ occur often in the geriatric population because of the loss of bone density resulting from osteoporosis.

5. Because elderly patients suffer from a variety of chronic conditions, many of them take a large number of _____ every day.

6. A health care program that brings together a variety of caregivers to provide physical, spiritual, social, and economic care for patients who have terminal illnesses is called a _____.

7. _____ is a decrease in the density of bone that is common in postmenopausal women.

8. The most common type of dementia, _____, is a chronic degenerative disorder that attacks the brain and results in impaired memory, behavior, and thinking.

9. In a hip fracture, the injured leg is usually (but not always) _____ than the other leg.

10. There are two major types of respiratory diseases: chronic and _____.

True/False

For each statement, write the letter "T" if you believe it to be more true than false, or write the letter "F" if you believe it to be more false than true.

_____ 1. Cancer is a frequent cause of disability and death in elderly patients.

_____ 2. If you think an elderly person cannot hear what you are saying, you should shout directly into his or her ear to make sure you are understood.

_____ 3. All elderly people are disabled in some way.

_____ 4. You should make sure that elderly patients' eyeglasses are kept with them if possible.

_____ 5. Most elderly people have trouble reading lips because they usually cannot see well.

_____ 6. You should support elderly patients as they move because most are afraid of falling.

_____ 7. If a patient who is senile becomes uncooperative or hostile toward your attempts to help, you should remain calm and keep talking.

_____ 8. Loss of bowel or bladder control is common among the elderly and should not interfere with your care.

_____ 9. If possible, you should send all medications to the hospital with elderly patients.

_____ 10. Elderly patients and their spouses seldom need as much emotional support as younger people when faced with serious illness or death.

_____ 11. Many of the medical conditions that commonly occur in elderly patients can result in altered mental status.

_____ 12. If you do not know sign language, the best way to communicate with a deaf person is to gesture or write a note.

_____ 13. The best way to determine if a person is deaf is to ask "Can you hear me?" while turned away from the patient.

_____ 14. Because elderly patients suffer from a variety of chronic conditions, many of them take a large number of medications every day.

_____ 15. If the patient is being transported to a medical facility, you should gather up his or her medications and bring them to the hospital with the patient.

_____ 16. During an emotional or medical crisis, the reassurance of your touch may be even more important to a blind person than to a person who can see.

_____ 17. Today, most patients with serious chronic medical conditions are treated in hospitals or rehabilitation centers and, as a result, their lifespan has increased.

_____ 18. Patients with chronic breathing difficulty may have pacemakers and automatic defibrillators under their skin.

_____ 19. Three types of mental problems seen frequently in older people are depression, suicide, and dementia or Alzheimer's disease.

_____ 20. Depression is the most common psychiatric condition experienced by older adults.

_____ 21. Elder abuse is generally easy to detect.

_____ **22.** One of the goals of a hospice is to provide pain relief through the use of needles and IVs.

_____ **23.** Living wills and do not resuscitate (DNR) orders are examples of advance directives.

_____ **24.** When dealing with patients suffering from dementia, it is important to speak clearly to them using their names.

_____ **25.** Older men have a low rate of suicide in the United States.

Short Answer

Write a brief response to each of the following questions.

1. List at least three disabilities that may occur with age.

_____

_____

_____

2. Name three signs that would suggest that an elderly person has a broken hip.

_____

_____

_____

3. List three important ways you can ease communication with deaf patients.

_____

_____

_____

4. Name three signs of elder abuse.

_____

_____

_____

5. List three factors that may contribute to suicide among older patients.

_____

_____

_____

You Make the Call

The following scenario provides an opportunity to explore the concerns associated with patient management. Read the scenario, then describe the best way to handle the situation.

You arrive on the scene to find an 80-year-old woman complaining of dizziness. After assessing the situation, taking a patient history, and performing an exam, you find out that the patient has Alzheimer's disease and may have overdosed on her medication. What should you do?

CHAPTER

18 EMS Operations

Matching

Match each of the items in the left column to the appropriate description in the right column.

_____ **1.** Hot zone

_____ **2.** National Incident Management System (NIMS)

_____ **3.** Golden hour

_____ **4.** Casualty sorting

_____ **5.** Chocking

A. Classifying patients for treatment and transportation

B. Contaminated area

C. Concept of emergency patient care that attempts to place a trauma patient into definitive medical care within 1 hour of injury

D. Structure for managing an emergency incident that may require a response from many different agencies

E. Piece of wood or metal placed in front of or behind a wheel to prevent vehicle movement

Multiple Choice

Read each item carefully, then select the best response.

_____ **1.** When you are approaching a helicopter, you should avoid:

   A. the front of the helicopter.

   B. raising your arms above your head.

   C. walking upright.

   D. all of the above.

_____ **2.** When using the START system, what is the maximum amount of time you should spend determining how seriously any one victim has been injured?

   A. 15 seconds

   B. 30 seconds

   C. 1 minute

   D. 2 minutes

_____ **3.** The first step in the START system is to:

   A. begin casualty sorting immediately.

   B. get up and walk among the patients.

   C. call out loudly that any patient who can should walk to a specific area.

   D. ask each patient whether he or she can walk to a different area.

_____ **4.** The second step in the START system is to:

    A. begin casualty sorting.

    B. call out loudly that any patient who can should walk to a specific area.

    C. move through the patients to quickly assess and tag them .

    D. move among the patients, stopping only to place red tags on patients who need immediate care.

_____ **5.** Once you have gained access to patients in a vehicle, you should first:

    A. begin your assessment.

    B. perform a primary patient survey.

    C. remove them from the vehicle.

    D. clear all broken glass from the inside of the vehicle.

_____ **6.** Dispatch information should include:

    A. number of patients.

    B. name of closest relative.

    C. mental status of patient.

    D. all of the above.

_____ **7.** Upon arrival at the scene of an accident or medical emergency:

    A. consider the need for additional help.

    B. park your vehicle as close as possible to patients who may need to be transported.

    C. begin treatment of patients immediately.

    D. all of the above.

_____ **8.** As more highly trained EMS personnel arrive on the scene, the first responder should:

    A. tell what treatment has been given.

    B. report on observations of the situation.

    C. assist EMS personnel.

    D. all of the above.

_____ **9.** Post-run activities include:

    A. cleaning equipment.

    B. replacing supplies that were used.

    C. documenting the situation and treatment provided.

    D. all of the above.

_____ **10.** The landing zone for a helicopter at the scene of an accident:

    A. may be designated by emergency vehicles.

    B. may be determined by first responders.

    C. must be free of loose debris and obstacles.

    D. all of the above.

_____ **11.** Removal of a patient from a difficult situation or position, such as a wrecked car, is called:

    A. excrescence.

    B. exothermicity.

    C. extrusion.

    D. extrication.

_____ **12.** The role of the first responder in the process of extrication includes which of the following?

    A. Providing initial emergency care

    B. Helping to remove patients

    C. Conducting an overview of the scene

    D. All of the above

_____ **13.** Which of the following is not considered part of the extrication process?

    A. Gaining access to the patient

    B. Rapid transport of the patient

    C. Preparation of the patient for removal

    D. All of the above

_____ **14.** If an electrical wire is in contact with an automobile, the first responder should:

    A. call for additional help.

    B. tell the passengers in the car to stay inside.

    C. leave the wire alone.

    D. all of the above.

_____ **15.** Vehicles can be stabilized by:

    A. chocking.

    B. deflating tires.

    C. making use of hubcaps.

    D. all of the above.

_____ **16.** Side and rear windows of a car:

    A. are made of tempered glass.

    B. may be the primary access routes to reach passengers.

    C. can be broken with a spring-loaded center punch.

    D. all of the above.

_____ **17.** The concept of the golden hour means:

    A. you must stabilize the patient within an hour.

    B. the patient's chance for survival decreases over time.

    C. you have 1 hour to remove a patient from the scene of an accident.

    D. all of the above.

_____ **18.** A situation involving more patients than can be handled with the initial resources available:

    A. is called a mass-casualty incident.

    B. is called a multiple-casualty incident.

    C. calls for the use of triage.

    D. all of the above.

_____ **19.** As you work to sort the patients in a multiple-casualty incident, you should:

    A. treat only critical patients.

    B. correct airway and severe bleeding problems.

    C. spend no more than 3 minutes with each patient.

    D. all of the above.

_____ **20.** The first step in START is to:

    A. color code all patients.

    B. do a visual examination of all patients.

    C. tell people to get up and walk if they are able.

    D. none of the above.

_____ **21.** If patients have walked to a designated area as part of the START system:

    A. they are tagged with a green tag.

    B. they are designated a priority three.

    C. it is assumed that they do not have life-threatening injuries.

    D. all of the above.

_____ **22.** The last step of the BCM series of the triage tests is the test of the patient's:
  A. ability to move unassisted.
  B. mental status.
  C. motor skills.
  D. all of the above.

_____ **23.** If a patient in a multiple-casualty situation has adequate breathing and circulation, the patient should be:
  A. tested for mental status.
  B. asked to follow simple verbal commands.
  C. tagged priority two (yellow) if responsive.
  D. all of the above.

_____ **24.** With the START system, a patient who is unresponsive, cannot follow a simple verbal command, and is considered unresponsive to verbal stimuli should be tagged with what color?
  A. Red
  B. Yellow
  C. Green
  D. Black or gray

_____ **25.** You can stabilize a vehicle by:
  A. overinflating the tires.
  B. chocking the front or back of each wheel.
  C. removing the doors and using them to wedge the vehicle securely.
  D. tying the hood down with a rope.

Fill-in-the-Blanks

Read each item carefully, then complete the statement by filling in the missing word(s).

1. As a general guideline, a helicopter requires an open, unobstructed landing area of about _____ feet by _____ feet.

2. There are two types of fires related to automobile crashes: impact fires and _____ fires.

3. Many fire departments and rescue squads carry wooden _____ and "step-chocks" to help stabilize vehicles.

4. _____ are used by EMS systems to reach patients, transport patients to medical facilities, or remove patients from inaccessible areas.

5. _____ are substances that are toxic, poisonous, radioactive, flammable, or explosive and can cause injury or death with exposure.

True/False

For each statement, write the letter "T" if you believe it to be more true than false, or write the letter "F" if you believe it to be more false than true.

_____ **1.** Your first priority in responding to the scene is to get there quickly and safely.
_____ **2.** The first responder can be of great assistance as ground support during helicopter ambulance operations.
_____ **3.** Triage was developed to help emergency medical personnel care for a large number of accident victims who all need treatment at the same time.
_____ **4.** In multiple-casualty incidents, a casualty sorting system helps you decide which patients need treatment and transport to the hospital first.
_____ **5.** Casualty sorting must be done rapidly but requires that you stay calm and use your skills as a first responder.

_____ **6.** Your goal as a first responder at a multiple-casualty incident should be to do the most good for the greatest number of patients.

_____ **7.** Often it is difficult to know when to switch from a normal emergency care approach to a casualty-sorting system approach.

_____ **8.** You should always try to plan ahead what you might need to do when responding to a reported multiple-casualty incident.

_____ **9.** You should immediately begin casualty sorting as soon as you arrive at the scene of a multiple-casualty incident.

_____ **10.** When sorting patients in a multiple-casualty incident, you may not have time to follow cervical spine guidelines when opening patients' airways.

_____ **11.** Before opening the airway of a patient who is not breathing, you should quickly clear the patient's mouth of any foreign matter.

_____ **12.** A patient who does not breathe on his or her own should be tagged as dead only after you have checked for a pulse.

_____ **13.** During a multiple-casualty incident, you should wait for EMS personnel to control severe bleeding in a patient.

_____ **14.** "Close your eyes and squeeze my hand" is an example of a simple command to give a patient to check mental status.

_____ **15.** Patients who have adequate breathing and circulation but who do not follow simple commands should be given a yellow tag.

_____ **16.** If you are called to a multiple-casualty incident but are not the first to respond, you should just pitch in and help wherever you think help is needed.

_____ **17.** If additional rescue workers have not arrived by the time you have sorted all patients, you should go back and recheck the patients with yellow and green tags.

_____ **18.** Most fatalities and serious injuries in hazardous materials incidents occur from breathing problems.

_____ **19.** If you suspect a hazardous material is involved in an incident, you should look for a placard identifying the material before assisting the patients.

_____ **20.** You should never attempt to rescue patients at a hazardous materials incident unless you have the necessary training and protective equipment.

_____ **21.** The overview of an accident scene should be as complete as possible before you leave your vehicle.

_____ **22.** When stabilizing a scene, you should first be concerned with traffic near and around the accident scene.

_____ **23.** If other emergency personnel have already arrived and secured an accident scene, you can park your vehicle in a place that is convenient for you.

_____ **24.** The majority of accident victims can be accessed by stabilizing the vehicle and then opening a door or window.

_____ **25.** You should try to open the door of a vehicle, even if it looks badly damaged.

_____ **26.** Damaged automobile doors are likely to open only if you try the inside handle.

_____ **27.** Entry through the windshield of a vehicle should be attempted before any other window is tried.

_____ **28.** The glass in the rear and side windows of an automobile is tempered, which means it will break into small pieces that usually pose little danger.

_____ **29.** You should always warn passengers before you break the glass of the vehicle's window.

_____ **30.** A first responder life support kit should contain two different kinds of gloves.

_____ **31.** Your first and only priority in responding to a scene is to reach the scene as quickly as possible.

_____ **32.** When more highly trained medical personnel arrive on the scene, the first responder should leave the patient and analyze other possible needs.

_____ **33.** If a patient is turned over to EMS personnel, and the first responder has given all necessary information, it is the responsibility of the EMS personnel to complete all paperwork.

_____ **34.** It is the responsibility of the first responder to notify the dispatching center or supervisor when ready to respond to another call.

_____ **35.** At the scene of an accident, a first responder may be responsible for determining the need for a helicopter and, if necessary, calling for one.

_____ **36.** Setup and preparation of a landing site for a helicopter at the scene of an accident may be the responsibility of a first responder.

_____ **37.** Loading patients into a helicopter requires the same procedures as loading patients into any emergency vehicle.

_____ **38.** The extrication process requires at least a helmet with face shield and gloves.

_____ **39.** The extrication process sometimes requires coordination with a utility company.

_____ **40.** Anticipating and planning the response to an incident begins with the dispatcher's message.

_____ **41.** The work of a first responder begins with initial contact with the patient or observer.

_____ **42.** Additional help should be called for only after casualty sorting has taken place.

_____ **43.** Body substance isolation precautions very seldom are a consideration at the scene of an automobile crash.

_____ **44.** It may be necessary and advisable for an emergency vehicle to block traffic at the scene of a crash.

_____ **45.** Asking bystanders to assist in keeping other people away from the scene of a crash should not be necessary and may lead to legal problems.

_____ **46.** If spilled fuel is present at a crash scene, the first responder should take no action until the fire department arrives.

_____ **47.** If an electrical wire shows flashes or sparks, it is to be avoided, but it is safe to approach one that does not show sparks, arcs, or flashes.

_____ **48.** If a vehicle is upright and on all four wheels, there is no need to stabilize it before removing injured passengers.

_____ **49.** A vehicle that is upside down is usually extremely unstable.

_____ **50.** Two types of fires related to automobile crashes are called impact fires and postimpact fires.

_____ **51.** Upon arriving at the scene of an automobile accident, you observe a car on fire and passengers inside; your first action should be to use a dry chemical fire extinguisher.

_____ **52.** A fire extinguisher should be directed first at the top of the fire, then moved downward as the fire subsides.

_____ **53.** At the scene of an automobile crash, an attempt should be made to open all doors before using any other equipment.

_____ **54.** The windshield should be considered the primary access to reach passengers trapped inside a vehicle.

_____ **55.** If a window must be broken to gain access to a patient trapped in an automobile, the window closest to the patient should be used if possible.

_____ **56.** Once access is gained to a damaged vehicle, the next action needed is to remove the patient from the vehicle.

_____ **57.** The two primary goals of first responders are gaining access to the patient and stabilizing the patient.

_____ **58.** Looking for a placard on a vehicle may be the first step in identifying a potentially hazardous material.

_____ **59.** An area contaminated by a hazardous material may be called a hot zone.

_____ **60.** The single most important step in handling any hazardous materials incident is to identify the substance(s) involved.

_____ **61.** The triage system depends on accurate diagnosis of each patient's problems.

_____ **62.** The triage system uses the three primary observations of breathing, circulation, and mental status.

_____ **63.** The triage system allows a first responder to assess a patient in 60 seconds or less.

_____ **64.** The START system allows first responders to open blocked airways and stop severe bleeding quickly.

_____ **65.** In the triage system, a green color code means that the patient must immediately go to a medical facility for treatment.

_____ **66.** In the triage system, a red color code means that the medical personnel can stop giving any treatment.

_____ **67.** In the triage system, a yellow color code means that the patient is critical and extreme caution should be used in transporting.

_____ **68.** In the triage system, a black or gray color code means that the patient is dead and no care is required.

_____ **69.** The second step in the START system is to begin where you stand, moving through the patients to perform a quick assessment and tagging.

_____ **70.** A patient being evaluated in the START system who is breathing at a rate of more than 30 breaths a minute should be tagged as a priority three.

_____ **71.** Cervical spine injuries call for different treatment in multiple-casualty situations than in other situations.

_____ **72.** If a patient in a START system observation is not breathing and does not start to breathe with simple airway maneuvers, the patient should be tagged with a black or gray tag.

_____ **73.** The second step of the BCM series of the triage tests is to test the pulse.

_____ **74.** In the BCM series of the triage tests, if the carotid pulse is weak, the patient should be tagged with a red tag.

_____ **75.** In the BCM series of the triage tests, if the carotid pulse is absent, the patient should be tagged with a black or gray tag.

_____ **76.** Once patients at a multiple-casualty incident have been assessed and color-coded, it may be assumed that the conditions of these patients will remain the same until additional help arrives to treat them.

_____ **77.** Patients at the scene of a multiple-casualty accident may be retriaged for further evaluation, treatment, stabilization, and transportation as additional help arrives.

_____ **78.** There are very few specific antidotes or treatments for most hazardous materials injuries.

Short Answer

Write a brief response to each of the following questions.

1. List three common hazards found at automobile crash scenes.

_____

_____

_____

2. List the five phases of response.

_____

_____

_____

3. Name five things you should include in your initial radio or telephone report after surveying the scene of a multiple-casualty incident.

_____

_____

_____

4. What three letters will help you remember the three primary signs you need to observe on each victim during casualty sorting?

_____

_____

_____

5. Name your two primary goals when assisting in the extrication process.

_____

_____

_____

6. Name the seven steps of the extrication process that are the responsibility of the first responder.

_____

_____

_____

7. What one word should you always keep in mind when participating in an extrication?

_____

_____

_____

8. At a minimum, what three items of protective clothing should a first responder have and use for extrication processes?

_____

_____

_____

9. Name three ways that dispatch information can be received.

_____

_____

_____

10. What safety precautions should be taken before loading a patient into a helicopter?

_____

_____

_____

Labeling
Label the following diagrams with the correct terms.

1. Label the stages of use for a dry chemical fire extinguisher.

A. _____   B. _____

C. _____   D. _____

Skill Drills

Test your knowledge by filling in the correct words in the photo captions.

A. Accessing the Vehicle Through the Window

1. Place the spring-loaded center punch at the _____ corner of the window.

2. Press on the center punch to _____ the window.

3. Remove the glass to the _____.

4. Enter the vehicle through the _____.

B. Airway Management in a Vehicle

1. Place one hand under the
_____ and the other
hand on the _____
of the victim's head.

2. Raise the head to
_____ position to
open the airway.

You Make the Call

The following scenario provides an opportunity to explore the concerns associated with patient management. Read the scenario, then describe the best way to handle the situation.

You are dispatched to a scene where a single car has hit a tree. The car has sustained major front-end damage. What should you do?

CHAPTER

19 Terrorism Awareness

Matching

Match each of the items in the left column to the appropriate description in the right column.

_____ **1.** Blister agents

_____ **2.** Biological agents

_____ **3.** Chemical agents

_____ **4.** Nerve agents

_____ **5.** Metabolic agents

_____ **6.** Pulmonary agents

A. Substances that produce respiratory distress or illness

B. Compounds that can be used by terrorists to inflict harm

C. Disease-causing bacteria or viruses that might be used by terrorists to intentionally cause epidemics of disease

D. Chemicals that cause the skin to blister

E. Toxic substances that attack the central nervous system

F. Substances that are intended to produce injury or death by disrupting chemical reactions at the cellular level

Multiple Choice

Read each item carefully, then select the best response.

_____ **1.** Which of the following symptoms could be caused by a nerve agent?

A. Urination

B. Excessive tearing

C. Gastric upset

D. All of the above

_____ **2.** When arriving on the scene of a suspected terrorist event, your first responsibility is to:

A. assess scene safety.

B. set up the incident command system.

C. start triage.

D. request additional resources.

_____ **3.** Safety considerations for first responders dealing with incidents involving radiation include:

A. staying away from source of radiation until specially trained teams arrive.

B. using body substance isolation (BSI) precautions.

C. remaining downwind of the blast site.

D. all of the above.

_____ **4.** Which of the following is an example of terrorism?
   A. Bombing of an abortion clinic
   B. Intimidating national event where property was damaged but no lives were lost
   C. Attacks on the World Trade Center and the Pentagon on September 11, 2001
   D. All of the above
_____ **5.** Infrastructure that may be affected by weapons of mass destruction includes:
   A. bridges and tunnels.
   B. airports and seaports.
   C. power plants.
   D. all of the above.
_____ **6.** Shortness of breath, flushed skin, rapid heartbeat, seizures, coma, and cardiac arrest are possible symptoms of exposure to:
   A. insecticides.
   B. cyanides.
   C. blister agents.
   D. radiation.
_____ **7.** SLUDGE is an acronym to help remember:
   A. common hazardous materials.
   B. important safety considerations.
   C. symptoms of exposure to insecticides or nerve agents.
   D. steps in response to suspected terrorist events.
_____ **8.** Common targets of terrorists include all of the following EXCEPT:
   A. farms.
   B. undeveloped land.
   C. housing developments.
   D. churches.
_____ **9.** Common signs of low levels of exposure to radiation include:
   A. hair loss.
   B. cancer.
   C. vomiting.
   D. death.
_____ **10.** Important BSI safety precautions include the use of:
   A. HEPA masks.
   B. proper breathing apparatus.
   C. quarantine.
   D. vaccinations.

Fill-in-the-Blanks
Read each item carefully, then complete the statement by filling in the missing word(s).

1. A/An _____ is any agent designed to bring about mass death, casualties, and/or massive damage.

2. An agent used to produce a concussion that destroys property and inflicts injury and death is a/an _____.

3. A personal _____ measures the amount of radiation to which an individual is exposed.

4. Anthrax and smallpox are examples of _____ agents.

5. A/An _____ period is the time from a person's exposure to a disease organism to the time symptoms appear.

True/False

For each statement, write the letter "T" if you believe it to be more true than false, or write the letter "F" if you believe it to be more false than true.

_____ **1.** Radiation is a hidden hazard that is similar to electricity.

_____ **2.** Unless there was a warning issued about such an event, rescuers might not know about the presence of radiation.

_____ **3.** Explosives are sometimes used to start fires.

_____ **4.** When vapors of blistering agents are inhaled, they can cause burns in the digestive system.

_____ **5.** Chlorine is an example of a pulmonary agent.

_____ **6.** Metabolic agents tend to have a fruity smell or no smell at all.

_____ **7.** Reactions to metabolic agents are usually immediate.

_____ **8.** The primary route of exposure to pulmonary agents is vapor hazard.

_____ **9.** Pulmonary agents are the most lethal chemical agents.

_____ **10.** When weapons of mass destruction have been used, it is generally safe to enter where the event has occurred.

Short Answer

Write a brief response to each of the following questions.

1. List the five categories of chemical agents.

_____

_____

_____

2. Name three symptoms of exposure to an organophosphate insecticide or nerve agent.

_____

_____

_____

3. Name the three common signs of acute radiation sickness with low exposure.

_____

_____

_____

4. Identify three locations in which radiation is commonly used.

_____

_____

_____

5. What are the signs and/or symptoms of cyanide exposure?

_____

_____

_____

You Make the Call

You respond to a frantic call from dispatch stating that a white powder has been found in the post office downtown. You respond to the call within 2 minutes of initial dispatch and arrive to find several employees screaming and running around with small particles of white powder on their clothes. What should you do?

CHAPTER

20 Special Rescue

Matching

Match each of the items in the left column to the appropriate description in the right column.

_____ **1.** Decompression sickness	**A.** Can obstruct blood vessels
_____ **2.** Flotation device	**B.** Includes life rings and buoys
_____ **3.** Reach-throw-row-go	**C.** Unusually strong surface currents flowing outward from the seashore that can carry swimmers out to sea
_____ **4.** Riptides	**D.** Condition seen in divers in which gas, especially nitrogen, forms bubbles in blood vessels and obstructs them
_____ **5.** Air embolism	**E.** Four-step reminder of the sequence of actions that should be taken in water rescue situations

Multiple Choice

Read each item carefully, then select the best response.

_____ **1.** In a water rescue, you should enter the water only if you:

    A. are sure the person will not panic and drag you under.

    B. do not have a flotation device available.

    C. know the struggling person cannot swim.

    D. are a capable swimmer trained in lifesaving techniques.

_____ **2.** The best way to turn an unresponsive patient who is face down in the water is to:

    A. lift up on the patient's chest with both hands.

    B. hold the patient by both shoulders and then push up on one shoulder and down on the other.

    C. pull the patient's head up out of the water.

    D. roll the patient over while supporting the head and neck.

_____ **3.** If you must rescue someone who has fallen through the ice, you should tie a rope around your waist and secure it to a sturdy object on shore. Next, you should:

    A. crawl out to the victim.

    B. walk quickly out to the victim.

    C. push yourself across the ice on your stomach.

    D. slowly walk across the ice.

_____ **4.** If you are called to rescue people from a car on the ice, you should ask them to open the car doors so that:

   A. the car will sink more slowly if the ice breaks.

   B. the windows will be less likely to break and cause damage to the car's occupants.

   C. you will be able to see the people in the car more clearly.

   D. the door jams won't freeze.

_____ **5.** The "throw" step of the water rescue sequence can be used:

   A. by rescuers who cannot swim.

   B. if the victim is too far out to be reached.

   C. if the victim is in a swimming pool.

   D. all of the above.

_____ **6.** Scuba gear consists of:

   A. an air tank.

   B. a regulator.

   C. a mouthpiece and face mask.

   D. all of the above.

_____ **7.** The two specialized injuries associated with diving are:

   A. air embolism and decompression sickness.

   B. air embolism and suffocation.

   C. decompression sickness and hyperventilation.

   D. decompression sickness and suffocation.

_____ **8.** Signs and symptoms of a diving accident may be similar to those of:

   A. a heart attack.

   B. a stroke.

   C. flu.

   D. choking.

_____ **9.** Signs and symptoms of a diving accident include all of the following EXCEPT:

   A. difficulty speaking.

   B. difficulty breathing.

   C. abdominal pain.

   D. vomiting.

_____ **10.** During an ice rescue, you may be at risk for:

   A. hypothermia.

   B. hyperthermia.

   C. air embolism.

   D. the bends.

Fill-in-the-Blanks

Read each item carefully, then complete the statement by filling in the missing word(s).

1. At a swimming pool, dock, or supervised beach, a/an _____ device may be available.

2. The four steps of a water rescue are reach, throw, _____, and go.

3. If you are in a water rescue situation, your primary concern must be to open the _____, establish breathing and circulation, and stabilize spinal cord injuries.

4. When turning a patient in the water, start by supporting the _____ and _____ with one hand.

5. Two specialized injuries are associated with diving: _____ embolism and _____ .

6. In confined space rescues, you must be careful of hazards, including insufficient _____ and danger of collapse.

7. In farm rescues, reporting of the emergency may be _____ .

8. _____ are unusually strong surface currents flowing outward from the seashore that can carry swimmers out to sea.

9. When you see a person struggling in the water, your first impulse may be to _____ in to assist, but this is a mistake.

10. If a swimmer has suffered _____ , quickly stabilize the head and neck and remove the patient from the water.

True/False

For each statement, write the letter "T" if you believe it to be more true than false, or write the letter "F" if you believe it to be more false than true.

_____ 1. A person who has suffered a diving injury may have signs and symptoms of a person who has had a stroke.

_____ 2. It is not always necessary to turn patients who are face down in the water face up.

_____ 3. You should use the jaw-thrust technique to open the airway of a patient in the water, but the head should be kept in a neutral position.

_____ 4. A patient who you believe has a spinal cord injury should be removed from the water on something that will provide support for the back.

_____ 5. Neck pain and numbness or tingling in the arms or legs are signs of spinal cord injury in a responsive patient needing rescue from the water.

_____ 6. If no rigid support is available to move an unresponsive person from the water, you and one other rescuer can provide adequate support to lift the person out of the water.

_____ 7. In a bus rescue, patients and equipment should be passed through the same window for maximum efficiency and speed.

_____ 8. Reach, throw, row, and go are rescue steps used primarily when it is too cold for the rescuer to enter the water.

_____ 9. Reach, throw, row, and go are water rescue steps used primarily by rescuers without swimming skills.

_____ 10. A towel can be used for the "reach" step of the water rescue sequence.

_____ 11. If no buoy is on hand, skip the "throw" step of the water rescue sequence.

_____ 12. You should enter the water to save a victim as a last resort and only if you are a capable swimmer trained in lifesaving techniques.

_____ 13. If your water rescue patient has suffered cardiac arrest, you should immediately begin CPR.

_____ 14. You should treat a patient who is unconscious in the water as if a spinal cord injury were present.

_____ 15. You should remove a patient from the water before beginning rescue breathing.

_____ 16. In diving accidents, pink or bloody froth coming from the mouth may be a sign of a collapsed lung.

_____ 17. In diving accidents, severe abdominal pain may be a sign of recompression.

_____ 18. In a bus collision involving multiple casualties, one responder can be expected to handle the command functions.

_____ 19. Confined spaces are structures that are designed to keep something in or out.

_____ 20. Rescue situations involving confined spaces are hazardous because there may be insufficient oxygen or a poisonous gas may be present.

Short Answer

Write a brief response to each of the following questions.

1. List, in order, the four steps you should follow when attempting a water or ice rescue.

_____

_____

_____

2. Name three common signs or symptoms of common diving injuries.

_____

_____

_____

3. List five confined spaces you might encounter as a first responder.

_____

_____

_____

4. What are the two deadly hazards you may face when involved with a confined space rescue?

_____

_____

_____

5. What are the seven steps of extrication?

_____

_____

_____

Skill Drills

A. Turning a Patient in the Water

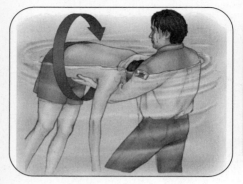 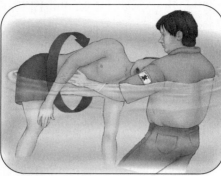 

1. Support the _____ and _____ with one hand. Place the other hand on the _____ of the patient.

2. Carefully turn the patient as a _____.

3. Stabilize the patient's _____ and _____.

You Make the Call

The following scenario provides an opportunity to explore the concerns associated with patient management. Read the scenario, then describe the best way to handle the situation.

You are dispatched to a farm for the report of an injured person. When you arrive, you find the patient in a farm silo. He has fallen about 15 feet from the top of the silo and appears to be unconscious. A co-worker of the patient says he thinks he had a heart attack. What should you do?

CHAPTER

21 Supplemental Skills

Matching
Match each of the items in the left column to the appropriate description in the right column.

_____	**1.** Systolic	**A.**	High blood pressure
_____	**2.** Hypotension	**B.**	Arterial pressure during relaxation
_____	**3.** Auscultation	**C.**	Taking a blood pressure with a cuff but no stethoscope
_____	**4.** Palpation	**D.**	Arterial pressure during contraction
_____	**5.** Diastolic	**E.**	Low blood pressure
_____	**6.** Hypertension	**F.**	Listening to sounds with a stethoscope

Multiple Choice
Read each item carefully, then select the best response.

_____ **1.** A patient who has a systolic blood pressure reading of 90 mm Hg or lower should be:
   A. treated for shock immediately.
   B. reported as having high blood pressure.
   C. examined and prepared for treatment of shock.
   D. examined and prepared for treatment of stroke.

_____ **2.** Which of the following is the appropriate way to report a blood pressure?
   A. 100 and 60
   B. 95 to 75
   C. 100 over 60
   D. 95 out of 100

_____ **3.** A bag-mask device can supply up to _____ oxygen.
   A. 75%
   B. 80%
   C. 90%
   D. 100%

_____ **4.** Supplemental oxygen can be used around all of the following, EXCEPT?

   A. Water

   B. Lightning

   C. Fire

   D. High-altitude environments

_____ **5.** Compared with a blood pressure taken by auscultation, a blood pressure taken by palpation will:

   A. always be lower.

   B. always be higher.

   C. consist of the diastolic pressure only.

   D. consist of the systolic pressure only.

_____ **6.** The blood pressure cuff should be placed on a patient's upper arm with the arrow of the cuff pointing:

   A. up toward the brachial artery, with the bottom of the cuff 1 or 2 inches above the elbow.

   B. down and over the brachial artery, with the bottom of the cuff 6 or more inches above the elbow.

   C. down and over the brachial artery, with the bottom of the cuff 1 or 2 inches above the elbow.

   D. down and over the brachial artery, with the bottom of the cuff even with the elbow.

_____ **7.** Systolic pressure is:

   A. the pressure exerted during contraction of the heart.

   B. the pressure exerted while the heart is at rest.

   C. the bottom of the two numbers.

   D. not a good indicator of hypertension.

_____ **8.** Hypertension exists when blood pressure consistently exceeds:

   A. 120/80.

   B. 140/90.

   C. 100/80.

   D. 80/60.

_____ **9.** Hypotension exists when systolic pressure falls to _____ or below.

   A. 90

   B. 80

   C. 96

   D. 100

_____ **10.** To take a patient's blood pressure by palpation:

   A. place the patient in a prostrate position.

   B. find the patient's carotid pulse.

   C. apply a blood pressure cuff to an uninjured arm.

   D. all of the above.

_____ **11.** To take a patient's blood pressure by auscultation:

   A. apply the blood pressure cuff.

   B. place the diaphragm of the stethoscope over the site of the brachial pulse.

   C. inflate the blood pressure cuff to 30 mm over the pressure at which the brachial pulse disappears.

   D. all of the above.

_____ **12.** Supplemental oxygen can benefit patients who suffer from which of the following conditions?

   A. Heart attack

   B. Stroke

   C. Chronic lung disease

   D. All of the above

_____ **13.** In the United States, oxygen cylinders are marked with what color?

     A. Red

     B. Blue

     C. Green

     D. Yellow

_____ **14.** Each oxygen cylinder lasts for at least:

     A. 2 hours.

     B. 90 minutes.

     C. 20 minutes.

     D. 5 minutes.

_____ **15.** A nasal cannula delivers _____ liters of oxygen per minute.

     A. 20 to 26

     B. 8 to 15

     C. 2 to 6

     D. 10 to 15

_____ **16.** When using oxygen, care must be taken because:

     A. pure oxygen is dangerous to inhale.

     B. oxygen will easily explode.

     C. oxygen supports combustion.

     D. all of the above.

_____ **17.** A nonrebreathing face mask delivers _____ liters of oxygen per minute.

     A. 20 to 26

     B. 8 to 15

     C. 2 to 8

     D. 30 to 50

_____ **18.** A nonrebreathing face mask should be used for patients:

     A. requiring a high flow of oxygen.

     B. experiencing serious shortness of breath.

     C. showing signs or symptoms of shock.

     D. all of the above.

_____ **19.** One disadvantage of a bag-mask device is:

     A. it is difficult to use with a single rescuer.

     B. it must be used with supplemental oxygen.

     C. it is difficult to use on very large patients.

     D. it is a large piece of equipment.

_____ **20.** The device used to assess the amount of oxygen saturated in the red blood cells is a:

     A. pulse oximeter.

     B. bag-mask device.

     C. nasal cannula.

     D. flowmeter.

Fill-in-the-Blanks

Read each item carefully, then complete the statement by filling in the missing word(s).

1. A nasal cannula can deliver _____ percent oxygen to a patient.

2. A nonrebreathing mask can deliver as much as _____ percent oxygen to a patient.

3. _____ exists when blood pressure remains greater than 140/90 after repeated examinations over several weeks.

4. To take a patient's blood pressure by _____, apply the blood pressure cuff on the uninjured arm.

5. _____ is compressed by 2000 pounds per square inch (psi) and stored in portable cylinders.

6. A/An _____ has two small holes, which fit into the patient's nostrils.

7. To administer oxygen, you will need to adjust the _____ to deliver the desired liter-per-minute flow of oxygen.

8. The bag-mask device has three parts: a self-inflating bag, one-way valves, and a/an _____.

True/False

For each statement, write the letter "T" if you believe it to be more true than false, or write the letter "F" if you believe it to be more false than true.

_____ **1.** Oxygen tanks and equipment should be kept away from sparks, heat, and flames.

_____ **2.** If the pressure gauge on the flowmeter of an oxygen tank reads less than 500 psi, the amount of oxygen in the tank is too low to be useful in an emergency situation.

_____ **3.** A bag-mask device can be operated by one or two people.

_____ **4.** High blood pressure generally indicates one of various types of shock.

_____ **5.** Systolic pressure is the second of the two numbers reported with the blood pressure.

_____ **6.** The bottom number in a blood pressure reading is known as the diastolic pressure.

_____ **7.** The diastolic pressure represents the arterial pressure during the relaxation phase of the heart.

_____ **8.** If a patient's systolic pressure falls to 90 or below, he or she should be examined and treated for shock.

_____ **9.** Blood pressure cuffs that are too small can give falsely high readings.

_____ **10.** When blood pressure is taken by palpation, it is not possible to obtain a diastolic pressure.

_____ **11.** The human body operates efficiently with the 21% oxygen that is contained in the air.

_____ **12.** The pressure regulator increases the pressure in the cylinder from 50 to 2000 psi.

_____ **13.** The regulator and flowmeter are incorporated into a single unit that is attached to the outlet of the oxygen cylinder.

_____ **14.** Nasal cannulas have two small holes that fit into the patient's nostrils.

_____ **15.** Nasal cannulas consist of connecting tubing, a reservoir bag, one-way valves, and a face piece.

Short Answer

Write a brief response to each of the following questions.

1. What are the three main parts of the equipment for oxygen administration?

_____

_____

_____

2. Where is the brachial artery located?

_____

_____

_____

3. What are the three parts of a bag-mask device?

_____

_____

_____

4. What are the two ways to take a patient's blood pressure?

_____

_____

_____

5. For what patients should nonrebreathing masks be used?

_____

_____

_____

Skill Drills

A. Using a Bag-Mask Device with One Rescuer

1. Kneel at patient's _____ and maintain an open airway. Check the patient's _____ for fluids, foreign bodies, and dentures.

2. Select the proper _____ size.

3. Place the mask over the patient's _____.

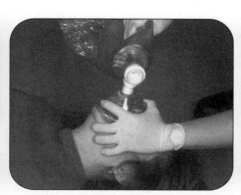

4. _____ the mask.

5. Squeeze the _____ with your other hand. Check for _____.

6. Add _____.

You Make the Call

You are called to a scene where a 60-year-old man is complaining of shortness of breath. Upon your arrival at the scene, the patient proceeds to tell you that he has hypertension and a history of strokes. By palpation, you are able to obtain a blood pressure reading of 160/100. The patient is visibly in pain and is very anxious. He also states that he sometimes uses home oxygen but does not have it with him. What should you do?

Chapter 1: Introduction to the EMS System

Matching

1. F (page 11)
2. G (page 11)
3. E (page 9)
4. C (page 13)

5. B (page 11)
6. A (page 11)
7. D (page 11)

Multiple Choice

1. D (page 16)
2. B (page 16)
3. D (page 13)
4. D (page 6)
5. A (page 9)
6. C (page 11)
7. A (page 11)
8. A (page 12)
9. C (pages 12–13)
10. A (page 13)
11. C (page 13)
12. A (page 13)
13. D (pages 13, 15)
14. C (page 15)
15. D (page 15)
16. C (page 16)
17. C (page 6)

Fill-in-the-Blanks

1. immediate care (page 13)
2. confidential (page 16)
3. improvise; assist (pages 7–8)
4. law enforcement (page 10)
5. Civil (page 12)

True/False

1. T (page 6)
2. F (page 15)
3. T (page 8)
4. T (page 6)
5. F (page 10)
6. F (page 11)
7. T (page 10)
8. T (page 16)
9. F (page 16)
10. T (page 16)
11. F (page 7)
12. F (page 6)

13. F (page 7)
14. F (page 7)
15. T (page 9)
16. F (page 9)
17. F (page 10)
18. F (page 10)
19. T (page 13)
20. T (page 15)

Short Answer

1. (See page 9.)
   1. Reporting
   2. Dispatch
   3. First response
   4. EMS response
   5. Basic or advanced life support
   6. Hospital care
   7. Medical oversight

2. First response; EMS response; hospital care (pages 10–11)

3. Any three of the following (page 15):
   • Condition of the patient when found
   • Patient description of injury and/or illness
   • Initial and subsequent vital signs
   • Treatment that you gave the patient
   • Agency and personnel that took over treatment
   • Any other helpful facts

4. (See pages 7–8.)
   1. Know what you should not do.
   2. Know how to use your first responder life support kit.
   3. Know how to improvise.
   4. Know how to assist other EMS providers.

5. To ensure that the patient receives appropriate medical treatment (page 16)

6. Any three of the following (pages 12–13):
   • Regulation and policy
   • Resource management
   • Human resources and training
   • Transportation equipment and system
   • Medical and support facilities
   • Communications system
   • Public information and education
   • Medical direction
   • Trauma system and development
   • Evaluation

7. Any five of the following (page 8):
   • Flashlight
   • Gloves
   • Face masks
   • Hand sanitizer
   • Mouth-to-mask resuscitation device
   • Portable hand-powered suction device
   • Oral airways
   • Nasal airways
   • Gauze strips or pads

- Universal trauma dressings
- Occlusive dressings
- Gauze rolls
- Bandages
- Adhesive tape
- Burn sheet
- Cervical collars
- Splints
- Spring-loaded center punch
- Heavy leather gloves
- Blankets
- Cold packs
- Scissors
- Protective clothing (helmet, eye protection, EMS jacket)
- Reflective vest
- Fire extinguisher
- *Emergency Response Guidebook*
- Fuses
- Binoculars

You Make the Call

Your answer should include the following steps and information (page 15).

- Communicate with the paramedics.
- Inform the paramedics of what you have discovered about the patient's condition and what treatment you have provided.
- Be prepared to assist the paramedics.
- Prepare documentation, including your observations about the scene, the patient's condition, and the treatment you provided.

Chapter 2: The Well-Being of the First Responder

Matching

1. D (page 23)
2. B (page 23)
3. C (page 23)
4. E (page 23)
5. A (page 23)

Multiple Choice

1. C (pages 24–25)
2. D (page 28)
3. C (page 27)
4. B (page 28)
5. D (page 23)
6. B (page 24)
7. B (page 24)
8. D (page 23)
9. A (page 23)
10. B (page 23)
11. B (page 23)
12. D (page 28)
13. A (page 28)
14. A (page 28)
15. C (page 28)
16. D (page 28)
17. D (page 29)
18. D (page 30)
19. A (page 31)
20. D (page 33)

Fill-in-the-Blanks

1. reducing (page 36)
2. 8 (page 24)
3. Preincident (page 27)
4. peer (page 27)
5. critical incident stress debriefing (CISD) (page 27)

True/False

1. F (page 22)
2. F (page 22)
3. T (page 24)
4. F (page 27)
5. T (page 26)
6. F (page 26)
7. T (page 24)
8. F (page 29)

9. F (page 29)
10. F (page 28)
11. T (page 35)
12. F (page 27)
13. F (page 29)
14. T (page 28)
15. F (page 28)
16. T (page 28)
17. T (page 28)
18. F (page 29)
19. F (page 31)
20. T (page 31)

Short Answer

1. Any three of the following (page 22):
   - Calls involving a patient who reminds you of a family member
   - Calls involving very young or old patients
   - Cases of death
   - Cases of violence
   - Mass casualty situations

2. Any five of the following (page 24):
   - Irritability
   - Inability to concentrate
   - Change in normal disposition
   - Difficulty in sleeping or nightmares
   - Anxiety
   - Indecisiveness
   - Guilt
   - Loss of appetite
   - Loss of interest in sexual relations
   - Loss of interest in work
   - Isolation

3. (See page 29.)
   1. Wearing gloves
   2. Wearing proper protective gear
   3. Washing hands and changing contaminated clothing
   4. Using puncture-resistant containers for "sharps"
   5. Using a face shield when providing resuscitation

4. Any three of the following (page 31.)
   - Protecting the area from traffic hazards
   - Checking that emergency warning lights are operating correctly
   - Carefully exiting the vehicle
   - Wearing reflective material in the dark
   - Leaving room for other arriving vehicles
   - Protecting the scene from further accidents

5. Water rescues; ice rescues; confined-space or below-grade rescues; mass casualty situations (page 35)

6. Any five of the following (pages 31–35):
   - Traffic
   - Crime or violence
   - Crowds
   - Electrical hazards
   - Fire
   - Hazardous materials

- Unstable objects
- Sharp objects
- Animals
- Environmental conditions
- Special rescue situations
- Presence of airborne and bloodborne pathogens

7. Denial; anger; bargaining; depression; acceptance (page 23)

You Make the Call

Your answer should include the following steps and information (page 31).

- Approach carefully, making sure the scene is secure before entering.
- Take a mental picture of the scene and avoid disturbing anything unless it is necessary to move objects to provide patient care.
- Perform a patient assessment and treat your patient.

Chapter 3: Medical, Legal, and Ethical Issues

Matching

1. D (page 41)
2. B (page 41)
3. A (pages 41–42)
4. E (page 42)
5. C (page 42)

Multiple Choice

1. B (page 46)
2. C (page 42)
3. D (page 43)
4. A (page 42)
5. D (page 40)
6. D (page 41)
7. D (page 43)
8. C (page 43)
9. D (page 40)
10. D (page 41)
11. C (page 41)
12. A (page 41)
13. A (page 42)
14. B (page 42)
15. D (page 42)
16. A (page 42)
17. A (page 42)
18. B (page 42)
19. D (page 42)
20. C (page 42)
21. A (page 43)
22. D (page 43)
23. D (page 43)
24. B (page 43)
25. D (page 46)

Fill-in-the-Blanks

1. living will (advance directive) (page 42)
2. negligence (page 43)
3. faith (page 45)
4. competent (page 42)
5. Expressed (page 41)

True/False

1. T (page 40)
2. F (page 41)
3. T (page 40)

4. T (page 45)

5. F (page41)

6. T (page 41)

7. T (page 45)

8. F (page 46)

9. T (page 40)

10. F (page 41)

11. T (page 42)

12. F (page 42)

13. T (page 45)

14. T (page 45)

15. F (page 46)

Short Answer

1. United States Department of Transportation (page 40)

2. To protect citizens from liability for errors or omissions in giving good faith emergency care (page 45)

3. Decapitation; rigor mortis; tissue decomposition; dependent lividity (page 43)

4. Any three of the following (page 45):
   - Knife wounds
   - Gunshot wounds
   - Motor vehicle accidents
   - Suspected child abuse
   - Domestic violence
   - Elder abuse
   - Dog bites
   - Rape

5. Any three of the following (page 46):
   - Condition of the patient when found
   - Patient's description of the injury or illness
   - Patient's initial and repeat vital signs
   - Treatment you gave
   - Agency and personnel who took over treatment of the patient
   - Any reportable conditions present
   - Any infectious disease exposure
   - Anything unusual regarding the case

You Make the Call

Your answer should include the following steps and information (page 46).

- Assess scene safety and take steps to protect yourself.
- Make patient care your first priority.
- Move the patient only if necessary, and take a mental "snapshot" of the scene before you do.
- Touch only what you need to touch to gain access to the patient.
- Preserve the crime scene for further investigation, and do not move anything unless it interferes with your ability to provide care.
- Be careful not to alter or destroy evidence when placing your equipment.
- Keep nonessential personnel such as curious neighbors away from the scene.
- After you have attended to the patient(s), write a short report about the incident and make a sketch of the scene that shows how and where you found the patient.

Chapter 4: The Human Body

Matching

1. C (page 57)
2. B (page 57)
3. E (page 57)
4. A (page 57)
5. D (page 57)

Multiple Choice

1. B (page 60)
2. C (page 61)
3. D (page 55)
4. C (page 56)
5. C (page 57)
6. A (page 53)
7. B (pages 54–55)
8. C (page 54)
9. B (page 53)
10. C (pages 60–61)
11. C (page 61)
12. D (page 59)
13. D (page 60)
14. B (page 56)
15. D (page 59)
16. D (page 57)
17. B (page 57)
18. A (page 59)
19. D (page 57)
20. D (page 57)
21. B (page 56)
22. D (page 56)
23. A (page 56)
24. B (page 56)
25. B (page 57)
26. B (page 55)
27. A (page 55)
28. D (page 56)
29. D (page 55)
30. A (page 52)
31. B (page 52)
32. C (page 53)
33. D (page 53)
34. C (page 53)
35. D (page 53)
36. A (page 53)
37. C (page 53)

Fill-in-the-Blanks

1. Twelve (page 57)
2. vertebrae (page 56)
3. spinal cord (page 56)
4. jawbone (page 56)
5. floating (page 57)
6. fibula (page 59)
7. joint (page 59)
8. heart (page 59)
9. abdomen (page 60)
10. mouth (page 60)

True/False

1. F (page 60)
2. T (page 60)
3. F (page 55)
4. F (page 55)
5. T (page 55)
6. F (page 52)
7. T (page 52)
8. T (page 52)
9. F (page 52)
10. T (page 52)
11. F (page 53)
12. F (page 55)
13. T (page 57)
14. F (page 57)
15. F (page 59)
16. F (page 59)
17. T (page 60)
18. T (page 60)
19. F (page 60)
20. T (page 60)

Short Answer

1. Nasal cavity or nasopharynx; mouth; epiglottis; larynx; trachea; lungs (page 53)
2. Protect against harmful substances; regulate temperature; receive information from the outside environment (page 61)
3. Support the skin; protect vital structures; manufacture red blood cells (page 56)
4. Contracting (shortening); relaxing (lengthening) (page 59)
5. Cervical spine; thoracic spine; lumbar spine; sacrum; coccyx (page 57)
6. Mouth; throat; esophagus; stomach; small intestine; large intestine; rectum; anus (page 60)
7. (See page 54.)
   A. Pediatric patients have smaller, more flexible respiratory systems.
   B. Because a child's airways are smaller, they are more easily blocked.
   C. Very young infants can breathe only through their noses.
8. Skull; spine; shoulder girdle; upper extremities; rib cage; pelvis; lower extremities (pages 56–57, 59)

Word Fun

Across

3. anterior (page 52)
5. skeletal (page 56)
6. medial (page 52)
7. proximal (page 53)
9. circulatory (page 54)
11. nervous (page 60)
12. distal (page 53)

Down

1. posterior (page 52)
2. muscular (page 59)
4. inferior (page 52)
8. lateral (page 52)
10. skin (page 61)

Labeling

1. (See page 53.)
   A. Upper airway
   B. Trachea
   C. Lung
   D. Diaphragm
2. (See page 53.)
   A. Nasal cavity (nasopharynx)
   B. Mouth (oropharynx)
   C. Epiglottis
   D. Larynx
   E. Esophagus
   F. Trachea
   G. Lung
3. (See page 55.)
   A. Lungs
   B. Heart
   C. Aorta (artery)
4. (See page 57.)
   A. Sternum
   B. Ribs
   C. Spinal column
   D. Xiphoid process

5. (See page 61.)
- **A.** Mouth
- **B.** Throat (pharynx)
- **C.** Esophagus
- **D.** Liver
- **E.** Stomach
- **F.** Gallbladder
- **G.** Pancreas
- **H.** Large intestine
- **I.** Small intestine
- **J.** Rectum
- **K.** Anus

You Make the Call

Your answer should include the following steps and information (page 55).

- Check the pulse at the carotid artery at either side of the neck.
- Check the radial artery at the wrist.
- Check the femoral artery on the inside of the upper leg.

Chapter 5: Lifting and Moving Patients

Matching

1. C (page 72)
2. B (page 72)
3. D (page 72)
4. A (page 73)
5. F (page 73)
6. E (page 74)

Multiple Choice

1. B (page 72)
2. D (pages 72–73)
3. C (page 72)
4. B (page 73)
5. D (pages 85, 88)
6. D (page 85)
7. C (page 84)
8. B (page 84)
9. D (page 82)
10. A (page 84)
11. A (pages 77–78)
12. A (page 74)
13. C (pages 74–75)
14. D (page 75)
15. B (page 75)
16. D (page 76)
17. C (page 81)

Fill-in-the-Blanks

1. log rolling (page 85)
2. immobilize (page 84)
3. Cervical collars (page 84)
4. scoop (page 82)
5. Soft (page 84)
6. head (page 70)
7. four (page 85)
8. airway (page 93)

True/False

1. F (page 73)
2. T (page 76)
3. F (page 76)
4. T (page 76)
5. F (page 79)
6. T (page 79)
7. T (page 79)

8. F (page 79)
9. T (page 81)
10. T (page 81)
11. F (page 81)
12. T (page 81)
13. F (page 82)
14. T (page 84)
15. F (page 84)
16. F (page 84)
17. F (page 84)
18. F (page 84)
19. F (page 82)
20. F (page 82)
21. T (page 88)
22. T (page 88)
23. F (page 89)
24. F (page 90)
25. F (page 93)
26. T (page 70)
27. T (page 70)
28. T (page 70)
29. F (page 70)
30. T (page 70)
31. F (page 73)
32. T (page 74)
33. T (page 74)
34. T (page 74)
35. T (page 70)

Short Answer

1. For the protection of the patient; if rescuers need more room to provide treatment (page 70)
2. Keep the patient's head and spine immobilized so he or she does not move (page 70)
3. To help maintain an open airway (page 71)
4. Any three of the following (pages 71–72):
   - Burning building
   - Confined space
   - Danger of fire, explosion, or structural collapse
   - Accident scene cannot be protected
   - Presence of hazardous materials
   - Need to gain access to other patients
5. Any three of the following (pages 79–82):
   - Wheeled ambulance stretcher
   - Portable stretcher
   - Stair chair
   - Long backboard
   - Short backboard
   - Scoop stretcher

Labeling

1. Arm-to-arm drag (page 73)
2. Two-person walking assist (page 79)
3. Two-person extremity carry (page 74)
4. Cradle-in-arms carry (page 75)
5. Two-person seat carry (page 75)
6. Blanket drag (page 73)
7. One-person walking assist (page 79)
8. Pack-strap carry (page 76)
9. Clothes drag (page 73)
10. Two-person chair carry (page 75)
11. Fire fighter drag (page 73)

Skill Drills

A. (See page 87.)
1. roll
2. side
3. backboard
4. Roll
5. secure

B. (See page 91.)
1. Stabilize
2. cervical collar
3. straps
4. blanket roll
5. neck
6. cravats

You Make the Call

Your answer should include the following steps and information (pages 75–76 and pages 78–79).

In this circumstance, you will want to use one of the following techniques:

1. Two-person walking assist:
   - Help the patient stand.
   - Have the patient place one arm around your neck and hold the patient's wrist (which should be draped over your shoulder). Put your free arm around the patient's waist and help the patient walk.
   - Have the patient do the same with the other rescuer.
   - Two rescuers can support the patient as they escort him or her from the building.

2. Two-person chair carry:
   - Rescuer One stands behind the seated patient, reaches down, and grasps the back of the chair close to the seat.
   - Rescuer One then tilts the chair slightly backward on its rear legs so that Rescuer Two can step back between the legs of the chair and grasp the chair's front legs.
   - The patient's legs should be between the legs of the chair.
   - When both rescuers are correctly positioned, Rescuer One gives the command to lift and walk away.

3. Two-person seat carry:
   - The rescuers kneel on opposite sides of the patient near the patient's hips.
   - The rescuers raise the patient to a sitting position and link arms behind the patient's back.
   - The rescuers then place the other arm under the patient's knees and link with each other.
   - If possible, the patient puts his or her arms around the necks of the rescuers for additional support.

Chapter 6: Airway Management

Matching

1. D (page 105)
2. B (page 105)
3. E (page 106)
4. C (page 105)
5. A (page 110)

Multiple Choice

1. A (page 108)
2. D (page 108)
3. D (page 109)
4. C (page 111)
5. A (page 112)
6. B (page 114)
7. C (page 114)
8. B (page 125)
9. C (page 106)
10. A (page 118)
11. A (page 118)
12. D (page 118)
13. C (page 118)
14. A (page 118)
15. D (page 123)
16. B (page 123)
17. A (page 123)
18. B (page 120)
19. C (pages 126–127)
20. C (page 127)

21. B (page 128)
22. A (page 123)
23. C (page 119)
24. A (page 105)
25. B (page 105)
26. D (page 105)
27. B (page 106)
28. C (page 107)
29. D (pages 109–111)
30. B (page 110)
31. D (page 116)
32. D (page 116)
33. D (page 112)
34. B (page 112)
35. D (page 118)
36. D (pages 118–119)
37. A (page 119)
38. D (page 119)
39. A (pages 126–127)
40. A (page 127)

Fill-in-the-Blanks

1. manual, mechanical (pages 109–110)
2. recovery (page 112)
3. cyanosis (or blue skin) (page 113)
4. respiratory arrest (page 116)
5. breathing (page 116)

True/False

1. T (page 105)
2. T (page 105)
3. T (page 127)
4. F (page 127)
5. F (page 108)
6. T (pages 126–127)
7. T (page 126)

8. T (page 127)
9. T (page 131)
10. F (pages 131–132)
11. T (page 132)
12. T (page 107)
13. F (page 110)
14. T (page 109)

15. T (page 112)   **36.** T (page 115)
16. T (page 113)   **37.** T (page 116)
17. T (page 116)   **38.** T (page 118)
18. F (page 119)   **39.** F (page 118)
19. F (page 121)   **40.** T (page 122)
20. T (page 112)   **41.** T (page 121)
21. T (page 136)   **42.** F (page 124)
22. T (page 105)   **43.** F (pages 123–124)
23. F (page 106)   **44.** F (page 123)
24. F (page 106)   **45.** F (pages 123–124)
25. T (page 107)   **46.** T (pages 123–124)
26. F (page 108)   **47.** T (page 126)
27. T (page 108)   **48.** T (page 125)
28. F (page 108)   **49.** T (pages 126–127)
29. T (page 109)   **50.** F (page 126)
30. T (page 112)   **51.** T (page 127)
31. T (page 112)   **52.** F (pages 127–128)
32. T (page 113)   **53.** T (page 127)
33. F (page 112)   **54.** T (pages 128–129)
34. T (page 113)   **55.** T (page 129)
35. T (page 116)   **56.** T (page 129)

Short Answer

1. Any three of the following (page 106):
   - Structures of respiratory systems are smaller
   - Tongue is proportionally larger
   - Trachea is more flexible
   - Head is proportionally larger
   - Lungs are smaller
   - Cardiac arrest usually results from airway problems

2. Any three of the following (page 109):
   - Secretions (vomitus, mucus, or blood)
   - Foreign body (candy, food, or dirt)
   - Dentures or false teeth
   - Tongue

3. Maintain airway; maintain pathway for suction (page 112)

4. (See page 113.)
   1. Select the proper size.
   2. Open the mouth with one hand.
   3. Hold the oral airway upside down with the other hand.
   4. Insert the airway gently along the roof of the mouth until it meets resistance.
   5. Rotate the airway 180 degrees.

5. (See pages 113–116.)
   1. Select the proper size.
   2. Coat the airway.
   3. Select the larger nostril.
   4. Gently stretch the nostril open with your thumb.
   5. Gently insert the airway until the flange rests against the nose.

6. (See page 119.)
   1. Position yourself at the patient's head.
   2. Open the patient's airway.
   3. Place the mask over the mouth and nose of the patient.
   4. Grasp the mask and the patient's jaw.
   5. Maintain an airtight seal.
   6. Take a deep breath and seal your mouth over the mouthpiece.
   7. Breathe slowly into the patient.
   8. Monitor the patient's breathing.
7. Any two of the following (page 116):
   • Noisy respirations (including wheezing or gurgling)
   • Rapid or gasping respirations
   • Cyanosis (blue skin)
   • Lack of chest movements
   • Lack of breath sounds
8. Mild (partial); severe (complete) (page 126)
9. Roll the patient to the side, supporting the head, and place the patient's face on its side so that secretions can run out of the mouth (page 112).

Word Fun

Across
2. oropharynx (page 105)
3. mandible (page 105)
6. alveoli (page 106)
8. nasopharynx (page 105)
10. esophagus (page 105)
11. larynx (page 106)

Down
1. capillaries (page 106)
4. trachea (page 105)
5. bronchi (page 106)
7. lungs (page 106)
9. oxygen (page 104)

Labeling

1. (See page 105.)
   A. Nasopharnyx
   B. Mouth
   C. Oropharynx
   D. Trachea
   E. Lung
   F. Diaphragm
2. (See page 111.)
   A. Manual suction device
   B. Battery-powered suction device
   C. Rigid suction tip
   D. Flexible suction catheter
3. (See page 127.)
   A. Tongue blocking airway
   B. Injury
   C. Swelling
   D. Foreign object

Skill Drills

A. (See page 114.)
   1. earlobe
   2. oral airway
   3. 180 degrees
B. (See page 115.)
   1. airway
   2. larger
   3. nose

You Make the Call

Your answer should include the following steps and information (pages 128–129).

- Ask "Are you choking? Can you speak?"
- Stand behind the patient
- Position your hands for abdominal thrusts
- Repeat abdominal thrusts until the object is expelled or the patient becomes unconscious

Chapter 7: Patient Assessment

Matching

1. E (page 157)

2. A (page 158)

3. C (page 157)

4. D (page 158)

5. B (page 157)

6. F (page 157)

Multiple Choice

1. D (page 147)

2. C (page 151)

3. C (page 153)

4. A (page 152)

5. A (page 152)

6. D (page 158)

7. B (pages 157–158)

8. C (page 158)

9. C (page 162)

10. C (page 164)

11. D (page 151)

12. D (page 150)

13. B (page 152)

14. D (page 152)

15. A (page 153)

16. D (page 153)

17. A (page 153)

18. C (page 153)

19. D (page 147)

20. B (page 148)

21. A (page 148)

22. D (page 162)

23. C (page 162)

24. B (page 162)

25. A (page 162)

26. D (page 154)

27. B (page 157)

28. D (page 157)

29. C (page 158)

30. D (page 159)

31. A (page 159)

32. D (page 159)

33. C (page 159)

34. A (page 157)

35. C (page 162)

36. B (page 162)

37. D (page 164)

38. B (page 165)

39. C (page 172)

40. B (page 172)

Fill-in-the-Blanks

1. introduce yourself (page 151)

2. unresponsive (page 151)

3. head tilt–chin lift (page 152)

4. rate; quality (page 152)

5. airway (page 150)

6. symptom (page 157)

7. sign (page 157)

8. serious illness (page 158)

9. shock (page 158)

10. rate; rhythm; quality (page 158)

11. 98.6 °F (page 159)

12. respiratory rate; pulse; skin condition and temperature (page 160)

13. (See page 150.)
  1. C
  2. B
  3. F
  4. A
  5. D
  6. E
  7. G

True/False

1. T (page 147)   **21.** F (page 152)
2. T (page 147)   **22.** T (page 152)
3. T (page 147)   **23.** T (page 153)
4. F (page 147)   **24.** T (page 153)
5. T (page 148)   **25.** T (page 154)
6. F (pages 148–149) **26.** F (page 148)
7. T (page 152)   **27.** F (page 160)
8. F (page 151)   **28.** T (page 157)
9. T (page 152)   **29.** T (page 157)
10. F (page 153)   **30.** T (page 157)
11. F (page 154)   **31.** T (page 157)
12. T (page 160)   **32.** T (page 157)
13. F (page 167)   **33.** F (page 157)
14. T (page 144)   **34.** F (page 158)
15. F (page 172)   **35.** T (page 158)
16. F (page 151)   **36.** F (page 161)
17. T (page 151)   **37.** F (page 161)
18. T (pages 152–153) **38.** F (page 162)
19. F (page 151)   **39.** T (page 163)
20. T (page 152)   **40.** T (page 165)

Short Answer

1. (See page 144.)
  1. Scene size-up
  2. Initial patient assessment
  3. Physical exam
  4. Taking the patient's medical history
  5. Ongoing assessment
2. Any three of the following (page 147):
  • Location of incident
  • Type of incident
  • Number of persons involved
  • Safety level of the scene
3. (See pages 147–149.)
  1. Review dispatch information
  2. BSI
  3. Scene safety
  4. Mechanism of injury/nature of illness
  5. Determine need for additional resources

4. Any four of the following (pages 147–148):
   - Electrical wires
   - Traffic
   - Spilled gasoline
   - Unstable building
   - Crime scene
   - Crowds
   - Unstable surfaces (ie, slopes, ice, water)
   - Electricity
   - Hazardous materials
   - Poisons

5. How the accident happened; type of accident; extent of damage (page 148)

6. Alert; verbal; pain; unresponsive (page 152)

7. Place the side of your face by the patient's nose and mouth and look, listen, and feel for breath (page 152).

8. (See pages 153–154.)
   A. Decreased circulation or shock
   B. Fever or sunburn
   C. Lack of oxygen
   D. Liver problems

9. Deformity; open injuries; tenderness; swelling (page 160)

10. (See page 157.)
    1. Radial artery, found on the wrist; used for responsive adult patients
    2. Carotid artery, found on the sides of the neck; used for unresponsive adult patients
    3. Brachial artery, found on the arm; used for infants

11. Squeeze the patient's nail bed firmly between your thumb and forefinger, then release the pressure. Determine the length of time it takes for the nail bed to become pink again (page 158).

12. Signs/symptoms; allergies; medications; pertinent medical history; last oral intake; events leading up to the injury or illness (pages 167–168)

13. Head; eyes; nose; mouth; neck; face; chest; abdomen; pelvis; back; extremities (pages 160–165)

14. Fingernail beds; whites of eyes; inside of mouth (page 154)

Word Fun

Across

3. BSI (page 147)
5. carotid (page 153)
7. ABC page (pages 152–153)
10. respiratory (page 157)
12. SAMPLE (page 167)
15. LOC (page 151)

Down

1. assessment (page 151)
2. sign (page 157)
4. mechanism (page 148)
5. cyanotic (page 162)
6. capillary (page 158)

8. brachial (page 157)
9. symptom (page 157)
11. radial (page 157)
13. AVPU (page 152)
14. exam (page 157)
16. CC (page 154)

Labeling

1. (See page 159.)
   A. Normal pupil
   B. Dilated pupil
   C. Constricted pupil

You Make the Call

Your answer should include the following steps and information (pages 151–172).

- Position the patient on her side or stomach.
- Consider that the information given by the patient's husband may be inaccurate.
- Assess the patient's airway, breathing, and circulatory status.
- Move the patient if necessary. (If the patient is breathing adequately and secretions are draining adequately, there may be no reason to move the patient. The patient should be moved if movement is needed to improve the airway or to support breathing or circulation.)
- Complete a thorough patient assessment.
- Obtain a pertinent medical history from family members.
- Provide ongoing assessment as needed, and arrange for transport to a nearby medical facility.

Chapter 8: Communications and Documentation

Matching

1. E (page 180)
2. B (page 181)
3. C (page 182)
4. D (page 181)
5. A (page 181)

Multiple Choice

1. C (page 183)
2. B (page 183)
3. A (page 183)
4. D (page 184)
5. C (page 185)
6. C (page 187)
7. B (page 187)
8. B (page 188)
9. A (page 188)
10. C (page 192)

Fill-in-the-Blanks

1. printed; written (page 181)
2. mobile (page 180)
3. one (page 187)
4. Federal Communications Commission (page 180)
5. deaf (page 189)

True/False

1. T (page 193)
2. T (page 193)
3. F (page 193)
4. F (page 192)
5. T (page 191)
6. T (page 190)
7. F (page 190)
8. T (page 188)
9. F (page 190)
10. T (page 190)

Short Answer

1. A base station is a powerful stationary two-way radio that is attached to one or more fixed antennas. A mobile radio is mounted in a vehicle and draws electricity from the electrical system of the vehicle (page 180).
2. Data; voice (page 180)
3. Two-way radio with a self-contained battery; built-in microphone; built-in antenna (page 181)
4. Paging systems; mobile data terminals; fax machines (page 181)
5. To transmit electrocardiograms and other patient data to online medical control (page 182)

6. This gives the patient, family members, and bystanders an idea of who you are and lets them know your qualifications (page 185).

7. They may frighten or confuse the patient (page 185).

You Make the Call

(See page 183.)

1. Provide the age and sex of the patient.
2. Describe the history of the incident.
3. Describe the patient's chief complaint.
4. Describe the patient's level of responsiveness.
5. Report the status of the vital signs, airway, breathing, and circulation (including severe bleeding).
6. Describe the results of the physical examination.
7. Report any pertinent medical conditions with the SAMPLE format.
8. Report the interventions provided.

Chapter 9: Professional Rescuer CPR

Matching

1. C (page 203)
2. I (page 219)
3. J (page 209)
4. G (page 205)
5. A (page 201)
6. F (page 208)
7. B (page 201)
8. H (page 205)
9. D (page 205)
10. E (page 206)

Multiple Choice

1. A (page 202)
2. D (page 201)
3. C (page 205)
4. B (page 206)
5. D (page 207)
6. D (page 209)
7. D (page 212)
8. C (page 209)
9. B (page 209)
10. B (page 205)
11. D (page 215)
12. D (page 214)
13. D (page 216)
14. D (pages 215, 217)
15. A (page 206)
16. C (page 219)
17. D (page 219)
18. B (page 210)
19. D (page 212)
20. D (page 212)
21. A (page 209)
22. C (page 222)
23. D (page 204)
24. D (pages 203–204)
25. B (page 200)
26. C (page 203)
27. D (page 217)
28. D (page 219)
29. D (page 201)
30. B (page 200)
31. A (page 226)

Fill-in-the-Blanks

1. 100 (page 205)
2. brachial (page 205)
3. (See pages 210–212.)
    A. V
    B. V
    C. C
    D. V
    E. C
    F. C
4. pump (page 200)
5. four (page 200)
6. lungs (page 200)

True/False

1. T (page 207)
2. T (page 223)
3. T (page 205)
4. T (page 205)
5. T (page 205)
6. F (page 205)
7. T (page 219)
8. T (page 219)
9. F (page 219)
10. T (page 219)
11. T (page 203)
12. F (page 203)

13. T (page 200)	**29.** T (page 205)
14. T (page 203)	**30.** F (page 205)
15. F (page 204)	**31.** F (page 205)
16. T (page 203)	**32.** T (page 206)
17. F (page 209)	**33.** T (page 207)
18. T (page 209)	**34.** T (page 203)
19. F (page 210)	**35.** T (page 210)
20. F (page 212)	**36.** F (page 209)
21. T (page 212)	**37.** T (page 209)
22. F (page 212)	**38.** F (page 209)
23. F (page 219)	**39.** T (page 209)
24. T (page 220)	**40.** T (page 213)
25. F (page 223)	**41.** T (page 201)
26. F (page 205)	**42.** F (page 202)
27. T (page 205)	**43.** F (page 209)
28. T (page 205)	

Short Answer

1. Maintain the head tilt (page 207)
2. Just below the nipple line over the sternum (page 205)
3. Too much air delivered too fast; partial obstruction of the airway (page 219)
4. Neck or carotid artery, groin or femoral artery, wrist or radial artery, and arm or brachial artery (page 201)
5. Decapitation, rigor mortis, evidence of tissue decomposition, and dependent lividity (page 203)

Labeling

(See page 202.)
A. Neck; carotid pulse
B. Wrist; radial pulse
C. Arm; brachial pulse
D. Groin; femoral pulse

Skill Drills

A. (See page 206.)
  1. sternum
  2. center
  3. interlock
B. (See page 208.)
  1. responsiveness
  2. airway
  3. breathing
  4. rescue breathing
  5. circulation
  6. chest compressions

You Make the Call

Your answer should include the following steps and information (pages 207–209).

- Introduce yourself.
- Check responsiveness.
- Check and correct the airway (including use of proper techniques for opening the airway).
- Check and correct breathing (including use of proper method of performing rescue breathing).
- Check and correct circulation (including correct steps of external cardiac compressions).
- Establish the need for additional resources.
- Establish the need to arrange immediate transportation.

Chapter 10: Medical Emergencies

Matching

1. H (page 248)
2. B (page 245)
3. G (page 241)
4. F (page 235)
5. E (page 249)
6. D (page 244)
7. I (page 248)
8. J (page 239)
9. C (page 245)
10. A (page 242)

Multiple Choice

1. A (page 249)
2. C (page 242)
3. D (page 244)
4. B (page 242)
5. D (page 243)
6. C (page 242)
7. A (page 243)
8. D (page 243)
9. A (page 242)
10. A (page 245)
11. D (page 245)
12. C (page 246)
13. C (page 246)
14. A (page 246)
15. C (page 247)
16. D (page 247)
17. B (page 247)
18. A (page 247)
19. C (page 236)
20. D (page 238)
21. D (page 238)
22. B (page 241)
23. B (page 240)
24. B (page 241)
25. C (page 235)
26. D (page 236)
27. B (page 234)
28. B (page 236)
29. B (page 238)
30. A (page 239)
31. B (page 239)
32. A (page 240)
33. A (page 240)
34. D (page 241)
35. D (page 242)
36. B (page 242)
37. D (page 242)
38. D (page 243)
39. A (page 244)
40. C (page 244)
41. A (page 244)
42. D (page 247)
43. C (page 248)
44. A (page 247)
45. D (page 247)
46. D (page 248)

Fill-in-the-Blanks

1. mental (page 235)
2. (See pages 238–239.)
   A. HE
   B. HE
   C. HS
   D. HE
   E. HS
   F. HS
   G. HE
   H. HE
   I. HS
3. atherosclerosis (page 241)
4. Seizures (page 235)
5. asthma attack (page 245)

True/False

1. T (page 243)	**28.** F (page 240)
2. F (page 236)	**29.** T (page 241)
3. F (page 236)	**30.** F (page 240)
4. T (page 237)	**31.** T (page 241)
5. T (page 236)	**32.** T (page 240)
6. F (page 236)	**33.** T (page 241)
7. T (page 236)	**34.** T (page 241)
8. F (page 236)	**35.** F (page 235)
9. T (page 236)	**36.** T (page 238)
10. T (page 248)	**37.** F (page 239)
11. T (page 249)	**38.** T (pages 239–240)
12. T (page 247)	**39.** T (page 238)
13. F (page 246)	**40.** F (page 238)
14. F (page 246)	**41.** F (page 236)
15. T (page 246)	**42.** F (page 236)
16. F (page 246)	**43.** T (page 235)
17. T (page 247)	**44.** F (page 235)
18. T (page 246)	**45.** F (page 237)
19. T (page 250)	**46.** T (page 240)
20. T (page 239)	**47.** F (page 240)
21. F (page 239)	**48.** T (page 241)
22. T (page 239)	**49.** T (page 242)
23. F (page 239)	**50.** T (page 242)
24. T (page 240)	**51.** T (page 244)
25. T (page 239)	**52.** F (page 245)
26. F (page 239)	**53.** T (page 245)
27. T (page 240)	**54.** T (page 246)

Short Answer

1. Diabetic coma; insulin shock (pages 247–248)

2. "Are you a diabetic?"; "Did you take your insulin today?"; "Have you eaten today?" (page 247)

3. Cola or orange drink; honey (page 248)

4. Initial level of consciousness; any change in the patient's level of consciousness (page 235)

5. Any of the following (page 235):
   - Head injury
   - Shock
   - Decreased level of oxygen to the brain
   - High fever
   - Infection
   - Poisoning
   - Drugs
   - Alcohol
   - Diabetic emergencies
   - Psychiatric condition
   - Insulin reaction

6. Face, fingers, ears, toes (page 239)

You Make the Call

Your answer should include the following steps and information (page 235):

- Complete assessment
- Maintain ABCs
- Provide a safe scene
- Keep her warm
- Place her in the recovery position
- Prepare for prompt transportation

Chapter 11: Poisoning and Substance Abuse

Matching

1. G (page 261)
2. F (page 267)
3. I (page 267)
4. J (page 267)
5. C (page 267)
6. A (page 261)
7. E (page 267)
8. H (page 263)
9. D (page 260)
10. B (page 264)

Multiple Choice

1. B (page 259)
2. D (page 258)
3. A (page 259)
4. B (page 261)
5. D (page 264)
6. B (page 264)
7. B (page 268)
8. D (page 267)
9. B (page 258)
10. A (page 258)
11. D (page 258)
12. C (page 258)
13. D (page 260)
14. D (page 260)
15. A (page 260)
16. B (page 261)
17. B (page 263)
18. D (pages 261–262)
19. A (page 263)
20. A (page 263)
21. D (page 263)
22. D (page 265)
23. C (page 265)
24. B (page 267)
25. D (page 267)

Fill-in-the-Blanks

1. A. ingested (page 260)
   B. inhaled (page 261)
   C. inhaled (page 262)
   D. injected (page 263)
   E. ingested (page 260)
   F. inhaled (page 262)
   G. absorbed (page 265)
2. ammonia; chlorine (page 261)
3. (page 267)
   A. H
   B. U
   C. U
   D. D
   E. D
   F. H
   G. U
   H. H
4. inhalants (page 265)
5. suicide (page 268)

True/False

1. F (page 258)	**20.** T (page 261)
2. T (page 259)	**21.** T (page 262)
3. F (page 259)	**22.** T (page 258)
4. T (page 263)	**23.** T (page 263)
5. F (page 260)	**24.** F (page 258)
6. F (page 260)	**25.** T (page 263)
7. T (page 259)	**26.** F (page 264)
8. F (page 259)	**27.** T (page 264)
9. F (page 263)	**28.** T (page 264)
10. T (page 259)	**29.** T (page 265)
11. F (page 259)	**30.** T (page 264)
12. T (page 260)	**31.** F (page 264)
13. F (page 260)	**32.** T (page 264)
14. T (page 259)	**33.** T (page 265)
15. F (page 260)	**34.** F (page 265)
16. F (page 260)	**35.** F (page 265)
17. F (page 261)	**36.** F (page 267)
18. F (page 261)	**37.** T (page 267)
19. F (page 262)	

Short Answer

1. Ingestion (page 259)
2. Will produce vomiting (page 260)
3. Respiratory distress, cough, dizziness, headache, and confusion (page 263)
4. Remove everyone from the dwelling, suspect carbon monoxide poisoning, and administer oxygen if available (page 261).
5. Remove him or her from the source of the gas (page 262).
6. Use of proper encapsulating suit with a SCBA (page 262)
7. Any three of the following (page 263):
   - Itching
   - Hives
   - Swelling
   - Generalized weakness
   - Unconsciousness
   - Rapid, weak pulse
   - Rapid, shallow breathing
   - Drop in blood pressure
   - Cardiac arrest
8. Any three of the following (page 265):
   - Shock
   - Dizziness
   - Itching
   - Burning
   - Skin rash
   - Inflammation or redness of the skin
9. Provide basic life support, keep the patient from hurting himself or herself and others, and arrange for prompt transport to a medical facility (page 267).
10. Any contact with water is made (page 264)

Word Fun

Across

3. amphetamine (page 267)
5. injection (page 258)
6. inhalation (page 258)
8. alcohol (page 265)
10. carbon monoxide (page 261)
12. ingestion (page 258)
13. poison (page 267)

Down

1. barbiturate (page 267)
2. absorption (page 258)
4. overdose (page 267)
7. uppers (page 267)
9. cough (page 262)
10. cocaine (page 267)
11. hives (page 267)

You Make the Call

Your answer should include the following steps and information (page 259):

- Assessment and maintenance of ABCs
- Identification of the poison or type of medication that was taken
- Contact with local poison control for direction of necessary care
- Following directions from poison control
- Arrangement of transport to an appropriate medical facility

Chapter 12: Behavioral Emergencies

Matching

1. B (page 277)
2. D (page 274)
3. F (page 275)
4. H (page 284)
5. I   (page 279)
6. J (page 279)
7. G (page 278)
8. E (page 282)
9. C (page 277)
10. A (page 274)

Multiple Choice

1. C (page 275)
2. C (page 276)
3. D (page 276)
4. A (page 279)
5. D (page 279)
6. D (page 274)
7. D (page 274)
8. A (page 275)
9. D (page 275)
10. C (page 275)
11. C (page 277)
12. B (page 277)
13. A (page 278)
14. D (page 279)
15. D (page 282)
16. D (page 282)
17. B (page 284)

Fill-in-the-Blanks

1. situational crisis (page 274)
2. Communication (page 276)
3. Redirection (page 277)
4. empathy (page 278)
5. cries for help (page 282)

True/False

1. T (page 274)
2. T (page 274)
3. T (page 274)
4. F (page 275)
5. T (page 277)
6. T (page 277)
7. F (page 277)
8. T (page 277)
9. T (page 277)
10. T (page 277)
11. F (page 277)
12. F (page 279)
13. T (page 280)
14. T (page 274)
15. T (page 274)
16. T (page 274)
17. T (page 274)
18. F (page 274)
19. F (page 274)
20. F (page 275)
21. F (page 275)
22. F (page 275)
23. T (page 275)
24. F (page 276)
25. F (page 276)
26. T (page 276)
27. F (page 277)
28. T (page 276)
29. T (page 276)
30. F (page 276)
31. F (page 277)
32. F (page 278)
33. T (page 278)
34. T (page 277)
35. T (page 278)
36. F (page 278)
37. F (page 278)
38. T (page 278)
39. F (page 278)
40. T (page 277)
41. T (page 278)
42. F (page 278)
43. T (page 279)
44. F (page 279)
45. F (page 279)
46. F (page 280)
47. F (page 282)
48. T (page 282)
49. T (page 282)
50. T (page 282)
51. F (page 282)
52. T (page 282)
53. T (page 283)
54. F (page 283)
55. T (page 283)
56. F (page 283)
57. F (page 284)

Short Answer

1. Medical conditions; physical trauma; psychiatric illness; mind-altering substances; and situational stresses (page 274)
2. Anger is a normal response to emotional overload or frustration (page 275).
3. Perform scene size-up, initial patient assessment, physical exam, obtain medical history, ongoing assessment (page 276)
4. When the patient is going to do harm to himself or herself (page 282)
5. Any three of the following:
   - Ingesting poison
   - Jumping from heights
   - Shooting, hanging
   - Cutting wrists
   - Jumping in front of cars or trains (page 282)
6. Natural, accidental, and intentional (page 283)
7. Any three of the following:
   - Depression
   - Inability to sleep
   - Weight change
   - Increased alcohol consumption
   - Inability to get along with family or coworkers
   - Lack of interest in food or sex (page 284)
8. To bring rescuers and trained personnel together to talk about rescuers' feelings (page 284)
9. (See page 277.)
   A. "You seem to be worried about getting home to take care of your children."
   B. "You are very concerned about the woman you hit. My partner is taking care of her now."
   C. "You miss your mommy, don't you? We can go and talk with her as soon as the paramedics finish fixing her leg."
10. (See page 277.)
    A. "You seem worried about getting home to take care of your children. Can you give me the name of a friend or neighbor we can call to help take care of them?"
    B. "You are concerned about the woman you hit. My partner is taking care of her and the paramedics will be here soon. Now we need to examine you to make sure you are not injured."
    C. "You miss your mommy don't you? When the ambulance gets here, you can ride with your mommy to the hospital. Have you ever been in an ambulance before?"

You Make the Call

Your answer should include the following steps and information (page 276):
- Remain calm
- Reassure the patient
- Take time with the patient
- Make eye contact
- Touch the patient for reassurance, if appropriate
- Use a calm and steady voice
- Use methods of restatement or redirection to communicate

Chapter 13: Bleeding, Shock, and Soft-Tissue Injuries

Matching

(See pages 293–294.)

1. D
2. B
3. E
4. E
5. G
6. F
7. A

Multiple Choice

1. C (page 292)
2. C (page 293)
3. B (page 293)
4. D (page 293)
5. B (page 293)
6. A (page 293)
7. D (page 293)
8. D (page 294)
9. D (page 294)
10. D (page 295)
11. D (page 295)
12. C (page 295)
13. B (page 295)
14. A (page 295)
15. D (page 296)
16. B (page 296)
17. C (page 296)
18. D (page 296)
19. D (page 296)
20. D (page 297)
21. C (page 299)
22. D (page 297)
23. D (page 299)
24. D (page 299)
25. D (page 298)
26. C (page 299)
27. D (page 299)
28. C (page 302)
29. D (page 303)
30. C (page 304)
31. B (page 305)
32. D (page 313)
33. D (page 317)
34. A (page 319)
35. C (page 294)
36. B (page 299)
37. A (page 295)
38. C (page 297)
39. C (page 309)
40. D (page 310)
41. C (page 316)
42. C (page 318)
43. D (page 320)

Fill-in-the-Blanks

1. (See page 317.)
   A. 30%
   B. 28%
   C. 18%
   D. 27%
   E. 19%

2. (See pages 316–317.)
   A. 1
   B. 3
   C. 2
   D. 3
   E. 1
   F. 3
   G. 1
   H. 2
   I. 2
   K. 3

True/False

1. T (page 292)	33. T (page 298)	65. F (page 296)
2. T (page 292)	34. T (page 298)	66. T (page 298)
3. T (page 292)	35. F (page 298)	67. T (page 298)
4. T (page 293)	36. T (page 298)	68. F (page 296)
5. F (page 293)	37. T (page 298)	69. T (page 296)
6. F (page 293)	38. T (page 299)	70. T (page 296)
7. T (page 293)	39. F (page 300)	71. T (page 296)
8. F (page 293)	40. T (page 300)	72. T (page 296)
9. F (page 293)	41. T (page 301)	73. T (page 299)
10. F (page 293)	42. T (page 301)	74. T (page 310)
11. T (page 293)	43. T (page 301)	75. T (page 310)
12. T (page 293)	44. F (page 302)	76. F (page 313)
13. T (page 294)	45. F (page 303)	77. T (page 313)
14. F (page 294)	46. F (page 304)	78. T (page 316)
15. T (page 294)	47. T (page 304)	79. T (page 306)
16. T (page 294)	48. T (page 305)	80. T (page 306)
17. T (page 294)	49. T (page 309)	81. F (page 306)
18. T (page 294)	50. T (page 311)	82. F (page 306)
19. T (page 295)	51. F (page 314)	83. T (page 307)
20. T (page 295)	52. F (page 315)	84. F (page 306)
21. F (page 295)	53. T (page 316)	85. T (page 307)
22. F (page 295)	54. T (page 316)	86. T (page 307)
23. T (page 296)	55. F (page 316)	87. T (page 308)
24. F (page 296)	56. T (page 318)	88. T (page 309)
25. T (page 296)	57. T (page 319)	89. T (page 319)
26. T (page 296)	58. F (page 319)	90. F (page 320)
27. F (page 297)	59. F (page 320)	91. T (page 320)
28. T (page 297)	60. T (page 294)	92. T (page 320)
29. T (page 297)	61. T (page 294)	93. T (page 320)
30. F (page 298)	62. F (page 294)	94. T (page 321)
31. F (page 298)	63. T (pages 294–295)	95. F (page 320)
32. F (page 298)	64. F (page 295)	96. T (page 320)

Short Answer

1. The pump (heart); the pipes (veins and arteries); the fluid (blood) (page 292)
2. Pump failure; pipe failure; fluid loss (pages 294–295)
3. Any three of the following (page 313):
   - Clear plastic cover
   - Aluminum foil
   - Plastic wrap
   - Special occlusive dressing
4. Superficial (first-degree); partial thickness (second-degree); full thickness (third-degree) (pages 316–317)
5. Dry sterile dressing (page 318)

6. Any three of the following (page 319):
   • Burns around the face
   • Singed nasal hair
   • Soot in mouth and nose
   • Difficulty breathing
   • Pain while breathing
   • Unconscious as a result of a fire
7. Capillary oozes; venous has a steady flow; arterial spurts or surges (page 299)
8. Brachial artery and femoral artery pressure points (page 301)
9. Control bleeding; prevent further contamination of the wound; immobilize the injured part; stabilize any impaled object (page 306).

Word Fun

Across
1. laceration (page 307)
4. chemical (page 321)
6. exit (page 306)
7. abrasion (page 306)
8. thermal (page 320)
9. gunshot (page 306)
11. closed (page 305)

Down
2. electrical (page 322)
3. puncture (page 306)
5. impaled (page 304)
6. entrance (page 304)
7. avulsion (page 305)
10. open (page 305)

Labeling

1. (See page 293.)
   A. Capillaries
   B. Vein
   C. Aorta
   D. Artery
   E. Atrium
   F. Heart
   G. Ventricle
2. (See page 300.)
   A. Capillary
   B. Venous
   C. Arterial

3. (See pages 304–305.)
   A. Abrasion
   B. Puncture wound
   C. Laceration
   D. Avulsion

You Make the Call

1. Your answer should include the following steps and information (page 318):
   - Cooling the area if still warm
   - Handling the blistered area carefully
   - Covering the area with a dry, sterile dressing
   - Removing the clothing from the burn site if it is not stuck
   - Arranging for transport
   - Completing the appropriate assessment

2. Your answer should include the following steps and information (page 299):
   - Direct pressure
   - Elevation of the extremity
   - Use of the brachial pressure point
   - Placing the patient in a supine position
   - Treatment for shock

Chapter 14: Injuries to Muscles and Bones

Matching

1. C (page 330)
2. F (page 332)
3. D (page 332)
4. H (page 332)
5. J (page 350)
6. B (page 330)
7. E (page 344)
8. A (page 352)
9. I (page 366)
10. G (page 351)

Multiple Choice

1. D (page 330)
2. A (page 330)
3. B (page 330)
4. C (page 330)
5. D (page 330)
6. D (page 332)
7. C (page 332)
8. B (page 332)
9. C (page 334)
10. D (page 334)
11. A (page 335)
12. C (page 335)
13. A (page 338)
14. C (page 338)
15. B (page 339)
16. D (page 351)
17. C (page 352)
18. C (page 354)
19. D (page 355)
20. D (page 361)
21. C (page 332)
22. C (page 332)
23. B (page 332)
24. B (page 335)
25. D (page 335)
26. A (page 335)
27. B (page 335)
28. C (page 335)
29. B (page 338)
30. C (page 339)
31. C (page 345)
32. D (page 345)

Fill-in-the-Blanks

1. rigid collar (page 356)
2. obstruction (page 353)
3. mechanism (page 330)
4. dislocation (page 332)
5. Battle's (page 352)
6. abdominal (page 355)
7. flail (page 360)
8. Osteoporosis (page 366)
9. CPR (page 357)
10. traction (page 338)

True/False

1. T (page 328)	25. F (page 339)	49. F (page 334)
2. T (page 329)	26. T (page 339)	50. T (page 333)
3. F (page 329)	27. T (page 344)	51. T (page 334)
4. T (page 330)	28. F (page 344)	52. F (page 333)
5. T (page 330)	29. T (page 344)	53. F (page 333)
6. T (page 330)	30. T (page 345)	54. T (page 334)
7. F (page 331)	31. T (page 345)	55. T (page 334)
8. F (page 332)	32. F (page 335)	56. F (page 334)
9. T (page 332)	33. F (page 348)	57. F (page 335)
10. T (page 332)	34. F (page 350)	58. T (page 335)
11. F (page 333)	35. T (page 351)	59. F (page 335)
12. F (page 333)	36. F (page 351)	60. T (page 338)
13. T (page 334)	37. T (page 351)	61. T (page 338)
14. F (page 334)	38. T (page 351)	62. F (page 338)
15. T (page 335)	39. T (page 353)	63. T (page 338)
16. F (page 335)	40. F (page 353)	64. T (page 344)
17. T (page 335)	41. T (page 355)	65. F (page 344)
18. F (page 335)	42. T (page 355)	66. T (page 344)
19. T (page 335)	43. F (page 355)	67. F (page 344)
20. F (page 335)	44. T (page 356)	68. T (page 344)
21. F (page 338)	45. F (page 356)	69. T (page 345)
22. T (page 339)	46. F (page 357)	70. F (page 363)
23. F (page 339)	47. T (page 360)	
24. F (page 339)	48. F (page 360)	

Short Answer

1. Support the body, protect vital structures, assist in body movement, and manufacture red blood cells (page 328).
2. Fractures, dislocations, and sprains (page 332)
3. Open wound, deformity, swelling, and bruising (page 334).
4. "Where does it hurt?" and "Is it tingling?" (page 334)
5. Pulse and capillary refill (page 335)
6. Any three of the following (page 355):
   • Laceration or bruise to head, neck, or spine
   • Tenderness over any point on spine or neck
   • Extremity weakness, paralysis, or loss of movement
   • Loss of sensation or tingling in the body below the neck
7. Any three of the following (page 335):
   • Pulse
   • Capillary refill
   • Sensation
   • Movement
8. Understanding of how injuries occurred (page 330)
9. (See page 330.)
   1. Direct force: a pedestrian struck by a car suffers a broken leg
   2. Indirect force: a woman falls on her shoulder and fractures her collar bone
   3. Twisting force: a football player is tackled while turning and twists his leg

10. (See page 328.)
   A. Head
   B. Spinal column
   C. Shoulder girdle
   D. Upper extremities
   E. Rib cage
   F. Pelvis
   G. Lower extremities

11. Splint the elbow joint in the position found (page 340).

12. Any four of the following (page 352):
   - Confusion
   - Unusual behavior
   - Unconsciousness
   - Nausea or vomiting
   - Blood from an ear
   - Decreasing consciousness
   - Unequal pupils
   - Paralysis
   - Seizures
   - Raccoon eyes
   - Battle's sign
   - External head trauma (bleeding, bumps, contusions)

13. Immobilize the head, maintain an open airway, support the patient's breathing, monitor circulation, control any bleeding, treat any other injuries, and arrange for prompt transport to an appropriate medical facility (page 352).

14. Any three of the following (page 333):
   - Pain at the injury site
   - An open wound
   - Swelling and discoloration (bruising)
   - Patient's inability or unwillingness to move the part
   - Deformity or angulation
   - Tenderness at the injury site

Labeling

1. (See page 328.)
   A. Head
   B. Spinal column
   C. Shoulder girdle
   D. Upper extremity
   E. Rib cage
   F. Pelvis
   G. Lower extremity

2. (See page 329.)
   A. Cervical
   B. Thoracic
   C. Lumbar
   D. Sacrum
   E. Coccyx

3. (See page 330.)
   A. Cardiac muscle
   B. Skeletal muscle
   C. Smooth muscle

Skill Drills

A. (See pages 336–337.)
1. radial
2. posterior ankle
3. capillary refill
4. Pink
5. sensation
6. sensation
7. movement
8. movement

B. (See page 358.)
1. neutral
2. screwdriver
3. trainer's tool

C. (See pages 359–360.)
1. airway; breathing
2. lower jaw
3. lower jaw; head
4. halfway
5. back
6. cervical spine

You Make the Call

Your answer should include the following steps and information (pages 333–335):

- Determining the mechanism of injury
- General patient assessment
- Stabilizing airway, breathing, and circulation
- Examining the injured leg
- Evaluating circulation and sensation in the leg
- Treatment (including proper steps for bandaging and splinting)

Chapter 15: Childbirth

Matching

1. E (page 372)
2. C (page 381)
3. D (page 381)
4. B (page 373)
5. A (page 372)

Multiple Choice

1. B (page 373)
2. B (page 383)
3. C (page 373)
4. D (page 373)
5. A (page 373)
6. C (page 373)
7. A (page 374)
8. A (page 376)
9. D (page 373)
10. B (page 377)
11. D (page 377)
12. D (page 383)
13. C (page 384)
14. C (page 372)
15. B (page 373)
16. A (page 373)
17. B (page 373)
18. D (page 376)
19. D (page 383)
20. D (pages 381–382)
21. D (page 377)

Fill-in-the-Blanks

1. placenta (page 372)
2. one (page 373)
3. crowning (page 374)
4. assist (page 372)
5. umbilical (page 378)
6. breech (page 381)
7. miscarriage (page 383)
8. multiple or twin (page 384)
9. beginning (page 374)
10. premature (page 384)

True/False

1. T (page 376)
2. T (page 376)
3. F (page 376)
4. F (page 376)
5. F (page 381)
6. F (page 383)
7. F (page 383)
8. F (page 379)
9. T (page 383)
10. F (page 383)
11. F (page 373)
12. F (page 373)
13. T (page 373)
14. T (page 373)
15. F (page 374)
16. F (page 373)
17. T (page 373)
18. T (page 376)
19. F (page 376)
20. F (page 376)
21. F (page 376)
22. F (page 377)
23. T (page 379)
24. F (page 380)
25. T (page 381)

Short Answer

1. (See page 373.)

   A. Stage one: contractions, water breaks, bloody show, no crowning

   B. Stage two: baby's head crowning; birth

   C. Stage three: delivery of placenta

2. (See pages 379–381.)

   1. Tilt the infant so the head is down and to the side to clear the airway.

   2. Gently snap your fingers on the soles of the infant's feet.

   3. Begin rescue breathing.

   4. Check for a brachial pulse.

   5. Begin chest compressions using the middle and ring fingers.

3. (See page 377.)

   1. Head begins to deliver

   2. Delivery of the head

   3. Delivery of upper shoulder

   4. Delivery of lower shoulder

4. (See pages 374–375.)

   1. Carefully open the sterile glove package without touching the gloves.

   2. Pick up the first glove by grasping one edge.

   3. Pull on the first glove, being careful not to touch the outside.

   4. Grasp the second glove by sliding two fingers of your hand into the rolled edge.

   5. Put on the second glove.

   6. Keep the gloves as sterile as possible.

5. Any three of the following (see page 383):

   • Save the fetus and tissue to transport with the mother

   • Control bleeding

   • Treat for shock

   • Prompt transport

   • Provide emotional support

Word Fun

Across

1. fetus (page 372)

2. placenta (page 372)

4. prolapsed (page 383)

5. amniotic sac (page 373)

8. breech (page 381)

9. miscarriage (page 383)

Down

1. fallopian tubes (page 372)

3. birth canal (page 372)

6. crowning (page 373)

7. uterus (page 372)

Labeling

1. (See page 372.)
   A. Placenta
   B. Uterus
   C. Rectum
   D. Vagina
2. (See page 377.)
   A. Head begins to deliver
   B. Delivery of head
   C. Delivery of upper shoulder
   D. Delivery of lower shoulder

Skill Drills

1. head
2. soles
3. rescue breathing
4. brachial
5. chest compressions

You Make the Call

Your answer should include the following steps and information (see pages 373–374):

- Assess the frequency of contractions.
- Determine if the baby's head is crowning.
- Either arrange for transport or prepare for delivery.
- Calm and reassure the patient.

Chapter 16: Pediatric Emergencies

Matching

1. C (page 407)
2. B (page 396)
3. A (page 398)
4. E (page 408)
5. D (page 404)

Multiple Choice

1. A (page 393)
2. B (page 399)
3. A (page 411)
4. B (page 411)
5. C (page 412)
6. A (page 403)
7. B (page 404)
8. C (page 397)
9. B (page 394)
10. B (page 393)
11. C (page 393)
12. D (page 394)
13. C (page 395)
14. A (page 394)
15. A (page 394)
16. C (page 394)
17. D (page 396)
18. D (page 398)
19. B (page 399)
20. D (page 399)
21. D (page 401)
22. D (page 402)
23. D (page 403)
24. C (page 404)
25. B (page 406)
26. C (page 406)
27. D (pages 407–408)
28. B (pages 407–408)
29. A (page 408)
30. C (page 409)
31. A (pages 408–409)
32. D (page 411)
33. A (page 411)

Fill-in-the-Blanks

1. 3 weeks; 7 months (page 410)
2. Pallor (page 396)
3. pediatric assessment triangle (page 395)
4. 90 to 180; 30 to 60 (page 394)
5. pediatric trauma (page 410)

True/False

1. T (page 392)
2. T (page 392)
3. F (page 393)
4. T (pages 408–409)
5. F (page 409)
6. F (page 409)
7. T (page 409)
8. F (page 407)
9. T (page 408)
10. T (page 407)
11. T (page 407)
12. T (page 410)
13. F (page 410)
14. T (pages 410–411)
15. F (page 411)
16. T (page 398)
17. T (page 398)
18. F (page 398)
19. T (page 399)
20. T (page 399)
21. T (page 407)
22. F (page 393)

23. T (page 393)   **40.** T (page 404)
24. T (page 394)   **41.** F (page 404)
25. F (page 394)   **42.** T (page 406)
26. T (page 395)   **43.** T (page 406)
27. F (page 394)   **44.** F (page 406)
28. T (page 394)   **45.** F (page 406)
29. T (page 396)   **46.** T (page 406)
30. F (page 396)   **47.** T (page 406)
31. F (page 398)   **48.** T (page 408)
32. F (page 398)   **49.** T (page 408)
33. T (page 400)   **50.** T (page 408)
34. F (page 401)   **51.** F (page 410)
35. F (page 401)   **52.** T (page 395)
36. T (page 402)   **53.** T (page 410)
37. T (page 402)   **54.** T (page 412)
38. F (page 403)   **55.** F (page 412)
39. F (page 404)

Short Answer

1. (See page 394.)
   1. Respiration
   2. Pulse
   3. Temperature
2. (See page 401.)
   1. Sharp or straight objects
   2. Bobby pins
   3. Bones
3. (See page 411.)
   1. Open and maintain the airway.
   2. Control bleeding.
   3. Arrange for prompt transport.
4. (See page 407.)
   1. Undress the child.
   2. Use wet sheets with a fan to cool the child.
   3. Transport immediately.
5. (See pages 407–408.)
   1. Uncover the child.
   2. Undress the child.
   3. Fan the child to cool him or her.
   4. Protect the child during seizures.
6. Treat every child with a sore or tender abdomen as an emergency and transport (page 408).
7. (See page 412.)
   1. Multiple fractures
   2. Bruises
   3. Human bites
   4. Burns
   5. Reports of bizarre accidents
8. Summon law enforcement and explain the situation (page 412).
9. If the infant is still warm (page 410)

You Make the Call

Your answer should include the following steps and information (pages 410–411):

- Assessing the child for level of responsiveness
- ABCs and head-to-toe examination
- Controlling bleeding; stabilizing the head and neck
- Treating for shock
- Keeping the child warm
- Giving oxygen if available
- Arranging for immediate transport

Chapter 17: Geriatric Emergencies

Matching

1. B (page 427)
2. D (page 422)
3. A (page 427)
4. C (page 428)
5. E (page 427)

Multiple Choice

1. A (page 422)
2. D (page 422)
3. C (page 420)
4. A (page 421)
5. D (pages 421–422)
6. C (page 420)
7. D (page 420)
8. D (page 420)
9. A (page 422)
10. C (page 422)

Fill-in-the-Blanks

1. more (page 420)
2. bladder (page 420)
3. Hearing loss (page 421)
4. Fractures (page 422)
5. medications (page 424)
6. hospice (page 428)
7. Osteoporosis (page 422)
8. Alzheimer's disease (page 427)
9. shorter (page 422)
10. acute (page 423)

True/False

1. T (page 423)
2. F (page 421)
3. F (page 420)
4. T (page 422)
5. F (page 421)
6. T (page 422)
7. T (page 427)
8. T (page 420)
9. T (page 424)
10. F (page 421)
11. T (page 424)
12. T (page 421)
13. F (page 421)
14. T (page 424)
15. T (page 424)
16. T (page 422)
17. F (page 424)
18. F (page 424)
19. T (page 425)
20. T (page 425)
21. F (page 428)
22. F (page 428)
23. T (page 428)
24. T (page 427)
25. F (page 427)

Short Answer

1. Any three of the following (pages 420–425):
   - Loss or impairment of hearing
   - Loss or impairment of sight
   - Slowed movements; fractures
   - Senility
   - Loss of bowel and bladder control

2. (See page 422.)
   1. Injured leg is shorter
   2. Injured leg may be externally rotated
   3. Patient is in too much pain to move the injured leg (page 422).

3. Any three of the following (page 421):
   - Face the patient.
   - Identify yourself.
   - Touch the patient.
   - Speak slowly.
   - Watch the patient's face.
   - Repeat or rephrase your comments.
   - Write down your comments.
   - Use sign language.

4. Any three of the following (page 427):
   - Bruises, especially on the buttocks, lower back, genitals, cheeks, neck, and earlobes
   - Multiple bruises in different stages of healing
   - Burns
   - Trauma in the genital area
   - Signs of neglect, such as malnourished appearance

5. Any three of the following (page 427):
   - Physical illnesses
   - Loss of a loved one
   - Alcohol abuse
   - Hopelessness
   - Depression

You Make the Call

Your answer should include the following steps and information (pages 424 and 427):

- Speak clearly and calmly to the patient.
- Find out what medications the patient is taking and what was taken when.
- Arrange for transport to the hospital.
- Gather up the patient's medications and bring them to the hospital.
- Let the patient know what you are doing at each step of your assessment.
- Ask family members or caregivers for a medical history.
- Try to avoid asking the patient if it is all right to do something; instead, gently inform him or her of the treatment.

Chapter 18: EMS Operations

Matching

1. B (page 450)
2. D (pages 458–459)
3. C (page 448)
4. A (page 453)
5. E (page 443)

Multiple Choice

1. D (page 438)
2. C (page 456)
3. C (page 456)
4. C (page 456)
5. A (page 440)
6. A (page 436)
7. A (page 437)
8. D (page 437)
9. D (page 438)
10. D (pages 438–439)
11. D (page 439)
12. D (page 440)
13. B (page 440)
14. D (page 442)
15. D (page 443)
16. D (pages 445–446)
17. B (pages 448–449)
18. D (page 450)
19. D (pages 450–453)
20. C (page 456)
21. D (page 456)
22. B (pages 456–457)
23. D (page 458)
24. A (page 457)
25. B (page 443)

Fill-in-the-Blanks

1. 100; 100 (page 438)
2. postimpact (page 443)
3. cribbing (page 443)
4. Helicopters (page 438)
5. Hazardous materials (page 450)

True/False

1. T (page 436)	**27.** F (pages 445–446)	**53.** T (page 445)
2. T (page 438)	**28.** T (pages 445–446)	**54.** F (page 445)
3. T (page 453)	**29.** T (page 446)	**55.** F (page 445)
4. T (page 453)	**30.** T (page 437)	**56.** F (page 448)
5. T (page 453)	**31.** F (page 436)	**57.** T (page 448)
6. T (page 453)	**32.** F (page 438)	**58.** T (page 450)
7. T (page 453)	**33.** F (page 438)	**59.** T (page 450)
8. T (page 453)	**34.** T (page 438)	**60.** T (page 450)
9. F (page 453)	**35.** T (page 438)	**61.** F (page 453)
10. T (page 457)	**36.** T (page 438)	**62.** T (page 456)
11. T (page 457)	**37.** F (page 439)	**63.** T (page 456)
12. F (page 457)	**38.** T (page 439)	**64.** F (page 456)
13. F (page 458)	**39.** T (page 440)	**65.** F (page 456)
14. F (page 458)	**40.** T (page 440)	**66.** F (page 457)
15. F (page 457)	**41.** F (page 440)	**67.** T (page 457)
16. F (page 458)	**42.** F (page 453)	**68.** T (page 457)
17. T (page 458)	**43.** F (page 437)	**69.** T (page 456)
18. T (page 450)	**44.** T (page 441)	**70.** F (page 457)
19. T (page 450)	**45.** F (page 441)	**71.** T (page 457)
20. T (page 450)	**46.** F (page 442)	**72.** T (page 457)
21. T (page 440)	**47.** F (page 442)	**73.** T (page 457)
22. T (page 440)	**48.** F (page 442)	**74.** T (page 458)
23. F (page 441)	**49.** F (page 443)	**75.** T (page 458)
24. T (page 445)	**50.** T (page 443)	**76.** F (page 458)
25. T (page 445)	**51.** T (page 444)	**77.** T (page 458)
26. F (page 445)	**52.** F (page 444)	**78.** T (page 450)

Short Answer

1. Any three of the following (pages 436–450):
   - Infectious diseases
   - Traffic
   - Bystanders
   - Spilled gasoline
   - Automobile batteries
   - Downed electrical wires
   - Unstable vehicles
   - Vehicle fires
2. (See pages 436–438.)
   1. Dispatch
   2. Response to the scene
   3. Arrival at the scene
   4. Transferring the patient to other EMS personnel
   5. Postrun activities
3. (See page 436.)
   1. Location of the incident
   2. Type of incident
   3. Any hazards
   4. Approximate number of victims
   5. Type of assistance required

4. BCM (page 456)

5. Obtain safe access; ensure patient stabilization (page 440)

6. (See page 440.)
   1. Overview the scene.
   2. Stabilize the scene.
   3. Gain access.
   4. Provide initial emergency care.
   5. Help disentangle patients.
   6. Help prepare patients for removal.
   7. Help remove patients.

7. Safety (page 440)

8. Helmet; face shield or goggles; gloves (page 439)

9. Any three of the following (page 436):
   • Telephone
   • Radio
   • Pager
   • Computer terminal
   • Computer printout

10. Any of the following (page 439):
   • Secure all loose clothing, sheets, and instruments.
   • Use eye protection.
   • Approach a helicopter from the front and only after the pilot or a crew member signals that it is safe.

Labeling

1. (See page 444.)
   A. Check the pressure gauge.
   B. Release the hose.
   C. Pull the locking pin.
   D. Discharge at the base of the fire.

Skill Drills

1. (See page 447.)
   1. lower
   2. break
   3. outside
   4. window

2. (See page 449.)
   1. chin; back
   2. neutral

You Make the Call

Your answer should include the following steps and information (see pages 436–450):

- Park your vehicle in a safe location and use your vehicle warning lights.
- Overview the scene for safety.
- Take into account the number of patients and determine if you need additional resources.
- Follow the patient assessment sequence.
- Identify any hazards (gasoline, power lines or wires, or hazardous materials).
- Control those hazards for which you are trained and equipped.
- Gain access to the patients.
- Provide patient care and stabilization.
- Help disentangle patients and prepare patients for removal.
- Help remove patients.
- Prepare a report for EMS personnel once they arrive on the scene.
- Offer to assist EMS personnel in caring for the patients.

Chapter 19: Terrorism Awareness

Matching

1. D (page 470)
2. C (page 472)
3. B (page 469)
4. E (page 470)
5. F (page 469)
6. A (page 469)

Multiple Choice

1. D (page 469)
2. A (pages 473–474)
3. A (page 473)
4. D (page 466)
5. D (page 466)
6. B (page 469)
7. C (page 469)
8. B (page 467)
9. C (page 473)
10. B (page 472)

Fill-in-the-Blanks

1. weapon of mass destruction (page 466)
2. explosive (page 468)
3. dosimeter (page 473)
4. biologic (page 472)
5. incubation period (page 472)

True/False

1. T (page 473)
2. T (page 473)
3. T (page 468)
4. F (page 470)
5. T (page 470)
6. F (page 468)
7. T (page 468)
8. T (page 468)
9. F (page 468)
10. F (page 468)

Short Answer

1. (See page 469.)
   1. Pulmonary agents
   2. Metabolic agents
   3. Insecticides
   4. Nerve agents
   5. Blister agents

2. Any three of the following (page 469):
   - Salivation
   - Sweating
   - Lacrimation (excessive tearing)
   - Urination
   - Defecation or diarrhea
   - Gastric upset
   - Emesis (vomiting)

3. Nausea; vomiting; diarrhea (page 473)

4. Any three of the following (page 473):
   - Hospitals
   - Research facilities
   - Nuclear power plants
   - Manufacturing sites for military weapons

5. Any of the following (page 469):
   - Shortness of breath
   - Flushed skin
   - Rapid heartbeat
   - Seizures
   - Coma
   - Cardiac arrest

You Make the Call

Your answer should include the following steps and information (pages 473–474):
- Carefully survey the scene for safety.
- Recognize that a specially trained hazardous materials response team will be needed.
- Establish an incident command system as soon as possible.
- Do not treat any patients who have come into direct contact with the powder until they have been decontaminated.
- Be sure to take proper BSI precautions before treating patients.

Chapter 20: Special Rescue

Matching

1. D (page 485)
2. B (page 482)
3. E (page 482)
4. C (page 483)
5. A (page 485)

Multiple Choice

1. D (page 482)
2. D (page 483)
3. C (page 486)
4. A (page 486)
5. D (page 482)
6. D (page 485)
7. A (page 485)
8. B (page 485)
9. D (page 485)
10. C (page 486)

Fill-in-the-Blanks

1. flotation (page 482)
2. row (page 482)
3. airway (page 483)
4. back; head (page 483
5. air; decompression sickness (page 485)
6. oxygen (page 487)
7. delayed (page 488)
8. Riptides (page 483)
9. jump (page 482)
10. cardiac arrest (page 484)

True/False

1. T (page 485)
2. F (page 483)
3. T (page 483)
4. T (page 484)
5. T (page 484)
6. F (page 485)
7. F (pages 490–491)
8. F (page 482)
9. F (page 482)
10. T (page 482)
11. F (page 482)
12. T (page 482)
13. F (page 484)
14. T (page 484)
15. F (pages 483–484)
16. T (page 485)
17. F (pages 485–486)
18. F (page 491)
19. T (page 485)
20. T (page 487)

Short Answer

1. (See page 482.)
  1. Reach
  2. Throw
  3. Row
  4. Go

2. Any three of the following (pages 485-486):
- Dizziness
- Difficulty speaking
- Difficulty seeing
- Decreased level of consciousness
- Difficulty maintaining an open airway
- Chest pain
- Shortness of breath
- Pink or bloody froth coming from the mouth or nose
- Severe abdominal pain
- Joint pain

3. Any five of the following (page 486):
- Manholes
- Below-ground utility vaults
- Storage tanks
- Old mines
- Cisterns
- Wells
- Industrial tankers
- Farm storage silos
- Water towers

4. Respiratory hazards (including insufficient oxygen or poisonous gases); danger of collapse (page 487)

5. (See page 489.)
1. Overview the scene and call for sufficient help.
2. Stabilize the scene and any hazards.
3. Gain access to patients, if possible.
4. Provide initial emergency care.
5. Help disentangle patients.
6. Help prepare patients for removal.
7. Help remove patients.

Skill Drills

1. (See page 484.)
1. back; head; front
2. unit
3. head; neck

You Make the Call

Your answer should include the following steps and information (pages 488–489):
- Carefully overview the scene to determine the scope of the problem.
- Treat the silo as a confined space and do not enter without proper self-contained breathing apparatus and proper training.
- Call for adequate assistance from fire, rescue, and EMS organizations.
- If possible, gain access to the patient.
- Provide initial emergency care to the patient, including establishing responsiveness, supporting the patient's ABCs, controlling bleeding, and maintaining the patient's body temperature.
- Talk with the patient and provide psychological support.
- As other rescuers arrive on the scene, help them to disentangle the patient, prepare the patient for removal, and remove the patient.

Chapter 21: Supplemental Skills

Matching

1. D (page 498)
2. E (page 498)
3. F (page 499)
4. C (page 498)
5. B (page 498)
6. A (page 498)

Multiple Choice

1. C (page 498)
2. C (page 498)
3. C (page 503)
4. C (page 502)
5. D (page 498)
6. C (page 498)
7. A (page 498)
8. B (page 498)
9. A (page 498)
10. C (page 498)
11. D (page 499)
12. D (page 500)
13. C (page 500)
14. C (page 500)
15. C (page 502)
16. C (page 501)
17. B (page 502)
18. D (page 502)
19. A (page 503)
20. A (pages 505–506)

Fill-in-the-Blanks

1. 35 to 50 (page 502)
2. 90 (page 502)
3. Hypertension (page 498)
4. palpation (page 498)
5. Oxygen (page 500)
6. nasal cannula (page 501)
7. flowmeter (page 500)
8. face mask (page 503)

True/False

1. T (page 501)
2. T (page 501)
3. T (page 503)
4. F (page 498)
5. F (page 498)
6. T (page 498)
7. T (page 498)
8. T (page 498)
9. T (page 498)
10. T (page 498)
11. T (page 500)
12. F (page 500)
13. T (page 500)
14. T (page 501)
15. F (page 501)

Short Answer

1. Oxygen cylinder; pressure regulator/flowmeter; nasal cannula or face mask (pages 500–502)
2. On the inside of the arm at the crease of the elbow (page 498)
3. Self-inflating bag; one-way valve; face mask (page 501)
4. Palpation; auscultation (pages 498–499)
5. Patients requiring higher flows of oxygen, such as those experiencing serious shortness of breath, severe chest pain, carbon monoxide poisoning, congestive heart failure, or signs and symptoms of shock (page 502)

Skill Drills

1. (See page 504.)
   1. head; mouth
   2. mask
   3. face
   4. Seal
   5. bag; chest rise
   6. supplemental oxygen

You Make the Call

Your answer should include the following steps and information:

- Check airway, breathing, and circulation.
- Administer oxygen.
- Keep the patient comfortable.
- Obtain further medical history.
- Call for advanced life support